By revealing the common ideas and assumptions that underlay three distinct cultural developments in Britain after 1945 – the fantasy literature of C. S. Lewis and J. R. R. Tolkien and the response it provoked, the protests that emerged in the late 1950s against Britain's possession of the Bomb, and the early Green movement of the 1960s and 1970s – this work illuminates the importance of the romantic tradition in shaping significant aspects of contemporary middle-class culture. It is an exercise in intellectual history: an exploration of the continuing prominence of romantic protest in modern Britain. It is also, however, an essay in cultural history, an effort to outline the often unarticulated yet powerful beliefs and understandings that undergirded the British middle-class experience in the decades after the Second World War.

Fantasy, the Bomb,
and the Greening of Britain

Fantasy, the Bomb, and the Greening of Britain

Romantic Protest, 1945–1980

MEREDITH VELDMAN
Louisiana State University

CAMBRIDGE
UNIVERSITY PRESS

Published by the Press Syndicate of the University of Cambridge
The Pitt Building, Trumpington Street, Cambridge CB2 1RP
40 West 20th Street, New York, NY 10011-4211, USA
10 Stamford Road, Oakleigh, Melbourne 3166, Australia

First published 1994

Printed in the United States of America

Library of Congress Cataloging-in-Publication Data
Veldman, Meredith.
Fantasy, the bomb, and the greening of Britain :
romantic protest, 1945–1980 / Meredith Veldman
p. cm.
Includes bibliographical references.
ISBN 0-521-44060-2 – ISBN 0-521-46665-2 (pbk.)
1. Great Britain – Civilization – 1945–   2. Literature and society –
Great Britain – History – 20th century.   3. Antinuclear movement –
Great Britain – History – 20th century.   4. Fantastic literature,
English – History and criticism.   5. Green movement – Great Britain –
History – 20th century.   6. Middle classes – Great Britain –
History – 20th century.   7. Protest literature, English – History and
criticism.   8. Romanticism – Great Britain – History – 20th century.
9. Environmental protection in literature.   I. Title.
DA589.4.V45   1994
941.085 – dc20   93-12772

A catalog record for this book is available from the British Library.

ISBN 0-521-44060-2 hardback
ISBN 0-521-46665-2 paperback

Copyright page continues on page xi.

For Gram
and
Jem

Contents

Acknowledgments

I am very pleased to have the chance to acknowledge the many individuals, organizations, and institutions who assisted in the making of this book.

The Louisiana State University Council on Research and the American Council of Learned Societies supplied funding that allowed me to complete the research. For use of their collections and for the patient assistance provided by their staffpersons, I thank the BBC Written Archives Centre, the British Library, the Marion E. Wade Center at Wheaton College, the Modern Records Centre at the University of Warwick, the National Coal Board Library, the National Library of Scotland, the Special Collections of the Library of Political and Economic Science at the London School of Economics, and the Tolkien Collection at Marquette University.

I owe a special debt to several participants in the peace and environmental movements. Many of the following individuals not only consented to be interviewed but also opened up their homes and offered me lunch, lodgings, and, frequently, friendship: my thanks to Michael Allaby, Colin Blythe, Peter Bunyard, David Collins, John Davoll, Paul Ekins, Edward Goldsmith, Ruth Harrison, George McRobie, John Papworth, Christian Schumacher, Diana Schumacher, Graham Searle, Barbara Wood, and, most especially, Robert and Sue Waller. I am also grateful to Maxwell MacLeod for allowing me to examine his father's papers; George Charlton, Ron Ferguson, and Hamish Walker for helping me understand the Iona Community's role in the British peace movement; Peter Cadogan for giving me access to his collection of press reports on the Committee of 100; and Chris Church for providing me with the manuscript copy of his then-unpublished history of Friends of the Earth. The staffs of the Conservation Society, the Green Party, the Intermediate Technology Development Group, the Iona Community House, and the Soil Association tolerated with considerable grace my rummaging through their libraries and file cabinets.

Although any and all mistakes in the following pages are of course my own, a great many individuals assisted me in writing this book. My advisor and friend T. W. Heyck, who first encouraged me in the crazy idea that maybe

C. S. Lewis and CND had something in common, read countless drafts and offered unending encouragement. He can play E. P. Thompson in the film version if he wants to. Harold Perkin has also been with this project from the beginning and helped shape my argument. Michael Bess, Anne Hyde, and Benjamin Martin all supplied much-valued critical readings. Edward Muir helped with the Introduction, and Dena Goodman forced me to see what this book is really about. My student worker Genevieve Hamner performed the heroic task of checking the footnotes. Frank Smith of Cambridge University Press recognized a book in my work long before I did. The comments of the Press's anonymous reviewer were extremely helpful in highlighting necessary revisions. Thank you all.

I also thank Lynn Voskuil and Randy Nichols. Lynn gave me the benefit of a literary scholar's reading of Part I; even more important, however, was the sustenance provided by her friendship over the last several years. Randy not only read and commented on the entire manuscript but also committed the foolhardy act of marrying me in the midst of the revision process.

I am also grateful to a number of persons who were not directly involved in this work but who encouraged it nonetheless. Betty Birner wrote terrific letters. Victor Stater has been the ideal colleague: challenging, entertaining, and always ready for a chocolate break. Margaret and Neville Ashton, Joan and Harold Perkin, and Deborah Perkin and Mark Smithies welcomed me into their homes and families during my trips to Britain. My own family was consistently supportive of, if also puzzled by, this work: special thanks to Edith Veldman, Carol VanDenBerg, Russ and Jeanine Veldman, and Dirk and Henrietta DeGroot. Thanks also to Jason, Lissa, Rachel, Joshua, Kristen, and Jessica, who helped more than they can ever know.

Finally, I thank two very important people. The companionship offered by my grandmother Jennie Veldman helped me cope with the isolation of scholarly work. I'm very sorry that she did not live to see this book completed. The fact that it *was* completed depended a great deal on my son, Jeremy Nichols, whose birth imposed a much-needed deadline on the final draft. Gram and Jem, this book is for you.

Baton Rouge, Louisiana
August 1992

Permission acknowledgments

I thank E. J. Mishan for permission to quote from *The Economic Growth Debate: An Assessment* (London: Allen and Unwin, 1977); Adrian Mitchell for permission to quote from his poem "The Liberal Christ Holds a Press Conference"; Iris Murdoch for permission to quote from "Morality and the Bomb"; E. P. Thompson for permission to quote from *There Is a Spirit in Europe: A Memoir of Frank Thompson* (London: Gollancz, 1947); Maxwell MacLeod for permission to quote from his father's unpublished writings; and David Widgery for permission to include the song "Don't You Hear the H-Bomb's Thunder?"

I also thank Curtis Brown Ltd. for permission to quote from Barbara Ward's *Progress for a Small Planet;* as well as Elizabeth Stevens of Curtis Brown, John Farquharson Ltd. for the C. S. Lewis Estate, and Marjorie Lamp Mead, acting director of the Marion E. Wade Center of Wheaton College, for permission to use C. S. Lewis's unpublished letters. The quotations from C. S. Lewis's unpublished letters to Owen Barfield are reproduced by permission of Curtis Brown, London, on behalf of C. S. Lewis Pte. Ltd.

I am also grateful to the following for granting permission to quote from material first published by them:

Allen and Unwin, now Unwin Hyman (HarperCollins Publishers UK Ltd.), for permission to quote from J. R. R. Tolkien's *The Fellowship of the Ring, The Letters of J. R. R. Tolkien, The Monsters and the Critics, The Return of the King,* and *The Two Towers;*

Bodley Head (Random House UK Ltd.), for permission to quote from C. S. Lewis's *Out of the Silent Planet, Perelandra,* and *That Hideous Strength;*

Cambridge University Press, for permission to quote from C. S. Lewis, *The Discarded Image;*

Jonathan Cape (Random House UK Ltd.), for permission to quote from E. F. Schumacher's *A Guide for the Perplexed* and *Schumacher on Energy,* and from Barbara Wood, *Alias Papa: A Life of Fritz Schumacher;*

G. K. Chesterton Estate, for permission to quote from G. K. Chesterton, *The Bodley Head G. K. Chesterton;*

Collins Fount (HarperCollins Publishers UK Ltd.), for permission to quote from C. S. Lewis's *All My Road before Me,* "Christianity and Literature," *The Four Loves, The Last Battle, The Magician's Nephew, Of This and Other Worlds, Prince Caspian,* and *They Stand Together;*

Columbia University Press, for permission to quote from Barbara Ward, *Spaceship Earth;*

Eerdmans Publishers, for permission to quote from C. S. Lewis's "Christianity and Literature" and *The Pilgrim's Regress;*

Victor Gollancz Publishers, for permission to quote from Victor Gollancz, *The Devil's Repertoire;*

Harcourt Brace Jovanovich, for permission to quote from C. S. Lewis's *All My Road before Me, The Four Loves, The Letters of C. S. Lewis, Of Other Worlds: Essays and Stories, On Stories and Other Essays on Literature,* and *Surprised by Joy;*

Harper and Row (HarperCollins Publishers USA, Inc.), for permission to quote from E. F. Schumacher, *Small Is Beautiful;*

HarperCollins Publishers UK Ltd., for permission to quote from C. S. Lewis's *The Abolition of Man: How Education Develops Man's Sense of Morality, The Letters of C. S. Lewis, The Lion, the Witch and the Wardrobe, Mere Christianity, Miracles: A Preliminary Study, Surprised by Joy, They Asked for a Paper,* and *The Voyage of the Dawn Treader;*

HarperCollins Publishers USA, Inc., for permission to quote from E. F. Schumacher's *Good Work* and *A Guide for the Perplexed;*

Houghton Mifflin Company, for permission to quote from Humphrey Carpenter's *Tolkien: A Biography* and J. R. R. Tolkien's *The Fellowship of the Ring, The Letters of J. R. R. Tolkien, The Monsters and the Critics, The Two Towers,* and *The Return of the King;*

Hutchinson Publications (Random House UK), for permission to quote from E. F. Schumacher, *Small Is Beautiful;*

Ignatius Press, for permission to quote from G. K. Chesterton, *The Outline of Sanity: The Collected Works of G. K. Chesterton,* vol. 5;

Macmillan Publishing Company, for permission to quote from Walter Hooper, ed., *They Stand Together: The Letters of C. S. Lewis to Arthur Greaves;*

New Statesman and Society, for permission to quote from J. B. Priestley, "Britain and the Nuclear Bombs," *New Statesman,* 2 November 1957, pp. 554–6;

W. W. Norton and Company, for permission to quote from Barbara Ward, *Progress for a Small Planet;*

Oxford University Press, for permission to quote from A.W. Wright, *G.D.H. Cole and Socialist Democracy;*

Pantheon Books (Random House Inc.), for permission to quote from Henry Abelove, ed., *Visions of History;*

Peter Owen Ltd., for permission to quote from David Boulton's *Voices from the Crowd against the H-Bomb;*

A. D. Peters and Co. Ltd., for permission to quote from Hilaire Belloc's *The Servile State.*

Abbreviations

BBC-WAC   British Broadcasting Corporation Written Archives Centre, Reading

BL   British Library, London

BLPES   Special Collections, British Library of Political and Economic Science, London School of Economics and Political Science, London

ITDG   E. F. Schumacher Papers, Intermediate Technology Development Group, Rugby

NCB   Hobart House, National Coal Board (now British Coal), London

NL/ML   George MacLeod Papers, National Library of Scotland, Edinburgh

Wade   C. S. Lewis Papers, Marion E. Wade Center, Wheaton College, Wheaton, Illinois

Warwick   Modern Records Centre, University of Warwick, Warwick

Introduction

This work was born several years ago on a Chicago elevated train, somewhere between the suburb of Evanston and the city's North Side. To pass the time on the "el" I was reading J. R. R. Tolkien's *The Lord of the Rings*.[1] At the same time, as part of my preparations for doctoral candidacy examinations, I had immersed myself in E. P. Thompson's *The Making of the English Working Class*.[2] But shifting from Thompson to Tolkien and back again had a strange effect: I began to feel like I was reading the same book. I decided that I must need a vacation. For what could Thompson have to do with Tolkien? What could a Marxist share with a supporter of Franco? On what common ground could the politically active, cause-oriented Thompson meet a man who spent much of his life in a world of his own making? Yet the sensation of sameness, the belief that Thompson and Tolkien *did* meet on common ground, that Thompson's depiction of the world in which the working class made themselves shared certain deep structures with Tolkien's Middle-earth, remained with me and eventually led to the doctoral dissertation that formed the first draft of this study.

This work examines the ideas, attitudes, and values that link three very different cultural developments or movements in post-1945 Britain: the fantasy literature of C. S. Lewis and J. R. R. Tolkien and the response it provoked, the protest that emerged in the late 1950s against Britain's possession of the Bomb, and the early Green movement of the 1960s and 1970s. This study is not, however, about three different cultural developments; it is about the thing they share in common, the variable x that identifies them with each other.

Again and again within these cultural phenomena certain common patterns and themes surface, a shared series of affirmations and denials. With varied emphases and accents, all three affirmed and sought to strengthen the bonds between humanity and the natural world, endeavored to restore the

---

1 J. R. R. Tolkien, *The Fellowship of the Ring, The Two Towers, The Return of the King* (1954, 1955; New York: Ballantine Books, 1974).
2 E. P. Thompson, *The Making of the English Working Class* (1963; New York: Vintage Books, 1966).

ties between individual human beings and their histories, and struggled to rebuild community life and spirit in a society they believed to be increasingly atomized. They insisted that in a world dominated by large structures and the veneration of expertise, the ordinary individual retained the right and the responsibility to shape his or her corner of the universe. Asserting that material, empirical reality did not encompass the whole of truth, they looked for ways to acknowledge and expand intuitive, emotional, and spiritual understandings. Thus they rejected many of the fundamental assumptions of contemporary society and sought, in very different ways, to save their worlds from decay and destruction.

These shared themes together form x, that which unites cultural products as diverse as Tolkien's *The Lord of the Rings*, the Campaign for Nuclear Disarmament's Aldermaston Marches, and E. F. Schumacher's *Small Is Beautiful*.[3] This variable, of course, needs a name, but playing Adam has proven difficult because the obvious name, romantic, is one of the most problematic labels in intellectual and cultural history. More than twenty years ago H. G. Schenk noted that over one hundred definitions of "romanticism" existed, and none of them were satisfactory. In 1943 Jacques Barzun cited twenty-two assorted meanings of the term, and Ernest Bernbaum listed twenty-eight definitions in his once widely used college textbook.[4] Even when the term is confined to the small circle of English poets active in England between 1780 and 1830 – "Romanticism" with a capital R – critics fail to agree on its meaning.[5]

Despite such confusion, I have chosen the label "romanticism" because no other label will do. In the following pages, "romantic" refers neither to an artistic stand nor to a historical period, but instead to a world view, an outlook. At the heart of the romantic world view is the belief that the empirical and analytical methods of modern science cannot comprehend all of reality, that truth in its wholeness extends beyond the reach of the physical senses. Associated with this sense of "otherness" is a tendency toward transcendence: transcending *time*, first of all, in the sense that each human being owes a responsibility and allegiance to both the past and the future. This

---

3 E. F. Schumacher, *Small Is Beautiful: Economics as if People Mattered* (New York: Harper and Row, 1973).
4 H. G. Schenk, *The Mind of the European Romantics* (New York: Ungar, 1966), p. xxi; Jacques Barzun, *Classic, Romantic, and Modern* (1943; Chicago: University of Chicago Press, 1975), pp. 155–9; Ernest Bernbaum, *Guide through the Romantic Movement* (1930; New York: Ronald Press Co., 1949), pp. 301–2.
5 E.g., in his essay in *Romanticism and Consciousness*, Alfred Cobban stated the familiar argument that the English Romantic poets sought to unite themselves with nature. In his introductory essay, however, Harold Bloom asserted that the Romantics wrote "anti-nature poetry" and were not questing for unity with nature or with any greater or higher force. See Harold Bloom, ed., *Romanticism and Consciousness: Essays in Criticism* (New York: Norton, 1970), pp. 3–23, 132–48.

transcendent tendency extends also to the question of *identity*, in the sense that the human being is called to an awareness and an appreciation of the nonhuman realms, what we commonly call the natural world, and even, at times, the supernatural.

My use of the label "romantic" also has a specifically English, or better, British, sense. This study weaves together three diverse postwar cultural phenomena by placing them within what is here called the romantic tradition of protest. As Chapter 1 shows, this tradition originated with the Romantic poets of the late eighteenth and early nineteenth centuries.[6] Rooted in a suspicion of industrialization and empiricism, romantic protest has served as a continuous thread in the tapestry of British intellectual and cultural life to this day.

The fantasies of Lewis and Tolkien, the campaigns against the British H-bomb, and the warnings of the early Greens were fundamentally romantic in this sense. They shared a suspicion of technology and technocracy, and a reluctance to recognize empiricism and pragmatism as paths to truth. Together they affirmed that the past should serve as a guide for the future. They also insisted that reality extended beyond the material realm and that nature was a living entity worthy of respect. Fundamental to these postwar romantics was the faith that community had once existed, that it had disappeared from postwar Britain, and that it needed to be restored. These ideas formed a coherent whole, a protest against the dominant structures and assumptions of contemporary Britain.[7]

By exploring the coherence of these ideas within the intellectual tradition of romanticism, I emphasize the continuing vitality of the romantic critique amidst changing economic, social, and cultural conditions. Although it was not immediately evident, after 1945 Britain had a much smaller role to play on the world stage than the nation had become accustomed to in previous centuries. The steady dwindling of British imperial possessions provided only the most dramatic evidence of Britain's loss of world power.[8] The economic might of the United States and the advent of the cold war meant that British aims and ambitions had to be reconciled to the dictates of the superpower. At the root of this onset of impotence lay Britain's economic decline. Although the seeds of Britain's economic decay were sown in the

---

6 See Raymond Williams, *Culture and Society, 1780–1950* (1958; New York: Columbia University Press, 1983).

7 For two important interpretations of contemporary British and European history that use romanticism as a significant theme, see Samuel H. Beer, *Britain against Itself: The Political Contradictions of Collectivism* (New York: Norton, 1982), esp. pt. III; H. Stuart Hughes, *Sophisticated Rebels: The Political Culture of European Dissent, 1968–1987* (Cambridge: Harvard University Press, 1988).

8 See Bernard Porter, *Britain, Europe, and the World, 1850–1986: Delusions of Grandeur*, 2d ed. (London: Allen and Unwin, 1987).

Victorian period, the full fruits were not harvested until the decades after 1945, when Britain's productivity problem manifested itself in a series of financial crises and an ever-worsening manufacturing slump.[9] British responses to this loss of power varied; one response, shaped by the romantic tradition, was to assert that the British nation, if it remained rooted in the past, could play the role of moral leader in the U.S.-dominated, postwar world.

Economic decline was only one of the forces that shaped the romantic experience of postwar Britain; the expansion of the welfare state and the rise of a consumer society also defined British life after 1945. Between 1945 and 1951 the Labour government set in place the basic outlines of Britain's social democratic system, outlines that remained fundamentally unchanged until the election of Margaret Thatcher in 1979: a commitment to a mixed economy, the belief that the state should intervene in economic life for the maintenance of full employment, a nationalized health service, and a social security system that guaranteed a minimum standard of living for all.[10] This political and economic consensus rested upon Britain's transformation into a consumer society. Despite its relative decline, the British economy in the 1950s and 1960s succeeded in delivering more goods to more workers than ever before. The availability of affordable, mass-produced consumer products transformed the exteriors of workers' lives and challenged the Left to redefine socialism to suit the reality of a consumption-focused society. For some of the romantic protesters studied in the following pages, the construction of the welfare state and the improved working-class standard of living constituted at least the first step toward the building of a moral society that could lead the world; for others, these achievements signaled the road to social disintegration. The assumptions that led to these contradictory positions, however, grew out of the same soil: a desire to ensure that both individual agency and community life remained vital realities in contemporary Britain.

A third force that shaped Britain after 1945 was the continuing technological revolution. Like Britain's economic decline, the construction of the welfare state, and the emergence of a consumer society, this revolution began

9 For explanations of Britain's economic decline, see ibid.; Aaron Friedberg, *The Weary Titan: Britain and the Experience of Relative Decline, 1895–1905* (Princeton: Princeton University Press, 1989); Sidney Pollard, *Britain's Prime and Britain's Decline: The British Economy, 1870–1914* (London: Edward Arnold, 1989); Sidney Pollard, *The Development of the British Economy, 1914–1980,* 3d ed. (London: Edward Arnold, 1983); Martin Wiener, *English Culture and the Decline of the Industrial Spirit* (Cambridge: Cambridge University Press, 1981). See also Bruce Collins and Keith Robbins, eds., *British Culture and Economic Decline* (New York: St. Martin's Press, 1990).

10 See Paul Addison, *The Road to 1945* (London: Cape, 1975); Dennis Kavanagh, *Thatcherism and British Politics: The End of Consensus?* (Oxford: Oxford University Press, 1987).

well before 1945. In the years after the Second World War, however, the pace of technological change accelerated and changed the face of Britain. Technology appeared to hold the key to both social peace and economic prosperity. It promised to provide inexpensive and limitless sources of energy, to make the luxurious affordable, and thus to bring about the equitable society that had proven so elusive. Some Britons, however, perceived these promises to be hollow. They began to question the capacity of both human and natural resources to withstand the strain of rapid technological change. Skeptical about the ability and trustworthiness of the experts who were supposed to be directing the new Britain, they also questioned the sustainability of a society that devoted much of its technological capabilities to producing weapons of mass annihilation. The romantic tradition supplied these protesters with the concepts and criteria they needed; its long history of suspicion of the scientific method, revulsion against the social and cultural by-products of industrialization, and effort to restore humanity's links with the natural world proved easily adaptable for the fight against technology and the technocracy.

For protest to be effective, however, it must be heard. The common culture of Victorian Britain, a culture that largely excluded the working class, had ensured earlier romantic protesters of an audience. The fragmentation of this common culture, and the emergence of a mass culture shaped by commercial forces and dominated by the previously disenfranchised working class, made communication more difficult.[11] Postwar romantic protesters had to find new means of articulating their objections to the dominant values of British society. The problem of communication, which arises again and again in the movements examined below, was exacerbated by the British class system. The existing evidence, admittedly scanty in the case of the response to fantasy literature, indicates that these romantic protesters came from the middle class and, to a large degree, from the professional sectors of middle-class society. Operating outside the market economy, their interests and concerns differed from those of most workers, as well as most business leaders in both commerce and finance.[12]

By revealing the common ideas and assumptions that underlay three distinct cultural developments in Britain after 1945, this work illuminates the importance of the romantic tradition in shaping some aspects of contemporary middle-class culture. It is an exercise in intellectual history: an exploration of the continuing significance of romantic protest in modern Britain. It is

11 For more on the fragmentation of British intellectual and cultural life, see T. W. Heyck, *The Transformation of Intellectual Life in Victorian England* (London: Croom Helm, 1982); and D. L. LeMahieu, *A Culture for Democracy: Mass Communication and the Cultivated Mind in Britain between the Wars* (Oxford: Clarendon Press, 1988).

12 For a fascinating interpretation of contemporary British history that illumines the important role of professional values, see Harold Perkin, *The Rise of Professional Society since 1880* (London: Routledge, 1989).

also, however, an essay in cultural history, an effort to outline the often unarticulated yet powerful beliefs and understandings that undergirded the British middle-class experience in the decades after the Second World War. This book is also *not* a number of things. It is not a narrative history or a series of linked biographies. In addition to C. S. Lewis's and J. R. R. Tolkien's fictions, scholarly works, published letters, and, in the case of Lewis, autobiography, substantial and significant biographies already exist.[13] The history of the Campaign for Nuclear Disarmament has been told by Richard Taylor; moreover, Taylor's work closely examines the political significance and context of the Campaign.[14] No such narrative account exists for the early Green movement, but a number of important studies, both popular and scholarly, that relate various aspects of the history of radical environmentalism in Britain have been and are being published.[15]

This study, then, does not offer new "facts" about C. S. Lewis and J. R. R. Tolkien, nor does it attempt to outline the history of fantasy literature after 1945. It also does not seek to enter the battle about the boundaries of the literary canon. I am not arguing that *The Lord of the Rings* should be studied in literature seminars. I am arguing that the astoundingly large audience for these fantasies presents historians with a cultural development worthy of notice. This book recognizes and analyzes Lewis's and Tolkien's fantasies as cultural artifacts, valuable because of the light they shed on postwar British

---

13 See Humphrey Carpenter, *The Inklings: C. S. Lewis, J. R. R. Tolkien, Charles Williams, and Their Friends* (London: Allen and Unwin, 1978); Humphrey Carpenter, *Tolkien: A Biography* (Boston: Houghton Mifflin, 1977); George Sayer, *Jack: C. S. Lewis and His Times* (London: Macmillan, 1988); A. N. Wilson, *C. S. Lewis: A Biography* (New York: Norton, 1990). See also chap. 6, "The Oxford Fantasists," in Norman Cantor, *Inventing the Middle Ages* (New York: William Morrow, 1991), pp. 205–45.

14 Richard Taylor, *Against the Bomb: The British Peace Movement 1958–1965* (Oxford: Clarendon Press, 1988). See also Richard Taylor and Colin Pritchard, *The Protest Makers: The British Nuclear Disarmament Movement of 1958–1965, Twenty Years On* (Oxford: Pergamon Press, 1980); Richard Taylor and Nigel Young, *Campaigns for Peace: British Peace Movements in the Twentieth Century* (New York: St. Martin's Press, 1987).

15 See, e.g., Michael Allaby, ed., *Thinking Green: An Anthology of Essential Ecological Writing* (London: Barrie and Jenkins, 1989); H. W. Arndt, *The Rise and Fall of Economic Growth* (Melbourne: Longman Cheshire, 1978); H. W. Arndt, *Economic Development: The History of an Idea* (Chicago: University of Chicago Press, 1987); Anna Bramwell, *Ecology in the Twentieth Century: A History* (New Haven: Yale University Press, 1988); Chris Church, *Coming of Age: The First Twenty Years of Friends of the Earth in Britain* (London: Gollancz, 1992); David Evans, *A History of Nature Conservation in Britain* (London: Routledge, 1992); John McCormick, *Reclaiming Paradise: The Global Environmental Movement* (Bloomington: Indiana University Press, 1989); Roderick Frazier Nash, *The Rights of Nature: A History of Environmental Ethics* (Madison: University of Wisconsin Press, 1989); Max Nicholson, *The New Environmental Age* (New York: Cambridge University Press, 1987); David Nicholson-Lord, *The Greening of the Cities* (London and New York: Routledge and Kegan-Paul, 1987); Donald Worster, *Nature's Economy: A History of Ecological Ideas* (San Francisco: Sierra Club Books, 1977). See also Barbara Wood, *Alias Papa: A Life of Fritz Schumacher* (London: Jonathon Cape, 1984).

culture. It seeks to place Lewis and Tolkien within their intellectual and cultural context in twentieth-century British history.

It endeavors to do the same for the Campaign for Nuclear Disarmament and the related movements that emerged in the late 1950s to protest Britain's possession of the hydrogen bomb and, ultimately, participation in a nuclear alliance. This study neither rejects nor repeats Richard Taylor's important work. Instead, it seeks to set the protest against the Bomb in a different focus, to explore the unarticulated assumptions that place certain sections of the Ban-the-Bomb movement within the romantic tradition. Made up of diverse and often contradictory elements, this movement was not wholly romantic. But as Part II will show, important segments of it voiced their protest in romantic terms.

The early Greens also comprised both romantic and antiromantic elements. Part III explores the depth of this diversity but concentrates on those organizations and individuals whose call for an alternative economics governed by ecological priorities resonated with the romantic tradition. Because no comprehensive history of the early Green movement in Britain yet exists, Chapter 10 provides an overview of the important events and documents that helped shape Green awareness from 1950 on. But rather than providing a history of the movement, this study attempts to explore the value system that the movement both reflected and sought to create. As with both Parts I and II, Part III is an examination of an important manifestation of romantic protest in the postwar period.

Why these three movements? In keeping with the romantic tradition, my selection of fantasy literature, the Campaign for Nuclear Disarmament, and the early Green movement was much more intuitive than scientific. I was interested in these movements and so I began to study them; it was only in the course of this study that I became aware of x, of the common tradition that contributed to each of them. In the case of each of these three very different cultural phenomena, x does not constitute the primary reality: When Tolkien wrote his fantasy, when Campaigners embarked on four-day marches across the southern English countryside, when early Greens dumped hundreds of bottles on the doorstep of Cadbury-Schweppes, they were not consciously joining the romantic tradition. Their explicit intentions were much different, much more concrete. The details of their actions and writings, however, indicate a submerged reality that this study aims to explore.

At the core of this book is the effort to discern the unwritten values that helped shape middle-class culture in the years after the Second World War. The amount of written evidence for this period is immense. Yet, the contemporary historian faces a challenge not wholly unlike that which early modern historians have confronted so brilliantly over the last two decades. For the historian of seventeenth-century French non-elites, for example, the problem is how to discern the voices obscured by the written records of the minority. For the historian of the contemporary middle classes, the problem is how to hear the voices lost in the cacophony of mass culture. The contemporary historian, as much as the early modernist, is embarked on what Carlo Ginzburg has described as a Holmesian hunt, an effort to read the significance in the "inadvertent little gestures." Ginzburg argues that "the historian's knowledge . . . is indirect, based on signs and scraps of evidence, conjectural." Conjecture – but not incomprehension: "The existence of a deep connection which explains superficial phenomena can be confirmed when it is acknowledged that direct knowledge of such a connection is impossible. Reality is opaque; but there are certain points – clues, signs – which allow us to decipher it."[16] In this effort to decipher the cultural reality of post–World War II Britain, I have looked to three popular and middle-class cultural developments for the clues, the signs, the inadvertent little gestures that give away the game.

In addition, the often astonishing popularity of these movements and their continuing influence make them natural objects of study for the cultural historian. The fictions of Lewis and Tolkien sparked an explosion of fantasy literature, created a cult of fantasy fanatics among the British middle classes, and gave greater respectability to the writing and study of fantasy. The Campaign for Nuclear Disarmament originated important symbols and styles of protest and inaugurated a decade of middle-class street protest at the same time as it challenged conventional and consensual politics. The early Green movement went beyond challenging political structures to questioning the entire economic foundations of industrial society while it continued, like the Campaign, to create new symbols of romantic protest. Other movements could have been chosen, but to do so would have drawn this already-lengthy project on interminably. I do not argue that these three movements constituted the whole of romantic protest in Britain after the Second World War; they do, however, demonstrate the diversity of this protest and the strengths and weaknesses of this tradition.

16 Carlo Ginzburg, "Morelli, Freud and Sherlock Holmes: Clues and Scientific Method," trans. Anna Davin, *History Workshop* 9 (1980): 5–36; quotations from pp. 9, 16, 27. A revised version of this article under the title "Clues: Roots of an Evidential Paradigm" is in Ginzburg's *Clues, Myths, and the Historical Method*, trans. John and Anne Tedeschi (Baltimore: Johns Hopkins University Press, 1989), pp. 96–125.

1

The romantic protest tradition before 1945

The fantasies of C. S. Lewis and J. R. R. Tolkien, the campaign to ban the British Bomb, and the early Green movement belong to a protest tradition that emerged in the final decades of the eighteenth century. Economic developments from approximately the 1780s onward reshaped Britain's social and political structures and eventually brought to the vast majority of its people a degree of material affluence beyond the comprehension of most British men and women at the beginning of the nineteenth century. From the very onset of industrialization, however, and throughout the next two centuries, an important minority dared to question the direction in which Britain was headed and to propose alternative routes to a better future. In fiction, prose, and poetry, in painting and architecture, in economic and political programs, a wide variety of individuals sought to forge anew the links between British society and its natural environment, its past, and some sense of spiritual or nonmaterial reality. As a brief survey of the more important figures in this tradition reveals, this minority voiced its protest against industrial Britain in fundamentally romantic terms.

A new world

By the end of the eighteenth century, capitalism had triumphed in Britain and had cleared the way for what would be mislabeled the Industrial Revolution, in actuality an evolutionary process that slowly transformed Britain's production and consumption patterns. Although between 1780 and 1830 significant sectors of Britain's economy, such as the iron and the textile industries, shifted to the mechanized, large-scale productive processes characteristic of modern industrialization, the majority of British workers remained employed in traditionally organized industries. The shape of the future, however, was clear. The suddenly sprawling cities of the industrial North could not be contained; the vast plains of the traditional economy would soon be eroded to scattered islands within an industrial sea.[1]

The new world shaped by industrialization both rested on and reinforced the triumph of the machine and the victory of the middle class. Although industrialization is much more than the substitution of mechanical for human or animal power, the machine stands at its core. The machine guaranteed standardization, uniformity, interchangeability, and therefore a reduction in the costs of both production and consumption. It promised to turn luxury goods for the elite into standard products for the masses, and thus to turn a substantial profit for its owners. It also promised to remake labor itself. It could operate day and night, with no regard for holidays, holy days, or seasonal change. It held the potential of freeing the laborer from arduous work – and for greater productivity. By the middle of the nineteenth century, the Age of the Machine had arrived.

The Age of the Machine was also the Age of the Middle Class. Although Britain's aristocracy did not scorn moneymaking or profit taking and took full advantage of the economic opportunities provided by industrial expansion, it was the middle class that catapulted to economic dominance with Britain's industrial takeoff. This economic might did not translate into direct political dominance. Throughout the nineteenth century and to an astonishing degree into the twentieth, the traditional elites retained political power. But, as Harold Perkin has shown, by the middle of the nineteenth century, the middle class ruled Britain by remote control. The traditional elites still governed, but they did so at the behest of the bourgeoisie, whose values and standards shaped Victorian society. What Perkin labeled the "entrepreneurial ideal" – a vision of society as a competitive arena in which the productive individual would climb to the top – pushed aside, although never succeeded in eliminating entirely, contending world views.[2]

The industrial revolution was the most important force that transformed traditional into modern society; it was not, however, the only one. The new world also rested on an intellectual revolution that elevated respect for and trust in human reason and observation to new heights. Together, the contending epistemological theories of rationalism and empiricism provided secular solutions to the world's woes. Beginning with the scientific revolution of the seventeenth century and culminating in the eighteenth-century Enlightenment, the educated classes of Europe embraced a this-worldly focus that replaced divine authority with human intellect. The nonmaterial realms of existence and metarational modes of understanding were dismissed as irrelevant or attacked as illusory. Because this intellectual revolution never as-

---

1 I have borrowed the plains/islands metaphor of industrialization from T. W. Heyck.
2 Harold Perkin, *The Origins of Modern English Society* (London: Routledge, 1969; Ark Edition, 1985), pp. 218–340.

sumed in Britain the violently antireligious cast that it took on in France and other Continental countries, it was incorporated more easily into respectable thought and culture. Its mechanistic view of the universe provided a sturdy foundation for the Age of the Machine.

A third force that shaped the new world was that of political revolution. The French Revolution set the political agenda for the nineteenth century in Britain. It was at first welcomed as a sister to the "Glorious" Revolution of 1688, a God-ordained upheaval that would overthrow irrational absolutism and replace it with a limited monarchical system devoted to protecting the privileges of the propertied. The Jacobin, or radical, phase of the Revolution, however, shifted elite Britain into the antirevolutionary camp and provoked counterrevolutionary measures at home as well. These measures succeeded in suppressing radical and democratic agitation in the first decades of the nineteenth century but could not eradicate radical and democratic ideas. Although universal adult suffrage eluded Britain until 1928, throughout the nineteenth century the threat or promise of democracy remained a potent force in shaping modern Britain.

As this new world solidified and expanded over the next two centuries, a significant undercurrent of protest solidified and expanded as well. Rooted in a romantic world view, this protest challenged the seemingly inevitable outcomes of the industrial and intellectual revolutions. It offered contradictory assessments and definitions of democracy but sought a common aim: the enhancement of the quality of life for the ordinary individual as well as for the elites. The romantic protest tradition argued that much of value and significance had been lost in the transition to modern society. These protesters sought to regain what they perceived as the spiritual, communal, and aesthetic strengths of traditional society.

Poetry as protest

The industrial, intellectual, and political revolutions provided the context in which the English Romantic movement emerged. The poetry of Blake, Wordsworth, Southey, Coleridge, Keats, and Shelley was written in an age of "violent and inclusive change," a time when anything seemed possible, a period of revolutionary exaltation.[3] As Jacques Barzun has shown, despite their many differences, these poets formed a single movement because they attempted to solve a shared problem: "to create a new world on the ruins of the old." They were all occupied with the task of reconstruction. This task

---

3 M. H. Abrams, "English Romanticism: The Spirit of the Age," in *Romanticism and Consciousness: Essays in Criticism*, ed. Harold Bloom (New York: Norton, 1970), pp. 92–103.

led them in two seemingly opposite directions: toward political and social involvement aimed at changing and re-creating the outer reality and toward individual regeneration and the discovery of the inner reality. In Barzun's words, "romantic life led in two directions – union with God, conceived either traditionally or pantheistically or metaphysically; and work for mankind, conceived in the form of either social improvement, or the creation of art, or the application of science."[4] These two paths, however, intersected at key points. Renewing society and restoring one's soul were seen as complementary rather than contradictory. According to Raymond Williams, for the Romantics "a conclusion about personal feeling became a conclusion about society."[5]

At the heart of English Romantic poetry lay what H. G. Schenk called the quest for reintegration.[6] The Romantics sought to reconnect, in new ways, the fragments of a society and a soul shattered by the economic, political, social, and cultural changes of the previous decades. This quest led them to assert a belief in an organic universe, a belief with far-reaching intellectual consequences, and one that distinguished the Romantics from their eighteenth-century counterparts. No longer was the world a perfectly running machine, conforming to ideal and perhaps divine patterns. Instead, the Romantics perceived their world as a growing organism, capable of change and infinite diversity.[7] This organic perception of the universe, defined by Rene Wellek as the "root metaphor" of Romanticism, led to new concepts of nature, history, and community that would serve as continuous themes in the romantic protest tradition.[8]

Poetry became a form of resistance, a means of standing in opposition to the progress of industrial society and reclaiming, and at the same time remaking, traditional meaning and values. The Romantic poets fought against the mainstream in an increasingly industrialized society that reduced whole human beings to "hands," to appendages of machines, to factors of production that could be quantified. In their demand for wholeness, they rejected a materialist world view. To confine reality to the material world was to limit humanity's potential and to deny humanity's deepest longings. The Romantics perceived that "materialism narrows down the world to a fraction

---

4 Jacques Barzun, *Classic, Romantic, and Modern* (Chicago: University of Chicago Press, 1975), pp. 14, 94.
5 Raymond Williams, *Culture and Society* (New York: Columbia University Press, 1983), p. 30.
6 H. G. Schenk, *The Mind of the European Romantics* (New York: 1966), chap. 4.
7 See Morse Peckham, "Toward a Theory of Romanticism," *PMLA*, Feb. 1951, pp. 9–13.
8 Rene Wellek, "The Concept of 'Romanticism' in Literary History," *Comparative Literature* 1/1 (Winter 1949): 1–23 and 1/2 (Spring 1949): 147–72; Peckham, "Toward a Theory of Romanticism," p. 12.

of itself." Embarked on "the search for the infinite reality that corresponds to man's infinite longings," they sought to expand the boundaries of experience and so to expand their own souls.[9]

This antimaterialism resulted in less-than-wholehearted approval of scientific endeavor. Barzun has argued that the Romantics were not opposed to science in and of itself but perceived that scientific investigation revealed "a restricted field of experience."[10] In the Romantic world view, science could not embrace the whole of reality, or even its most significant aspects. To reach such realms demanded the heart and the soul rather than the mind and the senses.

The Romantics were not, however, irrationalists, just as they were not escapists. Rather, as Harold Bloom has argued, "the great enemy of poetry in the Romantic tradition has never been reason, but rather those premature modes of conceptualization that masquerade as final accounts of reason in every age."[11] For the English Romantics, utilitarianism, with its smug assurances that human reason could weigh the pleasures and pains of human society and thus calculate the greatest good for the greatest number, stood as the preeminent "premature mode of conceptualization" that had to be attacked. By dismissing the nonmaterial as contrary to fact and observation and therefore as irrelevant to social happiness, the utilitarians ignored and threatened to destroy the most significant aspects of human experience.

The utilitarians also erred in their materialistic and reductionist approach to the natural environment. To the Romantics, nature was more than material reality.[12] Nature was not an entity out there to be studied, classified, and objectified; rather, it was a living being with which and in which to participate. Whether the Romantic poet sought union with God through nature or union with nature itself, he or she viewed the natural world as a source of spiritual wisdom and as a means of achieving the reintegration of self and society that stood as the goal of his or her quest. This sacralization of nature served as a form of protest against materialist, industrializing society and its view of nature as insignificant apart from its utility as a resource to be plundered.

The organic concept of the world led not only to a revitalized sense of what Northrop Frye has termed nature's "numinous power"[13] but also to

9 Barzun, *Classic, Romantic, and Modern*, pp. 66, 93–4. See also Schenk, *Mind of the European Romantics*, pts. 2 and 3.
10 Barzun, *Classic, Romantic, and Modern*, p. 65. See also Peter Thorslev, Jr., "Romanticism and Literary Consciousness," *Journal of the History of Ideas*, July–Sept. 1975, p. 568.
11 Harold Bloom, *The Ringers in the Tower* (Chicago: University of Chicago Press, 1971), p. 323.
12 See Northrop Frye, *A Study of English Romanticism* (New York: Random House, 1968), p. 16.
13 Ibid.

a new vision of the past. Romantic emphasis on change and uniqueness led to an appreciation of the individuality of human cultures and historic periods. In addition, part of the process of reintegration involved the linking of the present reality with past manifestations. The Romantics celebrated change but did not embrace the Enlightenment view of human development as a progression from the darkness of superstition and ignorance into the sunshine of rationality. Instead, they saw in past societies important values that must be restored if the task of reintegration was to succeed.

Romantic medievalism arose out of this conviction that important values had been lost in the process of industrialization. Despite the new emphasis on closely examining past cultures, the Romantics painted a heavily idealized picture of the Middle Ages. As a result, Frye has argued that the Romantic historical sense was in fact *antihistorical* because the Romantics used the past to construct utopias.[14] Medievalism, however, was more than mere escapism or nostalgia; the Romantics may have created a utopia or social ideal out of the Middle Ages, but they utilized this social ideal in an effort to renew and re-create their social reality.

At the heart of this social ideal lay a concept of community. What appealed to the Romantics about the Middle Ages was what they perceived as its corporate life. By the early years of the nineteenth century, the existence of such a corporate spirit and experience appeared threatened in Britain. Secularization meant the fragmentation and marginalization of religious community, the fraying of one of the threads that linked individuals to something larger and more permanent than themselves. At the same time, as urbanization increased the anonymity of British society, it was easy to believe that in the preindustrial rural villages a web of community life had existed that securely bound individuals with mutual ties of obligation and dependency. Threatened by the standardizing impact of industrialization, the variety and richness of local and regional customs that gave this web its strength seemed in danger of disappearing altogether.

In their poetry, then, the Romantics did more than express new ideas about art and the artist. They offered a social and cultural critique, the major themes of which would continue to be articulated by protesters in the romantic tradition throughout the nineteenth and into the twentieth century. They rejected mechanistic and materialist theories for an organic conception of the universe that served as the starting point for their quest of reintegration and their task of reconstruction. They viewed human reason as essentially limited, and they endeavored, in their efforts to connect with nature and the past, to offer an expanded vision of experience and existence.

14 Ibid., p. 37.

Thomas Carlyle and the preservation of wonder

By the time the young Victoria assumed the throne and the Victorian Age began, most of the Romantic poets had died. The romantic who lived on was Thomas Carlyle, the Victorian sage who continued to voice the romantic critique of industrial society through the 1870s. Carlyle's immense and varied writings proclaimed the core message of antimechanism.[15] His first essay of social criticism, *Signs of the Times*, labeled the nineteenth century the "Age of Machinery." He recognized the material benefits conferred by mechanical progress but doubted whether the triumph of mechanism signaled an improvement in the spiritual and social aspects of existence. Warning against what he perceived to be a narrowing and limited view of reality, a mind-set in which "what cannot be investigated and understood mechanically cannot be investigated and understood at all," Carlyle contended that mechanical science could never comprehend the "primary, unmodified forces and energies of man, the mysterious springs of Love, and Fear, and Wonder, of Enthusiasm, Poetry, Religion, all of which have a truly vital and *infinite* character." The exaltation of the mechanical meant the degradation of the spiritual so that "by our skill in Mechanism, it has come to pass that in the management of external things we excel all other ages; while in whatever respects the pure moral nature, in true dignity of soul and character, we are perhaps inferior to most civilised ages."[16]

Carlyle made the contrast between the morally superior past and the mechanically able present explicit in *Past and Present*, written fourteen years after *Signs of the Times*. In this important work he rejected the Victorian assumption of progress and painted a picture of his society as spiritually declining and socially divided. Even in material goods Victorian Britain fell short: "In the midst of plethoric plenty, the people perish; with gold walls, and full barns, no man feels himself safe or satisfied." "Mammonism," the making of money, turned the wheels of Victorian society but could not guarantee social cohesion. Human relations demanded more than financial transactions: "We have profoundly forgotten everywhere that *Cash-payment* is not the sole relation of human beings."[17] In contrast, Carlyle held up the medieval monastic community as a social ideal that revealed the existence of other points of juncture apart from the cash nexus.

For Carlyle, history served as a storehouse of moral and spiritual wisdom. The true historian was not an objective fact gatherer but rather a poet, one

---

15 See John Holloway, *The Victorian Sage: Studies in Argument* (Hamden: Archon Books, 1962), pp. 1–47.

16 Thomas Carlyle, *Selected Writings*, ed. Alan Shelston (Harmondsworth: Penguin, 1971), pp. 64, 70, 72 (emphasis in original), 77.

17 Ibid., pp. 263, 277 (emphasis in original).

who could penetrate the deeper realities and mysteries of former ages. To read the past the historian had to rely on intuition and inspiration. Human reason alone was not sufficient, because "the healthy Understanding . . . is not the Logical, argumentative, but the Intuitive; for the end of Understanding is not to prove and find reasons, but to know and believe."[18] For Carlyle, as Brian John has argued, a "Fact" was "that which is recognized by the whole man rising up in a creative oneness of self, to an intuition . . . of the eternal realities."[19] The writing of history was essentially the same as the construction of a Romantic poem, a quest for reintegration.

Carlyle's definition of the "Facts" contrasted sharply with that offered by the utilitarians, his key opponents. Unlike the followers of Jeremy Bentham, Carlyle saw the powers of human reason as severely limited, and so viewed the utilitarian faith in social progress via fact gathering and statistical analysis as wrongheaded and dangerous, part of the intrusion of the Machine into all aspects of life. Numbers could not save the world. Statistics created a universe peopled by abstractions rather than by real individuals with genuine needs and hopes. Carlyle also condemned the utilitarian approach because it sought to eradicate mystery from human experience. Deprived of wonder, the human being ceased to be fully human. In the Age of Machinery, wonder gave way to systems and diagrams and rational reform, and thus society faced spiritual degradation and finally internal ruin. The man who described Britain's "industrial existence" as "one huge poison-swamp of reeking pestilence physical and moral; a hideous *living* Golgotha of souls and bodies buried alive. . . . that putrefying well of abominations,"[20] did not deny the need for reform. But he believed that utilitarian reform would destroy, rather than save, society.

Although he abandoned the strict Calvinism of his upbringing, Carlyle remained committed to a belief in God as an active and involved force in the universe and in human affairs. For Carlyle, "it [was] impossible to believe otherwise than that this world is the work of an Intelligent Mind." Despite bouts with despair and depression, he never lost his faith "that all things are governed by Eternal Goodness and Wisdom."[21] Carlyle's social and cultural critique offered a vision of the preindustrial past as a repository of much-needed wisdom and as an example of authentic community. By repeating and extending the themes of the protest first voiced by the Romantic poets, Carlyle ensured its continued importance in British cultural and intellectual life.

18 Carlyle, "Characteristics," in *A Carlyle Reader*, ed. G. B. Tennyson (New York: Modern Library, 1969), p. 71.
19 Brian John, "The Fictive World," in *Thomas Carlyle*, ed. Harold Bloom (New York: Chelsea, 1986), p. 87.
20 Carlyle, *Latter-Day Pamphlets #1*, in *Carlyle Reader*, pp. 442–3.
21 Quoted in Fred Kaplan, *Thomas Carlyle: A Biography* (Ithaca: Cornell University Press, 1983), p. 531.

The lure of the Middle Ages

In *Past and Present* Carlyle used the contrast between his idealized vision of the Middle Ages and his present reality to voice his anti-industrialism. The medieval period held a central position in the Victorian imagination, and particularly in the romantic protest. As Alice Chandler has argued, for the Victorians the Middle Ages came to stand as a symbol of order and coherence in a swiftly changing world. Chandler shows how medievalism functioned in Victorian literature as a "program of resistance" against rationalism, materialism, and the glorification of self-interest. Nineteenth-century writers used the Middle Ages "as a symbol of a creative universe in which human energy can manifest itself freely, purposefully, generously" and as an embodiment of their faith that this creative universe possessed meaning.[22] Within this meaningful, purposive universe, individuals existed not as competing self-contained units but rather as interdependent parts of an integral whole. Reintegration and reconnection lay at the heart of the medievalist vision just as they undergirded the Romantic quest.

Medievalism can be traced in British thought back to the Tudor period, but the origins of Victorian medievalism lay in the eighteenth century, in the interplay of three developments: the rise of the cult of the picturesque, the emergence of antiquarian studies, and the revival of history writing as a popular genre aimed at a literate and increasingly powerful middle-class audience.[23] The rejection of classical order involved in appreciation of the picturesque opened the way toward a new understanding of Gothic architecture and so toward greater sympathy for the period that had produced this architecture, at the same time as antiquarianism and a new approach to history writing illuminated the "Dark Ages." The result was the formation of an ideal that expressed a protest against empiricism and industrialism and that merged with the romantic critique.

Most nineteenth-century readers met medievalism through the works of Sir Walter Scott, whose fictions entranced the literate classes. In 1820, for example, the London theatergoer had a choice of five different dramatized versions of *Ivanhoe* to attend.[24] In Scott's pages the main themes of not only nineteenth-century medievalism but also the wider romantic protest appear again and again. He depicted a world of interdependence, in which leaders and led interacted in a vital community that sustained and promoted both social cohe-

22 Alice Chandler, *A Dream of Order: The Medieval Ideal in Nineteenth-Century English Literature* (Lincoln: University of Nebraska Press, 1970). Quotations from pp. 152, 233.
23 See Roy Strong, *Recreating the Past: British History and the Victorian Painter* (London: Thames and Hudson, 1978), pp. 11–72.
24 Mark Girouard, *The Return to Camelot: Chivalry and the English Gentleman* (New Haven: Yale University Press, 1981), p. 90.

sion and individual acts of heroism. In such a universe, the power of passion and tradition limited the domain of human reason and revealed the inadequacy of a purely rational or materialistic approach to social well-being.[25]

While Scott's novels presented a coherent and convincing alternative society to his readers and helped cement medievalism into the intellectual structure of the nineteenth century, the material structures of the Gothic Revival revealed the potency of medievalism in nonliterary aspects of nineteenth-century culture. By the middle of the nineteenth century, Gothicism held sway across the British Isles. For example, of the 214 churches built as a result of the Church Building Act of 1818, 174 were constructed in the Gothic style. Michael Bright places the Gothic Revival within the context of the Victorian quest for identity in a world of rapid change. Linked to the rise of modern historical inquiry, the Gothic Revival represented an effort by architects to "turn architecture back to the true and natural course from which it had been diverted" by the essentially foreign styles of the Renaissance and neoclassicism.[26]

Bright has shown that this effort to reconnect Britain's architecture to the nation's history appealed to a wide public whose tastes had been shaped by the aesthetic theories of Romanticism.[27] These theories taught, first, that architecture, like poetry, should reveal the spiritual essence of reality through the use and stimulation of the imagination. For this task, the soaring spires and playful unpredictability of the Gothic style proved eminently suitable. Second, architecture, like poetry, should be true to nature – nature seen romantically as an organic being rather than as the machine of eighteenth-century sensibility. Symmetry and perfection in design gave way to changeability, fluidity, a sense of change and incompleteness. Finally, in the Romantic vision beauty could not be separated from truth and from naturalness. Gothic architecture could stimulate the imagination to comprehend beauty and so elevate the moral impulses of the observer.

The Gothic Revival concerned more than just buildings. Not only were its aesthetic principles shaped by Romanticism, but its churches and train stations and remodeled country homes expressed a protest against industrializing society that was rooted in Romanticism. In a time of change the Gothicists asserted the importance of attending to the products of the past in order to move forward in the right direction. As they looked to the medieval past, they discerned the need to revive not only the Gothic style but central principles and values of the era that gave birth to Gothicism.

---

25 Chandler, *Dream of Order*, pp. 25–51.
26 Michael Bright, *Cities Built to Music: Aesthetic Theories of the Victorian Gothic Revival* (Columbus: Ohio State University Press, 1984), p. 34.
27 Bright, *Cities Built to Music*. The rest of this paragraph summarizes Bright's argument.

Art and society: Ruskin, Morris, and the
Arts and Crafts movement

One of the most important statements of the values and aims of the Gothic Revival was written by John Ruskin in his "The Nature of the Gothic." In this chapter from *The Stones of Venice* Ruskin articulated not only a theory about architecture but also a critique of industrial society and, in particular, a critique of the kind of work required by industrialization. In Ruskin's view, the defining characteristics or "moral elements" of Gothic – savageness, changefulness, naturalism, grotesqueness, rigidity, and redundance – were rooted in and revealed the moral framework of medieval society. For example, the savageness or imperfection of Gothic architecture, Ruskin argued, grew out of the Christian basis of society. In Christian society, workers were not reduced to servile status and forced to copy the master workman. They were granted freedom of creation, a freedom that could and did result in a rude rather than a finished product. Ruskin contended, "You must either make a tool of the creature, or a man of him. . . . Men were not intended to work with the accuracy of tools, to be precise and perfect in all their actions. If you will have that precision out of them, and make their fingers measure degrees like cog-wheels, and their arms strike curves like compasses, you must unhumanize them." This process of "unhumanization," the "degradation of the operative into a machine," that characterized industrialization threatened to destroy the spiritual basis of society and could only lead to social and cultural disintegration.[28]

Ruskin's quest for wholeness led him to write the series of essays that made up *Unto This Last*, the publication of which had to be curtailed because of the public outcry. *Unto This Last* dared to question the foundations of Victorian society: the so-called science of political economy. In his attack on the leading economic doctrines of his day, Ruskin articulated the major themes of the romantic critique. He rejected the abstraction that stood at the heart of political economy: the idea of "economic man," motivated solely by economic self-interest. No such being existed, Ruskin argued. Instead, the human being's "motive power is a Soul" and so "the force of this very peculiar agent, as an unknown quantity, enters into all the political economist's equations, without his knowledge, and falsifies every one of their results." One false result was the doctrine that laissez-faire economic policies would lead to both social and individual progress. True progress would come only when human society guided the flow of wealth for the benefit of all. Morality and justice, not the invisible hand of competition, must guard

28 John Ruskin, "The Nature of the Gothic," in *"Unto This Last" and Other Writings* (London: Penguin, 1987), pp. 79, 84, 86.

and govern economic relations. Laissez-faire policies would destroy the connections that held society together and, by so doing, would destroy the
foundations of real wealth. Wealth was not money, capital, or things, Ruskin
argued, but instead an accumulation of the "truly valuable . . . that which
leads to life with its whole strength."[29] Economics should be about discrimination, the discrimination of life from destruction, of wholeness from fragmentation, of the eternal from the transient. A society that based its economic attitudes and actions on the illusion of the economic man and the
reductionism of laissez-faire principles could only destroy itself.

Ruskin believed firmly that social cohesion depended on a community of
spirit and purpose between the leaders and the led: No democrat or Liberal,
he insisted that a natural hierarchy of authority existed. Nevertheless, his
attack on the major economic assumptions of his day became a foundational
text in British socialism: For example, the first twenty-nine Labour MPs
elected in 1906 pointed to *Unto This Last* as the book that most influenced
them.[30] Ruskin's ideas also helped shape the career of William Morris,
arguably one of the most important figures in twentieth-century British socialism, although he died in 1896. While still an Oxford undergraduate,
Morris read Ruskin's "The Nature of the Gothic." Under its influence he
resolved to give up his plans for the ministry and to become an architect.[31] It
was through Ruskin, Morris testified, "that I learned to give form to my
discontent. . . . Apart from the desire to produce beautiful things, the leading
passion of my life has been and is hatred of modern civilization."[32] Like
Ruskin, Morris was led through art to reject the mainstream economic and
social assumptions of his day. Like Ruskin, Morris used his idealized vision
of the Middle Ages to highlight the shortcomings of industrial society and to
illuminate the path forward out of the industrial and capitalist wasteland.

A man of tremendous energy, Morris often seems to have lived several
lives. After Oxford, he began to study as an architect under George Edmund
Street, an important influence on the architecture of the later Arts and Crafts
movement.[33] In 1856, after only nine months with Street, Morris met Dante
Gabriel Rossetti and resolved to become a painter. His contact with Rossetti
led to the formation of the second phase of the Pre-Raphaelite Brotherhood.
The Brotherhood was founded in 1848 by John Everett Millais, Holman
Hunt, Thomas Woolner, and Rossetti in order to revive painting through
"personal observation, and the intimate study of and strict adherence to

29 Ruskin, "Unto This Last," in ibid., pp. 170, 209.
30 Clive Wilmer, Introduction to ibid., p. 30.
31 Peter Davey, *Arts and Crafts Architecture: The Search for Earthly Paradise* (London: Architectural Press, 1980), pp. 21–2.
32 William Morris, "How I Became a Socialist," in *"News from Nowhere" and Selected
   Writings and Designs* (Harmondsworth: Penguin Books, 1980), pp. 35–6.
33 Davey, *Arts and Crafts Architecture*, pp. 15–19.

nature."[34] The group chose to call itself Pre-Raphaelite "out of banter, defiance, and a belief that the art of the Middle Ages provided a greater truth to nature than had been seen since the days of Raphael."[35] With Rossetti, his friend Edward Burne-Jones, and several other young men, Morris set out to continue the work of the Pre-Raphaelite Brotherhood. His career as a painter was short-lived, however. In 1857, he and Burne-Jones discovered that they could not find satisfactory furniture for their joint lodgings. Scorning what they perceived as the cheap and shoddy goods of industrial society, they chose to design their own, medievalist-looking pieces. This choice led Morris to embark on his most-lasting career: as a designer of not only furniture but also paintings, wallpapers, carpets, stained glass, embroidery, domestic utensils, and jewelry. In 1890, Morris expanded his already-exhausting range of activities to include bookbinding and printing and founded the Kelmscott Press, an effort to revive the art of making beautiful books. The publication of the Kelmscott Chaucer in the year of Morris's death marked the culmination of his efforts not only in bookmaking but also in the revitalization of dying handcrafts in a machine-oriented society.

During his busy years as painter, designer, and bookmaker, Morris also pursued a career as a writer. Like his early paintings, his early writings reveal a longing for the beauty and coherence that he perceived in the Middle Ages. *The Defense of Guinevere*, published in 1858, retells the Arthurian legend from a distinctly anti-Victorian viewpoint, in which Guinevere's passion is accepted rather than abhorred. His most popular poem during the Victorian era, "The Earthly Paradise," expressed his longing for escape from industrial reality:

> Forget six counties overhung with smoke,
> Forget the snorting steam and piston stroke,
> Forget the spreading of the hideous town;
> Think rather of the pack-horse on the down,
> And dream of London, small, and white, and clean.[36]

In this poem, written at the end of the 1860s, Morris sought only escape. He described himself as a "dreamer of dreams, born out of my due time," and asked, "Why should I strive to set the crooked straight?"[37]

By the early 1880s, Morris had answered his own question. He embraced socialism and spent the rest of his life striving to set the crooked straight. His socialist commitment, however, did not eradicate his longing for the past. In

---

34 William M. Rossetti, ed., *Pre-Raphaelite Diaries and Letters* (London, 1900), p. 205. Quoted in Chandler, *Dream of Order*, p. 193.
35 Chandler, *Dream of Order*, p. 193.
36 "The Earthly Paradise," in *"News from Nowhere" and Selected Writings*, p. 68.
37 Ibid., p. 67.

a series of prose romances written in the 1880s and 1890s, Morris looked backward even beyond the medieval era to explore imaginary worlds of community and vitality.[38] They were based in part on Morris's fascination with ancient northern Germanic and Icelandic literature and on his respect for the independence and hardiness of the people he met on his visit to Iceland in 1871. In both contemporary Iceland and in ancient northern sagas Morris perceived a classless society, a true community that fostered individual strength and creativity. The contrast between such communities and the atomized society of industrial, urbanized Britain, like the contrast between the good art of the medieval era and the shoddy commercialism of the nineteenth century, helped shape and motivate his socialism.

At the center of his condemnation of industrial Britain rested Morris's vision of work. Morris defined good work as labor that involved hope: "hope of rest, hope of product, hope of pleasure in the work itself."[39] Industrial capitalism denied the worker rest in sufficient quantity and of sufficient quality. Existing rather than living, the worker spent most of his or her energies in the mindless and soulless production of unnecessary goods, products without hope. Such work possessed no pleasure. It could not satisfy the human need to create, to color the world, to imitate the variety and playfulness of nature.

Nor could it create real wealth. Like Ruskin, Morris did not define wealth as the accumulation of things; rather, "wealth is what Nature gives us and what a reasonable man can make out of the gifts of Nature for his reasonable use." Wealth included "works of art, the beauty which man creates when he is most a man, most aspiring and thoughtful – all things which serve the pleasure of people, free, manly, and uncorrupted."[40] Morris concluded that capitalist society could never be truly wealthy. For both good work and good art to thrive, society itself would have to be good. Only the abandonment of capitalism and the establishment of a socialist system would restore authentic and meaningful community and consumption to modern society.

Although interested more in art than in economics, Morris read Marx and embraced his theory of revolutionary socialism. Nevertheless, his vision of socialism remained primarily romantic, an effort to overcome the disintegration and fragmentation of modern industrialism and scientific empiricism. When he sketched his hopes for a future socialized Britain in *News from Nowhere*, he painted a picture of a largely deindustrialized, deurbanized world, a fourteenth-century society without the church or famine or social hierarchy (but which included traditional gender roles). Not only the owner-

38 *The House of the Wolfings, The Roots of the Mountains, The Wood beyond the World,* and *The Well at the World's End.*
39 "Useful Work versus Useless Toil," in *"News from Nowhere" and Selected Writings,* p. 118.
40 Ibid., p. 121.

ship of the means of production but the means themselves have been changed, brought back to human scale, with machinery used only to eliminate the most unpleasant, mindless, and backbreaking tasks. It is socialism defined as "peace and rest, and cleanness and smiling goodwill."[41]

Although Morris played a key role in shaping British socialism, his political ideas were not embraced by the artistic movement that he helped create and that carried his aesthetic vision forward. Rooted in the ideals of the Gothic Revival and Morris's theories about good art, the Arts and Crafts movement of the late nineteenth and early twentieth centuries did, however, articulate a protest against industrial society and its products. In describing the movement's aims, Walter Crane explained it as "a revolt against the hard mechanical conventional life and its insensibility to beauty . . . [and] a protest against the turning of men into machines."[42]

The medievalism of Morris and his associates did not survive long in the works of their Arts and Crafts heirs, who branched off into experiments in the Queen Anne and Georgian styles and even full-blown classicism and modernism.[43] The unifying thread that tied together this diverse and often contradictory movement was, according to Peter Davey, the effort to oppose the compartmentalization of life and work imposed by industrialization.[44] In their architectural and artistic experiments, these artisans sought to reintegrate the individual with both the best of the past and the promise of the future, to treat all of life as a coherent whole. By constructing buildings that were both functional and beautiful, they sought to overcome the artificiality and fragmentation of industrial society. By seeking to build in vernacular styles and with local materials, they fought against the standardization and mass-produced uniformity of a world they found both materially and spiritually ugly.

The protest against the alienation inherent in industrial production led many supporters of the Arts and Crafts movement to search for ways to restore the spirit of community to the modern world. In 1902 the eminent Arts and Crafts architect C. R. Ashbee led his Guild of Handicraft from London to Chipping Camden in the Cotswolds, in an eventually abortive attempt to counter industrial alienation by building a rural community devoted to the principles of good work.[45] Three decades earlier Ruskin had undertaken a similar experiment in alternative living with the Guild of St. George; it, too, quickly failed. Not all of the Arts and Crafts guild endeavors

41 "News from Nowhere" and Selected Writings, p. 184.
42 Quoted by Davey, Arts and Crafts Architecture, p. 54.
43 E.g., one of the early leaders of the movement, William R. Lethaby, eventually embraced machine production. See ibid., pp. 56–67.
44 Ibid., p. 212.
45 See Fiona MacCarthy, The Simple Life: C. R. Ashbee in the Cotswolds (Berkeley and Los Angeles: University of California Press, 1981).

were residential communities. Some were less ambitious efforts to create a fellowship of artists and artisans that would further the ideals of the movement. The choice of the label "guild" indicated the medievalism at the core of the movement, a medievalism that embodied the struggle against the main currents of industrial society.

G. D. H. Cole and a different kind of socialism

Not surprisingly, when *Guild Socialism* emerged in the Edwardian era, it found many of its early supporters among the followers of the Arts and Crafts movement. It, too, was produced by a sense of revulsion against industrial society and a quest for alternatives. Often dismissed as reactionary, it offered a radical critique of modern British capitalism that posed an important challenge to mainstream assumptions and values.

Guild Socialism can be traced to Arthur Penty's *The Restoration of the Gild* [sic] *System*, published in 1906. A socialist inspired by William Morris as well as an architect influenced by Arts and Crafts ideals, Penty looked with horror on the type of socialism advocated by the Fabian Society. Dominated by Sidney and Beatrice Webb, the Fabians defined socialism in economic terms, as a more efficient means of production, and insisted that it could be achieved through legislative action and parliamentary reform. Penty found the Fabian emphasis on efficiency and expertise an affront to his more emotional and artistic political commitment and so sought to formulate a type of socialism more in accordance with his ideals. Penty argued that to recapture cohesion and vitality, modern society would have to revive the organizational framework of the medieval "gilds," which, because they were "social, religious, and political as well as industrial institutions," comprehended "the essential unity of life."[46]

Part of the constellation of ideas and movements that rejected the parliamentary route of change and sought new avenues of reform in the years before the Great War,[47] Guild Socialism found its chief spokesman in G. D. H. Cole, one of Edwardian Britain's leading young socialist intellectuals. Cole quickly became Guild Socialism's foremost thinker and activist. Although the movement had collapsed by 1923, Guild ideals and principles remained the primary motivating forces throughout Cole's long and signifi-

---

46 Quoted in James Webb, *The Occult Establishment* (La Salle, Ill.: Open Court, 1976), p. 107.
47 See George Dangerfield, *The Strange Death of Liberal England, 1910–1914* (1935; New York: Perigee Books, 1980). Dangerfield did not examine Guild Socialism in this brilliant work.

cant career as a socialist writer, educator, economist, and historian. Cole explicitly identified himself with the losing tradition in British socialism. Against the Fabian stress on management by experts, on parliamentary processes, and on nationalization, Cole stood for a socialism that emphasized participation, activism by ordinary people, decentralization, and workers' control. In Cole's view, although the socialist solution offered by the Fabians would alleviate much of the suffering imposed by capitalism, it and other forms of collectivist socialism "were somehow things one wanted for other people rather than for oneself." In contrast, Cole explained, Guild Socialism "offered me a kind of Socialism that I could want as well as think right" because it saw people "as having personalities to be expressed as well as stomachs to be filled."[48]

Cole came to his socialism through William Morris's *News from Nowhere.* In the pages of Morris's fantasy, Cole discerned "the vision of a society in which it would be a fine and fortunate experience to live."[49] For Cole, as for Morris, aesthetics rather than economics led him to socialism, which he always regarded as far more than an economic or political doctrine. He saw it as an entire, and better, way of life, one that guaranteed good work for all individuals. Cole did not denigrate "the common-sense ideal of high wages," but he believed socialism must also hold up "the other ideal of enabling men somehow to express, in the daily work of their hands, some part of that infinitely subtle and various personality which lives in each one of them, if we can but call it out."[50] Socialism meant enablement. It meant restoring to the ordinary worker the physical and creative control over his or her labor, control that had been lost in the course of industrialization.

Cole's concern with the conditions and quality of work in the industrial world led him to embrace and help define Guild Socialism. In 1915 he resigned from the Fabian Society and formed the National Guilds League, an organization that endeavored, but failed, to establish in Britain a socialist alternative to Fabianism and the Labour Party. Through Guild Socialism Cole envisaged a radical reorganization of society. At the core of Cole's vision stood the guilds, democratically run workplace organizations that made all the decisions regarding production and goods and services. These guilds included drastically reformed trade unions. In their unreformed state, the unions were organized according to branch, with a large bureaucratic

---

48 "Guild Socialism Twenty Years Ago and Now," *New English Weekly,* Sept. 1934; quoted in A. W. Wright, *G. D. H. Cole and Socialist Democracy* (Oxford: Clarendon Press, 1979), pp. 268–9.

49 *William Morris as a Socialist* (London: William Morris Society, 1960), p. 1; quoted in Gerald Houseman, *G. D. H. Cole* (Boston: Twayne, 1979), p. 21.

50 *The World of Labour: A Discussion of the Present and Future of Trade Unionism* (London: G. Bell and Sons, 1913), p. 9.

structure making all the decisions. In contrast, the locus of power in Guild Socialism lay in the workplace, among the actual workers involved in day-to-day production. In the Guild vision, consumers, too, were organized into representative and democratic groupings. The important and vital decisions of society were made at the local level, by ordinary citizens rather than bureaucrats. The state continued to exist, but with quite limited powers. Central government, concerned almost exclusively with foreign policy, defense, and justice, was organized on federalist lines, with its powers dispersed among decentralized units.

Through such reorganization, Guild Socialism sought to realize "a union of industrial self-government and community control."[51] Cole believed that nationalization, as advocated by the Fabians, was meaningless for the achievement of socialism because it would not give real industrial control to the workers. Similarly, he dismissed parliamentary democracy as a sham. Authentic democracy demanded the active participation, at local levels, of all its citizens. Democracy could be achieved only by a more radical reworking of society than that envisaged by either the Fabians or Labour's politicians. But Cole was no communist. He did not advocate violent revolution; Guild Socialism was to come about through a process of "encroaching control" whereby workers would take charge, bit by bit, of the structures and processes of production.

In the years immediately preceding and during the First World War, the advent of an apparently strong industrial movement seemed to affirm the relevance of Guild Socialism for British society. In the aftermath of the war and particularly the continuing economic depression of the 1920s, however, the workers were in retreat, and Cole's vision seemed hopelessly utopian. By 1923 the National Guilds League had disintegrated. Some scholars see the twenties as the "point of real disjuncture" in Cole's thought because during the later 1920s and the 1930s he embraced the Labour Party as the agent of socialist change in Britain and conceded the primacy of political, as opposed to economic, action.[52] But Cole never abandoned the ideals that had motivated his embrace of Guild Socialism. He believed, however, in working within the realm of the possible. Before 1923, the reorganization of society on the basis of guilds had appeared possible; afterward, the ideals such reorganization aimed to achieve had to be sought by other means. With Labour in the ascendancy after 1945, Cole returned to many of the themes and ideas of his Guild years.

Although the emphases and specifics of Cole's socialism changed during the five decades in which he played an active role in British politics and

51 Wright, *G. D. H. Cole*, p. 80.   52 Ibid., p. 106.

thought, the basic elements remained the same. Like the Fabians, Cole believed in the importance of careful research, of getting the facts correct; however, as Asa Briggs wrote shortly after Cole's death, "He was the Enlightenment on the surface: the Romantic Movement underneath."[53] In his attitude toward economics, his ambivalence toward technology, his desire to establish a sound basis for community life, his emphasis on individual agency, and his respect for the peculiarities of the past, Cole placed himself squarely within the romantic tradition of protest.

A. W. Wright has written that "in a very fundamental sense, Cole did not *like* economics." For Cole, appointed as a Reader in Economics at Oxford, economics did not constitute a science but rather a branch of morals, and so capitalist economics stood condemned not because it was inefficient but because it was unjust and inhumane.[54] Cole rejected the claims of economists to the status of scientists and argued that no study of human society could be reduced to an objective set of facts, figures, and predictable laws. He did not deny the power of human reason, but neither did he deny its limitations: As early as 1909 he asserted that "however much we may strive to give all things a materialistic explanation, some will always recede from our grasp into an unfathomed track whither the reason cannot follow them."[55] Human beings were complex, mysterious totalities, spiritual beings with needs incomprehensible to any economic calculation.

Cole's concern with restoring opportunities for good work to the British laborer undergirded his ambivalence toward technology. Like Penty and advocates of Guild Socialism, Cole had deep sympathy for the preindustrial age and believed that the values and techniques of craftsmanship would have to be restored to modern society if men and women were to be given the chance to do good work. He did not, however, wish to return to the past or to scrap all modern technology. He saw technology as the means of eliminating what he called "dirty work" and thus of humanizing the workplace.[56] Much more often, however, technology was used as a tool of dehumanization, glorified in a belief system that saw economic efficiency as the supreme good.

Cole condemned the Fabian emphasis on efficiency because he believed it omitted the central strength of socialism: its ideal of fellowship. From Morris's *News from Nowhere* Cole had acquired a vision of fellowship that remained his goal for the rest of his life. He saw socialism as the only means of overcoming the fragmentation and alienation of industrial life and of restoring to Britain the sense of community that had been eradicated by the

---

53 *The Listener*, 20 Oct. 1960, p. 672.
54 Wright, *G. D. H. Cole*, pp. 181 (emphasis in original), 206.
55 "Faith-Making," *Oxford Reformer*, Nov. 1909; quoted in ibid., p. 17.
56 Houseman, *G. D. H. Cole*, p. 87.

processes of urbanization and industrialization. Such community, however, could not be achieved without the implementation of participatory rather than parliamentary democracy, a democracy in which each individual played an active and vital role.

In Cole's view, individual freedom and authentic community were inextricably linked; the negation of one would lead to the disintegration of the other. A libertarian rather than a Marxist, Cole defined socialism in terms of individual fulfillment rather than class hostilities. He resisted Marxism because he perceived it as a deterministic creed, one that failed to account for the existence and power of human free will. The socialist society was not inevitable. It would come only through the courageous action of free individuals.

Cole also condemned Marxism because it reinforced the tendency of modern society toward "bigness," and thus it, like industrial capitalism, denied individual human beings the right to participate and to act. A constant theme in Cole's work was the relationship between the bigness of modern industrial society and the alienation that most men and women experienced in their working and political lives. Cole insisted that "democracy had to be small, or broken up into small groups, in order to be real."[57] One of his objections to Fabianism was its tendency to build overly large structures, just as he criticized the Soviet Union for its erection of a leviathan socialist state. In the last year of his life, Cole explained, "I am neither a Communist nor a Social Democrat because I regard both as creeds of centralisation and bureaucracy, whereas I feel sure that a Socialist society . . . must rest on the widest possible diffusion of power and responsibility, so as to enlist the active participation of as many as possible of its citizens in the tasks of democratic self-government."[58] Community and democracy were thus linked in Cole's vision and stood at the heart of his call for socialism and his critique of modern industrialism. In words that foreshadowed E. F. Schumacher's *Small Is Beautiful*, Cole argued that the socialist's task was "to find democratic ways of living for little men in big societies. For men are little, and their capacity cannot transcend their experience or grow except by continuous building upon their historic past."[59]

Respect for the historic past formed an important theme in Cole's work and in his romantic protest. Cole was a historian as well as an economist, political and social theorist, journalist, philosopher, and writer of popular detective novels. Cole strove for scholarly accuracy in his history writing, but he also recognized and claimed this work for the socialist struggle. Cole

---

57 Undated and untitled manuscript; quoted in ibid., p. 61.
58 *A History of Socialist Thought*, vol. 5: *Socialism and Fascism, 1931–1939* (London: Macmillan, 1960), p. 337; quoted in Wright, *G. D. H. Cole*, p. 282.
59 *Essays in Social Theory* (London: Macmillan, 1950), p. 94.

called for teachers to "go forth to preach the gospel of social history to every worker."[60] He wanted each worker to see that he or she existed within a historical tradition, within a community that spanned the generations and ensured each individual of a sense of belonging and purpose. Moreover, the past also offered alternatives to the present. Cole admitted that there was no historical link between the medieval guilds and his hope for reformed trade unionism; however, "it does not follow that, because there is no historical connection, there is not a spiritual connection, a common motive present in both forms of association."[61] Just as the medieval guilds had served to reinforce the cohesion of the medieval community, so their modern counterparts would work to restore fellowship to modern life.

Cole's respect for history led him to emphasize the reality and significance of national differences. He opposed any monolithic theory of socialism that failed to recognize the existence of differing national histories, which would produce varying versions of socialism. In Britain, socialists inherited a tradition, however incomplete, of democracy and individualism. In order to succeed, British socialists needed to build on this legacy rather than deny its potency. Cole's theory of Guild Socialism was one such attempt to define a distinctly British path and form of socialism.[62] Moreover, Cole, unlike many of the Left, possessed a strong love for things English. One of the reasons that he rejected violent revolution as a means to socialist ends was that he feared such revolution would destroy much that he cherished. He saw socialism not as a complete break with the past but rather as the culmination of the best in British culture and history and believed that gradualism stood a better chance of preserving the civilization he loved.[63]

As part of a minority tradition, Cole sought ways in which to communicate to the majority his protest against industrial society and his alternative vision. He achieved only limited success in this effort of communication. By the time of his death in 1959, his small-scale, antimaterialist ideal bore little resemblance to the actual achievements of the Labour Party. Cole's significance, however, has little to do with the issue of his political success or failure. His affiliation with the Campaign for Nuclear Disarmament reveals his direct link to the post–World War II romantic protest in Britain.[64] More important, the themes of his social critique echo those articulated by preceding romantic critics and appear again in the three movements examined in subsequent chapters here.

60 "The Importance of History to the Workers," *New Standards*, Mar. 1924; quoted in Wright, *G. D. H. Cole*, p. 147.
61 Introduction to Georges Renard, *Guilds in the Middle Ages: Reprints of Economic Classics* (1918; New York: Augustus M. Kelley Publishers, 1968), p. xi.
62 Wright, *G. D. H. Cole*, pp. 72, 235, 274–5.   63 Ibid., pp. 227–9, 277–8.
64 Houseman, *G. D. H. Cole*, p. 69.

Creating conservative community:
Distributism and Chesterbelloc

Throughout his career Cole aligned himself with the left wing of British socialism; yet, his libertarian conception of socialism led him to embrace many ideas that resonated with certain sectors of the British Right. In 1942 he warned socialists to be wary of "tearing up by the roots any small man's refuge that is left in a world so ridden as ours by hugeness. It should make them regard the farmer, the shopkeeper, the small manufacturer, not as obstacles in the way of universal centralisation, but as valuable checks upon a dangerous agglomerative tendency."[65] Cole's recognition of the value of small-scale private property placed him at odds with many fellow socialists and set him within the ranks of other seekers of change regarded as right wing or even fascist. The pages of the *New Age*, the first journal of Guild Socialism, featured not only contributions by leftists but also articles by Hilaire Belloc and G. K. Chesterton, British intellectuals usually placed on the right of the political spectrum. Labeling Belloc and Chesterton "rightist" is, however, problematic: Champions of the trade unions and the Labour Party throughout the 1920s, they regarded capitalism as a corrosive agent that threatened British society with ruin. Like Cole, they viewed Britain's parliamentary system as a failure and a sham. Like Cole, they rejected many of the assumptions and values of modern industrialism and sought to offer an alternative ideal. And like Cole, their protest was rooted in the romantic tradition.

Unlike Cole, "Chesterbelloc" looked not to Guild Socialism but to *Distributism* as a way out of the quagmire of industrial capitalism. Belloc's *The Servile State* (1912) presented the first systematic outline of the Distributist analysis and program. Often regarded as an early defense of capitalism against socialism, the work is actually an attack on capitalism, as well as a warning against the view that socialism offered a genuine alternative.[66] The central argument of this important work is that "the effect of Socialist doctrine upon Capitalist society is to produce a third thing different from either of its two begetters – to wit, the Servile State."[67] In a rather oversimplified version of European history, Belloc depicted medieval Britain as the first Distributive State, in which peasant traditions and the guilds worked both to limit the growth of an economic oligarchy and to protect the private property

---

65 *Great Britain in the Post-War World* (London: Victor Gollancz, 1942), p. 12.
66 Misunderstandings of the book's arguments and aims cropped up very early. In his preface to the second edition of the work, published in 1913, Belloc found it necessary to point out that the Servile State could not be equated with the Socialist State (*The Servile State* [Boston: LeRoy Phillips, 1913], p. vii).
67 Ibid., p. xii.

of ordinary people.[68] This "excellent consummation of human society," however, gave way to "the dreadful moral anarchy" called capitalism when the
monasteries were dissolved during the English Reformation and the balance
of power shifted from the Crown to the aristocratic families that seized the
enormous material resources of the church. By 1660 an economic and political oligarchy controlled not only the Crown but also the ordinary people, who
began to sink down the rank of a proletariat. Capitalism predated industrialization and determined the form that it assumed in Britain and the world.[69]
Because of its capitalist form, industrialization became "an almost unmixed
curse for the unhappy society in which it has flourished."[70]

This curse could not, however, endure. Belloc believed that he perceived
in the upheavals of Edwardian Britain another historic shift, from the Capitalist to the Servile State. The agency for this change was socialism. As a
remedy for the insecurity and inequalities of monopoly capitalism, socialism
offered the ideal of a society without private property. Such an ideal, however, did not yet exist and, according to Belloc, could never exist. The shift
from capitalism to servility would come about because socialists possessed a
two-pronged agenda: the dispossession of the capitalists and the improvement of the workers' lives. Faced with the impossibility of achieving the first
aim, they focused on the second and, in their effort to ameliorate conditions
for the masses, strengthened the hold of the capitalists on the workers. In the
end, Belloc warned, "you will have two kinds of men, the owners economically free, and controlling to their peace and to the guarantee of their liveli-
hood the economically unfree non-owners."[71] And such an end, he argued,
would soon be realized in Britain, where already the establishment of compul-
sory education and insurance contributions signaled the beginnings of the
Servile State.

Britain, however, had an alternative. Rather than opting for collectivist
theory that would produce, not the Socialist, but the Servile State, the British
could choose Distributism. Instead of removing property from the hands of
the few and placing it in the control of the state, Distributism advocated
spreading property among as many owners as possible through the elimina-
tion of monopoly capitalism but not of private property, the protection of the
small-scale trader at the expense of Big Business, the breakup of large
estates and the strengthening of family farms. Accused of hopeless idealism,
Belloc insisted that Distributism, unlike socialism, was based on genuine
historical experience. The Distributist State had once existed and could exist
again if men (there was little room for female choice in Belloc's world) chose
to recognize and repudiate the path to the Servile State.

68 Ibid., pp. 41–54.   69 Ibid., pp. 57–77; quotation from p. 52.
70 Ibid., p. 75.   71 Ibid., p. 127.

Belloc believed Distributism could save Britain from spiritual annihilation, but he did not believe that it would. A pessimist and a misanthrope with a great capacity for hatred, he possessed little hope that Britain would avoid the future he feared. He became convinced that this future was in the hands of Jewish bankers and financiers, whose race and religion blocked them from appreciating the European heritage of independent ownership. By the late-1930s, Belloc's fear of a Jewish conspiracy had led him to abandon his earlier support for Labour, to advocate the replacement of democracy with an authoritarian monarchical system, and to support Mussolini, although not Hitler.[72]

Belloc's extreme anti-Semitism and fascist tendencies help explain why his more than one hundred books on a wide variety of subjects and his countless newspaper and journal articles are rarely read today. In contrast, the work of the other half of Chesterbelloc, G. K. Chesterton, exerts a continuing influence. Although Chesterton, too, can be accused of anti-Semitism, it was not one of the central themes of his life and work.[73] Unlike Belloc, Chesterton was an optimist and a lover of humanity with little capacity for hatred. Although he embraced not only Belloc's Roman Catholicism but also his vision of history, Chesterton presented a much more hopeful picture of Distributism and its place in British society.

At the core of Chesterton's beliefs rested his faith in the ordinary man (like Belloc, Chesterton was a firm antifeminist) and his conviction that justice and equality could be secured only in a state of direct democracy. In 1902 Chesterton wrote that "Christ, St Francis, Bunyan, Wesley, Mr Gladstone, Walt Whitman, men of indescribable variety, were all alike in a certain faculty of treating the average man as their equal, of trusting to his reason and good feeling without fear and without condescension."[74] Throughout his life Chesterton sought to do the same. He took great delight in ordinary experiences and conversation. In his view, "It is not in the cold halls of cleverness where celebrities seem to be important that we should look for the great. . . . It is in our own homes . . . in old nurses, and gentlemen with hobbies, and talkative spinsters and vast incomparable butlers, that we may

---

72 For Belloc's anti-Semitism, see Jay Corrin, *G. K. Chesterton and Hilaire Belloc: The Battle against Modernity* (Athens: Ohio University Press, 1981), pp. 63–5; A. N. Wilson, *Hilaire Belloc* (London: Hamish Hamilton, 1984), pp. 187–9, 257–61. For his fascist sympathies, see Corrin, *Chesterton and Belloc*, pp. 167–8, 175–88; Wilson, *Belloc*, pp. 257, 289–92. By the end of the 1930s, the *Weekly Review*, edited by Belloc, was advocating an alliance with Germany and Italy against the Soviet Union; see Corrin, *Chesterton and Belloc*, p. 191.

73 For Chesterton's anti-Semitism, see Margaret Canovan, *G. K. Chesterton: Radical Populist* (New York: Harcourt Brace Jovanovich, 1977), pp. 136–40; Corrin, *Chesterton and Belloc*, pp. 65–7. On the question of Chesterton and fascism, see Canovan, *Chesterton*, pp. 126–45; Corrin, *Chesterton and Belloc*, pp. 167–8, 175–84, 191–2, 195–200.

74 "Thomas Carlyle," in *The Bodley Head G. K. Chesterton*, selected by P. J. Kavanagh (London: Bodley Head, 1985), p. 3.

feel the presence of that blood of the gods."[75] This sense of "the blood of the gods" in the veins of the most ordinary person led Chesterton to insist that things such as folk traditions, legends, and fairy tales should not be despised but rather respected and made use of as repositories of wisdom.[76] It also led him to contend that despite vast differences in wealth, power, and talent, the things that human beings shared outweighed the things that separated them. This shared identity formed the basis of democracy. Men should be trusted to make the decisions that concerned their lives and their societies. The "stupid public" did not exist.[77]

Chesterton's political views led him to embrace Christianity, eventually as a Roman Catholic, because he believed that the Christian religion taught the essential sacredness of every human being and the goodness of the world of ordinary experience.[78] For Chesterton, Christianity was an affirmation of common sense in a world made confused by experts and intellectuals. Yet, it was no dry-as-dust system but rather an endless mystery and source of wonder. Like "a huge and ragged and romantic rock" or like a Gothic cathedral, in Christianity "apparent accidents balanced."[79] The sense of wonder, however, was rapidly disappearing from modern life, with its faith in experts and answers, in systems and plans, in big machines and large organizations. The result was spiritual suffocation, a loss of vitality and color and, eventually, of the essential qualities of being human.[80]

Chesterton insisted that in order to understand and to defeat the forces of suffocation, human beings had to look to the past for alternatives to industrial capitalism.[81] He perceived history as "a hill or high point of vantage, from which alone men see the town in which they live or the age in which they are living."[82] To Chesterton, the medieval era offered the present an example of a vital community life, a cohesive society held together by a common religion and thus a shared sense of purpose. Yet, at the same time that medieval Europe exemplified unity, it also offered variety. Local and regional customs and traditions ensured the diversity of medieval society and reinforced the uniqueness of each particular place. Culture was not dictated by the cities or by an elite but arose spontaneously from the ordinary people.[83]

When Chesterton contrasted his present reality to his vision of the medieval past, he discovered a society of alienated individuals, subjected to mind-

---

75 "A Midsummer Night's Dream," in ibid., p. 62.
76 See "The Ethics of Elfland," in ibid., pp. 254–69.
77 See "The Fool," in "As I Was Saying": A Chesterton Reader, ed. Robert Knille (Grand Rapids: Eerdmans, 1985), pp. 259–62.
78 Canovan, Chesterton, pp. 63–4.
79 "Excerpts from Orthodoxy," in "As I Was Saying," pp. 115–16.
80 See "The Little Birds Who Won't Sing," in ibid., p. 89.
81 See "On Business Education," in ibid., p. 74.   82 From All I Survey, in ibid., p. 239.
83 See "Selections from What I Saw in America," in ibid., pp. 37–8.

dulling and spirit-destroying standardization, without the resources of a traditional culture.[84] In such a world, Chesterton insisted, democracy was an illusion. The parliamentary system emerged and existed to serve the interests of the Big People, the few who controlled the industrial and financial monopolies. "Politics" seemed far removed from the concerns and needs of ordinary people, and so bred passivity and apathy. Real democracy, in contrast, depended on participation. Such participation would be secured only in a decentralized, locally controlled system in which each citizen could see that his opinions and actions mattered.

Chesterton saw Distributism as a way of using the past to build this decentralized system and move forward into what he believed would be a more satisfying and sustainable future. It seemed to offer a way to refashion technology according to small-scale human needs while at the same time pointing humanity back to its spiritual foundations. Chesterton shared Belloc's vision of the past glory of a Distributist State, in which the guilds and peasant traditions ensured a wide distribution of property. He believed that both capitalism and socialism were heading in the same direction: toward ownership by the few, and the impoverishment and impotence of the many. The solution, then, was to return to wider property distribution, to a restoration of small proprietors: small farmers, shopkeepers, craftsmen. With the distribution of property would come the diffusion of power and the establishment of the conditions of true democracy.

To achieve this truly democratic Distributist State, individuals needed to begin acting. The first step lay in resisting the trend toward monopoly: in fighting for the small against the big. Ordinary people could take the small but necessary step of refusing to patronize the Big Shops, the department and chain stores. No pessimist, Chesterton declared that "it is not true that we can do nothing. Even now there is something that can be done, and done at once. . . . Even if we only save a shop in our own street . . . we may come in the nick of time and make all the difference." Such small actions, though, could not be imposed from the top. Chesterton envisaged the establishment of the Distributist State as "a thing that could be done *by* people. It is not a thing that can be done *to* people." Both socialist and Liberal reformers endeavored to do things to people, because both lacked the faith in the ordinary person that Chesterton believed to be fundamental to Christianity. To Chesterton, Catholicism stood for will and for choice; "it believed that ordinary men were clothed with powers and privileges and a kind of authority."[85]

The medievalism of Distributism won for it, as with Guild Socialism, the

<hr/>

84 See, e.g., Chesterton's "image of the Individualist" in *The Outline of Sanity*, vol. 5 of *The Collected Works of G. K. Chesterton* (San Francisco: Ignatius Press, 1987), pp. 74–5.

85 *Outline of Sanity*, pp. 108, 201 (emphasis in original), 207–8. See also "The Outline of Liberty," in *"As I Was Saying,"* p. 176.

reputation of being the crackpot ideology of antimachine fanatics who wished to force everybody back to the farm. Yet, Chesterton, like Cole, was not against machinery and technology per se. He opposed the tyranny of technology in modern life, but he did not wish to return the world to a pre-technological state. In cases where large-scale technology was essential (in coal mining, for example), Chesterton advocated worker shareholding, so that the machinery belonged to each worker.[86] What Chesterton sought was a change of mentality as much as machinery. He explained, "The best and shortest way of saying it is that instead of the machine being a giant to which the man is a pygmy, we must at least reverse the proportions until man is a giant to whom the machine is a toy."[87] Technology should be a tool, not a tyrant.

Chesterton saw the question of technology as primarily a spiritual question: He believed that humanity's attitudes toward and uses of technology revealed its assumptions about the nature of man and God. He did not see the charge of "medievalism" as one for which Distributists needed to be ashamed. In his view, much that was good in the modern world was a remnant of the Middle Ages.[88] Most important, the medieval era was a time of great spiritual vitality. Both Belloc and Chesterton believed that the Distributist State reflected the ideals and demands of Christianity, whereas both the capitalist and the socialist states denied those ideals and failed to satisfy those demands. Chesterton insisted that "there is a doctrine behind the whole of our political position . . . [and] it cannot be denied that it must in a sense be religious. That is to say, it must at least have some reference to an ultimate view of the universe and especially of the nature of man." Catholicism, Chesterton argued, upheld the fundamental and basic rights of individual human beings, including the right to the independence, security, and creativity that owning property ensured.[89] Both Belloc and Chesterton, then, perceived the need for spiritual as well as political and economic revolution, for restoring the soul as well as meeting the material needs of humanity.

Its links with fascism and its ultimate failure should not be allowed to obscure Distributism's significance in British intellectual and cultural history.[90] Chesterton and Distributism belong to the romantic protest tradition,

---

86 *Outline of Sanity*, pp. 148–9; Corrin, *Chesterton and Belloc*, pp. 132–5.
87 *Outline of Sanity*, p. 156.
88 See "On Turnpikes and Medievalism," in *"As I Was Saying,"* pp. 256–8.
89 *Outline of Sanity*, pp. 207–8; quotation from p. 207.
90 In its early days, the Distributist League, organized in 1926, usually backed Labour candidates and supported the trade unions, in particular during the General Strike. By 1929, however, the league had given up on both Labour politics and unionism as instruments of the Distributist revolution. For many members, including Belloc, fascism appeared to offer much of what the league had been hoping for. With the invasion of Ethiopia in 1936, the league split. Chesterton's death that same year meant that the

with Cole and the Guild Socialists, the Arts and Crafts movement, Morris, Ruskin, the Gothic Revival, Carlyle, and the Romantic poets. Unlike Cole, Chesterton abandoned Labour politics entirely and saw socialism in its twentieth-century forms as a greater threat to humanity than capitalism; however, both men shared an aversion to bigness and a desire to empower the ordinary citizen. Chesterton's Roman Catholicism clashed with the atheism of William Morris, the anti-Catholicism of John Ruskin, and the idiosyncratic religious faith of Carlyle. Nevertheless, he shared with these Victorians a romantic view of the world that led them to reject the assumptions and aims of industrial society and to seek out alternative social ideals. He was a journalist, not an architect, painter, or craftsman, but he shared with the Arts and Crafts movement a concern for the conditions of labor, the quality of products, and the growing gap between "Art" and "Society." With all these diverse cultural critics, Chesterton looked backward to the Middle Ages as a time of greater social, cultural, and spiritual cohesion, as an example of the sort of community in which individuals could achieve wholeness. The medieval past offered guidelines for shaping the future. It appeared to have been a time when the organic society really existed, when the ties linking human beings to the natural and spiritual worlds, as well as to each other and to their own inner beings, had not yet been broken.

The effort to reforge these connections, to reintegrate, stood at the heart of romantic protest before 1945. Several other themes are readily discernible: the ambivalence concerning technology, the effort to define good work, the hope of restoring independence and power to the ordinary individual, the resistance to the rule of the expert and the bureaucrat, the rejection of materialism, the belief in smallness. Each of these themes, however, served as part of the quest for reintegration. The three post-1945 romantic protest movements examined below shared these themes and this task of reintegration. But their articulation of these themes and definition of this task took on new tones and shapes in order to meet the historical context in which they emerged.

> league lost his crucial moderating influence and gained a reputation as a home for fascist sympathizers. It did not last long after Chesterton's death. See Corrin, *Chesterton and Belloc*, pp. 115–23, 172–200.

PART I

C. S. Lewis and J. R. R. Tolkien: fantasy as protest literature

In 1918, the European nations called a halt to their frenzy of self-destruction. Although the war had not been fought on its soil, Britain emerged from the trenches in a debilitated state. The war accelerated its relative economic decline, accentuated class tensions, and altered the political landscape. In Arthur Marwick's words, the Home Fit for Heroes became the Wasteland.[1] T. S. Eliot's masterful poem not only serves as a powerful symbol of Britain after the Great War, it also epitomizes the cultural transformation accentuated by the horrors of total war. Neither the heroic voice nor traditional poetic conventions could comprehend the uncut barbed wire of the Somme or the mud of Passchendaele. Irony, Paul Fussell has argued, became the modern mode of expression, the voice most suited to articulate the absurd agony of the twentieth century.[2]

The twentieth century, however, also witnessed the blossoming of fantasy literature, a genre in which the ironic voice is silenced and yet the outrage of contemporary life sounds clearly. For two British officers, the experience of the horror of the trenches served not as a prelude but as an interlude, not as an introduction to a new volume of ironic perception but as a parenthesis to heroic plots already chosen. C. S. Lewis and J. R. R. Tolkien emerged out of the trenches to eventually become two of the most popular writers in twentieth-century Britain. Their works of fantasy – *The Hobbit, The Lord of the Rings, The Chronicles of Narnia,* and Lewis's space trilogy – offered both juvenile and adult readers engrossing adventure stories. The response to these works, especially to *The Lord of the Rings,* demonstrates, however, that these fantasies were more than good stories. Lewis and Tolkien rejected many of the social, cultural, and political developments linked to the Great War.[3] Their fantasies protest against much of

1 Arthur Marwick, *The Deluge: British Society and the First World War* (London: Bodley Head, 1965), p. 284.
2 Paul Fussell, *The Great War and Modern Memory* (Oxford: Oxford University Press, 1975), chap. 1.
3 Contrast, e.g., the mockery of the heroic ideal of patriotic sacrifice in Wilfred Owen's famous "Dulce et Decorum Est" with C. S. Lewis's argument in *The Abolition of Man* (New York: Macmillan, 1955), pp. 31–2, 34.

the twentieth century and raise a call for resistance against industrial, secular society.

In uttering this protest, Lewis and Tolkien encountered the problem of communication. They perceived themselves as outsiders, as part of a small group of sympathetic souls in battle against a hostile society. The gap between these Oxford scholars and a popular audience loomed large in the class-divided and intellectually and culturally fragmenting society of twentieth-century Britain. Lewis and Tolkien needed, then, to find a form in which they could communicate their protest to an unsympathetic audience. For Lewis, the quest for the proper form was to a large degree intentional. As an apologist for orthodox Christianity in a secular society, he recognized and struggled to resolve the problem of communicating with a popular audience. In contrast, words, rather than communication, captivated Tolkien. Tolkien lost himself in language. Much more of a loner than Lewis, he was not as conscious of the problem of communication. Nevertheless, he succeeded, to a much greater degree than did Lewis, in reaching a mass audience.

Tolkien succeeded because he adopted fantasy literature (although Tolkien would probably have argued that fantasy adopted him). In choosing the fantasy genre, Tolkien, and Lewis as well, adopted a literary form that could and did speak to a mass audience at the same time that it connected them with a long and vital tradition in British intellectual life. Both the form and the content of Lewis's and Tolkien's fantasies place them within the romantic tradition. Lewis and Tolkien swam against the currents of contemporary Britain, but their protest flowed within the deeper stream of British romanticism. They viewed romantics such as William Morris as their literary forebears and, like Morris, revolted against the industrial world. Their fantasies articulated a rejection of materialism and empiricism deeply rooted in segments of British middle-class culture.

2

The escape of the prisoners

At the heart of the romantic protest from the early 1800s on was the fear that empiricism and industrialism together would confine reality to the material and the quantifiable, and would thus foster an antispiritual, aesthetically deprived culture. This protest appeared in a variety of forms, including the genre of fantasy literature. Fantasy developed in the nineteenth century in the works of Alfred Lord Tennyson, George MacDonald, Lewis Carroll, and William Morris, among others. It did not assume its contemporary form, however, until after World War II and after the publications of J. R. R. Tolkien and C. S. Lewis. Tolkien's and Lewis's works, both their fantasies and their theoretical essays, helped shape the modern genre of fantasy. As an examination of these works will show, Lewis and Tolkien used fantasy to articulate a romantic protest against the shape and structures of the contemporary world and to assert that humanity must renew its relationships with its past, the natural world, and the spiritual realm.

"We few"

The position of the protester came naturally to Lewis. Throughout his life he looked out onto a world divided into Us and the much more powerful Them. Born in 1898 in Ulster, Lewis descended from Protestants planted in the northern counties of Ireland during the seventeenth century in order to tighten England's hold on the bloodstained Irish hills. Surrounded by Roman Catholics, the Protestants of Northern Ireland assumed a fortress mentality.

Lewis's self-perception as an outsider was also rooted in the peculiar circumstances of his childhood. When Lewis was only ten years old, his mother died of cancer. Just two weeks later, his father packed him off to a poorly run English boarding school that violated even the lenient English standards for acceptable levels of public-school brutality. Albert Lewis was not a cruel man but he proved incapable of communicating with either of his two sons. In the difficult years of Lewis's later childhood and early adolescence, he relied almost exclusively on his brother, Warren, for support.

Reflecting on those years, Lewis admitted that "the vision of the world which comes most naturally to me is one in which 'we two' or 'we few.' . . . stand together against something stronger and larger."[1]

Lewis's sense of being isolated in a hostile universe was reinforced by his extraordinary intelligence. A voracious reader with a remarkable memory, Lewis found that his unusual literary interests and his inability to play games left him isolated in the world of the English public school; he was thrilled when his father agreed to send him to live with a private tutor instead. In 1916 Lewis finally found a world in which he belonged: the cloisters of Oxford. The Great War proved to be little more than an interruption in his Oxford years. Rushed to France in November of 1917 after only four weeks' training and into the trenches just twelve days later, Lewis was hit by a misdirected English shell in March 1918. The wound kept him in England for the duration of the war, so that he was able to resume his undergraduate studies. He received First Class Honours degrees in both Greats (classics) and English Language and Literature. In 1925, he was awarded a fellowship at Magdalen College, where he remained until 1954, when he left Oxford to become the first occupant of Cambridge's Chair of Medieval and Renaissance Literature.

By 1930, Lewis's definition of "we few" included a Christian component. An Anglican by birth and an atheist by choice, Lewis in the mid-1920s found that his embrace of philosophical Idealism forced him to reconsider the possibility that a god existed. As Lewis observed years later, ". . . a young Atheist cannot guard his faith too carefully. Dangers lie in wait for him on every side." For Lewis, those dangers, including Idealism's recognition of the possibility of the existence of spiritual realities, as well as Christian friends and the search for an ethical life, finally toppled his atheism and forced him, "the most dejected and reluctant convert in all England," to admit "that God was God. . . ."[2] Conversion to Christianity came two years later. Within two years after this acceptance of Christianity, Lewis had thrown himself into the task of asserting not only the rightness but also the relevance of Christianity in an increasingly secular age. He became the spokesman for the Christian few against something stronger and larger.

Although in Oxford Lewis found himself at home at last, his tendency to divide the world into Us and Them continued even there. He soon found himself an outsider within his college, which he described as "a cess pool, a stinking puddle . . . inhabited by . . . things in mens [sic] shapes . . . caring for

1 *Surprised by Joy – The Shape of My Early Life* (London: Harcourt Brace Jovanovich, 1955), p. 32.
2 Ibid., pp. 226, 228–9.

nothing less than learning."³ Lewis's sense of being besieged at Magdalen was not completely without foundation. Despite the high acclaim accorded to Lewis's scholarly works, Lewis never received an Oxford professorship. He committed two serious errors in Oxford's eyes: He became a popular writer, and he proselytized in print and in the Senior Common Room. Even friends and fellow Christians like J. R. R. Tolkien were at times offended by Lewis's outspoken Christianity. On at least one occasion the Roman Catholic Tolkien dismissed Lewis as "Everyman's Theologian." According to one of Lewis's colleagues and biographers, George Sayer, Lewis found himself increasingly isolated at Magdalen and eventually became obsessed with what he perceived as an anti-Christian conspiracy at work in the college.⁴

Lewis had not set out to become an apologist for what many critics believed to be an outdated version of Christianity; from early childhood, however, he had felt himself out of sympathy with the modern world. Motherless and often alone, as a child he turned for companionship and comfort to literature, to the products of past ages, which became for him in adulthood the standards against which he compared contemporary British society and found it wanting.

Like Lewis, John Ronald Reuel Tolkien considered himself an outsider and turned to the past for the fundamentals of his protest against the modern age. In Tolkien's case, as in Lewis's, religion played a decisive role in his self-definition as the outsider. Tolkien was born in 1892, the first child of an English couple married in South Africa one year earlier. In 1895, Tolkien's mother took him and his younger brother on what was supposed to be a holiday with the family in England. Tolkien's father died during the visit, however, and the widow and children remained in England. When Tolkien was eight years old, his mother converted to Roman Catholicism and so placed herself at odds with her extended family and, in a crucial sense, with most of England. Es-

3 Letter to Owen Barfield, Whitsunday [1928 or 1929], CSL/L-Barfield/10/Wade (quoted by permission of Curtis Brown, London, on behalf of C. S. Lewis Pte. Ltd.). The Marion E. Wade Center, Wheaton College, is the principal resource for Lewis scholars. Many of Lewis's letters are also held by the Bodleian, Oxford. Copies of most of the Bodleian's collection can be viewed in the Wade Center and vice versa. A number of selections of Lewis's letters have been published. See *The Letters of C. S. Lewis* (London: Geoffrey Bles, 1966); *Letters to an American Lady* (Grand Rapids: Eerdmans, 1967); *Mark versus Tristram: Correspondence between C. S. Lewis and Owen Barfield* (Cambridge, Mass.: Lowell House Printers, 1967); *They Stand Together: The Letters of C. S. Lewis to Arthur Greeves*, ed. Walter Hooper (New York: Macmillan, 1979).

4 George Sayer, *Jack: C. S. Lewis and His Times* (London: Macmillan, 1988), pp. 173–4. In his biography of Lewis, A. N. Wilson describes the extent to which Lewis's Christianity aroused the contempt of his colleagues. Wilson also shows, however, that the widespread loathing of Lewis stemmed at least in part from Lewis's tendency to see his colleagues in terms of Us and Them, as well as from his championship of his friends ("Us") for academic positions for which they were unqualified. See Wilson's *C. S. Lewis: A Biography* (New York: Norton, 1990), pp. 156–8, 181, 208–10, 231–2, 246.

tranged from her relatives, Tolkien's mother died in 1904. Her two sons were left in the care of a Roman Catholic priest, with the result that they spent their adolescence with no real home, only rooms in a boardinghouse. Tolkien blamed his anti–Roman Catholic relatives for his mother's early death and remained acutely sensitive to British anti-Catholicism all his life.[5] At the level most fundamental to his identity, his religious belief, Tolkien regarded himself as swimming against the tide.

Left to his own resources at a young age, Tolkien found comfort from the changeableness and chaos of the world by retreating to the predictable world of languages. While still a schoolboy he discovered that words brought him aesthetic as well as intellectual pleasure. The security offered by a world governed by grammatical law was compelling. Moreover, Tolkien soon found that he could control this world by inventing his own languages. This youthful passion for language shaped Tolkien's professional life. He took a First Class Honours degree in English Language and Literature from Oxford in 1915 and, after surviving the Somme offensive and being invalided home with trench fever in 1916, became a contributor to the *New English Dictionary*. Following a five-year stint at the University of Leeds, in 1925 Tolkien returned to Oxford as its professor of Anglo-Saxon.

Lewis's and Tolkien's stance as romantic protesters merged easily with their self-image as outsiders, their perception of the world in terms of "We versus They." Each had lost his mother at an early age and struggled through childhood in the company of a single brother: ". . . two frightened urchins huddled for warmth in a bleak world."[6] Bookish boys who regarded sports as a nuisance at best, Tolkien and Lewis early on came to treasure those few friends who shared their academic interests and to view the rest of society as a hostile force. Tolkien expressed this idea to his son Christopher when he wrote that "you and I belong to the ever-defeated never altogether subdued side."[7]

Pockets of Resistance

Lewis admitted that after his mother's death in 1908, "all settled happiness, all that was tranquil and reliable, disappeared from my life. . . . It was sea and islands now; the great continent had sunk like Atlantis."[8] In the midst of what they believed to be the nonnavigable sea of the twentieth century, Lewis and

---

5 Tolkien blamed the cooling of his friendship with Lewis in the 1950s at least in part on what he perceived as Lewis's Ulster "anti-Papism." See Humphrey Carpenter, *Tolkien: A Biography* (Boston: Houghton Mifflin, 1977), p. 151; Wilson, *Lewis*, p. 135–6.
6 Lewis, *Surprised by Joy*, p. 19.
7 Letter to Christopher Tolkien, 31 July 1944, in *The Letters of J. R. R. Tolkien*, ed. Humphrey Carpenter with Christopher Tolkien (Boston: Houghton Mifflin, 1981), p. 89.
8 *Surprised by Joy*, p. 21.

Tolkien discovered islands of refuge in the community of Oxford and particularly in the small circle of male friends in which they moved. Lewis remained a bachelor for most of his adult life; Tolkien was married but not always happily.[9] Both men turned to male friends for companionship and comfort. In his chapter on "Friendship" in *The Four Loves*, Lewis explained the importance he placed on his relationships with men.[10] For Lewis, friendship rested on a "relation between men at their highest level of individuality." True friendship strengthened and enhanced personality. Friendship was a bond of unity; it was also, however, a boundary marking off the friends from the rest of the world, a form of Us versus Them. To Lewis, "Every real Friendship is a sort of secession, even a rebellion. . . . In each knot of Friends there is a sectional 'public opinion' which fortifies its members against the public opinion of the community in general. Each therefore is a pocket of potential resistance."[11]

For Lewis and Tolkien, the Inklings served as the most important pocket of resistance. The "Inklings" was Lewis's half-joking title for a group of friends who met weekly in Lewis's Magdalen rooms and an Oxford pub for discussion and for fellowship, for communion based on religious and literary interests and a liking of male company. In addition to conversation and companionship, the Inklings' gatherings provided a forum for readings of works in progress: *The Hobbit*, the first chapters of *The Lord of the Rings*, and parts of Lewis's space trilogy had their first hearing in Lewis's Magdalen sitting room.[12] In his more generous moods, Tolkien admitted that neither *The Hobbit* nor *The Lord of the Rings* would have been published without the encouragement and prodding of his fellow Inklings, particularly Lewis.

9 A confirmed bachelor with something of a reputation for misogyny, Lewis shocked his friends by marrying Joy Davidman in 1957. Davidman was an ex-Marxist American Jew whose conversion to Christianity rested in part on Lewis's apologetics. Because Davidman was divorced, the marriage should not have been consecrated in the Anglican church. Already fatally ill with cancer when she married, Davidman died in 1960, and Lewis just three years later.

10 C. S. Lewis, *The Four Loves* (New York: Harcourt, Brace, World, 1960), p. 105. See also Lewis's letter to Bede Griffiths in *The Letters of C. S. Lewis*, edited, with a memoir, by W. H. Lewis (London: Geoffrey Bles, 1966), p. 197; original letter held by the Wade Center (CSL/L-Griffiths/16/Wade).

11 *The Four Loves*, pp. 90, 114–15.

12 Humphrey Carpenter, *The Inklings: C. S. Lewis, J. R. R. Tolkien, Charles Williams, and Their Friends* (London: Allen and Unwin, 1978); Carpenter, *Tolkien*, pp. 149–52; Roger Lancelyn Green and Walter Hooper, *C. S. Lewis: A Biography* (New York: Harcourt Brace Jovanovich, 1974), pp. 154–9; Wilson, *Lewis*, p. 142–3, 148–68. See also Kathleen Spencer, *Charles Williams* (San Bernardino: Borgo Press, 1987). According to Green and Hooper, Inklings regulars in the 1930s included Lewis's brother, Major Warren Lewis, English professor Nevill Coghill, Hugo Dyson, Owen Barfield, Adam Fox, and Dr. R. E. Havard. In 1939, Charles Williams became a regular as well. By the end of the 1940s, Williams had died and Fox had left Oxford. New regulars included Gervase Mathew, Colin Hardie, Christopher Tolkien, and John Wain.

Their fantasies, and Lewis and Tolkien themselves, were nourished by the friendly climate of this island of refuge from what they saw as the stormy seas of twentieth-century Britain.

The larger Oxford community, too, despite Lewis's sense of ostracism from Magdalen College and Tolkien's battles against the Literature and on behalf of the Language side of the English School, provided Lewis and Tolkien with a secure milieu, a place of refuge. Oxford made the Inklings possible. It gave Lewis and Tolkien a larger community, one connected with a centuries-old tradition. The social changes and economic decline accelerated by the impact of total war did not pass Oxford by, yet the university remained remarkably unaltered during the years of Lewis's and Tolkien's tenures.[13] Certainly by the 1950s important changes were evident: Lewis's biographers Walter Hooper and Roger Green argue that he found it impossible to adjust to the growth of the undergraduate population and the shift from "the young gentlemen" to "the students."[14] Nevertheless, throughout the 1950s Oxford remained a rather uncomfortable place for a working-class scholar but familiar terrain for males of Lewis's and Tolkien's background. The social composition of the undergraduate population was slowly changing with the arrival of government-financed education, but even by 1961, 50 percent of the undergraduates at Oxford and Cambridge were drawn from public schools, actually a greater percentage than in the 1930s. Oxford remained overwhelmingly male as well. Women were granted degrees in 1920, but by the beginning of the 1960s, only 13 percent of the undergraduate population at Oxford and Cambridge were women. (Colleges did not become coeducational until the 1970s.) In addition, Oxbridge's dominance in political life remained unchallenged during Lewis's and Tolkien's tenure. In 1961, less than 1 percent of the population attended either university, yet Oxbridge educated 80 percent of Britain's parliamentary secretaries, 40 percent of its members of Parliament, and 70 percent of the vice-chancellors of other universities.[15]

Despite important change, Oxford remained a place of privilege and, for Lewis and Tolkien, a refuge from the society outside its cloisters. Within the confines of the English School, in fact, Lewis and Tolkien played leading roles in ensuring that Oxford sheltered its students from the twentieth cen-

---

13 Tolkien retired from the Merton Professorship in 1959. Lewis left Oxford for Cambridge in 1954; he was forced by ill health to retire in 1961.
14 Green and Hooper, *Lewis*, pp. 279–80.
15 Anthony Sampson, *Anatomy of Britain* (New York: Harper and Row, 1965), pp. 218–48. The revolution in the English university system occurred after Lewis and Tolkien had withdrawn from university life. The Robbins Report produced by the Committee of Enquiry set up in 1961 cleared the way for the overhaul of the British university system: In the 1960s, eight new universities were established, and ten colleges of advanced technology were upgraded to university status.

tury by means of an English syllabus that virtually ignored contemporary literature. Neither man could begin to comprehend the possibility that university undergraduates might need assistance in reading the literary products of their own period, by which Lewis and Tolkien meant the nineteenth as well as the twentieth century. In the fight over syllabus reform Tolkien led the way in insisting that philology serve as the foundation of the English School. Although a "Literature," rather than a "Language," man, Lewis supported Tolkien. The syllabus reform, effected in 1931, ensured that Anglo-Saxon language and literature stood at the center of English studies at Oxford, and that contemporary literature was relegated to an optional paper.[16]

Lewis's and Tolkien's fantasies bear the marks of their Oxford origins. The roads to both Middle-earth and Narnia cut through the quads and common rooms of this elite university. A by-product of Tolkien's philological pursuits, Middle-earth reflects the themes and values of the Saxon and Icelandic literature he studied, and Lewis's world of Narnia re-creates in many aspects the medieval civilization he explored in lectures. More than this, though, the worlds of their fantasy fictions, like Oxford in the middle of the twentieth century, were male dominated, hierarchical, and communal; worlds in which the Good Life could be effortlessly lived, with little concern about such things as economic production and distribution. Before looking more closely at the fantasies of Narnia and Middle-earth, however, it is important to examine Lewis's and Tolkien's influential theoretical works on the genre.

The function of fantasy

Tolkien reported that Lewis once said to him, "Tollers, there is too little of what we really like in stories. I am afraid we shall have to try and write some ourselves."[17] What they "really liked," and what they wrote, was fantasy. To Lewis and Tolkien, the writing of fantasy was not only a respectable but also a religious act. The by-products of a literary theory shaped by Christian belief, *The Chronicles of Narnia* and *The Lord of the Rings* served as platforms for the voicing of romantic protest against a secular and materialist society.

16 Carpenter, *Tolkien*, pp. 136–7; Green and Hooper, *Lewis*, pp. 150–1; Wilson, *Lewis*, pp. 103–5, 208–9. See also C. S. Lewis, "Our English Syllabus," in *Rehabilitations and Other Essays* (London: Oxford University Press, 1939), pp. 81–93.

17 Letter to Charlotte and Denis Plimmer, 8 Feb. 1967, in *Letters of Tolkien*, Letter 294, p. 378. According to Warren Lewis, C. S. Lewis's brother, the conversation took place after Lewis read David Lindsay's space-travel novel *Voyage to Arcturus* and decided that the genre offered fruitful possibilities for Christian writers. He then suggested to Tolkien, "We shall have to write books of the sort ourselves" (24 May 1946, W. H. Lewis's diary, quoted in Sayer, *Jack*, pp. 152–3).

Although the exact outlines of the fantasy genre remain blurred, Tolkien and Lewis sculpted its general shape in their works of and about fantasy.[18] In his 1939 Andrew Lang Lecture "On Fairy-Stories," Tolkien gave a pivotal defense of fantasy, which Lewis amplified in essays written over the following two decades. Tolkien's theory of fantasy drew from the literary theory of Samuel Taylor Coleridge. He adopted Coleridge's view of literature as a lamp rather than a mirror; that is, literature created "Secondary Worlds," which illumine, rather than simply reflect, reality. The one essential element in fantasy is the quality of strangeness and wonder, usually realized through the presence of the marvelous or numinous, which not only defines fantasy but gives it its power.[19] This quality also serves as the stumbling block to critics and readers who regard fantasy as unreal, escapist, or childish.

Tolkien, however, believed fantasy to be "not a lower but a higher form of Art, indeed the most nearly pure form, and so (when achieved) the most potent." As Tolkien pointed out, anyone can write "the green sun"; but "to make a Secondary World inside which the green sun will be credible, commanding Secondary Belief, will probably require labour and thought, and will certainly demand a special skill, a kind of elvish craft." Fantasy succeeds not through the willing suspension of disbelief but rather through the creation of a believable secondary world: "You therefore believe it, while you are, as it were, inside. The moment disbelief arises, the spell is broken; the magic, or rather art, has failed." To sustain this belief, the fantasist cannot transgress the laws of reason and logic within the world he or she has created. A believable secondary world must be rational by its own standards of rationality. Fantasy thus stands realms apart from the absurd: "It certainly

18 For other attempts to define fantasy, see T. E. Apter, *Fantasy Literature: An Approach to Reality* (Bloomington: Indiana University Press, 1982); Sheila Egoff, *Worlds Within: Children's Fantasy from the Middle Ages to Today* (Chicago: American Library Association, 1988); Rosemary Jackson, *Fantasy: The Literature of Subversion* (London: Methuen, 1981); W. Irwin, *The Game of the Impossible: The Rhetoric of Fantasy* (Urbana: University of Illinois Press, 1976); Edmund Little, *The Fantasts: Studies in J. R. R. Tolkien, Lewis Carroll, Mervyn Peake, Nikolay Gogol, and Kenneth Grahame* (Amersham, England: Avebury, 1984); C. N. Manlove, *The Impulse of Fantasy Literature* (Kent: Kent State University Press, 1983); C. N. Manlove, *Modern Fantasy: Five Studies* (Cambridge: Cambridge University Press, 1975); Michael Moorcock, *Wizardry and Wild Romance: A Study of Epic Fantasy* (London: Gollancz, 1987); Eric Rabkin, *The Fantastic in Literature* (Princeton: Princeton University Press, 1976); Martha Simmons, *A Better Country: The Worlds of Religious Fantasy and Science Fiction* (New York: Greenwood Press, 1988); Ann Swinfen, *In Defence of Fantasy: A Study of the Genre in English and American Literature since 1945* (London: Routledge and Kegan Paul, 1984); Tzvetan Todorov, *The Fantastic: A Structural Approach to a Literary Genre* (Ithaca: Cornell University Press, 1975); Diana Waggoner, *The Hills of Faraway: A Guide to Fantasy* (New York: Atheneum, 1985).

19 For C. S. Lewis's definition of "numinous," see *The Problem of Pain* (London: Fontana Books, 1959), p. 5. Lewis listed as examples of the numinous in literature scenes from *The Wind in the Willows*, Wordsworth, Malory, Ovid, Vergil, Aeschylus, and the biblical books of Ezekiel and Genesis.

does not destroy or even insult Reason. . . . The keener and clearer is the reason, the better fantasy will it make."[20]

Tolkien and Lewis viewed fantasy not just as a genre worthy of critical attention and readers' respect but as the highest form of art. This rather startling assertion rested on their linkage of fantasy with mythmaking, and mythmaking with Christian worship and service. For Lewis and Tolkien, "myth" meant more than a story or an account of earth's beginnings. Clyde Kilby accurately described Lewis's view of myth as the belief that "there is a great, sovereign, uncreated, unconditioned Reality at the core of things, and myth is on the one hand a kind of picture-making which helps man to understand this Reality and on the other hand the result of a deep call from that Reality."[21] In Lewis's own words, ". . . Myth in general is . . . at its best, a real though unfocussed gleam of divine truth falling on human imagination."[22] Myth represents the spiritual reality that undergirds the physical world. When utilized in a story, myth serves to link the reader to this spiritual reality. As Lewis explained, "What flows into you from the myth is not truth but reality (truth is always about something, but reality is that about which truth is)."[23]

By presenting the reader with an alternative vision of reality, a successful fantasy enhances and clarifies ordinary experience. Lewis explained in his review of Tolkien's *Lord of the Rings* that the "value of [Tolkien's] myth is that it takes all the things we know and restores to them the rich significance which has been hidden by 'the veil of familiarity.' . . . By putting bread, gold, horse, apple, or the very roads into a myth, we do not retreat from reality: we rediscover it. . . . By dipping them in myth we see them more clearly."[24] Tolkien termed this process of clarification "Recovery." Fantasy takes ordinary things and makes them marvelous, enabling the jaded, blinded, and weary to strip the distorting varnish of the familiar and so encounter life afresh. After immersion in the secondary world of fantasy, the reader can no longer view the familiar as ordinary. He or she must look, and so recover wonder.

Children "born to . . . the atomic bomb" needed fantasy, according to

---

20 Quotations from Tolkien, "On Fairy-Stories," in *The Monsters and the Critics and Other Essays*, ed. Christopher Tolkien (London: Allen and Unwin, 1983), pp. 139, 140, 132, 144. Given as the Andrew Lang Lecture at the University of St. Andrews, 8 Mar. 1939. First published in *Essays Presented to Charles Williams* (Oxford, 1947). Reissued under the title *Tree and Leaf* (1964).
21 Clyde S. Kilby, *The Christian World of C. S. Lewis* (Grand Rapids: Eerdmans, 1964), p. 81.
22 C. S. Lewis, *Miracles: A Preliminary Study* (New York: Macmillan, 1947), p. 161, n. 1.
23 "Myth Became Fact," in *God in the Dock: Essays in Theology and Ethics* (Grand Rapids: Eerdmans, 1970), p. 66.
24 "Tolkien's The Lord of the Rings," in *On Stories and Other Essays on Literature*, ed. Walter Hooper (New York: Harcourt Brace Jovanovich, 1982), p. 90. First published as "The Gods Return to Earth," *Time and Tide*, 14 Aug. 1954; and "The Dethronement of Power," *Time and Tide*, 22 Oct. 1955.

Lewis. Its "brave knights and heroic courage" would provide much-needed support when its readers met with the inevitable cruelties that abounded in everyday experience.[25] What fantasy offered twentieth-century readers was not only relief from the sheer ugliness of so much of modern life but also a means of combating the ugliness. In Tolkien's terms, fantasy functioned as "the Escape of the Prisoner" rather than "the Flight of the Deserter."[26]

Tolkien argued that fantasy gives its readers not only recovery and escape but also the "Consolation of the Happy Ending," or the "Eucatastrophe." With the happy ending the fantasy draws its reader in to the experience of unexpected grace and so gives "a fleeting glimpse of Joy, Joy beyond the walls of the world, poignant as grief." The greatest, most perfect eucatastrophe, Tolkien believed, occurred in the Gospels, in the story of Christ's resurrection. The Christian joy is of the same quality as the joy produced by the fantasy's eucatastrophe, the joy of surprising and overwhelming grace. Nevertheless, the Christian joy is higher, even more joyous, because "this story is supreme; and it is true. Art has been verified. God is the Lord, of angels, of men – and of elves. Legend and History have met and fused." Christianity does not nullify or defeat other fairy stories: "The Evangelium has not abrogated legends; it has hallowed them."[27] The fantasist, in adding to God's creation, fulfills his or her role as the Image of the Maker and thus glorifies both the Maker and the made.

This understanding of fantasy as a form of worship, of mythmaking as a religious act, led Lewis and Tolkien to protest against the relegation of fantasy to the children's shelf. The conventional tendency to throw together children and fantasy arises from the conviction of both the child's greater gullibility and fantasy's inherent irrationality. This idea, however, that only children can or should abide fantasy denigrated the child while entirely missing the central purpose of fantasy. In Lewis's words, fantasy "arouses [in its reader] a longing for he knows not what. It stirs and troubles him (to his life-long enrichment) with the dim sense of something beyond his reach. . . ."[28] Children, Tolkien argued, are no more and no less suited for fantasy than adults. Although Tolkien himself "desired dragons with a profound desire," not all children want dragons or anything like dragons. Fantasy, Tolkien insisted, is a serious art form, not child's play: "If fairy-story as a kind is worth reading at all it is worthy to be written for and read by adults."[29] Lewis not only agreed with Tolkien that fantasy is worthy of adults but even viewed any division between

25 "On Three Ways of Writing for Children," in *Of Other Worlds – Essays and Stories*, ed. Walter Hooper (New York: Harcourt Brace Jovanovich, 1966), p. 31. First published in *Proceedings, Papers, and Summaries of Discussions at the Bournemouth Conference, 29th April to 2nd May 1952 of the Library Association* (London: Library Association, 1952).
26 "On Fairy-Stories," p. 148.   27 Ibid., pp. 153, 156.
28 "On Three Ways of Writing for Children," p. 29.
29 "On Fairy-Stories," pp. 135, 137.

children's and adult literature as false. He himself never lost his taste for such children's books as *The Wind in the Willows* or the works of Rider Haggard. According to Lewis, "No book is really worth reading at the age of ten which is not equally (and often far more) worth reading at the age of fifty."[30] He wrote his Narnia books in the form of a children's story because he regarded this form as the most suited for what he had to say, not because he believed Narnia "to be below adult attention."[31]

Both Tolkien and Lewis believed fantasy, or mythmaking, to be an effective form for communicating religious truths. Tolkien, in fact, used myth to lead Lewis to Christian orthodoxy. In 1926, the two met at a meeting of Oxford's English Faculty. Lewis found Tolkien "a smooth, pale, fluent little chap. . . . No harm in him: only needs a smack or so."[32] Lewis never administered the smack, however; in a sense the reverse occurred. The two men found they shared the same general revulsion for much of twentieth-century literature and the same passion for medieval romances, Icelandic and Nordic sagas, and the works of William Morris. This shared sympathy for what Lewis called "Pagan myth" led to Tolkien's smacking Lewis with Christianity. Tolkien opened the Christian faith to Lewis by arguing that Christianity both paralleled and fulfilled the pagan myths in which they found such delight. Lewis later explained that what "Tolkien showed me was this: . . . the story of Christ is simply a true myth . . . it is God's myth where the others are men's myths: i.e. the Pagan stories are God expressing Himself through the minds of poets . . . while Christianity is God expressing Himself through what we call 'real things.' "[33] This concept of Tolkien's answered the last of Lewis's arguments against Christianity. The shared passion for "myth," for stories that deal with a spiritual reality beyond the grasp of reason or empirical observation, led to shared faith. Out of this passion for myth came both men's contributions to fantasy literature.

Romantic roots

As Tolkien's reliance on Coleridge for his theory of fantasy suggests, he was a romantic in his view of the role of art and imagination in society. Both he

---

30 "On Stories," in *On Stories*, p. 14. First published in *Essays Presented to Charles Williams*.

31 Lewis, "Sometimes Fairy-Stories May Say Best What's to Be Said," in *Of Other Worlds*, p. 38. First published in *New York Times Book Review*, 18 Nov. 1956.

32 Entry in Lewis's diary for 11 May 1926 (W. H. Lewis, *Memoirs of the Lewis Family, 1850–1930*, vol. 9, p. 89; available in the Wade Center). The diary has been published as C. S. Lewis, *All My Road before Me: The Diary of C. S. Lewis, 1922–1927* (London: HarperCollins, 1992); quotation from p. 393.

33 Letter to Arthur Greeves, 18 Oct. 1931, in Hooper, *They Stand Together*, no. 171, p. 427 (original in Wade – CSL/L-Greeves/172/Wade).

and Lewis stood in the English romantic tradition. Although they swam against the currents of contemporary Britain, their protest flowed from this important stream in British culture.

Lewis's romanticism seems more problematic than Tolkien's. On several occasions he posed as an antiromantic. In his *Preface to Paradise Lost*, for example, Lewis charged that Milton's critics had so assimilated the romantic exaltation of human pride and individual achievement that they could not read *Paradise Lost* with sympathy.[34] In his approach to literature Lewis could be called a classicist: He believed that true freedom was achieved through restraint, through adherence to laws of form. Lewis couched his classicism in religious terms, arguing that because the New Testament teaches that "the art of life itself is an art of imitation" and that " 'Originality' . . . is quite plainly the prerogative of God alone," great literature was essentially derivative. Rejecting the romantic idea of literature as the product of the individual creative genius, Lewis believed that the artist's task was to embody in established forms "some reflection of eternal Beauty and Wisdom."[35]

Despite this apparently antiromantic approach to literature, however, romanticism permeated Lewis's life and thought. His biographer A. N. Wilson has described Lewis as a "Romantic egoist," a writer preeminently concerned with self-presentation who used his own experiences to create his mythological reality, and as a frustrated poet with "a vivid awareness of his own consciousness, a sense that the chief end of writing is to communicate sensation and experience."[36] Beginning in childhood, Lewis had a series of romantic experiences, usually resulting from meeting with either an aesthetic or a natural beauty and characterized by intense longing. In *The Pilgrim's Regress* (1938), he placed these experiences under the heading "romanticism," but he later found this term to be problematic[37] and so in his autobiography in 1955 called these encounters with the nonmaterial world "Joy" (hence the title of the autobiography, *Surprised by Joy*, a title drawn from Wordsworth). Lewis's quest for Joy drew him to the edge of the occult world and to fears that his romantic longings would drive him mad.[38] In the end, however, his romanticism made him vulnerable to Christianity. Struggling to retain his unbelief in the 1920s, Lewis found that "All the books were beginning to turn against me." Those that resonated were written by Christians, with one important exception: "The only Non-Christians who seemed

34 *A Preface to "Paradise Lost"* (New York: Oxford University Press, 1942), pp. 133–4.
35 "Christianity and Literature," in *Rehabilitations*, pp. 191, 192.
36 Wilson, *Lewis*, p. 290. See also pp. 146, 183, 210, 291–2.
37 See the Preface to the Third Edition, *The Pilgrim's Regress* (New York: Bantam, 1981), pp. vii–xvi.
38 Sayer, *Jack*, p. 50.

to me really to know anything were the Romantics. . . ."[39] From the time he had learned to read, he had "listened for the horns of elfland" and found them in Keats, Shelley, and Coleridge.[40]

Through his reading of both romantic and Christian works and through his quest for Joy, Lewis came to believe in the essential truth of religious faith. He concluded that "Joy" was, in fact, desire, a longing for unity with God. As he explained, ". . . the human soul was made to enjoy some object that is never fully given – nay, cannot even be imagined as given – in our present mode of subjective and spatio-temporal experience."[41] The Fall had shattered the unity between Creator and created but had not entirely obliterated humanity's desire to forge anew this right relationship. Joy pointed to God; it constituted an almost painful desire, expressed in Romantic poetry, for the completion and fulfillment that Lewis believed could be met partly through Christianity and fully when death reunites the Christian believer with God. Both Lewis and Tolkien saw this ineradicable longing for the unattainable, the experience of Joy, as a central aspect of fantasy literature. According to Tolkien, fairy stories concern not possibility but "desirability. If they awakened desire, satisfying it while often whetting it unbearably, they succeeded."[42] Lewis argued that by whetting this desire, romanticism can point the way to Christianity. Both Christianity and romanticism suggest this something beyond humanity's grasp. Both deny the modern assumption that the material world encompasses reality and thus assert the significance and centrality of the spiritual life.

Like the Romantic poets of the late eighteenth and early nineteenth centuries, Tolkien and Lewis believed that empiricism and industrialism threatened to reduce the whole of reality to its materialist aspects. They were horrified by the mechanical destruction of nature, by technological approaches to human experience, and by utilitarian assumptions about ethical conduct. Like the Romantic poets, they turned to works of imagination in order to express their protest against these horrors.

Heirs of William Morris

The most important romantic forebear of Lewis and Tolkien was not, however, one of the early Romantic poets but rather William Morris. Lewis discovered Morris during his school days; Tolkien while at university.[43] In

---

39 *Surprised by Joy*, pp. 213, 214. For Lewis's defense of the Romantics, see "To Roy Campbell," in C. S. Lewis, *Poems* (London: Harcourt Brace Jovanovich, 1964), pp. 66–7. See also "Shelley, Dryden, and Mr. Eliot," in *Rehabilitations*, pp. 33–4.
40 *Surprised by Joy*, p. 5.   41 *Pilgrim's Regress*, p. xii.   42 "On Fairy-Stories," p. 134.
43 Sayer, *Jack*, pp. 52, 58, 156.

1914, when Tolkien won the Skeat Prize for English awarded by Exeter College (Morris's college as well), he used his five-pound award to purchase books by Morris.[44] The experience of reading Morris drove Tolkien to write. The first draft of what became *The Silmarillion* imitated the narrative structure of Morris's "Earthly Paradise," and *The Lord of the Rings* drew on Morris's *The House of the Wolfings* and *The Roots of the Mountains*.[45] Like Morris, Lewis and Tolkien reveled in "northernness," the aesthetic, emotional, and spiritual qualities of Icelandic sagas and Germanic tales (the love of which drove all three to learn Old Icelandic).[46]

The appeal of the world of the saga was in part the lure of a lost, and they believed superior, civilization. Repelled by industrialism, Morris had turned to the past, to the world of the heroic saga and to the Middle Ages, for usable models of cultural coherence.[47] Tolkien and Lewis agreed with and were influenced by Morris's conclusion that good art demands a good society, and both believed that the twentieth century possessed neither and the medieval period produced both.[48] Lewis recognized that Morris built "his imaginary world on hints furnished by the Middle and the Dark Ages as these existed in the imagination of his own time and his own circle in particular." Despite the historical errors, Lewis argued that "his choice was poetically right simply because that misconception of the Middle Ages . . . already existed, and existed poetically, in the public imagination. It was, and to some extent still is, part of our mythology."[49] The fantasies of Lewis and Tolkien resonated with British readers at least in part because they, too, drew on this mythology, on this romantic vision of the past that is at its core a protest against industrial society.

For Lewis, Morris's appeal lay in his ability to both arouse and partially satisfy the romantic longing for unity with God. He saw Morris as the "most essentially *pagan* of all poets," whose writings nonetheless pointed toward the truth of Christianity.[50] In 1931 he explained to his childhood friend Arthur Greeves that Morris "has taught me things he did not understand himself.

44 Carpenter, *Tolkien*, p. 69.
45 Ibid., pp. 69–70, 90, 92. See also letter to Professor L. W. Forster, 31 Dec. 1960; and letter to Edith Bratt (Bratt became Tolkien's wife), Oct. 1911; in *Letters of Tolkien*, pp. 303, 7.
46 Lewis's and Tolkien's friendship, in fact, solidified when they became members of the Coalbiters, a club that met during term time in Oxford to read the Icelandic sagas in their original language. Lewis was first introduced to Morris through H. A. Grueber's *Myth of the Norsemen* (Sayer, *Jack*, p. 52).
47 See William Morris, *News from Nowhere* (1890; London: Routledge and Kegan Paul, 1970).
48 See Lewis's poem "On a Vulgar Error," in *Poems*, p. 60.
49 "William Morris," in *Rehabilitations*, p. 43.
50 Letter to Arthur Greeves, 31 June 1930, in Hooper, *They Stand Together*, no. 144, p. 366 (Wade – CSL/L-Greeves/143/Wade). See also Lewis's letter to Owen Barfield, 2 Sept. 1937, Wade – CSL/L-Barfield/40/Wade.

These hauntingly beautiful lands . . . push you onto the real thing because they fill you with desire and yet prove absolutely clearly that in Morris's world that desire cannot be satisfied."[51]

It may seem odd that Tories such as Lewis and Tolkien should find Morris, the revolutionary Marxist, so appealing, but the common quest for community overcame these political barriers and drew Lewis and Tolkien to Morris. Lewis argued that Morris's medievalism, despite its historical inaccuracies, remained of great intellectual and emotional relevance. Morris "has 'faced the facts.' . . . He seems to retire far from the real world and to build a world out of his wishes; but when he has finished the result stands out as a picture of an experience ineluctably true." Morris's work illumined the tension between the "unsatisfactoriness of mortal life and a conviction that the vigorous enjoyment and improvement of such life is infinitely worth while. . . ." Morris's reconciliation of this tension, Lewis argued, lay in his affirmation of community. Here, Lewis recognized, was the core of both Morris's socialism and his poetry: "The 'kindreds,' 'houses,' or 'little lands' of the romances are the points where Morris's career as a socialist touches his career as a poet." Although no socialist, Lewis admitted the validity and appeal of what Morris offered: "The great use of the idyllic in literature is to find and illustrate the good. . . . [Morris] brings back a sentiment that a man could really live by."[52] As orthodox Christians, Tolkien and Lewis could not embrace Morris's Marxism, and they shied away from the tendency, characteristic of twentieth-century versions of socialism, to treat individuals in terms of the "mass." They found in Morris's romantic fantasies, however, the spiritual enrichment and the sense of community for which they longed.

As the link with Morris illustrates, by choosing fantasy as their main medium of social and cultural criticism Lewis and Tolkien rooted themselves in a tradition of dissent that can be traced back to late-eighteenth-century Romanticism. Although Lewis himself believed that "romantic" is now "a word of such varying senses that it has become useless and should be banished from our vocabulary,"[53] the term *does* denote a particular – and, in the case of modern British history, a potent – world view. Lewis and Tolkien, with their anti-industrial stance and their rejection of mechanism and rationalism as forms of reductionism, articulated a romantic protest.

51 Letter to Arthur Greeves, 22 Sept. 1931, in Hooper, *They Stand Together*, no. 170, p. 422 (Wade – CSL/L-Greeves/170/Wade).
52 "William Morris," in *Rehabilitations*, pp. 54, 46–7, 48, 49. 53 *Pilgrim's Regress*, p. vii.

3

C. S. Lewis: bridging the Great Divide

Before 1950, the name C. S. Lewis conjured up not pictures of fauns in snowy woods or golden lions but rather two contrasting images: on the one hand, the lover of medieval and Renaissance literature whose work was both perceptive and poetic; on the other, the hearty, aggressive, popular defender of orthodox Christianity. Lewis's subtle and supple scholarship seems at odds with his simplified apologetics, in which analogy often took the place of argument and open contempt substituted for careful consideration of opposing views. These contrasting qualities come together in his fantasies, the works that have won Lewis his most enduring fame. Although often beautifully written and solidly based on decades of loving scholarship, Lewis's fantasies betray impatience with and even cruelty toward his opponents, who appear as crudely drawn caricatures. These fantasies also reveal the underlying message of both his apologetics and his scholarship. All of Lewis's works call on Britain to reevaluate, question, and retreat from contemporary values and to reclaim a rapidly disappearing cultural tradition.

Lewis regarded himself as a dinosaur still surviving from the lost age when, he argued, the material and the spiritual interacted to create a vital culture. Much of his scholarly work centered on the theme that the break between the Middle Ages and the Renaissance did not exist, that, in fact, the classical, medieval, and Renaissance societies formed an unbroken line that held together Western thought until at least the nineteenth century. In his inaugural lecture at Cambridge in 1954, Lewis identified himself as a specimen of this past culture. Four forces – the replacement of "rulers" by "leaders," the collapse of cultural consensus, the decline in religious belief, and the technological revolution – had ripped open a "Great Divide" between modern humanity and its predecessors. According to Lewis, he should be regarded as a chance survivor from the world on the other side of the Great Divide, which had opened up sometime "[b]etween Jane Austen and us" and "is not even now complete. . . ." Lewis urged his listeners to "use your specimens while you can. There are not going to be many more dinosaurs."[1]

1 C. S. Lewis, "De Descriptione Temporum," in *They Asked for a Paper* (London: Geoffrey Bles, 1962), pp. 20, 23, 25. Graham Hough wrote one of the more perceptive responses

With his scholarship, apologetics, and fantasies, Lewis sought to bridge the Great Divide and restore some of the broken bonds between humanity, its past, and the nonmaterial world.

The discarded image

Lewis wrote his fantasy fictions in the evenings, when he was too tired for "real work." His "real work," however, was the foundation on which his fantasies rested. Lewis's scholarly writings reveal his immense respect for and utter delight in a world view and cosmology alien to the twentieth century but fundamental to his fantasies.[2] Lewis saw himself as a historian of literature, but differing from the ordinary historian in that he was concerned "with the past not as it 'really' was . . . but with the past as it seemed to be to those who lived in it: for of course men felt and thought and wrote about what seemed to be happening to them."[3] Such an exclusively literary and therefore inherently elitist perception of the past left Lewis free to re-create vanished cultures in new ways. For Lewis, the past provided a variant reality; like a vision of utopia, it criticized the present by offering pictures of alternative actions and attitudes.[4]

Lewis's study of what he called the medieval "Model," the cosmology and world view of the Middle Ages, offers a powerful version of alternative reality. First given as a series of lectures at Oxford in 1938 and published posthumously as *The Discarded Image*, this masterful work breathes life into an ancient and discredited system of thought by re-creating the medieval image, or model, of the universe.[5] As a literary historian, Lewis believed that full appreciation of medieval literature required an understanding of the

to the lecture. See his "Old Western Man," *Twentieth Century*, Feb. 1955, p. 106; see also Hough's "The Scholar's Tale," *Times Literary Supplement*, 7 Jan. 1965, p. 1 (attribution by J. S. Ryan, *Tolkien: Cult or Culture* [Armidale: University of New England, 1969], p. 84).

2 See *The Allegory of Love: A Study in Medieval Tradition* (1936), *A Preface to "Paradise Lost"* (1942), *English Literature in the Sixteenth Century, Excluding Drama* (1954), *The Discarded Image* (1964), and the numerous essays and talks reprinted in *Rehabilitations and Other Essays* (London: Oxford University Press, 1939), *Studies in Words* (Cambridge: Cambridge University Press, 1960), *An Experiment in Criticism* (Cambridge: Cambridge University Press, 1961), *They Asked for a Paper, Studies in Medieval and Renaissance Literature* (London: Geoffrey Bles, 1962), and *Selected Literary Essays*, ed. Walter Hooper (Cambridge: Cambridge University Press, 1969). After this chapter was written, I read Norman Cantor's perceptive evaluation of Lewis's medieval scholarship, which recognizes the links between Lewis's historical and fictional writings. See Norman Cantor, *Inventing the Middle Ages* (New York: William Morrow, 1991), pp. 213–18.

3 *English Literature in the Sixteenth Century, Excluding Drama* (Oxford: Oxford University Press, 1954), p. 32.

4 See, e.g., *A Preface to "Paradise Lost"* (New York: Oxford University Press, 1942), chap. 9.

5 *The Discarded Image* (London: Cambridge University Press, 1964).

medieval mind: The past was a foreign country whose language and customs must be explained if the visitor was to be more than a tourist.[6] In *The Discarded Image* he embarked on a voyage of discovery.

What he discovered was a world of coherence and purpose. He admitted that "the old Model delights me as I believe it delighted our ancestors. Few constructions of the imagination seem to me to have combined splendour, sobriety, and coherence in the same degree."[7] Lewis did not argue that this model was factually true, but he insisted that the twentieth-century materialist model was not necessarily true either. Both are imaginative attempts to account for the world in which men and women find themselves.

Lewis believed that the medieval model outmatched its twentieth-century rival in that it gave significance to persons. In keeping with the model, for example, medieval chroniclers focused on the heroic deeds of persons rather than on impersonal forces or ideas. Even the pervasive medieval belief that the ages were declining lent significance to individuals: "Historically as well as cosmically, medieval man stood at the foot of a stairway; looking up, he felt delight. . . . There were friends, ancestors, patrons in every age. One had one's place, however modest, in a great succession; one need be neither proud nor lonely."[8] The medieval model, in Lewis's view, ordered human experience into a coherent and satisfying pattern.

Such an orderly pattern rested on a hierarchical understanding of the world. A democratic structure based on individualism is essentially chaotic; it could not provide the coherence, the sense of place, for which Lewis longed. Lewis failed to embrace the twentieth century's acceptance of democratic values and individual fulfillment as the ultimate good. In his vision, the loss of community outweighed the benefits offered by a society based on individualism. Humanity, Lewis believed, was part of the Great Chain of Being, an inherently hierarchical structure. By severing the links that joined it to the rest of the Chain, humanity threatened Being itself.

Lewis believed that the discarding of the medieval image of the world reflected the separation of men and women from the natural world. With the eyes of a poet Lewis reveled in natural beauty, but his pleasure transcended the aesthetic. As a Christian, he believed that the physical wonder of nature illumined the spiritual marvel of the Divinity. In describing an English woodland in springtime, for example, Lewis wrote that the scene "came nearer to one's idea of the world before the Fall than anything I ever hoped to

---

6 See *Studies in Medieval and Renaissance Literature*, pp. 2–4.
7 *Discarded Image*, p. 216. For a poetic expression of Lewis's delight in medieval cosmology, see "The Planets," in *Poems* (New York: Harcourt Brace Jovanovich, 1964), p. 12.
8 *Discarded Image*, p. 185.

see. . . ."⁹ Both Tolkien and Lewis argued that a life lived in harmony with nature remained closely linked to mythic and spiritual truth. Lewis noted,

> Tolkien once remarked to me that the feeling about home must have been quite different in the days when a family had fed on the produce of the same few miles of country for six generations, and that perhaps this was why they saw nymphs in the fountains and dryads in the woods. . . . We of course . . . are really artificial beings and have no connection (save in sentiment) with any place on earth. We are synthetic men, uprooted. The strength of the hills is not ours.¹⁰

In his writings, Lewis aimed to regain some sense of this connection, to enable his readers to draw again from the strength of the hills by reminding them of the beauty and power of the natural world.

The "discarded image" of the human community and the cosmos gave the individual a sense of place and purpose within both the human community and the natural environment. For Lewis, the past, as revealed in literary texts, provided an alternative reality, one that he believed surpassed the present in many respects. This vision of the past was lovingly yet precisely articulated in his academic work. Literary scholarship, however, is a limited form of communication. To reach beyond an academic audience, Lewis turned to other forms, including both Christian apologetics and fantasy literature.¹¹

Defender of the faith

Lewis announced his conversion to Christianity in print in 1933 with the publication of *The Pilgrim's Regress: An Allegorical Apology for Christianity, Reason, and Romanticism.* An often clumsy allegory that assumed the reader's knowledge of British intellectual developments and divisions, the book failed to reach a general audience.¹² Its limited sales highlight the problem of communication between an intellectual like Lewis and the great majority of Britons. *The Pilgrim's Regress* did, however, attract the attention of Ashley Sampson, editor of the Christian Challenge Series published by Geoffrey

9 Letter to Warren Lewis, 14 June 1932, *The Letters of C. S. Lewis*, ed. W. H. Lewis (London: Geoffrey Bles, 1966), p. 154; original in the Wade Center (CSL/L-Lewis/ Wade Index no. 0061).

10 Letter to Arthur Greeves, 22 June 1930, in *They Stand Together: The Letters of C. S. Lewis to Arthur Greeves*, ed. Walter Hooper (New York: Macmillan, 1979), no. 143, pp. 363–4 (original in Wade – CSL/L-Greeves/142/Wade).

11 Lewis was quite conscious of the problem of communication. See, e.g., his address to the Church of Wales Assembly in 1945, reprinted in *Undeceptions: Essays on Theology and Ethics* (London: Geoffrey Bles, 1971), and quoted in George Sayer, *Jack: C. S. Lewis and His Times* (London: Macmillan, 1988), p. 154.

12 It sold only 650 of its first printing of 1,000 copies (Sayer, *Jack*, p. 137).

Bles. Sampson commissioned Lewis to write *The Problem of Pain*, which quickly became a best-seller after it was published in 1940.[13] In *The Problem of Pain*, Lewis not only bridged the communications gap by replacing allegory with clear exposition and amusing anecdote, he also tackled a topic of intrinsic interest: the problem of evil in the universe. To a society confronting the horror of a second world war, Lewis's commonsensical manner and hearty confidence in the justice of God brought some measure of reassurance. Lewis's next apologetic work, *The Screwtape Letters*, was even more of a success. The book is a series of often extremely funny letters written by a devil to his nephew, who has been assigned the task of winning the soul of an unnamed Englishman in wartime Britain. It not only sold well but attracted the notice of Christians and non-Christians alike in Britain.[14]

It was, however, the radio rather than any book that established Lewis in the role of the outspoken, articulate, witty defender of Christian orthodoxy, the apologist who infuriated his opponents with his assumption that unbelievers just did not get it, that they really were not very bright. Between August 1941 and April 1944 Lewis gave a series of BBC talks on the fundamentals of the Christian faith. These fifteen-minute chats received a great deal of attention. Alistair Cooke, for example, attacked them for appealing to the worst of the British wartime spirit: a narrow-minded, simplistic moralism.[15] What Lewis offered to the 600,000 listeners of each of his broadcasts[16] was certainty: a certainty of faith and purpose that must have resonated with his hearers as the bombs rained down. Moreover, in these talks more than in any other of his works, Lewis presented himself as an ordinary man. Such a pose seems ridiculous: With his intimate knowledge of obscure sixteenth-century texts, Lewis was no ordinary person. This self-presentation was, however, extraordinarily effective. With it Lewis tapped into the wartime myth of a classless Britain and the victory of the little people of a little island over the vast might of an evil empire.

The wartime atmosphere gave Lewis a sense of urgency that translated into an impressive outpouring of religious works.[17] In these works, the war

13 Ibid., p. 162.
14 *The Screwtape Letters* first appeared in weekly installments in the Church of England's newspaper *The Guardian*. Geoffrey Bles published *The Screwtape Letters* in book form in February 1942; the first printing of 2,000 copies sold out immediately. The book has never been out of print and has sold over a million copies. See A. N. Wilson, *C. S. Lewis: A Biography* (New York: Norton, 1990), pp. 177–9. By September of 1947, *The Screwtape Letters* had gone through twenty British and fourteen U.S. printings, according to *Time* (8 Sept. 1947, p. 71).
15 Alistair Cooke, "Mr. Anthony at Oxford," *New Republic*, 24 Apr. 1944, pp. 578–80.
16 The figure of 600,000 is given in "Don v. Devil," *Time*, 8 Sept. 1947, p. 65. This issue of the magazine featured Lewis on its cover, with the caption "Oxford's C. S. Lewis. His heresy: Christianity."
17 In addition to his radio talks, published as *Broadcast Talks* (1942), *Christian Behaviour: A Further Series of Broadcast Talks* (1943), and *Beyond Personality: The Christian Idea of God*

served as a convincing backdrop and lent strength to Lewis's central argument: that a cosmic war is raging, a centuries-old conflict between the forces of Satan and the armies of God, with the earth as the battlefield and human souls as the spoils of victory. In both *The Problem of Pain* and *Miracles* Lewis depicted the human race as a bad regiment in rebellion against the rightful Commander. Lewis described humanity in a "frontier situation, in which everything looks as if Nature were not resisting an alien invader but rebelling against a lawful sovereign."[18] As Lewis explained during one of his radio talks, "Enemy-occupied territory – that is what this world is. Christianity is the story of how the rightful king has landed, you might say landed in disguise, and is calling us all to take part in a great campaign of sabotage."[19] In the climate of the war years, such a vision of human history seemed powerful.

Lewis, however, was seeking not to comfort or console his fellow Britons but rather to challenge them with what he defined as the hard truths of Christianity. The most important of Lewis's works in this context is *The Abolition of Man*, which originated as a series of lectures at the University of Durham in 1942 and was first published as a pamphlet in 1943.[20] In this work Lewis adopted the stance of the prophet who points out sin and warns of retribution. The sin was the contemporary tendency to dismiss moral values as subjective. Lewis wrote *Abolition* after receiving an upper-form English textbook in his mail in 1942.[21] Outraged by what he perceived as its authors' denial of an objective moral system, Lewis denounced the textbook as the product and purveyor of moral annihilation and as representative of

(1944), during the war years Lewis wrote *The Problem of Pain* (1940), *The Screwtape Letters* (1942), *The Abolition of Man* (1943), *The Great Divorce* (1945), and *Miracles* (1947 – but begun in 1943).

18 Quotation from *Miracles* (New York: Macmillan, 1947), p. 41. See also pp. 83, 131, 146, 152–3, 155, 159. Sayer describes the work as one of "the most philosophical of [Lewis's] books . . . [and] one of the least successful" (*Jack*, p. 186). In contrast, *The Problem of Pain* (1940; London: Fontana, 1957) remains one of Lewis's most popular books. It was reprinted twice in 1940, four times in 1941, and three times in 1942 and 1943 (Sayer, *Jack*, p. 162). For the war imagery in this book, see pp. 51–2, 79, 83.

19 *Mere Christianity* (London: Geoffrey Bles, 1952), p. 37. For other military metaphors, see pp. vi, 39, 45, 51–2, 104, 110. In *The Great Divorce* (New York: Macmillan, 1946), a state of war between Heaven and Hell serves as the backdrop for Lewis's rather vicious depiction of souls who have been given a vacation from Purgatory (see p. 46). In *The Screwtape Letters* (New York: Macmillan, 1952), the European war figures prominently in the failed efforts of the devil Wormwood to win the soul of the unnamed hero (see pp. 33, 40, 76, 98).

20 *The Abolition of Man: How Education Develops Man's Sense of Morality* (1943; New York: Macmillan, 1955).

21 *The Control of Language* by Alec King and Martin Ketley. Identified by Sayer (*Jack*, p. 182). Lewis did not identify the textbook's title or authors in either the oral or the written version of his lectures.

"the whole system of values which happened to be in vogue among moderately educated young men of the professional classes during the period between the two wars."[22] *The Abolition* presents a violent, ill-focused attack on this system of values. As John Beversluis has pointed out, the simplified version of ethical subjectivism presented in a textbook by "two modest practising schoolmasters" (Lewis's words) can hardly be considered a valid and definitive presentation of a significant and sophisticated philosophy.[23] In his ill-considered attack, however, Lewis revealed the outlines of his protest against contemporary British attitudes and developments.

The Abolition of Man takes its title from Lewis's central thesis: that the denial of what he called the Tao is leading to the abolition of man, the negation of human value and worth. Lewis defined the Tao as "the doctrine of objective value, the belief that certain attitudes are really true, and others really false, to the kind of thing the universe is and the kind of things we are." His use of the Chinese word emphasized that this doctrine was found not only in Christianity but in almost all traditional belief systems. He translated the Tao as "Natural Law or Traditional Morality or the First Principles of Practical Reason or the First Platitudes. . . . the sole source of all value judgements." Against the Tao, Lewis placed his oversimplified version of ethical subjectivism: a bleak vision of the universe consisting of "the world of facts, without one trace of value, and the world of feelings, without one trace of truth or falsehood, justice or injustice. . . ."[24] Out of this universe, Lewis insisted, would come the death of humanity.

Subjectivism's ethical confusion manifested itself in fundamental misconceptions concerning humanity's relationship to nature. In the twentieth century, men claimed to have conquered nature. Such a victory, Lewis argued, came at the cost of reducing the natural world to quantifiable abstractions. Although the gains of the modern scientific outlook are clear, something important was sacrificed: "It is not the greatest of modern scientists who feel most sure that the object, stripped of its qualitative properties and reduced to mere quantity, is wholly real. . . . The great minds know very well that the object, so treated, is an artificial abstraction, that something of its reality has been lost." The loss may be, and often is, necessary. But the final step of "conquering Nature," Lewis warned, was the conquering of human nature, the stripping of human beings of all nonquantifiable properties. Without the Tao to give meaning and value, human beings are left to their unrestrained instincts. And so, in the end, "Man's conquest of Nature turns out . . . to be Nature's conquest of Man."[25]

22 *Abolition*, pp. 40–1.
23 John Beversluis, *C. S. Lewis and the Search for Rational Religion* (Grand Rapids: Eerdmans, 1985), pp. 44–50.
24 *Abolition*, pp. 29, 56, 30.   25 Ibid., pp. 82, 80.

Moreover, the extension of human control over nature meant the extension of human control over other human beings. Lewis's essentially libertarian instincts recoiled from the multiplication of the means of control implied by technological and scientific developments: "the power of Man to make himself what he pleases means . . . the power of some men to make other men what *they* please." By stepping outside the Tao, men deluded themselves into thinking that they were freeing humanity from unnatural and irrational constraints when they were actually enslaving most men and women to the dictates and desires of the few, be the few fascists, capitalists, or socialists.[26]

Science provided the weapons by which the few conquered nature, humanity, and themselves. It is ironic that Lewis was writing these lectures at the time when the British and American governments were beginning to organize their scientific communities to create the atomic bomb.[27] Lewis never grasped the unique horror of atomic weapons; for him, the Bomb was simply one more tool of slaughter in a world of weapons.[28] He saw the atomic bomb as mad but dismissed the call for British unilateral nuclear disarmament as even madder.[29] Yet, the making of the atomic bomb represents the subjugation of science to power politics and the enhancement of the ability of the few to control the lives of the many that Lewis warned against.

The weaknesses or dangers of the scientific outlook, Lewis contended, arose from the birth of modern science in the sixteenth and seventeenth centuries, the same period in which magic flourished.[30] The conjunction of the birth of modern science and the heyday of magic was more than coincidence: Both discovered the efficacy of technique as a path to power, and both aimed "to subdue reality to the wishes of men" rather than to pursue wisdom, "to conform the soul to reality. . . ."[31] Lewis argued that in order to

26 Ibid., pp. 68, 72, 85.
27 See Richard Rhodes, *The Making of the Atomic Bomb* (New York: Simon and Schuster, 1986), pt. 2.
28 See "On the Atomic Bomb," in *Poems*, pp. 64–5; Shirwood Wirt's interview with Lewis entitled "Heaven, Earth, and Outer Space," *Decision*, Oct. 1963; C. S. Lewis, *God in the Dock: Essays in Theology and Ethics* (Grand Rapids: Eerdmans, 1970), pp. 311–12; Lewis's letter to Mrs. Edward A. Allen, undated, in *Letters*, p. 225 (original dated 18 Dec. 1950: Wade – CSL/L-Allen/42/Wade); Lewis's "Letter to a Lady," 17 July 1953, in *Letters*, p. 250 (copy of the original in the Wade Center: letter to Mrs.[?] Johnson, CSL/L-Johnson, 4/X, Wade Index no. 654); and Nevill Coghill's reminiscences in *Light on C. S. Lewis*, ed. Jocelyn Gibb (New York: Harcourt, Brace, and World, 1966), pp. 64–5.
29 See his letter to Edward and Mrs. Allen, 10 Dec. 1960, Wade – CSL/L-Allen/59/Wade.
30 For the interconnections between magic and early science, see Hugh Kearney, *Science and Change, 1500–1700* (New York: McGraw-Hill, 1971), chaps. 4 and 6; and works exploring the magical side of Isaac Newton: Gale Christianson, *In the Presence of the Creator: Isaac Newton and His Times* (London: Macmillan, 1984); Betty Jo Dobbs, *The Foundations of Newton's Alchemy; or, "The Hunting of the Greene Lyon"* (Cambridge: Cambridge University Press, 1975); and Betty Jo Dobbs, *The Janus Face of Genius: The Role of Alchemy in Newton's Thought* (Cambridge: Cambridge University Press, 1991).
31 *Abolition*, p. 88.

overcome its birth "in an unhealthy neighborhood and at an inauspicious hour," science must be reoriented, and its practitioners must repent.[32] An unrepentant science could bring the world to catastrophe, as power was concentrated in the hands of the "Conditioners," the "man-moulders of the new age . . . armed with the powers of an omnicompetent state and an irresistible scientific technique . . . who really can cut out all posterity in what shape they please."[33]

Spiritual space travel

Lewis's warnings of the dangers of technological tyranny and the erosion of ethical values reached few listeners or readers. *The Abolition of Man* sold poorly for a work of Lewis's and probably confused the few who bothered to read it. It illustrates the fundamental weaknesses of Lewis's apologetics and the limitations of this genre as a medium of communication. To be received, a protest must be expressed in a form comprehensible to more than the protester. The pamphlet format of *Abolition* failed to convey the message Lewis wished to communicate. Lewis, however, proved himself willing to use a variety of forms to articulate his protest: radio talks, academic lectures, book reviews, essays, fiction, and fantasy. A. N. Wilson has noted that Lewis's apologetics present a curious picture. Lewis had come to his faith through myth and through imagination, yet, in his apologetics, he attempted to defend Christianity by rational argument alone, by reason rather than by romanticism. Given his almost complete lack of knowledge of biblical scholarship as well as his outdated philosophical stance, Lewis's defenses of Christianity could be and have been easily breached.[34] His fantasies proved to be a more successful medium of communicating his protest against the modern world.

Lewis's defense of fantasy rested in part on his realization that it could serve as a means of communicating with the uneducated and with those readers who, unlike Lewis himself, did not turn instinctively to Spenser or Milton for refreshment. They turned to popular literature, for which Lewis expressed a surprising degree of respect. He believed that many critics were guilty of both social and temporal elitism: They condemned fantasy and much of contemporary popular literature because they misunderstood the *romance*. Fantasy, and popular literature in general, stem from this medieval genre and share its emphasis on "story." Modern literary criticism, in contrast, ignored "story," and thus ignored a fundamental aspect of good litera-

---

32 *Abolition*, p. 89. See also *Miracles*, p. 179.   33 *Abolition*, p. 73.
34 Wilson, *Lewis*, p. 166.

ture. A good story, Lewis argued, not only draws the reader in and on, it also allows him or her to experience beauty and joy; hence, ". . . any work which has ever produced intense and ecstatic delight in anyone" falls within the category of "good literature," according to Lewis.[35] Popular literature, including fantasy, demands serious attention, because "something which the educated receive from poetry can reach the masses through stories of adventure, and almost in no other way. . . ." In fantasy Lewis, and Tolkien as well, sought to rework the adventure story, to elevate it, yet to retain that link with a non-elite readership. Lewis hoped that he was "in a very small way contributing . . . to the encouragement of a better school of prose story in England: of story that can mediate imaginative life to the masses while not being contemptible to the few. . . ."[36]

In his space trilogy Lewis used fantasy as an additional weapon in his struggle to convince a skeptical and materialist age to return to the spiritual, eternal truths of orthodox Christianity.[37] By lifting the reader out of the world of the earthly and ordinary, and by placing the Christian story within a new context, Lewis hoped to break through the obstacles of familiarity and boredom. Besides moving beyond the familiar, fantasy enabled Lewis to spotlight the drama of the warfare between the forces of Christianity and the forces of evil. The motif of the universe at war, central to Lewis's apologetics, also provided the backdrop for Lewis's space trilogy. Impatient with complacent and comfortable religion, he aimed to shock his readers into a state of military preparedness. Earth, in his space fantasy, "turns out to be a kind of Ypres Salient in the universe. . . ."[38] Tragically, those down in the trenches fail to realize they are on the battlefield.

In *Out of the Silent Planet* (1938), *Perelandra* (1944), and *That Hideous Strength* (1946), Lewis wove his Christian apologetics and medieval scholarship into a powerful myth about the struggle between good and evil on both the cosmic and the individual levels.[39] In the alternative vision of reality

35 Lewis, "Different Tastes in Literature," in *On Stories and Other Essays on Literature*, ed. Walter Hooper (New York: Harcourt Brace Jovanovich, 1982), p. 124. First published as "Notes on the Way," *Time and Tide*, 25 May 1946 and 1 June 1946. One could argue that, by Lewis's definition, pornography thus constitutes "good literature."

36 Lewis, "On Stories," in *On Stories*, pp. 16, 17.

37 Lewis's space trilogy is often classified as science fiction but it belongs in the fantasy section. For Lewis on science fiction, see "An Expostulation," in *Poems*, p. 58.

38 *Out of the Silent Planet* (New York: Macmillan, 1965), p. 158. The Ypres Salient was one of the two main sectors on the British front lines during World War I. It projected about four miles into the German line and so "was notable for its terrors of concentrated, accurate artillery fire" (Paul Fussell, *The Great War and Modern Memory* [New York: Oxford University Press, 1975], p. 40).

39 In addition to *Out of the Silent Planet*, the space trilogy includes *Perelandra* (1944; New York: Macmillan, 1965) and *That Hideous Strength* (1946; New York: Macmillan, 1965). *That Hideous Strength* was first published in the United States in an edited version entitled *The Tortured Planet* (1952).

Lewis offered in the trilogy, Earth is the Silent Planet, cut off from communication with the rest of the universe by the rebellion of Satan. In the first volume, the philologist-hero (a bow to Tolkien), Ransom, defeats the efforts of two scientists to colonize Mars and to exterminate its inhabitants. Venus, called Perelandra, provides the setting for the second volume, in which Ransom again faces off against the evil scientist. In this book, the religious nature of Lewis's vision is much clearer: Weston, the scientist, has been possessed by the devil; in the paradise of Perelandra the temptation of Adam and Eve is replayed. This time, however, the couple passes through the temptation and Perelandra remains pure.[40] The final and least successful of the volumes of the trilogy is set on Earth. Once again scientists are depicted as devil worshippers, who are defeated by Ransom and his followers in a bloody massacre.

Lewis set his space trilogy in contemporary Britain; it is the medieval past, however, that structures the work. The medieval model detailed in *The Discarded Image* serves as the backdrop for the trilogy: Ransom discovers that medieval cosmology is true, both mythically and factually. For example, Ransom's space journey in *Out of the Silent Planet* reveals to him the falseness of the modern view of space as "the black, cold vacuity, the utter deadness. . . ."[41] Instead, the medieval concept of space as a pulsating plenum, the Deep Heaven, proves more apt. Medieval cosmology also moves the plot forward in the trilogy. The *eldila* of the fantasy are Lewis's versions of the planetary intelligences that move the celestial spheres. As in the Middle Ages, these intelligences in Lewis's story blend Christian and classical elements. They are both angels and the pagan deities associated with the planets. Hence, the *eldil* of Perelandra is the angelic power who guards Venus as well as the love goddess whose descent to Earth sparks the riot of lovemaking that closes *That Hideous Strength*.

Lewis used his fantastic re-creation of the medieval model to illumine the failings of twentieth-century society. The medieval model had provided a coherent cosmos, a world in which humanity and nature were linked in an unbreakable chain. In the twentieth century, this chain has been snapped. Lewis detailed the consequences of the severing of the connection between humanity and the natural world in the trilogy. In *That Hideous Strength*, the villains are the members of N.I.C.E., the National Institute for Coordinated Experiments, who have cut themselves off from the natural state of sympathy with other living creatures. One scientist at N.I.C.E. aims to cleanse the

---

40　The germ of the idea that led to *Perelandra* can be seen in *The Problem of Pain*, published four years earlier (see pp. 72–3).
41　*Out of the Silent Planet*, p. 32.

earth of man's "rivals" such as animals and vegetables, and another dreams of a world scoured clean like the moon.[42] Lewis's most effective condemnation of the antiecological perspective of those in the service of the Enemy takes place in the scenes describing the construction of N.I.C.E.'s headquarters in the previously charming town of Edgestow. Here the Enemy effects "the conversion of an ancient woodland into an inferno of mud and noise and steel and concrete. . . ."[43]

Although Lewis's condemnation of such abuse pulsates in these three volumes, affirmation dominates the books: affirmation of the marvelous variety of creation and of a life lived in sympathy with the natural world. In his descriptions of the imagined worlds of Malacandra (Mars) and Perelandra (Venus), Lewis reveals his delight in color, in form, in the endless variety of creatures, and in the interactions of such creatures. Malacandra is an ecological tour de force, a complex and intricate ecosystem in which the three rational species coexist in mutual dependence and respect. In Perelandra, as on Earth, the only rational creature is humanity; however, in this unfallen world the king and queen, like the pre-Temptation Adam and Eve, live in harmony with the creatures they rule. Ransom's confrontation with a gigantic insectlike creature in the caves of Perelandra, for example, dissolves the barriers established at the Fall between humanity and the insect world. He could never "understand again why one should quarrel with an animal for having more legs or eyes than oneself. All that he had felt from childhood about insects and reptiles died that moment. . . . Apparently it had all, even from the beginning, been a dark enchantment of the enemy's."[44]

Lewis sought to highlight not only God's intended harmony between humanity and nature but also the sanctity of nature itself, apart from any relationship with humanity. Nature, in Lewis's view, is not simply a script in which the Christian reads the drama of God's actions. Nature reveals God to humanity, but this natural revelation is not nature's reason for being. Like many ecologists two decades later, Lewis asserted nature's right to exist, its holiness as a living entity, apart from its utility to humanity. Man's appropriation of nature as a thing, rather than respect for it as a fellow creation, violates the divine plan. The splendors of the Perelandrian world had existed for centuries before the advent of humans on that planet. Ransom discovers, "Though men or angels rule them, the worlds are for themselves. . . . You

---

42 *That Hideous Strength*, pp. 42, 172–3.
43 Ibid., p. 90. For Lewis's condemnation of the destruction of the natural environment, see also "Pan's Purge," "The Future of Forestry," "Lines during a General Election," and "The Condemned," in *Poems*, pp. 5–6, 61–3.
44 *Perelandra*, p. 182.

are not the voice that all things utter, nor is there eternal silence in the places where you cannot come."[45] Ransom learns to view nature as holy in and of itself.[46]

The figure of Merlin in *That Hideous Strength* highlights Lewis's sacramental view of nature. Both the Enemy's followers in N.I.C.E. and Ransom's company mistakenly believe that Merlin can be roused and utilized as a tool for evil in twentieth-century Britain. Merlin is roused but immediately aligns himself with the company because his view of nature is diametrically opposed to that of the scientists of N.I.C.E. For Merlin, "every operation on Nature is a kind of personal contact. . . . After him came the modern man to whom Nature is something dead – a machine to be worked. . . ." Merlin has power over nature because he is part of nature himself, he uses nature as an ally rather than as a tool. The members of N.I.C.E. wish to use Merlin to bolster their mechanical subjugation of the natural world; but, as they discover to their peril, Merlin and a utilitarian world view cannot be combined. Ransom's company realizes that Merlin's intimate relationship with nature "represents what we've got to get back to. . . ."[47] Humanity must recognize the sanctity of nature and seek to rebuild a right relationship with it.

In Lewis's view, this sense of the correct relationship between humanity and nature, a fundamentally ecological perspective, led to a respect for not only the varied forms of nature but also the various individual bearers of God's image. The belief that abstractions are dangerous, that each person matters, serves as a pervasive theme in Lewis's works. The modern world violates the integrity of the individual by its inclination to generalize, categorize, and quantify. The tendency to think in abstractions and so violate the humanity of individual human beings underlies the villainy of the evil Weston in *Out of the Silent Planet*. He regards the survival of the human race as important but completely disregards the needs or rights of individual human beings.[48] Similarly, in *That Hideous Strength* Mark Studdock's sociology has taught him to view humanity in terms of classes and status groups rather than individual men and women. This flawed perception blinds him to the deceptions of N.I.C.E. until it is almost too late. Against the sociological assumption that humanity can be quantified, Lewis argued (in another context) that

---

45 Ibid., pp. 215–16. Lewis explained this view of nature more directly in *Miracles*, pp. 77–81.

46 Lewis's ideas were not always in accordance with an ecological perspective, however. In a rather controversial chapter on animal pain in *The Problem of Pain*, Lewis argued that domesticated, rather than wild, animals were the most "natural," the most in accordance with God's purposes for creation. See *Problem of Pain*, p. 126. Lewis also disagreed strongly with the pantheist current that runs on the fringes of the ecological movement. He believed that pantheism reduced not only God but nature. See *Miracles*, p. 81.

47 *That Hideous Strength*, pp. 285, 286.   48 *Out of the Silent Planet*, pp. 135–141.

"there isn't any crowd. No one is like anyone else. . . . each loved by God individually, as if it were the only creature in existence."[49]

Lewis believed each individual must be seen as a participant in "the great dance." Within the whirl of this powerful medieval image the center shifts, yet remains stable: ". . . each is equally at the centre and none are there by being equals, but some by giving place and some by receiving it, the small things by their smallness and the great by their greatness, and all the patterns linked and looped together by the unions of a kneeling with a sceptred love."[50] The great dance evokes a world of hierarchy and order; it is not, however, a rigid minuet depriving the dancers of all choice. In the dance each individual must choose how he or she will step; in the world each must choose to seek to restore wholeness to the world or contribute to its fragmentation. Although the war between good and evil occurs on the cosmic level, individual actions remain all-important. Ransom's efforts on Perelandra prevent a second Fall. Merely a middle-aged philologist, he is yet capable of acts of cosmic significance. Jane Studdock's choice of Ransom and his company makes her able to withstand the Enemy and so help save Britain from physical destruction and spiritual annihilation. To choose rightly, as Ransom and Jane do in Lewis's vision, means to affirm the individual wonder of each human being, of each created thing. It is to achieve an ecological perspective: to grasp the variety, the interdependence, the complexity, and the marvelousness that make up the universe, and thus to glimpse the spiritual reality that provides its foundation.

In the space trilogy, characters reveal themselves to be servants of the Enemy by their disregard for individual choice and happiness. The physicist Weston believes not in individual men or women but in "Life," a concept so abstract as to be utterly meaningless and thoroughly destructive.[51] In order to permit the human race to escape the confines of a finite world, Weston aims to colonize Malacandra, and to exterminate most of its inhabitants in the process.

Lewis used Weston as a representative for what he defined as "scientism," essentially the "belief that the supreme moral end is the perpetuation of our own species, and that this is to be pursued even if, in the process of being fitted for survival, our species has to be stripped of all those things for which we value it – of pity, of happiness, and of freedom."[52] Lewis argued that no

49 "To a Lady," 20 June 1952, in *Letters*, p. 243.
50 *Perelandra*, p. 217. The image of the great dance also appeared in Lewis's apologetics. See *Mere Christianity*, p. 139; *Miracles*, p. 150; *Problem of Pain*, p. 141.
51 *Out of the Silent Planet*, p. 27.
52 "A Reply to Professor Haldane," in *Of Other Worlds: Essays and Stories*, ed. Walter Hooper (New York: Harcourt Brace Jovanovich, 1966), p. 77. This article was a rejoinder to Prof. J. B. Haldane's "Auld Hornie, F.R.S.," a review of *That Hideous Strength* in *Modern Quarterly*, n.s., 1, no. 4 (Autumn 1946).

true scientist would embrace the error of scientism. In *Out of the Silent Planet* Weston claims to act as a scientist; yet he fails in the most elementary scientific observation. In *That Hideous Strength* the sociologist, Mark Studdock, proves susceptible to N.I.C.E. not because he is a scientist but because of his lack of scientific training.[53] Although taught to regard himself as a scientist, Mark, like Weston, lacked the faculty of observation: ". . . his education had had the curious effect of making things that he read and wrote more real to him than things he saw. Statistics about agricultural labourers were the substance; any real ditcher, ploughman, or farmer's boy, was the shadow."[54] Even worse than Mark's failure to observe is N.I.C.E.'s manipulation of scientific truth, or truth of any kind, for the sake of an "Order" that demands the reconditioning of the human race, including the extermination of weaker elements. To N.I.C.E., the rock face of the moon shines as one form of its ideal. The gruesome "Head" symbolizes another: the body eliminated, the brain bubbling over the skull, the mind free of the organic. Scientism, Lewis concluded, means perpetuating the human race at the cost of all that is human.

Although Lewis claimed to be attacking scientism rather than science in the trilogy, his fiction reveals his uneasiness with scientific assumptions and achievements. For Lewis, human rationality was fundamentally limited. For example, Ransom's reason should have prepared him for the suddenness and all-embracing blackness of the Perelandrian night; it could not, however, dictate a right response to the pleasures of the new paradise.[55] Lewis affirmed, even reveled in, the reality of the physical world, but he asserted throughout the trilogy that humanity ignores the reality of the spiritual realm to its everlasting peril. In the end, the scientists and the officials do not control N.I.C.E.; its direction rests in the ruthless grip of the spiritual enemy, who utilizes the self-deceptions and greed of humanity for his own pleasure.

Although *That Hideous Strength* concludes with the victory of Ransom's company of believers over N.I.C.E., it also ends with the assurance that the Enemy will rise again with new and more hideous strength. The trilogy, however, is much less defeatist than this conclusion suggests. In the three books, Lewis attempted to confront his readers with a fresh perspective on the Christian story and the idea (learned from Tolkien) that Christianity is the true myth in which all myth finds completion and that in the Gospels mythology and history unite. Ransom learns throughout the course of the trilogy the fundamental truth of much that he had dismissed as fancy. On Malacandra, for example, his encounters with the Malacandrians and the *eldila* teach him that "the distinction between history and mythology might be

53 "A Reply to Professor Haldane," p. 78.
54 *That Hideous Strength*, p. 87. For Lewis's fear of sociology, see also *Screwtape Letters*, p. 14.
55 *Perelandra*, p. 42.

itself meaningless outside the Earth."[56] On Perelandra Ransom grasps more fully the relationship between Christianity and myth. There he "had a sensation not of following an adventure but of enacting a myth" throughout. His first sight of the Lady standing amidst a crowd of creatures reveals "another myth coming out into the world of fact. . . ." She is, he realizes, both pagan goddess and Madonna, a fusion of the sacred and secular, the natural and supernatural.[57]

This fusion dominates the second volume of the trilogy. Again and again in *Perelandra*, Ransom encounters myths made physical fact: dragons, mermaids, and gigantic beetles intermingle with a replaying of the true myth of creation in which a new world comes alive, a new Temptation occurs, and a second Fall is averted. In the final pages of the book Ransom meets the *eldila* of Malacandra and Perelandra in the bodily forms of Mars and Venus. He finally understands that despite the Fall, despite Earth's condemnation to be the Silent Planet, "the traces of the celestial commonwealth are not quite lost. . . . Our mythology is based on a solider reality than we dream: but it is also at an almost infinite distance from that base." The mythology of Earth consists of "gleams of celestial strength and beauty falling on a jungle of filth and imbecility."[58]

For Lewis, the medieval model with its masterful synthesis of folktale, classical mythology, and Christianity shone as one of the brightest of these gleams of celestial strength and beauty. At the model's core Lewis perceived a coherent order in which humanity found its proper place, with vital links to the spiritual and natural realms, and to the mythic, which encompassed both. Lewis's space trilogy asserted the essential, although not factual, truth of this model and stressed the need to restore these links if humanity is to avoid the abyss to which misplaced faith in science leads. It articulated a romantic protest against the reduction of reality to the material and the quantifiable, and the consequences of such a reduction: the alienation of human beings, the abuse of the natural world, and the denigration of the past as irrelevant.

Into the wardrobe

In *The Chronicles of Narnia*, as in the space trilogy, Lewis created an otherworld that demonstrated the beauty and potency of the links that united humanity to the natural and spiritual realms. The space trilogy has remained in print and attracts a steady readership; Lewis's most enduring fame, however, rests not on these adult fairy tales but on the Narnia stories, written for

---

56 *Out of the Silent Planet*, pp. 144–5.   57 *Perelandra*, pp. 47, 54, 64.   58 Ibid., p. 201.

and marketed at a more juvenile audience. The fast-paced action, simple moral structure, and of course the youthful heroes explain much of the appeal of the Narnia books to children. Although the space fantasies reveal a much more sophisticated version of Lewis's social and cultural critique, it is the protest embedded in the children's stories that reached a truly popular audience. Moreover, the *Chronicles* were written at remarkable speed, sometimes in a single draft. In these stories Lewis's grievances against the age sit openly, without the cover of scholarly sophistication or subtlety.[59]

As with *That Hideous Strength*, the Narnia stories are in some ways the by-product of World War II. During the war, Lewis's rather odd household expanded to include a number of children evacuated from English cities. With practically no experience of small children, Lewis somewhat surprisingly enjoyed playing host to these young evacuees, although he was disturbed to discover that they read very little. When one small guest asked if she could enter his wardrobe to see what lay behind it, Lewis was inspired to write a story for children.[60] In 1950, this story appeared as *The Lion, the Witch and the Wardrobe*. Six sequels followed.

The books chronicle the history of the otherworld of Narnia from Creation to the Last Day by recounting the adventures of eight English children who fall into Narnia at various times and in various ways, but always find themselves faced with the task of saving Narnia from dire peril. Kings and queens rule Narnia, but they are subject to Aslan, the Christ-figure who calls the children into Narnia. Aslan is a lion, an appropriate incarnation in a world "peopled" by a host of creatures including talking animals, dwarfs, giants, dryads, fauns, and centaurs.

Not surprisingly, given Lewis's preference for medievalism over modernity, Narnia is a medieval world. Moreover, because the *Chronicles* constitute a fairy story or fantasy, awkward questions, such as who produces the wealth and by what means, can simply be ignored. Lewis's descriptions of Cair Paravel, the seat of Narnia's kings, evoke the splendor of the Middle Ages.[61] Hierarchy and authority, important medieval values, shape this ideal world. Again, because of his choice of genre, Lewis could embrace an unpalatable and problematic doctrine without arousing too much opposition. In Narnia's

---

59 Lewis began *The Lion, the Witch and the Wardrobe*, the first volume in the series, at the end of 1939 but set it aside and did not complete it until 1948 or 1949. He finished *The Voyage of the Dawn Treader* by February 1950, *The Horse and His Boy* by the middle of the same year, and *The Last Battle*, the final book in the series, by March of 1953 (Wilson, *Lewis*, p. 220). According to George Sayer, Lewis wrote *The Voyage of the Dawn Treader* in two months, *The Horse and His Boy* in five months, and *The Silver Chair* in about four months. See Sayer, *Jack*, pp. 190–1.

60 Sayer, *Jack*, p. 189.

61 *Prince Caspian* (1951; New York: Collier Books, 1971), p. 17; *The Silver Chair* (1953; New York: Collier Books, 1970), pp. 27–9.

hierarchy, as in the Great Chain of Being of the medieval world view, human beings stand near the top of the ladder. Although neither more intelligent nor more powerful than the talking beasts and other creatures, humanity must rule: ". . . Narnia was never right except when a Son of Adam was King."[62] The rightness of kingship goes without question. In *The Voyage of the Dawn Treader*, the unlikable Eustace's progressive republicanism, for example, forms one more line on the indictment sheet against him.[63] Hierarchical authority in Narnia does not, however, confer unrestrained power. All creatures are under Aslan, who Himself is subject to the Emperor's law.[64]

Although the seven books trace Narnia's history from start to finish, little historical development occurs. Little development is needed, according to Lewis, for the medieval society of Narnia represents society at its best. The books detail Narnia in various crises but in between were "whole centuries in which all Narnia was so happy that notable dances and feasts, or at most tournaments, were the only things that could be remembered, and every day and week had been better than the last."[65]

This idyll ends with *The Last Battle*, the seventh volume in the series, when Narnia falls into the hands of a corrupt Ape in league with Narnia's traditional enemy, the state of Calormen. The Ape has plans for Narnia, plans for modernization. With modernity comes the abuse of power. The previously independent creatures of Narnia find themselves forced into the cash nexus and a system of wage slavery. The Ape declares that under the new order Narnia will be "a country worth living in." This, he explains, means "roads and big cities and schools and offices and whips and muzzles and saddles and cages and kennels and prisons. . . ."[66] The Ape and his fellow modernizers push Narnia toward the Last Battle, the final Armageddon after which the world is destroyed and the company of the good find themselves in a new and everlasting Narnia.

As in the space trilogy, classical and medieval myth interact in the *Chronicles* with a reworking of the Christian Gospel, in order both to scrape the accretions of familiarity from Christianity and to illumine the glimmers of truth embedded in all myth. The *Chronicles* are not allegories of the Crucifixion and Resurrection but rather possible answer to the question of what form Christ would assume in a different world.[67] The stories thus make up a

---

62 *Caspian*, p. 65.
63 *The Voyage of the Dawn Treader* (1953; New York: Collier Books, 1970), p. 25.
64 *The Lion, the Witch and the Wardrobe* (1950; New York: Collier Books, 1970), pp. 139–40.
65 *The Last Battle* (1956; New York: Collier Books, 1970), p. 89.   66 Ibid., p. 30.
67 "Sometimes Fairy-Stories May Say Best What's to Be Said," in *Of Other Worlds*, pp. 36–7. See also "It All Began with a Picture," in *Of Other Worlds*, p. 42, first published in *Radio Times, Jr., Radio Times* 148 (15 July 1960); and Lewis's letter to Mrs. Phillip (Martha) Hook, 29 Dec. 1958, a copy of which is held in the Wade Center (CSL/L-Hook/X/Wade Index no. 586). In this letter Lewis explained that his fantasies were not

modern-day myth, one that questions conventional assumptions about reality and does not hesitate to draw on past myths for support. Lewis playfully asserted the tension between reality and "fact" in his description of a faun's study. The books bear such titles as *Men, Monks, and Gamekeepers: A Study in Popular Legend* and *Is Man a Myth?* In *The Lion, the Witch and the Wardrobe*, the children encounter as real much that they have been taught to regard as imaginary: fauns and witches, Silenus and Bacchus, Father Christmas.[68] These elements intermingle with the truths of Christianity in a riotous, mythic medley.

Myth provides the English children with the guidance they require to perform their tasks in Narnia. They know to follow the robin in *The Lion, the Witch and the Wardrobe* because, as the eldest boy, Peter, argues, "They're good birds in all the stories I've ever read."[69] In *The Voyage of the Dawn Treader* Eustace's lack of familiarity with myth hinders his acceptance of the joys of Narnia and nearly incapacitates him for his role on the seaborne quest. This unlovable character became the vessel into which Lewis poured many of his grievances with the modern world. The child of modern vegetarians, Eustace has received a progressive education that has taught him to call his parents by their Christian names and little else. When he first encounters a dragon, he has no idea what it is, for he "had read only the wrong books. They had a lot to say about exports and imports and governments and drains, but they were weak on dragons." The world of fantasy remains a foreign land, along with its subrealms of nature and imagination. Eustace liked animals "if they were dead and pinned on a card." He liked books, too, "if they were books of information and had pictures of grain elevators or of fat foreign children doing exercises in model schools." As a result, he "was quite incapable of making anything up himself."[70] Not surprisingly, he is the only one of the eight children called to Narnia in the series who finds the otherworld a horrible place. He longs for machinery until he is remade by Aslan's magic.

The failure of Eustace's education in the real world mirrors Lewis's assessment of the failure of twentieth-century Western culture to confront mythic truth. He argued that, like Eustace, modern man had read all the wrong books. Ignorance of myth, according to Lewis, not only stultifies the imagination but leaves men and women without the resources needed to interpret and respond to reality correctly. Like the Narnian men in *Prince Caspian* who no longer believed in the existence of the talking beasts they had driven underground, Western humanity lives in a world of self-created illusion.

allegories but rather suppositions: Suppose a world such as Narnia existed; what form would Christ take in such a world? See also Lewis's letter to Father Peter Milward, 22 Sept. 1956 (Wade – CSL/L-Milward/7/Wade).
68 *Lion*, pp. 12, 8, 27, 43–7, 102–5.   69 Ibid., p. 59.   70 *Voyage*, pp. 71, 1–2, 5.

Lewis believed that myth, by contrast, prepares the mind for belief. For example, Prince Caspian's love for stories about the supposedly unreal talking beasts leads him to faith in Aslan in the end.[71]

Belief constitutes a significant individual choice. Eustace's conversion may seem forced (he is, after all, trapped in dragon form), but as other episodes in the *Chronicles* show, Lewis argued that one can always refuse to believe and thereby blind oneself to reality. Lewis's apologetics stressed again and again his belief in free will. His fantasies reinforced this idea. The petty and unprincipled magician Uncle Andrew deprives himself of the joy of Narnia's creation and the wonders of Aslan by such refusal. He convinces himself that Aslan's song must be only a roar: "Soon he couldn't have heard anything else even if he had wanted to."[72] Uncle Andrew has made his choice; he cannot find the fusion of natural, physical, and spiritual glimpsed in myth. The most dramatic and even heartrending example of the choice not to believe, and not to share in the joy, comes in *The Last Battle* when (as in the Christian myth of Christ's birth) a stable proves to be the gateway to everlasting life. A group of obstinate dwarfs chooses not to believe in the new Narnia. The dwarfs' unbelief blinds them so that they cannot see the doorway into the better world. Instead, they continue to believe that they are confined to a dark and dirty stable. Not even Aslan can convince them of the truth: "They have chosen cunning instead of belief. Their prison is only in their own minds, yet they are in that prison; and so afraid of being taken in that they cannot be taken out."[73] According to Lewis, the dwarfs, like modern humanity, have chosen illusion and incompleteness.

Freedom to choose undergirds not only belief but also action in the stories. Aslan draws the English children into Narnia; they do not enter of their own accord. Nevertheless, the lack of choice in this matter does not negate free will once in Narnia. Often, the children take the wrong road. At the beginning of the series, Edmund chooses to align himself with the White Witch. Lucy chooses not to follow Aslan's call in *Prince Caspian*, and so much time is wasted on the quest. Jill and Eustace make a series of poor choices in *The Silver Chair* and continually "muff the Signs."[74] The children discover that in Lewis's authoritarian world fulfillment lies in obedience, yet obedience is a choice freely made, an offering freely given. Through his fantasy Lewis affirmed not only a hierarchical universe but also the uniqueness of each individual creature and the significance of each creature's choices, beliefs, and actions. In a world of "the mass," Lewis asserted the primacy and power of the individual. He argued that each being is significant in and of itself. Yet, he also argued that each is a piece of a larger unity as well, a uniquely

71 *Caspian*, p. 77.
72 *The Magician's Nephew* (1955; New York: Collier Books, 1970), p. 126.
73 *Battle*, p. 148. 74 *Lion*, chap. 4; *Caspian*, p. 137; *Chair*, p. 102.

individual piece complete only in right relation to the other members of this whole. Lewis sought to reconcile the conflicting ideals of community and individuality by claiming that only within the relationships that make for true community can the individual find purpose and significance.

Lewis created a myth that both affirmed the importance of the individual and insisted that the individual achieves fulfillment in context, in right relation to other human beings as well as to the natural and spiritual worlds. In the *Chronicles* Aslan calls no child to Narnia alone. Always he assigns a task to be achieved by group effort. The contribution each member makes to the company's task, the growth of fellowship and trust within the group, and the final accomplishment that transcends any individual's achievement serve as common themes throughout the seven stories and as Lewis's protest against the isolated protagonist of modern literature.

In the mythic world, not only the ties between human beings but also the bonds that connect the natural and the human worlds are forged anew. In Narnia, the speech of the beasts serves as a crucial link. Humans and animals exist in harmony; the mystery and power inherent in the animal world remain, but humanity's terror has gone. In contrast, talking beasts and mythical creatures like the fauns and dwarfs do not live in Calormen, Narnia's enemy across the desert. This land of cruelty and corruption has cut its ties to the natural world. In Narnia, however, even the trees, rivers, and stars communicate.75 Narnia's decay brings the fraying of the bonds between nature and humanity. The Calormenes' arrival in Narnia results in the reduction of horses and unicorns to beasts of burden, the dwarfs' enslavement, the murder of the trees. But in the new Narnia, Aslan restores the right relationships. Death, that final break between natural and spiritual, falls in defeat, and all the characters of the various *Chronicles* come together in a joyous celebration, the eucatastrophe Tolkien deemed essential to fairy stories.

In the Narnia stories Lewis created a fantasy that fulfilled his central aim of presenting the Christian Gospel in a new, fresh, and appealing form: *The Lion, the Witch and the Wardrobe* replays the Crucifixion and Resurrection; *The Magician's Nephew* reenacts the Creation story; in *The Voyage of the Dawn Treader* Aslan the Lion is revealed as the Paschal Lamb; in *The Last Battle* readers see Armageddon and the Second Coming. The *Chronicles* also, however, furthered the argument he established in the space trilogy: that modern Britain, and the modern West, had lost touch with mythical reality, and so with the spiritual and natural realms. Against the materialism and "massness" of twentieth-century culture Lewis built a fantasy bulwark, an affirmation of the uniqueness and significance of each individual, and of the coherent and meaningful universe peopled by such individuals. Lewis looked to

75 *Voyage*, p. 180.

the past, particularly to medieval civilization, for the building blocks of his fantasy. In the literature, art, and architecture of the Middle Ages he believed he had found a vibrant and vital culture, the product of a vibrant and vital civilization that had not yet lost touch with nonmaterial realities. The protest against the assumptions of contemporary society that Lewis expressed in his creation of Narnia reiterated the themes of the romantic social and cultural critique: a mistrust of mechanization, rationalization, and expertise, and an avowal of the need to reconstruct human community, preserve the natural world, and recognize the primacy of the spiritual realm.

4

Middle-earth as moral protest

The respect for a lost culture and the desire to restore to modern England its links with the natural and spiritual worlds that impelled Lewis to create Narnia also lay behind Tolkien's *Lord of the Rings*. A sort of epic fairy tale, the work grew out of Tolkien's lifelong passion for self-created languages and mythology. The mythological world underpinning *The Lord of the Rings* provided for Tolkien the vocabulary he utilized to articulate his experiences and order his world, and thus the expression of his critique of modern British culture and society. The major themes of this critique place it within the British tradition of romantic protest.

The road to Middle-earth

Tolkien's scholarly writings, unlike those of Lewis, are not extensive, although the scholarly work he published, particularly a new edition in Middle English of *Sir Gawain and the Green Knight* (1925) and a fresh look at *The Beowulf* (*Beowulf: The Monster and the Critics* [1937]), were well respected in the narrow world of Anglo-Saxon and philological studies.[1] The relatively small number of Tolkien's academic publications stems in part from his perfectionism. A tireless tinkerer, Tolkien was rarely satisfied enough with his work to regard it as publishable. Even more important than his perfectionism in explaining his failure to publish, however, was that Tolkien concentrated his energies and time not on academic scholarship but in the elaboration of a world of his own making.

In 1937, Oxford received its first hint that its Professor of Anglo-Saxon might be rather different from the ordinary academic. That year *The Hobbit* appeared, Tolkien's now much-loved children's story about a likable hobbit named Bilbo Baggins who discovers that, despite his love of hearty dinners

---

1 See the bibliography in Humphrey Carpenter, *Tolkien: A Biography* (Boston: Houghton Mifflin, 1977), for a list of Tolkien's scholarly publications. Norman Cantor examines the links between Tolkien's scholarly works and his fantasy in *Inventing the Middle Ages* (New York: William Morrow, 1991), pp. 225–33.

and cozy hearthsides, he is really an adventurer capable of outwitting dwarfs and dragons. Reviews in both the *Spectator* and the *Times Literary Supplement* (the latter written by C. S. Lewis) rightly predicted that the story would become a children's classic.[2] The origins of *The Hobbit* are well-known to fantasy readers: Sometime in the 1920s as Tolkien was grading School Certificate examination papers for extra income, he came upon a blank page. He wrote, "In a hole in the ground there lived a hobbit." He then decided he should find out what a hobbit was.[3] The outcome of his hobbit quest, a long-running bedtime story for his children, eventually became the best-seller published by Allen and Unwin.

The Hobbit is very much a children's story, although a delightful one. To the great surprise of its author, publisher, and first reviewers, however, *The Hobbit*'s intended sequel, *The Lord of the Rings*, is a very different sort of work.[4] Instead of a second good-natured adventure story about hobbits, Tolkien produced a vast work of over one thousand pages about the unending struggle between good and evil, a saga that, in C. S. Lewis's words, leaves "a final impression of profound melancholy."[5] What had happened was that Tolkien's hobbits had stumbled onto Middle-earth, an imaginary pre-England of epic proportions that Tolkien had created over the previous two decades. By the 1930s, Middle-earth occupied such a central place in Tolkien's imagination that it was, perhaps, inevitable that when Bilbo Baggins appeared, he did so in the Shire, an obscure corner of Tolkien's imagined universe.

Middle-earth had grown up out of Tolkien's hobby of inventing languages.[6] In order to develop a language fully, Tolkien discovered he had to devise an appropriate land, people, and past: Created words had led him to created worlds. Born during his school days, Tolkien's imaginary world blossomed with the nourishment of war. In the trenches of the Great War Tolkien discovered that his created languages and lore were more than a game, that they satisfied "the desire to express your feeling about good, evil, fair, foul in some way: to rationalize it, and prevent it just festering." Forced to confront evil head-on, Tolkien turned to his myth, "lots of early parts of which (and the languages) . . . were done in grimy canteens, at lectures in cold fogs, in huts full of blasphemy and smut, or by candle-light in bell-tents, even some down in dugouts under shell fire."[7]

2 L. A. G. Strong, "Pick of the Bunch," *Spectator*, 3 Dec. 1937, p. 1024; "A World for Children," *Times Literary Supplement*, 2 Oct. 1937, p. 714. For attribution of the latter review to Lewis, see Carpenter, *Tolkien*, p. 182.
3 Carpenter, *Tolkien*, p. 172.   4 See ibid., p. 186.
5 Letter to Tolkien, quoted in ibid., p. 204.
6 See "A Secret Vice," in J. R. R. Tolkien, *The Monsters and the Critics* (London: Allen and Unwin, 1983), pp. 198–223, esp. pp. 210–11.
7 Letter to Christopher Tolkien, 6 May 1944, in *The Letters of J. R. R. Tolkien*, ed. Humphrey Carpenter with Christopher Tolkien (Boston: Houghton Mifflin, 1981), Let-

By 1937, when *The Hobbit* appeared, this conjunction of invented words and worlds had resulted in the creation of an entire mythology, a cycle of stories that traced the corruption and decay of the noble and once-perfect civilization of the Elves, who were not the wee fairies of Arthur Rackham tales but stately, forbidding, and ultimately tragic figures. This cycle served as the prehistory to both *The Hobbit* and *The Lord of the Rings;* it gave the latter the depth, the sense of a many-layered past, that marked it off as a unique achievement in fantasy literature. Tolkien wrote *The Lord of the Rings* between 1937 and 1949;[8] the mythology on which it rested was, in contrast, the work of a lifetime, begun while Tolkien was in school and not yet finished when he died.[9] Tolkien's outward life was conventional, but while he carried on with the demands of academic life and a growing family, he also lived the secret, much more unorthodox existence of a creator of a world, the world of the epic prose poem published posthumously as *The Silmarillion.*[10]

This work and Tolkien's letters reveal that Tolkien spent much of his time in Middle-earth. His created world served Tolkien as a place of refuge, as the haven, he would have argued, for the escaping prisoner rather than the fleeing deserter. It enabled him to cope not only with the horrors of the trenches during World War I but also with what he perceived as the horrors of life outside the trenches in twentieth-century Britain. Middle-earth, his created country, both reflected and commented on contemporary British culture and society.

A hobbit's quest

In the pages of *The Lord of the Rings* and *The Silmarillion,* Tolkien endeavored to construct a literary monument to England, to "restore to the English an epic tradition and present them with a mythology of their own."[11]

ter 66 (FS 22), p. 78. In an interview with Philip Norman, however, Tolkien denied that he had done any writing in the trenches: "That's all spoof. You might scribble something on the back of an envelope and shove it in your back pocket but that's all. You couldn't write. This [his study] would be an enormous dugout. You'd be crouching down among flies and filth" ("The Hobbit Man," *Sunday Times Magazine,* 15 Jan. 1967, p. 36). The first drafts of the *Silmarillion* are dated 1917 (Humphrey Carpenter, "A World of His Own," *Sunday Telegraph Magazine,* 11 Sept. 1977, p. 32).

8 Problems with publishers meant that the work was not published until 1954–5.

9 After studying the manuscripts of various drafts of the *Silmarillion,* Humphrey Carpenter concluded that all the stories in the work were written by 1925. For the rest of his life Tolkien tinkered with the work – and never finished it. See Carpenter, "A World of His Own," p. 32.

10 J. R. R. Tolkien, *The Silmarillion* (Boston: Houghton Mifflin, 1977). See also *The Lost Road and Other Writings,* ed. Christopher Tolkien (London: Unwin Hyman, 1987).

11 Letter to Mr. Thompson, 14 Jan. 1956, in *Letters of Tolkien,* Letter 180, pp. 230–1.

Tolkien's studies in northern European languages and literature had convinced him that England lacked a mythology firmly rooted in the nation's language and traditions. He found the Arthurian legends too British; his country was England, and England needed an English myth. He declared that he was "from early days grieved by the poverty of my own beloved country: it had no stories of its own (bound up with its tongue and soil), not of the quality that I sought, and found . . . in legends of other lands." Tolkien the literary scholar and Tolkien the lover of England conflicted; he wished to reconcile his two passions with a mythology acceptable to both. He worked, he explained, "to make a body of more or less connected legend, ranging from the large and cosmogonic, to the level of romantic fairy-story . . . which I could dedicate simply to: to England; to my country." He saw his work as akin to Celtic legend but higher in tone, "purged of the gross, and fit for the more adult mind of a land long now steeped in poetry."[12] His England deserved nothing less.

By England Tolkien meant primarily the rural Midlands of the Edwardian era. He translated the setting of his boyhood into the world of the Shire, his imaginary land that he peopled with his three-foot-high hobbit heroes. C. S. Lewis, in a review of *The Lord of the Rings*, recognized the hobbits as "a myth that only an Englishman (or, should we add, a Dutchman?) could have created."[13] Except for their diminutive size and furry feet, the hobbits are stereotypical Englishmen: provincial and parochial, often petty, but with surprising reserves of strength. In a much-quoted letter to a reader, Tolkien explicitly identified himself with his hobbit heroes:

> I am in fact a Hobbit (in all but size). I like gardens, trees and unmechanized farmlands; I smoke a pipe, and like good plain food (unrefrigerated), but detest French cooking; I like, and even dare to wear in these dull days, ornamental waistcoats. I am fond of mushrooms (out of a field); have a very simple sense of humour. . . . I go to bed late and get up late (when possible). I do not travel much.[14]

The Shire, too, Tolkien admitted, "is a parody of . . . rural England, in much the same sense as are its inhabitants: they go together and are meant to."[15] Tolkien based his parody on the England he discovered when he arrived from South Africa at four years of age. The transition from the African heat and starkness to the pastoral beauty of the Midlands gave

---

12 Letter to Milton Waldman, late 1951, in ibid., Letter 131, pp. 144–5. For a discussion of Tolkien's desire to reconstruct England's missing mythology, see T. A. Shippey, *The Road to Middle-earth* (London: Allen and Unwin, 1982), pp. 27–33.
13 C. S. Lewis, "Tolkien's Lord of the Rings," in *On Stories and Other Essays in Literature* (New York: Harcourt Brace Jovanovich, 1982), p. 85.
14 Letter to Deborah Webster, 25 Oct. 1957, in *Letters of Tolkien*, Letter 213, pp. 288–9.
15 Letter to Rayner Unwin, 3 July 1956, in ibid., Letter 190, p. 250.

Tolkien an abiding love for the English countryside he knew during his childhood, a love he expressed in his creation of the Shire.[16] This love was reinforced by the tragedy of his mother's death a few years later. As Tolkien's biographer, Humphrey Carpenter, has noted, "There is no doubt that her death made Tolkien's imagination turn back time and time again to the idyllic years at Sarehole; it made him, indeed, primarily a backward-glancing man for whom a golden age had passed away forever."[17]

The Lord of the Rings

The Lord of the Rings stemmed from both Tolkien's personal past and his beliefs about the identity and history of England. The work contains at its core the central themes of the romantic protest. In it the good and the heroic treasure the past and traditional wisdom, see themselves as part of the natural world, affirm the power of individual agency to transform the course of history, and seek to create a community in which each individual has a place and a purpose. In contrast, Tolkien's villains reject the lessons of the past, regard nature as a resource to be exploited, revel in technology, and work to obliterate individuality while creating a universe characterized by self-interest and alienation. A delightful fairy tale, *The Lord of the Rings* is also Tolkien's romantic interpretation of England's past and his comment on its present.

In his best-selling mythology Tolkien painted a splendid and colorful world but one fading, rapidly, just as the England he loved was vanishing quickly. Although the evil Sauron is defeated when Frodo Baggins, nephew of the now-legendary Bilbo, succeeds in destroying the Ring, a thing of awesome evil and murderous power, this victory for the Good signals the end of the Age of the Elves. After Sauron falls, the Elves and other nonmortal beings such as Gandalf the wizard depart from Middle-earth. *The Lord of the Rings* chronicles the "fading time" during which the enchanted Age of the Elves gives way to the much more prosaic World of Men.[18] Like *The Beowulf,* on which Tolkien published a pivotal essay, *The Lord of the Rings* rests on "a past, pagan but noble and fraught with deep significance – a past that itself

---

16 See *Letters of Tolkien*, p. 235. See also John Ezard, "The Hobbit Man," *Oxford Mail*, 3 Aug. 1966, p. 4; Denys Geroult, "Now Read On," BBC Radio, 16 Dec. 1970, typescript, pp. 3–4, Wade Center; Charlotte and Denis Plimmer, "The Man Who Understands Hobbits," *Daily Telegraph Magazine*, 22 Mar. 1968, pp. 31–5. Shippey also discusses the link between the Shire and England. See *Road*, pp. 77–9.

17 Carpenter, "A World of His Own," p. 31.

18 *The Fellowship of the Ring* (1954; New York: Ballantine Books, 1974), p. 257.

had depth and reached backward into a dark antiquity of sorrow."[19] *The Silmarillion* described this antiquity of sorrow; in *The Lord of the Rings* it is only a shadow in the background, a sense of depth created by ancient ruins, lays about age-old heroes, and, most especially, the Elves. The "passing of the Elves" – their departure from Middle-earth and humanity's subsequent experience – represents a central theme of Tolkien's myth: the transience of life and the irrevocable loss of much good with the unfolding of history. Middle-earth, like the universe portrayed in Lewis's *Discarded Image*, was a declining world. In Tolkien's view, the Elves' passing, the loss of a sense of enchantment, dulled and impoverished the civilization of those left behind.

In the fading time chronicled by Tolkien the bonds linking myth to humanity's experience and definition of truth have begun to fray. Much of Elven enchantment in Middle-earth has assumed the quality of legend–stories for children and the gullible. In the Shire, for example, many hobbits have ceased to believe that Elves exist. In a neat turnabout, the hobbits discover that, in the lands of men, they themselves have been banished to the nursery, "only a little people in old songs and children's tales."[20] A central theme of *The Lord of the Rings* is that legend and reality interweave in a seamless web. Again and again Tolkien's characters discover that "the songs have come down among us out of strange places, and walk visible under the Sun."[21] Truth reveals itself not only in "the facts" but also in the mythological wisdom that transcends those facts tallied by ear and eye. The Elves in *The Lord of the Rings* possess such wisdom. An ancient race, they are in touch with prophecy, legend, and the past.

Although not the heroes of the story, the Elves provide it with an essential backdrop of mystery, beauty, and goodness. The most poetic of the races of Middle-earth and the closest in touch with the nonphysical realms, the Elves profoundly affect the lesser races of Middle-earth. Elven contact, for example, changes and deepens the hobbit-servant Sam Gamgee. A deferential servant who becomes a hero, Sam finds himself and his future transformed after his first encounter with Elves: "I don't know how to say it, but after last night I feel different. I seem to see ahead, in a kind of way. . . . I have something to do before the end, and it lies ahead, not in the Shire. I must see it through." The central character, Frodo Baggins, also realizes and accepts his mission through contact with Elves.[22]

In addition to impelling such self-realization, Elves provide much-needed solace. The Last Homely House, an Elven stronghold, stands guard against the wilderness and revives its guests with both the upward-reaching songs of

19 "Beowulf: The Monsters and the Critics," in *The Monsters and the Critics and Other Essays*, p. 27. Given as the Sir Israel Gollancz Lecture to the British Academy on 25 Nov. 1936. First published in vol. 22 of the *Proceedings of the British Academy*.
20 *The Two Towers* (1954; New York: Ballantine Books, 1977), p. 45.   21 Ibid., p. 197.
22 *Fellowship*, pp. 127, 116–24, 284–6, 353.

the Elves and such homely comforts as good beds, abundant food, and pipe tobacco. There Frodo not only recognizes his task but also finds healing and strength for the journey ahead.[23] Even Elven tales bring respite. In the wilderness at night Sam begs for "a tale about the Elves before the fading time" because "the dark seems to press round so close."[24]

The Elves shine out against the darkness at least in part because of their close connection with the natural realm. Their physical presence seems to embody such natural elements as moonlight and sunlight. They also maintain unbroken communication with other creatures. To "ride Elven-fashion," for example, means to ride without saddle or bridle. The Elf and the horse are partners rather than subduer and broken beast.[25] The Elves communicate with nonrational creation and possess the power to wake up even the trees.[26] With the passing of the Elves, however, comes the loss of such communication, the disappearance of the nonhuman races, and growing estrangement between humanity and nature.

Just as Tolkien paired the Elves with a respect for and understanding of the natural, so he linked the Elves' Enemy, the evil Sauron and his forces, with the nonnatural and the dead. Sauron's counterfeit Elves, the Orcs, take great pleasure in destroying living beings.[27] This delight in death and destruction characterizes Mordor, the domain of Sauron: "Here nothing lived, not even the leprous growths that feed on rottenness. The gasping pools were choked with ash and crawling muds, sickly white and grey, as if the mountains had vomited the filth of their entrails upon the lands about." Even outside Mordor, "a pit of uncovered filth and refuse" and "trees hewn down wantonly and left to die" signal the Enemy's presence.[28] The Enemy's infiltration of the hobbits' Shire produces a Mordor-in-the-making: a new and ugly mechanized mill, polluted water and air, senseless destruction of trees, all the results of the Enemy's desire to "hack, burn, and ruin."[29]

The Enemy's thrill in the destruction of nature results from his longing for absolute power over all living things. Nothing may grow, move, choose, or even die without his command. Tolkien noted to a reader that Sauron's Ring, the centerpiece of the story, represents this "will to mere power."[30] Whereas the Elves designed their Rings of Power for "understanding, making, and healing, to preserve all things unstained," Sauron created his Ring for destruction and tyranny.[31] The Elves sought enchantment; Sauron, however, desired magic. Although often confused, enchantment and magic have different purposes and conflicting results. In 1939, long before he published *The*

23 Ibid., pp. 289–368.   24 Ibid., p. 257.   25 *Two Towers*, p. 257.   26 Ibid., p. 90.
27 E.g., see ibid., p. 26.   28 Ibid., pp. 302, 328.
29 *The Return of the King* (1955; New York: Ballantine Books, 1974), p. 361.
30 Letter to Milton Waldman, late 1951, in *Letters of Tolkien*, Letter 131, p. 160.
31 *Fellowship*, p. 352.

Lord of the Rings, Tolkien explained the difference between the two. Magic, such as that realized in Sauron's Ring, "is not an art but a technique; its desire is power in this world, domination of things and wills." Enchantment, by contrast, "does not seek delusion, nor bewitchment and domination; it seeks shared enrichment, partners in making and delight, not slaves."[32] Thus, the Elves join nature in a partnership of affirmation and creation, whereas Sauron seeks to stifle such independence and build a lifeless world as the stage for his display of absolute power.

In contrast to the naturalness of the Elves, technology marked Sauron and his servants. "Wheels and engines and explosions always delighted" the Orcs, for example.[33] A similar technological obsession results in the downfall of Saruman. Once a leader of the forces of good in his role as head of the Council of the Wise (the chief wizard), Saruman comes to embody the spirit of Mordor against which Tolkien fought. He plots "to become a Power. He has a mind of metal and wheels; and he does not care for growing things, except as far as they serve him for the moment."[34] Hence, he diverts and then destroys a river in order to make his fortress of Isengard into a mechanical marvel. There a system of tunnels and dams, together with vents for the emission of poisonous gases and fires, provides Saruman with the illusion of invulnerability. But he falls – and, fittingly enough, to trees. He has violated the sanctity of the natural world, and nature has its revenge. The Ents, the tree-shepherds that are one of Tolkien's most original and inspired mythic creations, and their flocks of trees destroy Saruman's stronghold, strip him of "his precious machinery," and expose him as having "not much grit, not much plain courage alone in a tight place without a lot of slaves and machines and things."[35]

Saruman's faith in "a lot of slaves and machines and things" reflects his failure to see other beings in their wholeness and individuality. The Mordor spirit reduces individuals to an undifferentiated mass in need of regimentation. Saruman's fall begins with his desire for power in order to do good, but he demands to be able to dictate to others the timing, scope, and scale of this goodness. The warrior Boromir also falls prey to this desire to dictate. He longs for the power to determine the path of Frodo's quest and hence the destiny of Middle-earth. He, like Saruman, swallows the spirit of Mordor in his wish to deny others free choice.[36] Such a desire to dictate, even for the good, stems from the urge to dominate, the "will to mere power"

32 J. R. R. Tolkien, "On Fairy-Stories," in *The Monsters and the Critics and Other Essays*, p. 143. C. S. Lewis compared magic to science in *The Abolition of Man* (New York: Macmillan, 1955), pp. 87–9.
33 *The Hobbit* (1937; New York: Ballantine Books, 1974), p. 70.   34 *Two Towers*, p. 96.
35 Ibid., pp. 210–30; quotations from pp. 220, 219.   36 *Fellowship*, pp. 513–17.

embodied in the Ring and triumphant in Mordor and, according to Tolkien, in much of modern England.

Because it regards other creatures as slaves rather than allies, the "will to mere power" incarnate in Sauron annihilates individual freedom and choice. Sauron reduces those in his power to mere pawns to satisfy his own insatiable hunger for total domination. In contrast, the good achieve victory by recognizing the importance of individual choice and action. The corrupted Saruman would have "the Wise" determine the course of events, but the unfolding of *The Lord of the Rings* reveals the significance of the actions of small and weak individuals. Gandalf admits that "such is oft the course of deeds that move the wheels of the world: small hands do them because they must, while the eyes of the great are elsewhere."[37] As all the armies of Middle-earth gather for a cataclysmic encounter, the two small hobbits Frodo and Sam, acting of free choice, toil their way through Mordor to destroy the Ring in its fires. In the end, these two insignificant creatures, not the princes, wizards, and warriors, determine Middle-earth's fate. As Tolkien explained, *The Lord of the Rings* centers on the hobbits in order "to exemplify most clearly a recurrent theme: the place in 'world politics' of the unforeseen and unforeseeable acts of will, and deeds of virtue of the apparently small, ungreat, forgotten in the places of the Wise and Great."[38] *The Lord of the Rings* affirms that acts of will by small individuals matter. The quest seems doomed from the start but Frodo and the Fellowship refuse to surrender. Action must be taken, and it is.

The choice to act, however, is made within the context of a design, with the understanding that the choices made and actions taken occur as part of a much larger pattern. Despite the lack of clear references to Christianity such as are apparent in Lewis's fantasies, *The Lord of the Rings* is an intensely religious work.[39] It unfolds in pre-Christian times; hence, any religious practices would be either anachronistic or non-Christian, both choices anathema to Tolkien. Therefore, he explained to a fellow Catholic, he consciously omitted "practically all references to anything like 'religion,' to cults or practices, in the imaginary world. For the religious element is absorbed into the story and the symbolism."[40] The religiosity of *The Lord of the Rings* rests most firmly on the recurrent theme of an all-embracing design, the sense that Middle-earth is under the care of a supernatural power. The Ring's reappearance after lying hidden for centuries, Frodo's responsibility to de-

---

37 Ibid., p. 353.
38 Letter to Milton Waldman, late 1951, in *Letters of Tolkien*, Letter 131, p. 160.
39 A few religious elements are present. The people of Gondor observe a moment of silence before supper (*Two Towers*, p. 361; *Return*, p. 287); Gandalf reproaches the suicidal Denethor that only the heathen slay themselves (*Return*, p. 157); in moments of despair the various members of the Fellowship call on Gilthoniel (or Elbereth) (*Return*, p. 234).
40 Letter to Father Robert Murray, 2 Dec. 1953, in, *Letters of Tolkien*, Letter 142, p. 172.

stroy it, and the formation of the Fellowship to aid Frodo in this duty occur as part of this larger pattern.[41]

Despite the existence of a higher power at work in ordering the events of the world, free will remains a potent factor in *The Lord of the Rings*. Sauron uses slaves to effect his will, but those on the side of the good stand there willingly. Frodo has been chosen to carry the Ring to Mordor, and it is not a duty he welcomes, but he remains free to accept or refuse his role.[42] Toward the end he opts to step out of the ranks of the good and to keep the Ring for himself. At one point earlier in the story, Frodo puts on the Ring and thus stands in imminent danger of discovery by Sauron. He finds himself torn between the searching eye of Sauron and a voice "from some other point of power" (most likely Gandalf) commanding him to take off the Ring: "the two powers strove in him. For a moment, perfectly balanced between their piercing points, he writhed, tormented. Suddenly he was aware of himself again. Frodo, neither the Voice nor the Eye: free to choose, and with one remaining instant in which to do so. He took the Ring off his finger."[43] Not only Frodo but all beings in Middle-earth face "the doom of choice," but choice within the context of a pattern.[44]

Just as the small and weak make choices that have great significance for all of Middle-earth, so heroism in *The Lord of the Rings* centers on the little person. Neither Gandalf nor Aragorn are the heroes of the story; hobbits, not great men or wizards, determine the course of history and become the doers of heroic deeds. The mustering of armies, the mighty battles with flags waving and stallions rearing and swords dripping, pale in juxtaposition with the scenes of Frodo and Sam plodding step by step further into the wasteland of Mordor. Tolkien depicted the simple equation of heroism with military virtues as, in fact, a sign of the decline of Middle-earth. The men of Gondor, once an almost superhuman race, the "High," have slipped down to become "Middle Men" who mistakenly "now love war and valour as things good in themselves, both a sport and an end."[45]

The chief hero of *The Lord of the Rings* is the most unlikely at the outset, the servant Sam Gamgee. His support of Frodo through Mordor and, particularly, his taking up and later renunciation of the Ring reveal his heroism.

41 *Hobbit*, p. 286; *Fellowship*, pp. 88, 318. For a more extended discussion of religion in *The Lord of the Rings*, see Shippey, *Road*, pp. 149–54.

42 *Fellowship*, p. 95.

43 Ibid., p. 519. For Gandalf as the Voice, see his speech in *Two Towers*, p. 126: "I sat in a high place, and I strove with the Dark Tower; and the Shadow passed." I am indebted to T. A. Shippey for this reading (*Road*, p. 109).

44 *Two Towers*, p. 44.

45 Ibid., p. 364. For Tolkien's ambivalence toward the heroic code of the northern sagas, see also "The Homecoming of Beorhtnoth Beohthelm's Son," in *The Tolkien Reader* (New York: Ballantine Books, 1966), p. 25. First published in *Essays and Studies 1953*, collected for the English Association (London: John Murray, 1953).

Sam as chief hero reinforces Tolkien's "homely" view of heroism. *The Lord of the Rings,* Tolkien explained, describes " 'ordinary life,' springing up ever unquenched under the trample of world policies and events."[46] Heroic deeds often occur within the context of everyday actions. The chapter "Of Herbs and Stewed Rabbit," for example, relates one instance of this conjunction of ordinary life and world events, and of homely heroism. Sam's pride in his coney stew and his efforts to convince the horrid Gollum of the delights of fish and chips, in the shadows of Mordor, exemplify not only his unquenchable courage but also the wellspring of that courage: his unmatched ability to take pleasure in ordinary life, to find meaning in the mundane and hope in the homely.[47]

Tolkien affirmed not only the importance of individual choice and action, and the reality of a design in the world's past and future, but also the necessity of fellowship. *The Lord of the Rings* emphasizes that although each individual stands alone to choose his role in the larger pattern, each fulfills that role only with the aid of companions. The Fellowship of the first volume guides and protects Frodo on the first stage of his quest; the final volumes record the partnership of Sam and Frodo, and even the horrible Gollum, as they complete the journey. The fellowship and friendship that mark the relationships of the good contrast with the mistrust and internal battling of the Enemy's forces and, in Tolkien's eyes, with the alienation characteristic of twentieth-century culture.

Just as the recognition of individual action and free choice and the experience of fellowship distinguish those on the side of the good from those in service to Mordor, so the hobbits' Shire stands out in bright contrast to the technologically oriented, slavery-ridden, and quasi-rational land of Mordor. The conclusion of *The Lord of the Rings,* a riotous eucatastrophic vision, depicts the Shire in a utopic period. The trees grow again with the aid of enchantment, the crops burst from the ground, the mechanical monstrosity of the new mill falls, and "there seemed something more: an air of richness and growth, and a gleam of a beauty beyond that of mortal summers that flicker and pass upon this Middle-earth."[48] The scouring of the Enemy's servants from the Shire restores the country to a land fit for hobbits – a pastoral paradise, a "well-ordered and well-farmed countryside" with no machinery "more complicated than a forge-bellows, a water-mill, or a handloom."[49]

---

46 Letter to Milton Waldman, late 1951, in *Letters of Tolkien,* Letter 131, p. 160.
47 *Two Towers,* pp. 324–42.   48 *Return,* p. 375.
49 *Fellowship,* p. 19. Such a eucatastrophic ending was not, Tolkien believed, permanent. One of his students, Anthony Curtis (later the *Financial Times* literary editor), recalled Tolkien saying in reference to *The Lord of the Rings:* "I just couldn't go on with that story. It would have become too grim" ("Remembering Tolkien and Lewis," *British Book News,* June 1977, p. 430).

Mordor in the making

Tolkien believed England had moved irrevocably away from such a desired state. Feeling himself besieged by the technological age, he perceived Mordor's victory in his beloved country. In Tolkien's view, he and a small company of soul mates, which included his son Christopher and C. S. Lewis, faced a continuing onslaught by the forces of Mordor. Like Sam and Frodo, they struggled forward in a land occupied by the Enemy. As Tolkien explained to Christopher in 1943 when his son was in an RAF training camp: "We were born in a dark age out of due time. . . . [Yet] we have still small swords to use. 'I will not bow before the Iron Crown, nor cast my own small golden sceptre down.' Have at the Orcs."[50] Tolkien was not here equating the Orcs with Nazi Germany. In his view, regardless of the outcome of World War II, Mordor had already won. In 1945 he noted that "the first War of the Machines seems to be drawing to its final inconclusive chapter – leaving, alas . . . only one thing triumphant: the Machines."[51]

The lifeless, mechanical, tyrannical Mordor became for Tolkien a powerful symbol of what was wrong in twentieth-century England. Rooted in a world view that reduces people to objects, Mordor glorifies technology and the power it confers as the unquestionable and ultimate good. Only the spirit of Mordor could produce and use atomic weapons. Three weeks after the first British atomic bomb test in October of 1952, Tolkien made this view explicit in a letter to Rayner Unwin, his publisher. Tolkien began by mourning the arrival of heavy traffic in Oxford: "This charming house has become uninhabitable – unsleepable-in, unworkable-in, rocked, racked with noise, and drenched with fumes. Such is modern life. Mordor in our midst." He then shifted directly into his dismay at the news of the British atomic test: "And I regret to note that the billowing cloud recently pictured did not mark the fall of Barad-dur [the fortress of Sauron], but was produced by its allies – or at least by persons who have decided to use the Ring for their own (of course most excellent) purposes."[52] For Tolkien, the abuse of science and technology, the will to power, and the horrifying potential of destroying life embodied by the A-bomb signaled Mordor's expansion and its realization outside the world of fantasy.

The characters, languages, and history of Middle-earth supplied Tolkien with a framework for interpreting the world about him and a vocabulary with which to articulate his social and cultural criticism. The timing of the publica-

---

50 Letter to Christopher Tolkien, 29 Nov. 1943, in *Letters of Tolkien*, Letter 52, p. 64. Quotation from Tolkien's poem "Mythopoeia: For CSL."
51 Letter to Christopher Tolkien, 30 Jan. 1945, in ibid., Letter 96 (FS 78), p. 111.
52 Letter to Rayner Unwin, 24 Oct. 1952, in ibid., Letter 136, p. 165. The first British A-bomb test occurred on the Monte Bello Islands on 3 Oct. 1952.

tion of *The Lord of the Rings* led many readers and critics to believe that the work was intended as an allegory of Britain during World War II. Because Tolkien had created the Silmarillion mythology that underlay the work long before 1939, and because he abhorred allegory, such an interpretation is simplistic.[53] Tolkien insisted that it was the Great War, not World War II, that influenced the writing of *The Lord of the Rings*.[54] World War II did not shape Tolkien's myth; rather, his myth shaped his experience of the war. By 1939, Tolkien's private world had consumed him to such a degree that it came to define the way he viewed not only that war but also the other changes he saw occurring in Britain throughout the 1940s and 1950s.

In some ways, Tolkien viewed the war as a personal affront, an undermining of his life's work. Both his academic efforts and his fantasies were a celebration of what he called "Northernness," the context for the languages and myths of Old Icelandic and Anglo-Saxon that he adored, an indefinable mood very different from that radiated by Greek or Latin mythologies but shared by the Germanic tales and languages. The triumph of Hitler and of Nazi nationalism sullied Tolkien's love: "Ruining, perverting, misapplying, and making for ever accursed, that noble northern spirit, a supreme contribution to Europe, which I have ever loved, and tried to present in its true light."[55] Thus, a strange conjunction occurred: As Tolkien followed Frodo to Mordor and so pressed on with his task of composing a legend fit for England and its northern spirit, he watched that northern spirit effecting the destruction of civilized Europe.

Yet, despite his loathing for Hitler and all that Hitler stood for, Tolkien was no "my country right or wrong" patriot during the Second World War. More perceptive than many, he realized that both sides of the conflict were responsible for horror. His wartime letters to his son Christopher, an RAF pilot, reveal the way in which his private mythology allowed him to articulate his fears and beliefs. In 1944, for example, Tolkien mused that the British involved in the war must do "an ultimately evil job. For we are attempting to conquer Sauron with the Ring. And we shall (it seems) succeed. But the penalty is . . . to breed new Saurons, and slowly turn Men and Elves into Orcs. Not that in real life things are as clear cut as in a story, and we started

---

53 In the Foreword to the *Fellowship of the Ring*, Tolkien wrote, "The crucial chapter, 'The Shadow of the Past,' . . . was written long before the foreshadow of 1939 had yet become a threat of inevitable disaster. . . . Its sources are things long before in mind, or in some cases already written, and little or nothing in it was modified by the war that began in 1939 or its sequels" (*Fellowship*, p. x). This foreword first appeared in the American paperback edition in 1965.

54 See Tolkien's Foreword to *The Fellowship of the Ring*, p. xi. See also Barton Friedman, "Tolkien and David Jones: The Great War and the War of the Ring," *Clio*, Winter 1982, pp. 115–36.

55 Letter to Michael Tolkien, 9 June 1941, in *Letters of Tolkien*, Letter 45, pp. 55–6.

out with a great many Orcs on our side."⁵⁶ Tolkien found it especially hard to accept that Christopher was with the air force because, as he explained to his son, "it is the aeroplane of war that is the real villain. . . . My sentiments are more or less those that Frodo would have had if he discovered some Hobbits learning to ride Nazgul-birds [the flying steeds of the evil captains of Sauron], 'for the liberation of the Shire.' "⁵⁷ The bomber, even under Allied command, represented the awesome evil power of modern technology.

In Tolkien's myth, Sauron obtains the technology for creating his Ring from a branch of Elves Tolkien described as "always on the side of 'science and technology.' " He compared such Elves to "Catholics engaged in certain kinds of physical research (e.g. those producing, if only as by-products, poisonous gases and explosives)." Although their products are not necessarily evil, "things being as they are, and the nature and motives of the economic masters who provide all the means for their work being as they are," such people "are pretty certain to serve evil ends."⁵⁸ Fallible, fallen human beings cannot be trusted with the power that advanced technology confers. Tolkien argued that machinery "attempts to actualize desire, and so to create power in this World." Laborsaving devices often create worse labor; more tragically, humanity's fallen state "makes our devices not only fail of their desire but turn to new and horrible evil." As a result, "we come inevitably from Daedalus and Icarus to the Giant Bomber. It is not an advance in wisdom!"⁵⁹ Rather, Tolkien believed, it is the mark of a civilization doomed to destruction, of a culture swept up in the spirit of Mordor.

Tolkien's equation of modernity with Mordor stemmed from more than just a crotchety distaste for a too-quickly changing world. His antimachinery, antitechnology stance grew out of the soil of his world view: his religious belief in a fallen world and the consequent necessity of limiting the power of fallen human beings. In this crucial aspect of his thought he can be seen as deeply antiromantic: opposed to the concept of the unlimited potential of the individual. *The Lord of the Rings*, however, belongs nonetheless in the tradition of romantic protest. In its pages Tolkien protested against the basic assumptions of industrial Britain. He refused to draw the boundaries of reality at the material world and endeavored to assert the individual's right and responsibility to participate in and help shape the decisions and structures that determined his life.⁶⁰ In revulsion against the social and cultural atomization of the contemporary era, Tolkien presented in the Fellowship

56 Letter to Christopher Tolkien, 6 May 1944, in ibid., Letter 66 (FS 22), p. 78.
57 Letter to Christopher Tolkien, 29 May 1945, in ibid., Letter 100, p. 115.
58 Letter to Peter Hastings, Sept. 1954, in ibid., Letter 153, p. 190.
59 Letter to Christopher Tolkien, 9 July 1944, in ibid., Letter 76 (FS 39), pp. 87–8. See also pp. 145–6.
60 I have deliberately used the masculine pronoun in this sentence; Tolkien had no interest in allowing women to participate in or shape the governing structures of their lives.

gathered around Frodo a picture of a community of very different individuals drawn together by an identity of purpose. Decades ahead of the Greens, he denounced the exaltation of mechanization and the narrow definition of economic progress that resulted in the degradation of the natural environment, and he did so in romantic terms: In Tolkien's Middle-earth, nature expressed a reality beyond human comprehension and worthy of human respect. Through his creation of Middle-earth, Tolkien offered a vision of an alternative reality, one that he believed could never be achieved because of the sinfulness of humankind, but one that both drew on and nourished the romantic protest tradition.

5

Challenge and response

Tolkien and Lewis created alternative worlds in celebration of a vision of reality in which the spiritual and concrete formed an inseparable and consistent whole. In their works they sought to highlight both the strengths and the weaknesses of twentieth-century England. Their fantasies offered more than escape; they challenged the basic structures on which contemporary British society rested. The dwarfs and fauns and wicked wizards of Middle-earth and Narnia stood upon the bedrock of prophetic condemnation. Articulations of romantic protest, Lewis's and Tolkien's fairy stories are also important sources of evidence about middle-class attitudes in the postwar era. Did Tolkien and Lewis succeed in communicating their message? The reception of their fantasies reveals how a portion of the British people saw themselves and their world.

A Tory challenge

Tolkien once wrote to his son and fellow Inkling Christopher that although they were "born in a dark age out of due time," they still possessed "this comfort: otherwise we should not *know*, or so much love, what we do love. I imagine the fish out of water is the only fish to have an inkling of water."[1] In a world that they perceived as characterized by alienation and anomie, Lewis and Tolkien came to treasure community. In their view, fragmentation and conflict, rather than coherence and consensus, marked England both socially and culturally. The only bond, after the Second World War especially, appeared to be that of mass culture, a culture in which neither Lewis nor Tolkien could participate, a bond that both saw as illusory and degrading. Both men believed themselves to be in a position from which protest came naturally. Their protest, however, was more than the cranky complaint of the chronic outsider or the anguish of the aging observer who can no longer

1 Letter to Christopher Tolkien, 29 Nov. 1943, in *The Letters of J. R. R. Tolkien*, ed. Humphrey Carpenter with Christopher Tolkien (Boston: Houghton Mifflin, 1981), Letter 52, p. 64. Emphasis in original.

understand, let alone approve, the changes he sees about him. Scholarly immersion in the highest products of past ages, combined with conservative Christianity, gave Lewis and Tolkien the standards by which they evaluated the twentieth century and found it sorely wanting.

Much of their criticism focused on political trends of the mid-twentieth century, particularly the advance of collectivism. Neither Lewis nor Tolkien was politically active. Lewis did not bother to read a daily newspaper.[2] During the war, Tolkien followed current events, but here the personal outweighed the political: He had two sons in the services. In general, Tolkien, like Lewis, stood aside from contemporary politics. This disengagement, however, did not translate into either apathy or approval. Insulated by Oxford's cloisters from the social and economic problems that the coming of the welfare state alleviated, Tolkien and Lewis thought they could see in Attlee's government the beginnings of the end of personal freedom.[3] But, had they lived long enough to experience Thatcher's Britain, they would have recoiled from her brand of conservatism as well. Lewis, for example, dared to challenge the morality of usury, which he recognized as "the very thing on which we have based our whole life."[4] He and Tolkien were old-fashioned Tories – paternalistic, hierarchical, wedded to an ideal of community woven tightly together by mutually reinforcing threads of obligation and deference.[5]

What they feared in contemporary political developments was centralization, the expansion of an impersonal and bureaucratic state. As the war progressed, Tolkien suspected that wartime controls would become permanent and that the ordinary Englishmen whom he had honored in his creation of the hobbits would find their personal freedom threatened: "When it is all over, will ordinary people have any freedom left (or right) or will they have to fight for it, or will they be too tired to resist? The last rather seems the idea of some of the Big Folk."[6] In 1943, Tolkien reflected on the political scene and wrote, only partly tongue-in-cheek, "My political opinions lean more and more to Anar-

---

2 Lewis's letters to Vera Matthews (later Gebbert), written from 1947 through the 1950s, reveal a general awareness of political events and a keen concern about developments such as the Korean War. He evidently did not read the daily papers himself but relied on his brother Warren's synopses of current events (see Wade – CSL/L-Gebbert/51/ Wade). The Lewis–Matthews correspondence is housed in the Wade Center.

3 Lewis's letters during the years of the Attlee governments reveal his loathing of what he considered to be a socialist regime. Quite unfairly, although understandably, he blamed the Labour Party for the hardships that faced Britain in the immediate postwar years and believed that the Conservatives alone were responsible for ending the "Age of Austerity" and ushering in the "Affluent Fifties." See especially his letters to Vera Matthews (later Gebbert) and to miscellaneous correspondents (available in the Wade Center).

4 C. S. Lewis, *Mere Christianity* (London: Geoffrey Bles, 1952), p. 67.

5 Lewis described his ideal society in ibid., pp. 66–7.

6 Letter to Christopher Tolkien, 31 July 1944, in *Letters of Tolkien*, Letter 77 (FS 41), p. 89.

chy . . . or to 'unconstitutional' Monarchy. I would arrest anybody who uses the word State . . . and after a chance of recantation, execute them if they remained obstinate!" Tolkien wanted to restore a sense of the personal to public life: "If people were in the habit of referring to 'King George's council, Winston and his gang,' it would go a long way to . . . reducing the frightful landslide into Theyocracy."[7] The descent into "Theyocracy" frightened Lewis as well. In the *Observer*'s series entitled "Is Progress Possible?" Lewis criticized the planned society for its widening encroachment into the lives of ordinary people.[8] According to Lewis and Tolkien, "the growing exaltation of the collective and the growing indifference to persons," which they believed to be characteristic of modern Britain, could only lead to political and moral disaster as ordinary individuals lost their sense of both significance and responsibility, and as the powers of those few in charge grew ever larger.[9]

Lewis and Tolkien also protested against the expanding influence of the United States. Like many Tories, and many on the Left, they embraced a sturdy anti-Americanism. A pervasive theme in Tolkien's wartime letters to his son and soul mate, Christopher, was his certainty that regardless of its political and military outcome, the war would advance "Americo-cosmopolitanism."[10] Lewis's anti-Americanism was tempered by what he considered to be the better reception of his books across the Atlantic, as well as by the remarkable generosity of his American admirers during the wartime and immediate post-war years, when food rationing and shortages made daily existence both drab and frustrating.[11] He eventually married an American woman, but part of Joy Davidman's appeal was her Anglophilia and her mockery of her native land.[12]

The United States, with its stereotypical enthusiasm for and delight in technology, represented not only standardization but also modern humanity's misguided faith in scientific progress, which, Lewis and Tolkien believed, had led to irrevocable regress. Science had become the end rather than the means, the pattern to which all disciplines must conform. The cult of science

---

7 Letter to Christopher Tolkien, 29 Nov. 1943, in ibid., Letter 52, p. 63.
8 "Is Progress Possible? – 2. Willing Slaves of the Welfare State," *Observer*, 20 July 1958, p. 6.
9 C. S. Lewis, "Reply to Professor Haldane," in *Of Other Worlds: Essays and Stories*, ed. Walter Hooper (New York: Harcourt Brace Jovanovich, 1966), p. 83.
10 Letter to Christopher Tolkien, 9 Dec. 1943, in *Letters of Tolkien*, Letter 53, p. 65.
11 For the generosity of American admirers, see, e.g., his letters to Vera Matthews (later Gebbert) and Dr. W. M. Firor (originals are located in the Bodleian Library; copies are available in the Wade Center). For Lewis's perception of the better reception of his books in the United States, see Wade – CSL/L-Evans/22/Wade; Wade – CSL/L-Firor/1/Bodleian.
12 George Sayer, *Jack: C. S. Lewis and His Times* (London: Macmillan, 1988), p. 215. On Lewis's anti-Americanism, see p. 122. For Lewis's marriage, see Lyle Dorset, *And God Came In: The Extraordinary Story of Joy Davidman, Her Life, and Marriage to C. S. Lewis* (New York: Macmillan, 1983); and Brian Sibley, *Shadowlands: The Story of C. S. Lewis and Joy Davidman* (London: Hodder and Staughton, 1985).

and technology glorified such dangerous attitudes as a disregard for natural order and a disrespect for past achievements. It resulted in the denigration and eventual loss of the most valuable forms of knowledge and paths to wisdom. Made into such a monster, science and its even more hideous offspring, technology, now menaced humanity.

As an alternative to the cult of progress, Lewis and Tolkien offered faith in individual salvation, in intellectual effort, and in friendship. Both men regretted the fragmenting of Christendom but neither believed Christian Europe could be restored. Salvation lay with individuals, who must realize their faith in a world increasingly opposed to the basics of their beliefs. Hence the importance of choice in both men's works. The individual retained the power to choose, even in a world completely engulfed by Mordor. In addition, Lewis and Tolkien believed in the value of intellectual work. They found the life of the mind not only congenial but worthwhile. Scholarship offered a way to enter the otherwise sealed-off world of the past, with its still-intact ties to nature and the spiritual world.

Scholarship also served as a partial basis for the small companies of friends so critical to the development and happiness of both men. At gatherings of the like-minded they found the sense of coherence they perceived as lacking in twentieth-century society and culture. In the end, neither Tolkien nor Lewis retained much hope for this society or this culture, beyond individual spiritual renewal and acts of homely heroism. Lost community could not be restored in general society. Therefore, these two remained disengaged from contemporary affairs. Such things had ceased to matter. Lewis and Tolkien lived in the underground, so to speak, in an alternative society in which they could create meaning and find fellowship.

The response: incorporation into British culture

Although Lewis and Tolkien believed themselves to be alienated from contemporary British society, they produced works of fantasy that were taken up by and incorporated into British culture, at least into British middle-class culture. The evidence, admittedly impressionistic, that exists suggests that Tolkien's and Lewis's readers tended to be middle class. Critics and reviewers, for example, placed *The Lord of the Rings* within a middle-class framework.[13]

13 Donald Davie included *The Lord of the Rings* in his "attempt to define the political temper of the educated classes in England on the basis of the literature which they have produced and responded to in the last fifty years" (*Thomas Hardy and British Poetry* [New York: Oxford University Press, 1972], pp. vii–viii). Nigel Walmsley traced the links

They often viewed the work as shaded in uniquely Oxford tones and therefore possessing a special appeal to the Oxford-educated, who still, of course, belonged largely to the middle and upper classes.[14] More important, educational reform in Britain had failed to break down class barriers: Middle-class children in the second half of the twentieth century continued to receive higher quality educations, and thus an emphasis on reading continued to be regarded as evidence of a middle-class value system. In the early 1970s, the Schools Council Project's national survey of children's voluntary reading, which revealed a high level of readership for both the Narnia books and *The Lord of the Rings*, traced a not very surprising correlation between social class and reading.[15] It is a simple but not irrelevant fact that the British middle class tends to read, and in the postwar period, a significant portion of it read Lewis and Tolkien.

Despite such class correlations, Lewis's and Tolkien's fantasies were not only read by large numbers of Britons but were also absorbed into the fabric of British culture. *The Chronicles of Narnia* quickly rose to the status of a children's classic. In 1983 Naomi Lewis, author and critic of children's books, observed, "Ever since the first of the seven Narnia books appeared in 1950, C. S. Lewis has been perhaps the best-liked post-war 'quality' writer for children in Britain."[16] In the twenty years after Lewis's death in 1963, purchases of all his books, including his fantasies, increased sixfold. In 1988, one report stated

between *The Lord of the Rings* and middle-class students in the 1960s in a series of articles in the short-lived *New Tolkien Newsletter:* see "The Lure of the Rings," 1/1 (1 Aug. 1980): 4–6; "Soixante-huit," 1/4 (1 Mar. 1982): 8–12. See also Nigel Walmsley, "Tolkien and the 60s," in *J. R. R. Tolkien: This Far Land*, ed. Robert Giddings (London: Vision Press, 1983), pp. 73–86; Roger King, "Recovery, Escape, Consolation," in *J. R. R. Tolkien: This Far Land*, pp. 52–3; Robert Giddings, *J. R. R. Tolkien: The Shores of Middle-earth* (Frederick, Md.: Aletheia Books, 1982), pp. 4–6; Fred Inglis, *The Promise of Happiness: Value and Meaning in Children's Fiction* (London: Cambridge University Press, 1981), pp. 215–16; and Fred Inglis, "Gentility and Powerlessness: Tolkien and the New Class," in *J. R. R. Tolkien: This Far Land*, pp. 25–41.

14 See Lord David Cecil and Rachel Trickett, "Is There an Oxford School of Writing? A Discussion," *Twentieth Century* 157 (June 1955): 559–70; Francis Hope, "Welcome to Middle-earth," *New Statesman* 72 (11 Nov. 1966): 701–2; C. B. Cox, "The World of the Hobbits," *Spectator*, 30 Dec. 1966, p. 844; Mike Hebbert, "Tolkien Televised," *Isis* (Oxford University Magazine), 14 Feb. 1968, pp. 10–12; Roger Sale, "Tolkien and Frodo Baggins," in *Tolkien and the Critics: Essays on J. R. R. Tolkien's "Lord of the Rings,"* ed. Neil Isaacs and Rose Zimbardo (Notre Dame: University of Notre Dame Press, 1968), p. 249; John Grassi, "Professor J. R. R. Tolkien," *Oxford Times*, 7 Sept. 1973, p. 10; Alan Hindle, "Memories of Tolkien," *Amon Hen* 32 (June 1977): 4–6; John Gross, "Some Victorian Truths," *Observer Review*, 24 Apr. 1983, p. 34.

15 Frank Whitehead et al., *Children and Their Books: Final Report of the Schools Council Research Project on Children's Reading Habits, 10–15*, University of Sheffield Institute of Education (London: Macmillan Education, 1977), pp. 61–2, 78.

16 Naomi Lewis, "C. S. Lewis," in *Twentieth Century Children's Writers*, ed. D. L. Kirkpatrick (London: Macmillan, 1983), p. 475.

that about seventy million copies of Lewis's books have been sold.[17] The Narnia stories have never been out of print and continued in 1991 to sell at a rate that far exceeded any other novel for the eight-to-twelve age group on the Collins children's list.[18] A *Times* poll taken during the 1970s listed *The Lion, the Witch and the Wardrobe* as the second most popular children's book in Britain.[19] The Schools Council Research Project on Children's Reading Habits confirmed the high level of Narnia's appeal to British children.[20] By the mid-1980s, Narnia had embedded itself deeply enough into the soil of British culture for an episode of the BBC's "Young Ones" to parody Edmund's entry into Narnia and trust its viewers to respond accordingly.[21]

The continuing sales of the *Chronicles* and the high availability of *The Lion, the Witch and the Wardrobe* in school libraries were in part due to the inclusion of these fantasies, as well as *The Hobbit*, on school library lists[22] and on lists of recommended children's books since the 1950s. The Library Association, the National Book League, and children's literary critics, from the 1950s on, recommended Lewis and Tolkien's works to parents, teachers, and librarians. In 1958 the Library Association included the *Chronicles* (and *The Hobbit*) in its selection for the Chaucer House Library of Children's Literature collection and, in its catalog, described the Narnia stories as "perhaps the most original and powerful contribution in fantasy for children, within the last few years." Twenty years later, the National Book League recommended that children not only read but purchase *The Lion, the Witch and the Wardrobe*: "Despite becoming a 'set book' in many primary schools the quality of delight arising from the experiences in the land of Aslan through the ward-

17 "C. S. Lewis Goes Marching On," *Time* 110/23 (5 Dec. 1977): 92; Kathryn Lindskoog, *The C. S. Lewis Hoax* (Portland, Oreg.: Multnomah Press, 1988), p. 17.

18 Author's correspondence with Susan Dickinson, senior editor, Collins Children's Division, HarperCollins Publishers.

19 *Times* poll cited by Kathryn Lindskoog in *In Search of C. S. Lewis*, ed. Stephen Schofield (South Plainfield, N.J.: Bridge Publishers, 1983), p. 86. *Charlie and the Chocolate Factory* came in first.

20 Of the 7,557 books mentioned by the children surveyed, only 246 were read by ten or more children. *The Hobbit*, *The Lord of the Rings*, and all of the Narnia stories except *The Horse and His Boy* were included on this list. On the list of most widely read books by children aged ten and over, *The Lion, the Witch and the Wardrobe* came in sixth. According to Frank Whitehead and his associates, "among twentieth century children's writers the only two to achieve the distinction of having written a book which is read by 1% or more of this age group are C. S. Lewis with *The Lion, the Witch and the Wardrobe* and Enid Blyton with *The Secret Seven* and *Five on a Treasure Island*" (*Children and Their Books*, pp. 131–2). With girls aged twelve and over, *Lion* received (on a scale of 1 to 5) a "liking score" of 4.4 (the highest recorded in this category). Moreover, the survey discovered that although few modern titles were available in classroom libraries, *Lion* (eleventh on a list of sixty-five "quality" books recommended for class collections) was available in 143 schools – an unusually high availability rate for a postwar book (pp. 125–37).

21 Noted in *Amon Hen* 73 (May 1985): 17.

22 Author's correspondence with Susan Dickinson, senior editor, Collins Children's Division, HarperCollins Publishers.

robe door make this a book many children of 8 plus want to own. Destined to be described as a twentieth century classic."[23]

23 Library Association, Youth Libraries Section, *Children's Books of This Century: A First List of Books Covering the Years 1899 to 1956 Chosen for the Library of Children's Literature Now Being Formed at Chaucer House*, ed. Mary F. Thwaite (London: Library Association, 1958), pp. 28, 30, 21; quotation from p. 9. The Chaucer House collection comprised books published from 1899 to 1956 chosen as "typical examples of books of popular appeal" (p. 5). See also National Book League, *Children's Paperbacks, 5–11*, selected and annotated by Margaret Marshall (London: National Book League, 1978), p. 12. *The Hobbit*, described as "classic fantasy," is listed as well (p. 15). Neither Lewis's nor Tolkien's works were included in National Book League, *Children's Paperbacks, 11–16* (London: National Book League, 1977).

   See also (listed in chronological order, by date of publication):
   Library Association, *Books for Young People, Group I, Under Eleven* (London: Library Association, 1952), pp. 37, 51; *Group II, Eleven to Thirteen Plus* (1953), pp. 20, 29; *Group II, Eleven to Thirteen Plus*, rev. ed. (1954), pp. 22, 31; *Eleven to Thirteen Plus*, 3d ed. (1960), pp. 50, 62. *Books for Young People* was intended to be a working tool for educators. It aimed to include "only those books with some positive value" (*Books for Young People, Group I, Under Eleven*, p. 3).
   Kathleen Lines, *Four to Fourteen: A Library of Books for Children*, 2d ed. (London: Cambridge University Press, 1956), pp. 254, 283, 320. Lines devised her list as "a selection of interesting books from which a child's own library can be chosen" (p. xi).
   Sunday Times, The One Hundred Best Books for Children: A Special Sunday Times Survey, in Association with Kathleen Lines (London, 1958), pp. 6, 8–9.
   Schools Library Association, Primary Schools Book Panel, *Primary School Library Books: An Annotated List*, ed. H. C. Osborne (London: Schools Library Association, 1961), pp. 21, 25. *Primary School Library Books: An Annotated List*, 2d ed., ed. Felicity Sturt (London: Schools Library Association, 1965), pp. 28, 32. *Books for Primary Children: An Annotated List*, 3d ed., ed. Berna Clark (London: Schools Library Association, 1969), pp. 37, 40. This work, a compilation of books recommended by teachers and librarians, aimed to help primary school teachers select the books essential for their school libraries.
   Marcus Crouch, *Treasure Seekers and Borrowers: Children's Books in Britain, 1900–1960* (London: Library Association, 1962), pp. 7, 67, 103, 115.
   Boris Ford, ed., *Young Writers, Young Readers: An Anthology of Children's Reading and Writing* (London: Hutchinson, 1963), pp. 166, 168.
   Muriel Fuller, ed., *More Junior Authors* (New York: H. W. Wilson Co., 1963), p. 140. The 268 authors and illustrators of children's books whose biographical or autobiographical sketches make up this work were selected by a panel of 27 consultants consisting of children's librarians, school librarians, and other authorities on children's literature.
   Margery Fisher, *Intent upon Reading: A Critical Appraisal of Modern Fiction for Children* (Leicester: Brockhampton Press, 1964), pp. 80–4.
   Robert Geoffrey Trease, *Tales out of School* (London: Heinemann, 1964), pp. 40, 87.
   John Rowe Townsend, *Written for Children: An Outline of English Children's Literature* (London: Garnet Miller, 1965), pp. 113, 122–3.
   Library Association, Youth Libraries Group, *First Choice: A Basic Book List for Children*, ed. Eileen Colwell, L. Esme Green, and F. Phyllis Parrot (London: Library Association, 1968), pp. 34, 45. This work constituted a "list of books of high quality which could be recommended as the basic stock of any children's library" (p. 5).
   Elizabeth Cook, *The Ordinary and the Fabulous: An Introduction to Myths, Legends, and Fairy Tales for Teachers and Storytellers* (London: Cambridge University Press, 1969), pp. 46–7.
   Alec Ellis, *How to Find Out about Children's Literature* (Oxford: Pergamon Press, 1969), pp. 100, 117–18.

Like the *Chronicles*, the sales of *The Lord of the Rings* proved surprising. The work sold steadily after 1956 and was never out of print. By the mid-1960s, sales of *The Lord of the Rings* were booming, and Tolkien was clearly acquiring a fanatical cult following. In 1967, Tolkien received the A. C. Benson Silver Medal on behalf of the Royal Society of Literature for *The Lord of the Rings*. Two years earlier, Ace Books in New York had printed an unauthorized paperback edition of *The Lord of the Rings* in the United States. The edition sold briskly, especially on American college campuses. The publicity surrounding Tolkien's battle with Ace Books and the publication of the authorized Ballantine paperback edition later that year sent sales soaring. In 1966, world sales of *The Lord of the Rings* hit 2,750,000, and two years later, sales reached the three million mark. By 1972, the paperback edition was selling approximately 100,000 copies per year in Britain. If only two people read each copy, then 200,000 individuals were reading Tolkien in Britain each year. By 1980, eight million copies of *The Lord of the Rings*, in eighteen languages, had been sold.[24] In 1979, the *Evening News* claimed that only the Bible had sold more copies than Tolkien's trilogy.[25] The literary scholar and poet Donald Davie has argued, "There is evidence that, rightly or wrongly, this work has attracted and delighted more readers than any work in English verse since Eliot's *Waste Land*, and possibly more than any work of imaginative prose over the same period."[26] Perhaps the best indication of Tolkien's fame is the *Times Literary Supplement*'s seventy-fifth anniversary survey of writers, scholars, and artists, which twice mentioned Tolkien as the most overrated author in the past seventy-five years.[27]

The sales of *The Silmarillion* also indicate the extent of the Tolkien craze. Its publisher, Rayner Unwin, claimed that "there is no doubt that this is one of those occasions when one knows with certainty that one is producing a book that will stand as one of the monuments of the century's creative achievements in literature."[28] Unwin's assessment of the book seems laughable, although understandable coming from a man about to make a huge

Naomi Lewis, *Fantasy Books for Children* (London: National Book League, 1975), p. 32 (catalog for the winter 1975 National Book League exhibition Fantasy Books for Children, selected by Naomi Lewis).

Harry Blamires, ed., *Twentieth-Century Literature in English* (London: Methuen and Co., 1983), pp. 278–9, 158–9.

D. L. Kirkpatrick, ed., *Twentieth Century Children's Writers* (London: Macmillan, 1983), pp. 473–6, 765–7.

24　William Cater, "Lord of the Hobbits," *Daily Express*, 22 Nov. 1966, p. 10; Bill Cater, "Lord of the Legends," *Sunday Times Magazine*, 2 Jan. 1972, p. 24; Giddings, *Shores of Middle-earth*, p. 3.

25　*Evening News*, 2 July 1979, p. 22.　26　Davie, *Thomas Hardy and British Poetry*, p. vii.

27　"Reputations Revisited," *Times Literary Supplement*, 21 Jan. 1977, pp. 66–8. Tolkien was mentioned by Mary Douglas and John Sparrow.

28　Quoted in *Bookseller*, 30 July 1977, p. 451.

profit from a book that is virtually unreadable. *The Silmarillion*, the focus of Tolkien's creative and linguistic endeavors, attracts only the most hardy Tolkien reader. Much of it reads like the "begat" chapters of the Bible: long lists of unpronounceable names without personality or context. No hobbits appear in *The Silmarillion* and thus it lacks the celebration of the ordinary that enhanced the appeal and applicability of *The Lord of the Rings*.[29] Nevertheless, the work was a guaranteed best-seller. The publishing firm of Allen and Unwin, which had very wisely turned down an earlier version of *The Silmarillion* in 1950, released 600,000 copies in 1977, making it, according to one reviewer, the "biggest hardback fiction first edition in British publishing history."[30] Only the extraordinary appeal of *The Lord of the Rings* can account for such a phenomenon.

Works on children's literature reveal that *The Lord of the Rings* and *The Hobbit* quickly became accepted standards of reference in the field. Those who regarded fantasy as unsuitable reading for children found it necessary to attack Tolkien's work.[31] Other works used the *The Lord of the Rings* as example, with the assumption that a reference to Tolkien constituted a reference to a well-known work, to a part of the fantastic canon.[32] In Margery Fisher's

29 For favorable reviews of the *Silmarillion*, see Humphrey Carpenter, "Tolkien's Return," *Financial Times*, 15 Sept. 1977, p. 35; John Ezard, "Tolkien's Paradise Lost," *Guardian*, 15 Sept. 1977, p. 16; Rosemary Haughton, "Discovering New Worlds," *Tablet*, 24 Sept. 1977, p. 913; T. A. Shippey, *Oxford Mail*, 15 Sept. 1977, p. 4. For assessments more in agreement with my own, see Christopher Booker, "Bubble and Squeal," *Spectator*, 17 Sept. 1977, pp. 17–18; Anthony Burgess, "Hobbit Forming," *Observer Review*, 15 Sept. 1977, p. 25; Peter Conrad, "The Babbit," *New Statesman*, 23 Sept. 1977, pp. 408–9; Margaret Drabble, "Rebels against Iluvatar," *Listener*, 15 Sept. 1977, p. 346; Francis King, "Down among the Dwarves," *Sunday Telegraph*, 18 Sept. 1977, p. 14; "Mythbegotten," *Economist*, 17 Sept. 1977, p. 141; Auberon Waugh, *Private Eye*, 30 Sept. 1977, p. 17.

30 John Ezard, "Tolkien's Paradise Lost," *Guardian*, 15 Sept. 1977, p. 16. In April the *Guardian* reported an initial print run of 550,000 copies, with an additional 80,000 for the Commonwealth, and translations already begun (Michael Wainwright, "Guardian Diary – Celtic Binge," *Guardian*, 11 Apr. 1977, p. 11).

31 Bob Dixon, *Catching Them Young: Political Ideas in Children's Fiction* (London: Pluto Press, 1977), vol. 2, pp. 145–9 (for C. S. Lewis, see pp. 155–61); Andrew Stibbs, "For Realism in Children's Fiction," *Uses of English* 32/1 (1980): 18–24. For favorable evaluations of *The Lord of the Rings*, see Fisher, *Intent upon Reading*, pp. 84–7; Lewis, *Fantasy Books for Children*, p. 50; Blamires, *Twentieth-Century Literature in English*, pp. 278–9; National Book League, *Twenty-five Years of British Children's Books*, selected by John Rowe Townsend (London: National Book League, 1977), p. 53; Lines, *Four to Fourteen*, p. 283; *Sunday Times, One Hundred Best Books*, pp. 8–9; Ford, *Young Writers*, p. 168; Fuller, *More Junior Authors*, pp. 206–7; Trease, *Tales out of School*, p. 40; Kirkpatrick, *Twentieth Century Children's Writers*, pp. 765–7.

32 E.g., in a collection of essays on children's literature, Tolkien's works were used to examine reader response and to demonstrate the use of linguistic analysis, and were cited in a prolegomena to the study of children's literature. See Michael Benton, ed., *Approaches to Research in Children's Literature* (Southampton: University of Southampton, 1980), pp. 9, 25, 38.

Intent upon Reading (written in 1964 and described in 1976 as "still the best single British guide-book to children's literature"), Tolkien stood as the standard of excellence to which authors Joyce Gard and Alan Garner were compared. Fisher, a student of Tolkien's at Oxford, argued that "every child should read [*The Lord of the Rings*] somewhere between the ages of eleven and sixteen."[33]

Less expected references bear witness to the integration of Tolkien's myth into British life. A Midlands boating firm included the *Aragorn*, the *Pippin*, the *Merry*, and the *Frodo* in its fleet.[34] More important, by 1976, both the *Concise Oxford Dictionary* and the *Oxford English Dictionary Supplement* included "hobbit" as an entry. By 1977, the outpouring of posthumous Tolkien publications had become excessive enough to provoke a *Punch* spoof, which included announcement of works such as *Letters to My Son* (*the Envelopes*).[35] *Punch* later assumed its readers' knowledge of *The Lord of the Rings* to be deep enough to catch the meaning of a political satire entitled "The Lord of the Wings," which assigned Tolkienian names to cartoons of current political figures.[36] In 1980, T. A. Shippey's introduction to a new edition of William Morris's *Wood beyond the World* contained four references to Tolkien or his characters, references that presumed that Morris's readers were well acquainted with Tolkien's works.[37] Thus, Tolkien's fantasies, like Lewis's *Chronicles*, were read by a percentage of the British population so high as to ensure that the characters and concepts from these books became part and parcel of British culture.

Media adaptations aided this process of cultural absorption. BBC Radio adaptations of *The Lion, the Witch and the Wardrobe* appeared in 1959, 1960, and 1967.[38] As with all radio programming after the advent of television, however, the listener numbers for these adaptations were extremely low.[39] Tolkien's works also appeared in the British media, and so took root

33 Fisher, *Intent upon Reading*, pp. 352, 353, 85; description by Anthony Adams, *Teaching English* (London: National Book League, 1976), p. 30.
34 Reported in *Amon Hen* 22 (Oct. 1976): 23.
35 Jonathan Sale, "This One Will Rune and Rune," *Punch*, 24 Aug. 1977, pp. 304–5.
36 *Punch*, 8 Mar. 1981, pp. 406–7.
37 Tom Shippey, Introduction to William Morris, *The Wood beyond the World* (Oxford: Oxford University Press, 1980), pp. vii, ix, x, xvii.
38 The scripts for these broadcasts are deposited in the British Broadcasting Corporation Written Archives Centre, Reading. See BBC-WAC/Scripts/Children's Hour/Sept. 1959; and BBC-WAC/Scripts/Storytime/Aug. 1967.
39 *The Lion, the Witch and the Wardrobe* appeared on the "Children's Hour" in the summer of 1960. Broadcast from 5:15 to 5:55 p.m. on Sunday afternoons for six weeks, the program never drew an audience higher than 0.6% of the population. Its audience size was not unusually low for "Children's Hour." The subsequent program, an adaptation of *The Gleam in the North*, never drew an audience larger than 0.4% (BBC-WAC/R9/35/9). In 1957, the average audience for the Sunday broadcast of "Children's Hour" was 1%.

in a culture increasingly shaped by broadcasting rather than books. As early as 1956 *The Lord of the Rings* was adapted for radio and broadcast on the BBC's "Adventures in English" program for British schools. In 1961, *The Hobbit* was adapted for the same program, as well as abridged for the "Children's Hour." Two subsequent adaptations of *The Hobbit* followed, in 1968 and in 1974. In 1981, the BBC's Radio Four broadcast a twenty-six episode adaptation of *The Lord of the Rings*, which it repeated in 1987.[40] The audiences for these programs constituted only a very small percentage of the population, although not an unusually small listenership for radio presentations.[41] The animated film version of the first half of *The Lord of the Rings*, released in Britain in the summer of 1979, reached a much larger audience, despite being scorned by most critics.[42] The limited evidence that exists suggests that these media adaptations appealed most strongly to confirmed fantasy readers. Nonreaders often found such adaptations confusing and difficult to follow, although in some cases they were inspired to read the original texts. In a society increasingly influenced by the visual image, television broadcasts such as the ABC Television serialization of *The Lion, the Witch and the Wardrobe* in 1967[43] and the BBC Television adaptation of the first three *Chronicles* in 1989 and 1990 were much more significant. These programs revealed continuing interest in Lewis's books and stimulated further readership.[44]

40 See the BBC-WAC/Scripts/Schools/Jan. 1956; BBC-WAC/Scripts/Children's Hour/ Apr. 1961; BBC-WAC/Scripts/Schools/ Oct. 1961; BBC-WAC/Scripts/Storytime/ Sept. 1974.

41 An estimated 1% of the population of the United Kingdom listened to the broadcast of *The Lord of the Rings* on the "Adventures in English" program in 1956 (BBC-WAC/ R9/35/5). The BBC estimated that 0.4% of the whole population of the United Kingdom heard the first episode of *The Hobbit* broadcast on the "Children's Hour" in 1961 (BBC-WAC/LR/61/25). The Audience Research Report for the 1968 broadcast of *The Hobbit* calculated the listening audience at 0.3% of the population of the United Kingdom (BBC-WAC/LF/68/1587). In 1974, the audience for the adaptation of *The Hobbit* on "Storytime" was estimated to range from 0.4% to 1.0% (BBC-WAC/R9/ 36/9). The audience for the 1981 broadcast of *The Lord of the Rings* ranged from 1.1% to 2.1% of the U.K.'s population, with an overall average of 1.5% – 800,000 people (BBC-WAC/LR/81/149).

42 For a sampling of reviews, see *Yorkshire Evening Press*, 4 Sept. 1979, p. 3; *Guardian*, 5 July 1979, p. 8; *Daily Telegraph*, 6 July 1979, p. 13; *Daily Mail*, 6 July 1979, p. 13; *Financial Times*, 6 July 1979, p. 17; *New Musical Express*, 14 July 1979, pp. 26–7; *TV Times*, 21 July 1979, p. 83; *Sun*, 3 July 1979, p. 19; *Evening News*, 6 July 1979, p. 13; *Evening Standard*, 5 July 1979, p. 24.

43 Norman Hare, "Magic of C. S. Lewis Comes to Life on Screen," *Daily Telegraph*, 17 July 1967, p. 15.

44 Theater adaptations included the 1981 Westminster Theatre's *Song of the Lion*, a synthesis of Lewis's life and work, and the 1985 Westminster Theatre's dramatization of *The Lion, the Witch and the Wardrobe*. In 1990, *Shadowlands*, a play that dealt with Lewis's marriage and ran very successfully on the West End, moved to Broadway.

Published and public responses

That Lewis's and Tolkien's fantasies were read is clear; how they were read, the message readers received, is much more opaque. One set of accessible, but necessarily atypical, readings is provided by the published reviews. A survey of the reviews published in major national periodicals and newspapers reveals a mixed response to Lewis's and Tolkien's fantasy fictions. In their fantasies, Lewis and Tolkien protested against the dominant trends in post-war British culture: the emergence of a more egalitarian society, the advent of mass consumerism, the triumph of professionalization and specialization, the widening sphere of technology and technique, the movement of middle-class women beyond traditional roles, and steady secularization. An attack on such a wide front was bound to provoke counterattacks. Not surprisingly, reviewers often responded to Lewis's and Tolkien's fantasies with either inordinate enthusiasm or horrified hostility.

Both Lewis's space trilogy and *The Chronicles of Narnia* were widely reviewed upon publication. Lewis's fame as a radio broadcaster and popular Christian apologist was at its height during the years the trilogy appeared and so ensured that his first venture into fantasy did not pass unnoticed. Although by the 1950s Lewis had ended his radio career (much to the dismay of the BBC, which continued to request Lewis's broadcasting services until his death in 1963), the continuing sales of his religious works meant that he remained a well-known name. The widespread attention accorded to the Narnia books, however, owes more to the quality of the books than to Lewis's preceding reputation. The *Chronicles* were immediately recognized as quite exceptional in a genre characterized by mediocrity. Not all reviewers, however, believed that the books deserved the status of children's classic that was quickly bestowed upon them.

Most reviewers of Lewis's space trilogy and Narnia stories praised Lewis for his ability to create a good story.[45] As Lewis's own writings make clear, he

45 For the *Chronicles of Narnia:* C. T., "The Horse and His Boy," *Spectator,* 19 Nov. 1954, p. 658; M. S. Crouch, "Chronicles of Narnia," *Junior Bookshelf,* Nov. 1956, pp. 245–53; Mary Crozier, "Chance, Kings, and Desperate Men," *Guardian,* 8 July 1955, p. 8; Mary Crozier, "Fairies and Fantasies," *Guardian,* 6 Dec. 1951, p. 3; Gwendolyn Freeman, "History, Fantasy, and Verse," *Spectator,* 7 Dec. 1951, p. 784; Eleanor Graham, "The Silver Chair," *Junior Bookshelf,* Oct. 1953, p. 199; Naomi Lewis, "The Young Supernaturalist," *New Statesman,* 2 Oct. 1954, p. 404; Bel Mooney, "C. S. Lewis – Chronicles of Narnia," *Spectator,* 14 Mar. 1981, p. 23; Amabel Williams-Ellis, "Christmas for Small Children," *Spectator,* 4 Dec. 1953, p. 672; Amabel Williams-Ellis, "Traditional Tales," *Spectator,* 8 July 1955, pp. 51–2; "C. S. Lewis's Children's Classic," *Church Times Children's Books Supplement,* 30 Nov. 1951, p. i; "Children's Classic," *Church Times,* 18 Sept. 1953, p. 665; "The Magician's Nephew," *Junior Bookshelf,* July 1955, pp. 147–9; "The Little More, the Little Less," *Times Literary Supplement – Children's Books Supplement,* 28 Nov. 1952, p. vii;

regarded "Story" as the core of literary endeavor and sought first and foremost to tell a tale well.[46] The reviews indicate that he succeeded in his aim of enriching his readers' everyday lives by enabling them to participate in another world. Yet, in his fantasies Lewis sought to do more than tell a good story. He endeavored to create myth, to reveal the reality that lay beyond everyday experience, and thereby both to enhance the ordinary world and to expose its untruths. The available evidence suggests that many readers did not follow Lewis along the journey from story to myth.

One obstacle to a mythic reading of Lewis's works lay in their resemblance to religious allegory. Perhaps because of Lewis's writings on allegory and certainly because of his reputation as a Christian apologist, reviewers were inclined to approach his works as codes to be deciphered or puzzles to be worked.[47] Hence, Aslan = Christ; Ransom = Christ. Although such an interpretation could bring the reader at least part of the way toward realizing Lewis's intentions in the *Chronicles*, it could only confuse the reader of the space trilogy, and, more important, it robbed both works of their vitality and potency. An allegorical approach, at least where none is intended, flattens a work; it murders to dissect. Between Lewis and those reviewers who regarded his fantasies as allegories, the lines of communication were blocked.

The secularization of twentieth-century Britain presented a second obsta-

"Travellers in Fairyland," *Times Literary Supplement – Children's Books Supplement*, 27 Nov. 1953, p. iv; "The World of Magic," *Times Literary Supplement – Children's Books Supplement*, 19 Nov. 1954, p. vii; "The End of a Saga," *Times Literary Supplement – Children's Books Supplement*, 11 May 1956, p. v.

For the space trilogy: Tullis Clare, "New Novels," *Time and Tide*, 15 Sept. 1945, pp. 777–8; Tullis Clare, "Perelandra," *Time and Tide*, 1 May 1943, p. 362; H. P. E., "Technocracy Takes Charge," *Punch*, 29 Aug. 1945, p. 191; Graham Greene, "Strange Worlds," *Evening Standard*, 24 Aug. 1945, p. 6; J. B. S. Haldane, "Auld Hornie, F.R.S.," *Modern Quarterly*, Autumn 1946, pp. 32–40; Charles Marriott, "New Novels," *Guardian*, 30 Apr. 1943, p. 3; E. L. Mascall, "Out of the Silent Planet," *Theology*, Jan.–June 1939, pp. 303–4; Edwin Muir, "New Novels," *Listener*, 6 May 1943, p. 546; Edwin Muir, "New Novels," *Listener*, 6 Sept. 1945, p. 274; Kate O'Brien, "Fiction," *Spectator*, 14 May 1943, p. 458; George Orwell, "The Scientist Takes Over," *Manchester Evening News*, 16 Aug. 1945; Desmond Shawe-Taylor, "New Novels," *New Statesman*, 22 Oct. 1938, p. 662; Frank Swinnerton, "New Novels," *Observer*, 27 Nov. 1938, p. 6; "That Hideous Strength," *Times Literary Supplement*, 25 Aug. 1945, p. 401; "Visit to Venus," *Times Literary Supplement*, 1 May 1943, p. 209.

Not all reviewers of the space trilogy found the stories engaging. See J. D. Beresford, "Five Novels," *Guardian*, 24 Aug. 1945, p. 3; Alistair Cooke, "Mr. Anthony at Oxford," *New Republic*, 24 Apr. 1944, pp. 578–80; "Out of the Silent Planet," *Times Literary Supplement*, 1 Oct. 1938, p. 625.

46 See "On Story," in *Of Other Worlds: Essays and Stories*, ed. Walter Hooper (New York: Harcourt Brace Jovanovich, 1966), pp. 3–21.

47 E.g., "C. S. Lewis's Children's Classic," *Church Times Christmas Book Supplement*, 30 Nov. 1951, p. i; Annabel Farjeon, "Sense and Magic," *New Statesman*, 17 Nov. 1956, pp. 637–8; Amabel Williams-Ellis, "Traditional Tales," *Spectator*, 8 July 1955, pp. 51–2. See Wayland Hilton-Young's "The Contented Christian" for a perceptive critique of the misreading of the space trilogy as allegory (*Cambridge Journal*, July 1952, pp. 603–12).

cle to a mythic understanding of Lewis's fantasies. Despite Lewis's reputation as a Christian writer, and despite the overt religiosity of his fantasies,
many readers failed to grasp the spiritual implications of his fictions. Lewis
found this failure of communication quite frustrating. In a letter to a fellow
Christian, he mourned that out of approximately sixty reviews of *Out of the
Silent Planet*, only two displayed an understanding of the identity of the "Bent
One" with Satan.[48] In contrast, he rejoiced in what he perceived as the
surprising ability of his child readers to grasp the spiritual undercurrents of
the Narnia books.[49]

Many reviewers, however, recognized the mythic nature of Lewis's fantasies.[50] Some rejected his works precisely because they were myths.[51] For
these readers, myth could not meet the needs of the contemporary world,
particularly the needs of contemporary children. They argued that realism,
not romance, would enable a child to cope with the horrors of the twentieth
century. Other reviewers welcomed new additions to the mythological genre
but found themselves horrified by the values promoted in Lewis's otherworlds. They perceived the subcreations of Narnia, Malacandra, and Perelandra as the dumping grounds for Lewis's hostilities against and irritabilities
with the modern world.[52] Naomi Lewis, for example, believed the *Chronicles*
fatally weakened by Lewis's authoritarianism; for her, the championship of
hierarchy in the stories translated into the worst of the public-schoolboy
ethos.[53] Because Lewis's myths articulated a romantic protest against many

48 Letter to Sister Penelope, 9 July 1939, Wade – CSL/L-Penelope/3/Bodleian. See also
   his letter to a Miss Jacob, whose failure to comprehend the Christian elements in *Out of
   the Silent Planet* Lewis found incomprehensible (Wade – CSL/L-Jacob/1/Bodleian).
   The originals of these letters are held by the Bodleian. Photocopies are available in the
   Wade Center.

49 See Wade – CSL/L-Brady/2/Bodleian; Wade – CSL/L-Blamires/12/Bodleian. The
   originals of these letters are held by the Bodleian. Photocopies are available in the Wade
   Center.

50 See Gwendolen Freeman, "History, Fantasy, and Verse," *Spectator*, 7 Dec. 1951, p. 784;
   M. Hutton, "C. S. Lewis," *School Librarian*, July 1964, pp. 124–32; Bel Mooney, "C. S.
   Lewis – Chronicles of Narnia," *Spectator*, 14 Mar. 1981, p. 23; "The Myth-Makers,"
   Times Literary Supplement – Children's Books Supplement, 1 July 1955, pp. i–ii; "The
   Starry Threshold," *Times Literary Supplement – Children's Books Supplement*, 23 Nov.
   1951, p. viii; "Theme and Variations," *Times Literary Supplement – Children's Books Sup-
   plement*, 17 Nov. 1950, p. vi.

51 E.g., D. A. N. Jones, "Romans," *New Statesman*, 28 May 1965, p. 849; Alan Pryce-Jones,
   "New Novels," *Observer*, 25 Apr. 1943, p. 3.

52 J. B. S. Haldane's "Auld Hornie, F.R.S." is a lively example (*Modern Quarterly*, Autumn
   1946, pp. 32–40). For the *Chronicles*, see "The End of a Saga," *Times Literary Supplement –
   Children's Books Supplement*, 11 May 1956, p. v; Eleanor Graham, "The Silver Chair,"
   Junior Bookshelf, Oct. 1953, p. 199; "The Magician's Nephew," *Junior Bookshelf*, July 1955,
   pp. 147–9; "The World of Magic," *Times Literary Supplement – Children's Books Supplement*, 19 Nov. 1954, p. vii.

53 Naomi Lewis, "The Young Supernaturalist," *New Statesman*, 2 Oct. 1954, p. 404; and
   Naomi Lewis, "Dear Galahad, Yours Jack," *Observer*, 20 May 1979, p. 37.

of the values and structures of contemporary Britain, they posed a direct challenge to supporters of those values and structures.

In comparison to the favorable reviews of Lewis's fantasies, those praising Tolkien adopted a more breathless tone, perhaps because Tolkien's work was more astonishing in its crashing of the usual literary borders. Lewis's space trilogy could be labeled science fiction, and *The Chronicles of Narnia* clearly belonged on the children's shelves; in contrast, *The Lord of the Rings* slid easily into no single slot. Today, fantasy fiction written for adults fills entire walls of bookshops, in large part because of the popularity of Tolkien's work, but in the 1950s, the genre appeared much more problematic – hence the tone of admiring bewilderment in some of Tolkien's favorable reviews. For these critics the depth of Tolkien's created world was a cause of wonder and celebration, a revival of almost forgotten literary forms.[54]

The reviews of *The Lord of the Rings* published in the national press demonstrate both the limitations and the success of fantasy as a vehicle for the articulation of romantic protest. The coincidence of the trilogy's publication in the first half of the 1950s and both the ending of the Second World War and the beginning of the atomic age led many readers to misread Tolkien's fantasy as allegory, an intellectual exercise that neither Tolkien's disclaimer first published in the preface to the 1966 revised edition nor even the 1981 publication of his *Letters*, with their very definite refutation of allegorical meaning, put to rest. Allegory requires a one-to-one relationship between literary object and extraliterary meaning; Tolkien regarded it as a limited literary form and, in fact, disliked Lewis's Narnia stories in part because he viewed them as too allegorical.[55] The most common allegories assigned to *The Lord of the Rings* were the linking of the Ring with the atom bomb, and Mordor with socialism, nazism, bureaucracy, or industrialization. Certainly the work expressed Tolkien's critique of these things; nonetheless, as T. A. Shippey has pointed out, the work must be read as having "applicability" rather than allegorical meaning.[56] Many readers of *The Lord of the Rings*,

54 C. S. Lewis, "The Gods Return to Earth," *Time and Tide*, 14 Aug. 1954, pp. 1082–3; Naomi Mitchison, "One Ring to Bind Them," *New Statesman* 48 (14 Sept. 1954): 331; Hugh I'A. Faussett, "Magical," *Guardian*, 26 Nov. 1954, p. 9; H. A. Blair, "Myth or Legend," *Church Quarterly Review* 156 (Jan./Mar. 1955): 121–2; Francis Huxley, "The Endless Worm," *New Statesman* 50 (5 Nov. 1955): 587–8; R. C. Scriven, "Hobbit's Apotheosis," *Tablet*, 11 Feb. 1956, pp. 129–30; Francis Hope, "Welcome to Middle-earth," *New Statesman* 72 (11 Nov. 1966): 701–2; C. B. Cox, "The World of the Hobbits," *Spectator*, 30 Dec. 1966, p. 844; Julia Ballam, "Can Frodo Live Again?" *Times Literary Supplement*, 23 Nov. 1973, pp. 1427–8.

55 See Humphrey Carpenter, *Tolkien: A Biography* (London: Allen and Unwin, 1977), pp. 91–2, 189–90, 202–3, 243. Tolkien, however, tended to overstate his disliking of allegory; two of his short fairy stories – "Leaf by Niggle" and "Smith of Wooton Major" – are quite allegorical.

56 T. A. Shippey, *The Road to Middle-earth* (London: Allen and Unwin, 1982), pp. 126–30. See also *Letters of Tolkien*, p. 145.

however, found allegory-guessing to be an irresistible temptation. Maurice Richardson, in the *New Statesman*, was only one of many readers to wonder, "To what extent, if any, does the Ring tie up with the atomic nucleus. . . . Are the orcs at all equated with materialist scientists?"[57] According to the *Times Literary Supplement* reviewer, *The Fellowship of the Ring*, which ended with the breakup of the Fellowship, taught that "against Russia, the western world can draw together, but if the Iron Curtain vanished the rulers of Yugoslavia and Spain and Britain would find it hard to agree together on the next step." After publication of the final volume, however, the *TLS* concluded that "*The Lord of the Rings* cannot be read as a connected allegory" and decided instead that although in 1938 Tolkien had probably meant Mordor to symbolize nazism, he had changed his mind and meaning along the way.[58] The desire to decipher the code and to reduce Tolkien's work to an elaborate puzzle obscured the intentions of Tolkien's work from many readers; hence, the very thing that heightened its appeal, its applicability, limited its effectiveness as a medium of protest.

The outrage that *The Lord of the Rings* aroused among many readers also indicates the limitations of fantasy as a means of communication. Tolkien's imaginary world, seen by some readers as a many-layered mythic reality, was perceived by others as an immature illusion. Probably the most famous review of Tolkien's work was by the American Edmund Wilson. In a witty article entitled "Oo, Those Awful Orcs!" Wilson rightly predicted, and bewailed the fact, that *The Lord of the Rings* would win a wide readership. He concluded that "certain people – especially, perhaps, in Britain – have a life-long appetite for juvenile trash. They would not accept adult trash, but, confronted with the pre-teen-age article, they revert to the mental phase which delighted in *Elsie Dinsmore* and *Little Lord Fauntleroy*."[59] Similarly, Maurice Richardson conceded that *The Lord of the Rings* "will do quite nicely as an allegorical adventure story for very leisured boys" but admitted it made him want to "[slouch] through the streets with a sandwichman's board inscribed in jagged paranoid scrawl in violet ink: 'Adults of all ages! Unite against the infantilist invasion.' "[60]

Reviewers argued that at its most innocuous such an infantilist invasion served as a form of escapism; at its worst, it degraded the best of Britain and promoted elitist, imperialist, and sexist values. In such negative analyses, paradoxically, the success of Lewis's and Tolkien's efforts to communicate

57 Maurice Richardson, *New Statesman*, 18 Dec. 1954, p. 836.
58 "Heroic Endeavor," *Times Literary Supplement*, 27 Aug. 1954, p. 541; "The Saga of Middle Earth," *Times Literary Supplement*, 25 Nov. 1955, p. 704. See also the letters in response to the Nov. 1955 review: 9 Dec. 1955, p. 743; 23 Dec. 1955, p. 777.
59 Edmund Wilson, "Oo, Those Awful Orcs!" *Nation* 182 (14 Apr. 1956): 314.
60 Maurice Richardson, "New Novels," *New Statesman*, 18 Dec. 1954, p. 835.

their romantic vision of the world is clear. Not all the reviewers who stood outside Narnia and Middle-earth did so because they misunderstood what Lewis and Tolkien were about. Many did so precisely because they perceived the protest at the heart of these works. They recognized that Lewis and Tolkien had thrown down the gauntlet, that their fantasies were not simply stories written to entertain children but rather broadsides against much of modern British culture.

Hearing the horns of Elfland

In 1966, the *Spectator*'s review of the revised edition of *The Lord of the Rings* argued that Tolkien's story illuminated the unreality of the mechanical world, the innate religious sense of humanity, and the necessity of breaking down the barriers between the human race and the rest of the natural world. The reviewer, C. B. Cox, concluded, "Tolkien helps us poor benighted travellers in an industrial age to hear the notes of the horns of Elfland."[61]

To the surprise of some observers, particularly those familiar with Tolkien's political and social conservatism, the horns of Elfland harmonized well with the folk music, political chants, and rock rhythms of the culture of protest that emerged in the 1960s. *The Lord of the Rings* sold steadily in the 1950s, but it did not become a cultural phenomenon until the 1960s. The Tolkien cult and the culture of protest shared a common social origin: Both were rooted in the tremendous growth in the university populations in the industrialized nations. In Britain, the expansion of existing universities, the upgrading of existing technological institutions to technological universities, and the founding of eight new universities between 1961 and 1965 increased the British student population, which served as both the base of the protest movement and an easy market for Tolkien's fantasy.[62] Moreover, Middle-earth and the culture of protest also shared a common cultural origin: Both grew out of a reaction against the triumph of industrialism and empiricism in British thought and culture. Fundamentally romantic, they both asserted the primacy of the suprarational and the nonmaterial.

The links between Tolkien's fantasy and the resurgence of romanticism in the 1960s are most evident in the counterculture. Although the alliance of hippies and hobbits baffled some observers, this relationship emerged easily

---

61 C. B. Cox, "The World of the Hobbits," *Spectator*, 30 Dec. 1966, p. 844.
62 In Britain, the prewar university student population numbered roughly 50,000; in 1937–8, 1.7% of the population attended university. By 1961–2, the student population numbered 113,143; by 1967–8, 200,121. These statistics are taken from Michael Sanderson, "Higher Education in the Post-war Years," *Contemporary Record*, Winter 1991, pp. 417, 421.

and naturally.[63] Both the counterculture and the Shire affirmed human scale and values against the impersonal and inhumane.[64] Both offered opportunity for withdrawal from contemporary culture. Reading *The Lord of the Rings* led not to political engagement but to the "Escape of the Prisoner," in Tolkien's terms. Like the counterculture, Tolkien sought to deal with the problems he perceived in modern society by erecting an alternative world, one that refused accommodation with either the political or the economic structures of postwar Britain. The reenchantment Tolkien sought had to be, in the contemporary era, a personal and inner awakening, much the same as that desired by those who attempted to reject Western industrial society during the late 1960s and early 1970s.

The horns of Elfland, however, resonated beyond the confines of the counterculture. Like any utopia, Middle-earth served as an example of a world to be worked for, an ideal to be realized. *The Lord of the Rings* could serve as a text of not only withdrawal but also engagement, despite Tolkien's own political apathy. Its romantic attitudes toward the environment, technology, and the role of the individual and the community within society matched the context of the culture of protest.

As Part III of this book will show, the second half of the 1960s witnessed the first phase of post–World War II environmental activism in Britain, as well as in much of the Western world. To a society awakening to the reality of widespread environmental degradation and the possibility of wholesale environmental breakdown, the ecological undertones of Middle-earth rang true. The journal of David McTaggart's voyage into the French nuclear testing area in 1972 on behalf of Greenpeace testifies to this resonance: "I had been reading *The Lord of the Rings*. I could not avoid thinking of parallels between our own little fellowship and the long journey of the Hobbits into the volcano-haunted land of Mordor, home of the Dark Lord who lived in his fortress surrounded by fierce armies, his Evil Eye scanning, scanning, scanning for intruders."[65] Again and again in *The Lord of the Rings*, evil signals its presence by polluting the landscape. The foul ditches of Mordor, the dead bodies lurking beneath the surfaces of its oily pools, the black smoke that choked Sam and Frodo as they slogged through the wastes toward Mount Doom (itself reminiscent of John Martin's depiction of Victorian factories blazing against the evening sky in "The Day of His Wrath"), seemed sud-

63 See, e.g., "Peter Simple II," *Daily Telegraph*, 29 Aug. 1967, p. 12.
64 See Keith Brace, "In the Footsteps of the Hobbits," *Birmingham Post – Midland Magazine*, 25 May 1968, p. 1, for one account of the hippie–hobbit tie.
65 David McTaggart and Robert Hunter, *Greenpeace III – Journey into the Bomb* (London: Collins, 1978), p. 82. David Nicholson-Lord also discusses the links between Tolkien's mythology and the rise of environmental awareness in the 1960s, 1970s, and 1980s. See *The Greening of the Cities* (London and New York: Routledge and Kegan Paul, 1987), pp. 21, 42, 71–4, 86.

denly familiar as Britons in the 1960s began to tabulate the environmental costs of industrial progress. Even more familiar was Saruman's fortress of Orthanc, where trees had fallen to make way for the machinery of production and destruction. In a master stroke, Tolkien depicted the trees not as mere lumber but as living beings whose murder causes sorrow throughout the ancient forest of Fangorn.

In both Orthanc and Mordor, the victory of evil is made manifest by the triumph of technology. Mechanization in Middle-earth led not to progress but to the destruction of the good. Condemned as reactionary nostalgia by some, Tolkien's antitechnological stance was accepted by others as a legitimate position in a world in which technology appeared out of control. From the 1950s on, protests began to surface in Britain from both the Left and the Right against the unthinking development of technology, against the tendency to let technology dictate rather than serve.

This distrust of technology was rooted in not only environmental concern but also an awareness of alienation in the Marxist sense. At the core of the New Left that emerged in Britain in the late 1950s and in the United States in the early 1960s lay the demand for participatory democracy, for a re-creation of the political and social structures of industrialized society to allow individual men and women to regain control over their lives. Such a demand stemmed in part from a reaction against the bureaucratization and the exaltation of expertise that undergirded technological society. In *The Lord of the Rings*, the "experts" like Gandalf and Aragorn can guide and advise, but in the end it is the actions of the little people, the hobbits, who save the world. Middle-earth, the philological wonderland of a politically disengaged right-wing Roman Catholic, coincided in its deepest structures with the vision of a participatory political life that shaped the New Left. Middle-earth is, of course, no democratic utopia; even the unpretentious Shire has a clear social hierarchy. In *The Lord of the Rings*, individuals act, but they act within the context of a clearly defined community and as part of an all-embracing supernatural plan. Neither Tolkien's hierarchical vision nor his conservative religious commitment cohered with the New Left ideal. Nevertheless, the New Left, like Tolkien, protested against an increasingly bureaucratic, expert-oriented, mass society. Both affirmed the uniqueness and efficacy of individual action, and both drew on the romantic tradition in articulating their protest against modern British society.

In 1983 the historian, peace activist, and former New Leftist E. P. Thompson called Reagan and Thatcher "self-appointed Gandalfs" who could ruin the world.[66] By reaching into *The Lord of the Rings* for his terminology,

---

66 "Letters to the Editor," *Guardian*, 16 Mar. 1983, p. 12. Thompson evidently knows Middle-earth quite well. In "America's Europe: A Hobbit among Gandalfs," his preface

Thompson demonstrated that for many of his readers, Tolkien's work provided a vocabulary of moral protest. As Colin Wilson, the by-then middle-aged Angry Young Man, argued in the early 1970s, *The Lord of the Rings* "is at once an attack on the modern world and a credo, a manifesto. It stands for a system of values; that is why teenagers write 'Gandalf lives' on the walls of London tubes."[67] "Hobbit" meant more than a furry-footed, three-foot-high creature who lived in hillside holes; it represented a world view that refused to acquiesce in the orthodox evaluation of "progress." Hence, the supporter of a plan for construction of a bypass over part of the Dartmoor called his opponents "Middle Earth Hobbits," and an architectural writer argued that much current architectural criticism "assumes that any architecture that doesn't have pitched roofs, small windows and a general air of Hobbitry must be inhuman."[68] Similarly, Peter Davey introduced his study of the late-nineteenth-century Arts and Crafts movement by explaining that the "inhabitants of William Morris's visionary world have all the nice characteristics of Victorian gentlefolk, they are hobbits without furry feet."[69] Just as the hobbit came to represent one set of values, the villains of Middle-earth became packed with meaning as well. An orc was not just the hairy horror of a fairy story but an accepted symbol of the monumental cruelty and stupidity that gloried in destruction for its own sake. As a result, a letter writer to the *Guardian* who wanted to attack the editors' defense of the theory of mutually assured destruction could use Middle-earth to communicate his message: "This fantasy of mutual extermination describes the behaviour of Tolkien's orcs, not of human beings."[70] The letter writer did not go on to say that human beings should act more like hobbits, but if he had, he would have been understood. Tolkien, through his fantasy, provided like-minded protesters with the means to articulate their protest.

For many readers, the story of *The Lord of the Rings* encapsulated the struggle of humanity in the postwar era. Tolkien's work spoke to the fears and hopes of a generation that, like the hobbits' creator, looked at the industrialized world and found it severely wanting and so began to explore alternatives. The *Times* noted in its obituary of Tolkien that "it is doubtful how far he realized that these comfort-loving, unambitious (and in aspiration) unheroic creatures embodied what he loved best in the English character and saw

to excerpts from his *Protest and Survive* reprinted as the 24 Jan. 1981 issue of *Nation*, Thompson exhibited a familiarity with such lesser-known geographical details of Middle-earth as the territory of Eriador. See Chapter 9 for a discussion of Thompson.
67 Colin Wilson, *Tree by Tolkien* (London: Village Press, 1974), pp. 28–9.
68 *Western Morning News*, 19 Sept. 1978–cited in *Amon Hen* 35 (Oct. 1978): 17; Rayner Banham, "Hanging Gardens. N.W." *New Society*, 21 Sept. 1978, p. 635.
69 Peter Davey, *Arts and Crafts Architecture: The Search for Earthly Paradise* (London: Architectural Press), p. 9.
70 "Letters to the Editor," *Guardian*, 16 July 1980, p. 12.

most endangered by the growth of 'subtopia,' bureaucracy, journalism, and industrialization."[71] Lost in invented languages, Tolkien created a world that addressed a key issue of the postwar age: How can humanity cope with the rings of power it has created?

71 Quoted in Mary Salu and Robert Farrell, eds, *J. R. R. Tolkien, a Scholar and Storyteller: Essays in Memoriam* (Ithaca: Cornell University Press, 1979), p. 14. Humphrey Carpenter identified C. S. Lewis as the author of the obituary (*Tolkien*, p. 133).

Conclusion:
within the tradition

With the creation and use of atomic and nuclear weapons, Tolkien's fantastic rings of power appeared to have become horrible fact. Although the test explosion in the New Mexico desert in 1945 ushered in a new era, the advent of the industrial age had created earlier rings of power and in turn given rise to protests against their actual and potential destructive force. From the late eighteenth century on, critics cried out against the technological transformation of British society and culture. In his important and controversial study of British economic decline, Martin Wiener argues that the gradualness and incompleteness of Britain's social revolution allowed aristocratic anti-industrialism to capture the minds and hearts of the industrial and business classes. By the beginning of the twentieth century, Britain's self-image as the workshop of the world had been displaced by that of the green and pleasant land, a community of rural villages scattered across gently rolling hills.[1] Although the aristocratic nature of anti-industrialism is debatable and the links between it and Britain's economic decline are perhaps less solid than Wiener depicts, he clearly demonstrates the extent and significance of the "anti-industrial spirit" in modern British culture. Lewis's and Tolkien's fantasies resonated with British readers because these works shared in this deeply embedded protest against the industrial age.

Wiener has shown that a passion for the past was central to the spirit of anti-industrialism.[2] The appeal of Lewis and Tolkien's fantasies rested in part on their evocation of a past age, a time of greater security and stability. As discussed in Chapters 3 and 4, the medieval images of Narnia and Middle-earth came packed with concepts of community, beauty, and spirituality. Lewis's and Tolkien's fantasies, moreover, recalled another past, a myth as powerful as that of the Middle Ages in shaping contemporary British culture: the Edwardian era. Middle-earth and Narnia are both clearly the creations of British men who came of age before the First World War. Like

1 Martin Wiener, *English Culture and the Decline of the Industrial Spirit, 1850–1980* (New York: Cambridge University Press, 1981).
2 Ibid., pp. 42–6.

Kenneth Grahame's *The Wind in the Willows*, the books provide a fascinating glimpse into the world of the Edwardian upper-middle class. One of the Narnia stories, *The Magician's Nephew*, is actually set in Edwardian London, and it is, in fact, an Edwardian lamppost planted in Narnia that creates one of the most enduring images in modern children's fiction. The rest of the stories take place in England in the 1940s and 1950s; despite the contemporary dress, however, the children act and speak like Edwardian characters. Lewis drew more on his own memory than on his contact with contemporary children in writing the books. Narnia is itself an idealized blend of medieval and Edwardian England and sharply contrasts with the evil country of Calormen, which bears a rather suspicious resemblance to both Arabic and Indian civilizations. Similarly, the Shire is an idealized picture of Tolkien's memory of the Midlands before the Great War. The relation between Frodo and Sam, for example, is that of an Edwardian gentleman and his faithful manservant. And the Shire is threatened with destruction by Mordor, with its ruined landscape so like that of the Great War battlefields.[3]

The Edwardian era has supplied contemporary Britain with a powerful myth. The thought of counting the quotations of Sir Edward Grey's poetic prediction about the lamps going out in Europe is daunting, to say the least.[4] The image of a lamplit golden age, of a society and generation buried in the mud of northern France, haunts British thought and culture. By 1914, the precarious social balance of the mid-Victorian period had collapsed, and Britain's long slide from the peak of economic predominance was already under way. Nevertheless, in the folk and personal memory of the middle and upper classes, the time before the war appeared as the age in which they, and Britain, stood in unchallenged ascendancy. In Narnia and Middle-earth Lewis and Tolkien recalled this mythic world; they thus tapped into a folk memory of a harmonious, stable, and secure society that had been lost.

This lost neverland was, as Wiener has shown, a pastoral idyll of country manors and villages, covered bridges and wooded lanes, rather than the reality of highly urbanized, industrial Edwardian Britain. Such ruralism was possible, Wiener argues, *because of* urbanization: By the late nineteenth century, the English countryside was " 'empty' and available for use as an integrating cultural symbol."[5] Lewis's and Tolkien's fantasies reveal the power of the cultural symbol of the countryside and the integral role of ruralism in shaping the middle-class British cultural identity. In a revealing review of Paul Kocher's *Master of Middle-earth*, the *Times Literary Supplement* argued,

---

3 For an examination of Tolkien as a Great War writer, see Barton Friedman, "Tolkien and David Jones: The Great War and the War of the Ring," *Clio*, Winter 1982, pp. 115–36.
4 See Samuel Hynes, *A War Imagined: The First World War and English Culture* (New York: Atheneum, 1991), p. 3, esp. n. 1.
5 Wiener, *English Culture*, p. 49.

"There are signs that Professor Kocher, who is American, has missed a certain smell of the Shire – 'Meadowsweet, tansy, thyme, And fainthearted pimpernel' – in a word, its Englishness. . . . one nostalgic light falls over all: it is that of summer afternoons in the unravaged countryside of Puck of Pook's Hill."[6]

Chesterton was not the only English author with whom Tolkien was linked. According to reviewers and critics, Tolkien's hobbits, like Grahame's Mole and Toad or Milne's Pooh and Rabbit, "are based on recognisable English types"; his landscapes recall those of Shakespeare, Spenser, and Chaucer; his "refreshing tonalities" draw on Dickens and Wordsworth; he rests in the tradition of English landscape poetry or of English folklore and fairy tale.[7] He is, in other words, claimed as a quintessential English author, as part of a tradition that has helped shape the middle-class cultural identity. It is an intellectual tradition intrinsically linked to romantic protest, to a rejection of industrialism and the empiricist belief system that undergirds it. For Lewis and Tolkien, participating in this tradition served as a means of solace and escape. For other middle-class Britons in the postwar period, it drew them out into the streets and impelled them to try to change the world.

6 "Ring of Romanticism," *Times Literary Supplement*, 8 June 1973, p. 629; Paul Kocher, *Master of Middle-earth: The Achievement of J. R. R. Tolkien* (London: Thames and Hudson, 1973).

7 Roger Sale, "Tolkien and Frodo Baggins," in *Tolkien and the Critics: Essays on J. R. R. Tolkien's "Lord of the Rings,"* ed. Neil Isaacs and Rose Zimbardo (Notre Dame: University of Notre Dame Press, 1968), p. 249; see also Robert Giddings and Elizabeth Holland, *JRR Tolkien: The Shores of Middle-earth* (London: Junction Books, 1981), pp. 131–2, for parallels between *The Lord of the Rings* and *The Wind in the Willows;* Naomi Lewis, *Fantasy Books for Children* (London: National Book League, 1975), p. 50; Mark R. Hillegas, *Shadows of Imagination: The Fantasies of C. S. Lewis, J. R. R. Tolkien, and Charles Williams* (Carbondale: University of Illinois Press, 1979), pp. 95–6; Margery Fisher, *Intent upon Reading: A Critical Appraisal of Modern Fiction for Children* (Leicester: Brockhampton Press, 1964), p. 351; Fred Inglis, *The Promise of Happiness: Value and Meaning in Children's Fiction* (London: Cambridge University Press, 1981), p. 199; Jessica Jenkins, review of *The Lord of the Rings*, "Woman's Hour," 19 July 1967 (BBC-WAC/Films 93/94/Woman's Hour).

PART II

The Campaign for Nuclear Disarmament: romantic protest on the march

The Campaign for Nuclear Disarmament, born in Britain in 1958, played a leading role in outlining the patterns of postwar social and political protest. The distinctive peace symbol, a circle enclosing the semaphore signals for N(uclear) and D(isarmament), ⊕, was in itself an important legacy to protest movements throughout the world.[1] More significantly, CND embedded in the public imagination the image of the middle class on the march. After CND, protest was never quite the same. Although CND forged new weapons of protest, it deployed these weapons in a familiar fight. The speeches, literature, and the shape of the demonstrations themselves reveal that CND was more than a protest against nuclear weapons; it embraced a social and cultural critique of the whole of technological civilization, a critique that converged with the one expressed in the fantasy literature of Lewis and Tolkien.

It is important to note at the outset that the terms "CND" and "CNDers" imply a nonexistent homogeneity in the Campaign. CND served as an um-

---

1 The Aldermaston March of 1958, which introduced the peace symbol to the world, was sponsored not by CND but by the Direct Action Committee. See Michael Randle, "Non-violent Direct Action in the 1950s and 1960s," in *Campaigns for Peace: British Peace Movements in the Twentieth Century*, ed. Richard Taylor and Nigel Young (Manchester: Manchester University Press, 1987), p. 132.

The original sketches of the peace symbol are now held by the School of Peace Studies at Bradford University. The symbol was designed by Gerald Holtom. Holtom explained that the sign not only indicated the semaphore signals but also symbolized "the little man in despair" and "the triumph of good over evil" (Margaret Tims, "Nuclear Disarmament and the Artist," *Peace News*, 26 June 1959, p. 2). See also *Peace News*, 30 June 1961, p. 5; and Peggy Duff, *Left, Left, Left: A Personal Account of Six Protest Campaigns, 1945–1965* (London: Allison and Busby, 1971), p. 116. According to Frank Myers, the symbol's resemblance to the semaphore signals was coincidental. He writes that the symbol depicted a drooping cross as a sign of Holtom's despair at the failure of the Christian churches to speak out against nuclear weapons (Myers, "British Peace Politics: The Campaign for Nuclear Disarmament and the Committee of 100, 1957–1962" [Ph.D. diss., Columbia University, 1965], p. 107).

The Aldermaston plant remains a center of controversy. On 24 January 1993 the *Observer* reported that nearly one hundred people have been killed, injured, or contaminated with radioactivity over the last forty years. In addition, more than one thousand accidents occurred in that time period.

brella that sheltered a diverse assortment of individuals and groups: Labour Leftists, New Leftists, pacifists, anarchists, Marxists, Christians, liberal academics, and engaged artists and entertainers all marched under the CND banner. This diversity both raised CND to the heights of international acclaim and ensured its rapid decline. It also mines the waters about CND against generalization. On no specific issue, except the none-too-specific demand to "Ban the Bomb," did all CNDers agree. Yet, weaving its way through many of the various subgroups of the Campaign was the thread of romantic protest. Many CNDers wanted to make Britain not only safer but better, and they agreed that banning the Bomb marked a beginning in the building of this spiritually better Britain.

The decision in favor of an independent British atomic weapons program had provoked little opposition in Britain.[2] The advent of the *hydrogen* bomb proved to be the spark that burned through the apathy surrounding nuclear weapons and lit the fires of protest. The United States tested its first H-bomb in November of 1952 and the Soviets followed ten months later; more important in terms of public protest, however, was the American test in 1954 that dusted a Japanese fishing vessel with fallout and so killed one of its crew members. The almost incomprehensible destructive capacity of this new weapon, combined with growing apprehension over the effects of nuclear weapons testing, made the cold war seem more threatening than before. Anti–H-bomb activity in Britain smoldered and then flared up after the government announced in February 1955 that Britain would produce and maintain her own H-bomb arsenal. The heat of this protest forged the Campaign for Nuclear Disarmament.

---

2 It did, however, lead to the first and little-noticed Aldermaston protest. In 1949 the Peace Pledge Union set up a study group on nonviolence. Out of this study group came Operation Gandhi, later renamed the Non-Violent Resistance Group, which staged a sit-down outside the War Office on 11 January 1952 in response to the British decision to manufacture atomic bombs. Three months later, on 19 April 1952, the NVR Group marched outside the Atomic Energy (later Weapons) Research Establishment at Aldermaston. The NVR Group evolved into the Direct Action Committee. See Hugh Brock, "Evolution of the Aldermaston Resistance," *Peace News Supplement*, 20/27 February 1959, p. iii.

   In his fascinating study of the cultural effects of the atomic bomb in the United States, Paul Boyer argues that "the advent of the atomic bomb was very quickly recognized as one of those rare events that forever alter the human landscape." Americans initially responded to the fact of the atomic bomb with shock and horror. When the shock wore off, American reaction varied from optimistic predictions of a brilliant atomic-fueled future to dark visions of doom. After 1950, however, the news of the Soviet atomic tests, the reality of the cold war, the official policy of secrecy regarding the effects of radiation, and hope in the "peaceful atom" resulted in a muting of debate, a mood of "dulled acquiescence." The U.S. government's decision in 1950 to proceed with development of the hydrogen bomb was accepted – and barely noticed – by the majority of the American public. Paul Boyer, *By the Bomb's Early Light: American Thought and Culture at the Dawn of the Atomic Age* (New York: Pantheon, 1985), pp. 133–40, 291–302; quotations from pp. 133, 291.

To its founders' surprise, CND became a mass movement imitated in many countries. It publicized the health hazards of radiation, exposed the weaknesses of the British Civil Defence program, focused worldwide attention on the debate over nuclear weapons, and thus forced the world to confront the new nuclear reality. After 1962 the Campaign struggled with its direction and identity while its support and appeal rapidly diminished. Until its resurgence in 1980 in response to the NATO cruise missile deployment, CND functioned as a lobby group rather than a mass movement, one of a myriad of left-wing pressure groups on the British political scene.

In its first years, however, CND was something unique. A middle-class mass movement, it pulled ordinary men and women from their homes, offices, and university classrooms and pushed them onto the streets of Britain. Because CND had no national membership system until 1967, long after its peak, numbers are difficult to fix with certainty.[3] By 1960, more than 450 local groups existed around the country; by 1961, the number had reached 900. At its height, the CND monthly *Sanity* had a circulation of 45,000. Observers, supporters, and critics, however, gauged the strength of the Campaign not on number of groups or *Sanity* subscribers but on the turnout for the annual Easter weekend march between Aldermaston, the site of a nuclear weapons research plant, and London. The first march in 1958, the only one that went from London to Aldermaston rather than vice versa, exceeded all expectations when up to 10,000 supporters gathered in Trafalgar Square on Good Friday morning and perhaps as many as 8,000 marched on the first leg of the four-day protest.[4] The next year the numbers escalated; the final rally in Trafalgar Square drew between 12,000 and 35,000 people.[5] By 1960, perhaps as many as 100,000 supporters assembled in the square.[6] Such crowds had not gathered in Britain since before the war; hence, the Aldermaston March highlighted the uniqueness and the appeal of CND in the postwar period.

3 The estimated number of CND supporters in 1959 was between 40,000 and 50,000. See Allen Potter, *Organized Groups in British National Politics* (London: Faber, 1961), p. 132.
4 *Daily Mail*, 5 Apr. 1958, p. 1. The *Daily Telegraph* agreed with the *Mail's* estimate of 10,000 at the opening rally but reported that only half of these joined the march (5 Apr. 1958, p. 1). Other papers reported lower numbers: According to the *Scotsman's* account, 5,000–6,000 marched away from Trafalgar Square (5 Apr. 1958, p. 1). The *Times* reported 6,000 in the square and 4,000 marchers at the start (5 Apr. 1958, p. 6). The *Daily Worker* counted 8,000 at the opening rally and 5,000 on the march (5 Apr. 1958, p. 1). The *Guardian* estimated that 4,000 supporters gathered in Trafalgar Square on Good Friday (7 Apr. 1958, p. 1).
5 *Daily Mail*, 31 Mar. 1959, p. 7; *Daily Mirror*, 31 Mar. 1959, p. 3; *Daily Telegraph*, 31 Mar. 1959, p. 9; *Daily Worker*, 31 Mar. 1959, p. 1; *Guardian*, 31 Mar. 1959, p. 12; *Scotsman*, 31 Mar. 1959, p. 1; *Times*, 31 Mar. 1959, p. 4; *Tribune*, 3 Apr. 1959, p. 6.
6 *Daily Mail*, 19 Apr. 1960, p. 1; *Daily Mirror*, 19 Apr. 1960, p. 5; *Daily Telegraph*, 19 Apr. 1960, p. 11; *Daily Worker*, 19 Apr. 1960, p. 1; *Guardian*, 19 Apr. 1960, p. 1; *Scotsman*, 19 Apr. 1960, p. 1; *Times*, 19 Apr. 1960, p. 10; *Yorkshire Post*, 19 Apr. 1960, p. 1.

The Easter march, or "Aldermaston," was more than a matter of numbers, however. It proved a pivotal experience for CNDers, three days of community, camaraderie, hardship for the sake of the good, a taking of physical action to remedy what many perceived as a spiritual ill. When, as in 1960, the CNDers marched twelve abreast through London on Easter Monday, it seemed that, like the Risen Christ, they would do the impossible; they would turn the world upside down. For three days of the year, at least, the individual counted. And, for three days of the year, Britain seemed to count too. In the vision of the CNDers the British nation would seize the moral leadership of the world by abdicating the throne of Nuclear Power. Nuclear disarmament would allow Britain to revivify its own culture. Britain could then not only lead the neutral nations, particularly the developing areas, into a more peaceful and prosperous future but also serve as mediator between the two superpowers. A heady vision, it declared that in the nuclear age, the righteous and the realists stood together: The practical, the moral, and the possible were all one and the same.

6

Theme and variations

To their surprise and discomfort, CND's founders had created the means by which ordinary individuals could articulate their unease with, even their rejection of, the basic assumptions of the postwar era. The Campaign gave its supporters the illusion, at least, of communicating, of participating in shaping the governing structures of Britain and the world. Such an illusion seemed believable in the second half of the 1950s, when a series of pivotal events challenged the postwar status quo and it appeared that the world could be saved from itself. Under its umbrella, CND gathered together diverse groups of persons. They found themselves united for a short time by a sense of moral outrage against the Bomb, a conviction that Britain was on the path to not only physical but also spiritual destruction, and an ultimately misplaced hope that if their voices could be heard, they would redirect Britain's foreign and military policy, strengthen Britain's future, and save the earth.[1]

A new world order?

In the second half of the 1950s, the postwar international and political structure assumed a new shape. In response, Britain's economic, political and cultural life shifted and strained to fit this new outline. Five pivotal events or developments challenged the assumptions that had governed both national and international politics in the years since World War II. Four of these events occurred outside Britain: the emergence of neutralism as a force in the Third World, the Suez crisis, the Soviet suppression of the Hungarian Revolution, and the revolution in nuclear technology. The fifth was a domestic political matter: Aneurin Bevan's decision to support Labour Party leader

---

1 For a history of the Campaign, as well as a masterful analysis of its political impact and significance, see Richard Taylor, *Against the Bomb: The British Peace Movement, 1958–1965* (Oxford: Clarendon Press, 1988). This is a substantially revised and edited version of his Ph.D. dissertation: "The British Nuclear Disarmament Movement of 1958 to 1965 and Its Legacy to the Left" (University of Leeds, 1983).

Hugh Gaitskell and reject unilateral nuclear disarmament. These five events weakened Britain's postwar political structures and thus established the context for an extraparliamentary mass movement calling for far-reaching change. They created the conditions that made re-creating the world seem both necessary and possible.

The challenge of neutralism to the postwar status quo provided CND with a basis for hope as well as, for some CNDers, a plan for action. The Bandung Conference of April 1955 gathered together in Indonesia twenty-three Asian and six African nations. Led by Jawaharlal Nehru of India, Abdel Nasser of Egypt, and Achmad Sukarno of Indonesia, Bandung announced the impatience of the newly independent nations of the world with cold war hostilities and superpower hegemony. It marked the start of what would become the Non-aligned Movement, officially constituted in the first summit of nonaligned nations in Belgrade in 1961. Formed by anticolonialism and disturbed by the cold war, developing nations in Asia and Africa declared not only that true independence demanded a neutral stand in the international arena but also that, in concert, such neutral nations could become a countervailing force to the superpowers.[2] It was to the neutral nations that CND turned in its efforts to find a new role for Britain to play. Their declaration of independence seemed to signal that postwar positions were crumbling and that a revolt against the cold war, and the nuclear age that fed upon it, could succeed.

The neutral challenge took on a dangerous aspect one year after the Bandung Conference when the Suez crisis erupted. In 1956, Colonel Abdel Nasser, determined both to remove that last vestiges of British control from his nation and to win a place of influence among Arab and neutral nations, nationalized the Suez Canal. Although in strict violation of Anglo–Egyptian agreements, nationalization was a decisive and aggressive action that appealed to neutral and Arab anti-Western sentiment. In an ill-considered move, Anthony Eden's government, in collusion with France and Israel, agreed to military intervention to wrest the canal from Nasser's hands. On 25 October 1956, Israeli forces attacked Egypt. Five days later, the French and British governments issued a joint ultimatum calling for the belligerents to disengage and withdraw ten miles to the west and east of the canal, thereby leaving Israel one hundred miles deep within Egyptian territory and freeing

---

2 See A. W. Singham and Shirley Hune, *Non-alignment in an Age of Alignments* (Westport, Conn.: Lawrence and Hill, 1986), pp. 57–71. See also Singham and Hune's essay in *Dealignment: A New Foreign Policy Perspective*, ed. Mary Kaldor and Richard Falk (Oxford: Basil Blackwell, 1987), pp. 185–204; U. S. Bajpai, ed., *Non-alignment: Perspectives and Prospects* (Atlantic Highlands, N.J.: Humanities Press, 1986), pp. 1–17, 18–19, 61–2; Peter Lyon, *Neutralism* (Leicester: Leicester University Press, 1963), pp. 47–8, 56–7; Godfrey H. Jansen, *Afro-Asia and Non-alignment* (London: Faber, 1966), pp. 182–250, 363–84.

the canal from Egyptian control. Not surprisingly, Egypt failed to agree to the terms of the ultimatum, and Anglo–French forces followed a six-day bombing of Port Said with a military invasion.

Worldwide reaction was intensely negative; most significantly, both the United States and the USSR condemned Britain's and France's action. The Soviet Union threatened to turn long-range rockets against Britain if it did not call off the military action. Even more unsettling was the American use of economic compulsion. As a result of the invasion and, more specifically, of American disapproval, Britain saw its gold and dollar reserves rapidly depleted; about 15 percent of its reserves were lost in November. Britain had no choice but to accede to American demands and call off the invasion. An utter fiasco, the Suez episode left the canal in Egyptian hands, heightened Nasser's prestige, and discredited Britain in the eyes of the world.[3]

Suez helped to shatter the illusions and assumptions current in Britain after World War II. Although the crisis produced no immediate concrete political change – the Conservatives won the next general election easily, with scarcely a mention of Suez, and Britain remained committed to a role east of Suez until 1967 – it illustrated vividly that Britain was no longer an imperial power and was, in fact, a client state of the United States. The popularity of Eden's stand against Nasser, before the act of military intervention, demonstrated that many British men and women were uneasy with and angry about their nation's loss of influence and power. As F. S. Northedge explained, "The feeling of having been pushed out of one place abroad after another was bound to produce an outburst, especially if the pushing was dramatic and seemingly without excuse."[4] The years after Suez saw the British struggling with their lowered position in the world. The rise of CND bore witness to this struggle: Campaigners argued that unilateral nuclear disarmament would propel Britain to the position of moral leader of the world. This quest for moral leadership was made more urgent by what many British perceived as the essential immorality of their government's actions during the Suez crisis. CNDers marched to restore morality to the political arena.

The Suez crisis proved to be a factor in the third important event that reshaped the postwar international and political structure: the Soviet invasion of Hungary. In February of 1956, during a secret session of the Twentieth Congress of the Soviet Communist Party, the Soviet premier, Nikita Khru-

---

3 For the Suez crisis, see David Carlton, *Britain and the Suez Crisis* (Oxford: Basil Blackwell, 1989); Roger Louis and Roger Owen, eds., *Suez 1956: The Crisis and Its Consequences* (Oxford: Clarendon Press, 1989); F. S. Northedge, *The Descent from Power: British Foreign Policy, 1945–1973* (London: Allen and Unwin, 1974), pp. 98–141; and Hugh Thomas, *Suez* (New York: Harper and Row, 1967).

4 Northedge, *Descent from Power*, p. 131.

shchev, detailed and denounced the crimes committed during the long decades of Stalin's rule. The de-Stalinization process begun with Khrushchev's "Secret Speech" shook the fragile pillars on which Soviet control of Eastern Europe rested and aroused reform movements in both Poland and Hungary. Moving from reform to revolution, Hungarian students and workers marched in Budapest on 23 October 1956 to protest Hungary's subordination to the Soviet Union. Alarmed by this challenge to the postwar status quo, Khrushchev sent Soviet tanks to the edges of the city. To his and the world's surprise, the Hungarians poured into the streets of Budapest in defiance. On 28 October, he called back the Soviet troops and agreed to negotiate. The Anglo–French military intervention in Suez, however, strengthened Khrushchev's hand by diverting world attention from Budapest. On 3 November Soviet tanks entered the city and crushed the revolt.[5]

Soviet control in Eastern Europe would not face another significant challenge until the Prague Spring of 1968. In the West, the combination of Khrushchev's revelations of the atrocities of the Stalinist regime and the brutal crushing of the Hungarian revolt resulted in a mass exodus from the communist camp. In Britain, one-fifth of the total membership left the Communist Party. The hard Left faced some hard choices. The events of 1956 behind the Iron Curtain forced a reorientation of left-wing political activism. Like Suez, these events raised the question of morality in politics. To what moral legitimacy could post-Stalinist socialism lay claim? This effort to redefine socialism in the wake of Hungary was to lead former Communists to embrace CND as part of a new political consciousness in Britain and as the hope of British socialism.

Although they challenged British postwar political structures, Suez and Hungary were conventional military confrontations. The fourth factor in shaking up the postwar settlement and allowing CND to emerge was the combination of developments in nuclear weapons technology – the sort of technology that made conventional conflicts such as Suez and Hungary seem almost innocuous – and alterations in defense strategy. The period of the late 1950s and early 1960s was, according to Lawrence Freedman, a period of "great turmoil in weapons technology and strategic thinking."[6] In 1954 John Foster Dulles, the U.S. secretary of state, announced NATO's "New Look," a revised defense strategy that required the use of nuclear forces to respond to Soviet aggression, whether nuclear or not. The New Look gave

5   For a sampling of the many accounts of the uprising see George Mikes, *The Hungarian Revolution* (London: Andre Deutsch, 1957); Paul Kecskemeti, *The Unexpected Revolution: Social Forces in the Hungarian Uprising* (Stanford: Stanford University Press, 1961); Paul E. Zinner, *Revolution in Hungary* (New York: Columbia University Press, 1962); Noel Barber, *Seven Days of Freedom* (London: Macmillan, 1972); and Bill Lomax, *Hungary, 1956* (London: Allison and Busby, 1976).

6   Lawrence Freedman, *Britain and Nuclear Weapons* (London: Macmillan, 1980), p. 10.

added impetus to Britain's atomic and nuclear programs.[7] In the same year, NATO forces were equipped with American tactical nuclear weapons, and U.S. thermonuclear tests at Bikini Island doused at least three hundred people with high levels of radiation.[8] Both the strategic debate over the possibility and utility of a limited nuclear engagement and the growing public awareness of the health threat posed by nuclear fallout helped make this a time of controversy and confusion.

The shift from aircraft to missile delivery systems added to the tumult. The Soviets' successful launch of *Sputnik*, the first artificial space satellite, in October of 1957 demonstrated that the Soviet Union was capable of producing fast intercontinental missiles able to destroy American cities. With the United States vulnerable to Soviet nuclear attack and Britain a logical target of unstoppable Soviet nuclear warheads, "nuclear defense" seemed more and more an oxymoron in some circles. The Conservative government's Defence White Papers on both 1957 and 1958 accentuated the threatening possibilities of the new world situation.[9] The White Papers made clear Britain's reliance on nuclear weapons and bluntly admitted that Britain possessed no effective defense against a nuclear onslaught. The 1957 White Paper stated, "There is at present no means of providing adequate protection for the people of this country against the consequences of an attack with nuclear weapons."[10] The impact of the White Papers, combined with spreading realization of atmospheric contamination from nuclear testing, created a climate receptive to a campaign offering an escape from the nuclear madness.

That the way out had to be offered by a protest campaign and not a political party became clear after the Labour Party Conference of 1957, in which Aneurin Bevan disappointed his disciples and surrendered his leadership of the Labour Left by backing the official pronuclear policy of the Labour Party. This "betrayal" by Bevan, as it was seen, constitutes the final element that weakened the postwar political structure. The divide between Left and Right in the Labour Party is one of the significant political facts of the postwar years. From 1947 on, various leftist factions of the party had found themselves increasingly alienated by both the domestic moderation and the pro-American foreign policy of Attlee's government. Bevan's resigna-

---

7 Ibid., pp. 3–4.
8 Andrew Pierre, *Nuclear Politics: The British Experience with an Independent Strategic Force, 1939–1970* (London: Oxford University Press, 1972), p. 89; J. P. G. Freeman, *Britain's Nuclear Arms Control Policy in the Context of Anglo–American Relations, 1957–1968* (New York: St. Martin's Press, 1986), p. 26.
9 *Defence: Outline of Future Policy: 1957*, Cmnd. 124 (London: HMSO, 1957); *Report on Defence: Britain's Contribution to Peace and Security: 1958*, Cmnd. 363 (London: HMSO, 1958). See also Duncan Sandys's speech on 13 Feb. 1957 in the Commons: *Hansard*, 5th ser., pt. 1, vol. 564, [4–15 Feb. 1956–7], cols. 1306–12.
10 *Defence: Outline of Future Policy: 1957*, pp. 2–3.

tion in 1951 of his post as minister of labour, a resignation in protest against American-induced rearmament and the consequent cutbacks in social spending, provided these various factions with a leader and a focus.[11] The Bevanites believed "they were engaged in a struggle to preserve the soul of the Labour Party."[12]

Well before Britain possessed atomic or nuclear capability, the left wing of the Labour Party had aligned itself against the foreign and military policy pursued by both parties after the Second World War.[13] From 1951 until 1957, Bevan led the Left in its disarmament campaign. As a result, his actions at the Labour Party Conference in 1957 had a dramatic impact. At the conference, Harold Davies moved a resolution favoring Britain's unilateral abandonment of nuclear weapons. Bevan's speech guaranteed the defeat of the resolution. In words that have now become a cliché, Bevan attacked unilateralism as an "emotional spasm" that would send the British foreign secretary "naked into the conference chamber." For many on the Left, Bevan's speech signaled his treason, his betrayal of leftist principles for the perks of power.[14] It also signaled the need for an extraparliamentary campaign for nuclear disarmament. Although Labour Leftists believed that only a Labour government would effect nuclear disarmament, Bevan's speech prepared them to welcome a popular protest movement outside the stream of parliamentary politics as a means of forcing Labour into the nuclear disarmament current.

11 For Bevan's revolt, see Michael R. Gordon, *Conflict and Consensus in Labour's Foreign Policy, 1914–1965* (Stanford: Stanford University Press, 1969), pp. 222–45; Jonathan Schneer, *Labour's Conscience: The Labour Left, 1945–1951* (Boston: Allen and Unwin, 1988), pp. 196–207.

12 Schneer, *Labour's Conscience*, p. 207.

13 E.g., the Keep Left group in 1947 called on Britain "to renounce the manufacture and use of atomic bombs and to submit our armed forces and armament factories to inspections of UNO, irrespective of whether Russia or America reach agreement on this subject" (Richard Crossman, "The Job Abroad," in the pamphlet *Keep Left*, quoted by Schneer, *Labour's Conscience*, pp. 60–1).

14 Labour Party, *Report of the 56th Annual Conference, Brighton, September 30–October 4, 1957* (London: Labour Party, 1957), pp. 179–83. Bevan's speech is reprinted in Charles Wyatt Lomas, comp., *The Rhetoric of the British Peace Movement* (New York: Random House, 1971), pp. 41–54. Michael Foot provides an eyewitness account of the speech and an informed, yet puzzled, analysis of Bevan's motivations in *Aneurin Bevan, A Biography*, vol. 2, *1945–1960* (London: Davis-Poynter, 1973), pp. 566–84. Peggy Duff discussed the reasons behind Bevan's antiunilateralism in *Left, Left, Left: A Personal Account of Six Protest Campaigns, 1945–1965* (London: Allison and Busby, 1971), pp. 118–19, 170–1. See also Richard Taylor, "The Labour Party and the Campaign for Nuclear Disarmament," in *Campaigns for Peace: British Peace Movements in the Twentieth Century*, ed. Richard Taylor and Nigel Young (New York: St. Martin's Press, 1987), pp. 102–6. Mervyn Jones pointed out that Bevan was arguing that unilateralism logically meant withdrawal from NATO, and it was the prospect of Britain entering into negotiations without alliances, rather than without the Bomb, that Bevan described as walking "naked into the conference chamber" (Jones, *Chances* [London: Verso, 1987], pp. 144–6; see also Foot, *Bevan*, p. 578, n. 1).

On 17 February 1955, the British government announced its decision to produce the hydrogen bomb and soon encountered the fallout of protest. A Gallup Poll, taken in March 1955, found that 32 percent of those surveyed disagreed with the government's decision. Two months later, 53 percent said Britain should devote atomic energy solely to peaceful purposes. In April 1957, 44 percent disapproved of the government's decision to carry out its H-bomb test.[15] Although anti–H-bomb sentiment had been on the rise in Britain since 1954, the imminent arrival of a British Bomb made the nuclear issue more immediate than when the Bomb belonged only to the superpowers.[16] In addition, the announcement at the end of 1957 of the planned establishment of Thor missile sites in the United Kingdom heightened public awareness of Britain's likelihood of becoming a nuclear target in the event of war with the Soviet Union.[17]

The main elements of the movement

Although the contemporary context of discontent and disillusionment nourished the extraparliamentary mass movement that emerged in Britain, the roots of this movement extended deeply into the soil of romantic protest. The diversity of CND's supporters meant that its romanticism intermingled with and was often obscured by other intellectual and cultural traditions. In CND, respectable and apolitical middle-class mothers joined with perennial protesters, Gandhian pacifists, Labour Leftists, and ex-Communists to try to stop what they perceived to be imminent physical and spiritual annihilation. Examination of several of the Campaign's main elements, however, exposes certain familiar themes of romantic protest.

15 Leon Epstein, "Britain and the H-Bomb, 1955–58," *Review of Politics*, 21 July 1959, p. 512, n. 4.
16 The most important of the pre-CND protests against the H-bomb resulted in the formation of the Hydrogen Bomb Campaign Committee. On 7 April 1954, 300 delegates from a number of church, peace, and labor organizations, including the future chairman of CND, Canon L. John Collins, met with six Labour MPs. Out of this meeting came the Hydrogen Bomb Campaign Committee, which aimed to collect signatures for a petition asking for the convening of a disarmament conference and the strengthening of the UN. Although the organization gained some attention and some support, its limited aims failed to catch the public imagination (Christopher Driver, *The Disarmers: A Study in Protest* [London: Hodder and Staughton, 1964], pp. 26–7; A. J. R. Groom, *British Thinking about Nuclear Weapons* [London: Frances Pinter, 1974], p. 170; Taylor, *Against the Bomb*, p. 5). After 1954, resolutions favoring nuclear test bans became a regular feature at union conferences (Groom, *British Thinking about Nuclear Weapons*, pp. 168–9, 173).
17 Clive Rose, *Campaigns against Western Defence* (New York: St. Martin's, 1985), pp. 130–1. In 1957, the Liberal Party Assembly, the Labour Party Conference, and the Trades Union Congress called for a test ban and a postponement of the British H-bomb tests (Groom, *British Thinking about Nuclear Weapons*, pp. 176–7).

In the period before 1958, the National Committee for the Abolition of Nuclear Weapons Tests (NCANWT) was by far the most important of the attempts to alter Britain's nuclear policies.[18] NCANWT grew out of the concern expressed by the members of the Golders Green Women's Cooperative Guild over the radiation hazards of nuclear testing. That concern resulted in the formation of the Golders Green Committee for Abolition of Nuclear Weapons, which gave birth to a number of similar committees throughout the London area. On 7 February 1957, a national campaign was launched.[19] In order to gain the greatest number of supporters, NCANWT deliberately limited its aims to the abolition of nuclear tests.[20] It aroused support and interest, and embraced nonpacifists and nonunilateralists, but had no impact on governmental policy. The first British H-bomb test took place in May 1957 as planned.

NCANWT did have an impact on the shape and course of CND, however. When CND formed in January 1958, NCANWT voluntarily shut down; 28 of its 33 sponsors and 114 of its 115 local groups joined CND. It passed its organizational structure, a national organization working through regional and local councils, on to CND as well.[21] Even more important, NCANWT became one of four key groups that in combination gave to CND its peculiar and potent flavor.

NCANWT resulted from the same sort of grass-roots organization and initiative that later energized CND. In part, like CND, NCANWT was the product of the perennially protesting part of the middle class. For example, Gertrude Fishwick, the secretary of the original local group and the individual most responsible for initiating the campaign that led to the creation of NCANWT, possessed the résumé of a local left-wing activist: An ex-suffragette, she was a member of the Anglican Pacifist Fellowship and the

---

18 For the history of NCANWT, see Taylor, *Against the Bomb*, pp. 5–18. See also Richard A. Exley, "The Campaign for Nuclear Disarmament: Its Organization, Personnel, and Methods in Its First Year" (thesis, University of Manchester, 1959), chap. 2; Driver, *The Disarmers*, pp. 31–7; John Minnion and Philip Bolsover, eds., *The CND Story: The First Twenty-five Years of CND in the Words of the People Involved* (London: Allison and Busby, 1983), pp. 12–13.

19 *Peace News*, 15 Feb. 1957, p. 1. Throughout 1957, *Peace News* gave extensive coverage to NCANWT's activities. Richard Taylor writes that the founding meeting of NCANWT was held on 29 November 1956, at a conference sponsored by the National Peace Council (*Against the Bomb*, p. 7).

20 Exley, "Campaign for Nuclear Disarmament," p. 34; Taylor, *Against the Bomb*, p. 8.

21 NCANWT sold tickets to the 17 February mass meeting that launched CND (*Peace News*, 10 Jan. 1958, p. 1). At the press conference on 30 January announcing the formation of CND, NCANWT announced its merger with the new campaign. Its January *Bulletin* explained "that the Council's primary task ought now to be not merely to campaign against tests but to organize public opinion against the arms race" (*Peace News*, 31 Jan. 1958, p. 1). The merger of CND and NCANWT was not accomplished without controversy. See Peggy Duff's letter in *Peace News* (4 Dec. 1964, p. 11) and Sheila Jones's rejoinder (18 Dec. 1964, p. 11). See also Taylor, *Against the Bomb*, pp. 16–18.

Finchley Labour Party, and the secretary for Victory for Socialism, as well as a volunteer with the Movement for Colonial Freedom, the Union of Democratic Control, and the Socialist Medical Association.[22]

But NCANWT's significance for CND extended beyond funneling such dependable activists into the new campaign. The fact that the original group was a women's guild located in Golders Green, a respectable middle-class suburb in north London, foreshadowed CND's future constituency. CND drew on the British middle class for its support[23] and resonated especially strongly with women, still in traditional roles in 1958, who found the effects of radiation on the unborn particularly horrifying. Moreover, NCANWT demonstrated the appeal of an extraparliamentary campaign. It excluded MPs from leadership roles and so avoided the restraints and distractions of party politics. Richard Taylor has shown that although NCANWT welcomed the formation of local groups, it never envisaged itself as the head of a mass movement. Its members believed in the power of elite influence and saw the organization as a traditional lobby group.[24] Nevertheless, NCANWT both originated as and expanded into a grass-roots campaign and thus demonstrated the potential strength of the response of ordinary, not necessarily politicized, British citizens to the nuclear challenge. After CND replaced NCANWT, the Campaign's ability to continue to draw out these ordinary people, including those who were not necessarily pacifists or perennial protesters, gave it great uniqueness and power.

The second important grouping in CND resulted from Gandhi's influence on the Peace Pledge Union, a British peace organization. Since 1950, the Non-Violent Resistance Group of the PPU had been exploring ways to

22 *Peace News*, 7 Mar. 1958, p. 11; Driver, *The Disarmers*, pp. 31–2. According to Driver, "if any single person can be said to have triggered off the chain reaction which ended in CND it is Miss Fishwick" (p. 31). Fishwick died on 15 February 1958 – just two days before the first CND mass meeting at Central Hall.

23 Participants, observers, and later analysts all noted the middle-class composition of CND. See, e.g., Norman Birnbaum, "Great Britain: The Reactive Revolt," in *The Revolution in World Politics*, ed. Morton A. Kaplan (New York: Wiley, 1962), pp. 58–60; Ian Bradley, *The English Middle Classes Are Alive and Kicking* (London: Collins, 1982), chap. 9; Nigel Harris et al., "Labour and the Bomb," *International Socialism* 10 (Autumn 1962): 21–5; Robert Taylor, "The Campaign for Nuclear Disarmament," in *The Age of Affluence, 1951–1964*, ed. Vernon Bogdanor and Robert Skidelsky (London: Macmillan, 1970), p. 226. In his survey of former Campaign members in 1968, Frank Parkin found that 83 percent were in or came from families in nonmanual labour, and 54 percent had some form of higher education (*Middle-Class Radicalism: The Social Bases of the British Campaign for Nuclear Disarmament* [Manchester: Manchester University Press, 1968], pp. 17, 177). Ten years later, Richard Taylor and Colin Pritchard's findings confirmed Parkin's. Of their respondents, 90 percent were in the social classes labeled "Non-Manual," 56 percent had some form of higher education, and 73 percent had a degree or a professional qualification (*The Protest Makers: The British Nuclear Disarmament Movement of 1958–1965, Twenty Years On* [Oxford: Pergamon Press, 1980], pp. 147, 23).

24 Taylor, *Against the Bomb*, p. 12.

use Gandhian techniques of nonviolence to subvert Britain's nuclear defenses. In April 1957, the NVR Group set up the Emergency Committee for Direct Action against Nuclear War in order to raise funds to send a volunteer, Harold Steele, to Christmas Island in the Pacific, the site of the British nuclear test.[25] Steele failed in his effort to sail into the test area, but the Emergency Committee chose to stay in existence as the Direct Action Committee against Nuclear War (the DAC). In December of 1957, shortly before NCANWT gave way to CND, the DAC formulated plans for a three-day march from London to Aldermaston over the Easter weekend.[26] When CND formed at the beginning of 1958, the plans for the first Aldermaston March were already under way, and direct actionists were firmly entrenched in the antinuclear camp.[27]

The DAC drew into the Campaign a small but vital group.[28] Its members were pacifists, but pacifists of a new breed, Gandhians committed to civil disobedience and industrial action, with links to anarchism.[29] They aimed to create a nonviolent society through direct appeals to individuals and through symbolic but concrete actions. The goal was to bypass political processes and speak directly to those actually implementing Britain's nuclear policy: the workers, the soldiers, the police.[30] In its first well-publicized direct-action demonstration, for example, the DAC sat down outside the construction site of a U.S. Air Force missile base in Norfolk. By blocking access to the site with their bodies, DAC supporters hoped to break through the complacency of the construction workers and force them to confront their personal responsibility for nuclear weapons. Instead, the workers and the police responded to this threat to their livelihoods with physical brutality. Although the Swaffham demonstration failed in its ultimate aim, it succeeded in catching the public's attention. The demonstrations on 6, 7, and 20 December re-

---

25 *Peace News*, 12 Apr. 1957, p. 1; 10 May 1957, p. 1; 17 May 1957, pp. 1, 7.

26 *Peace News*, 3 Jan. 1958, p. 1.

27 *Peace News*, 1 Aug. 1958, p. 6. See also Michael Randle, "Non-violent Direct Action in the 1950s and 1960s," in *Campaigns for Peace*, ed. Taylor and Young, pp. 132–3.

28 For an extended discussion of the DAC, see Taylor, *Against the Bomb*, pp. 115–89. See also Taylor and Young, *Campaigns for Peace*, pp. 131–6; Taylor and Pritchard, *Protest Makers*, pp. 40–1, 75–7, 124–7.

29 The attitude of more traditional pacifists toward CND was ambivalent. Sybil Morrison, the chairperson of the PPU in 1958, opposed the formation of CND as an unnecessary organization that failed to address the core of the nuclear problem: Britain's failure to renounce war of any kind. See, e.g., Morrison's letter in *Peace News*, 3 Jan. 1958, p. 8; and Morrison's column in *Peace News*, 14 Feb. 1958, p. 8. At the Annual General Meeting of the PPU in April 1959, a majority rejected a motion instructing the PPU's National Council and officers to work with CND and the DAC. This decision aroused a great deal of controversy within the PPU. See the letters in *Peace News*, 8 May 1959, p. 5; 15 May, p. 5; 22 May, p. 5; 5 June, p. 7; 12 June, p. 5.

30 Philip Seed, "Three Ways to Revolution," *Peace News*, 19 May 1961, p. 9.

ceived widespread press, television, and radio coverage, as did the subsequent trial and imprisonment of over fifty of the protesters.[31]

The relationship between the DAC and the CND was never clearly defined. Both the contemporary press reports and subsequent political and historical analyses tended to place the direct actionists beneath the CND umbrella, although officially the DAC was a separate organization. CND's leadership condemned the use of illegal means of protest in a democratic society and sought, unsuccessfully, to distinguish the Campaign from the DAC.[32] The leadership could not block the appeal of direct action, however. At the grass roots, CNDers supported and often participated in DAC demonstrations.[33] As Christopher Driver explained, "From 1957 until 1961 . . . the DAC was the heart and soul, or the thorn in the flesh – according to taste – of CND."[34]

The DAC gave CND passion and creativity, best seen in the DAC creation that became the heart of CND's identity, the Aldermaston March. CND would never have had the impact it did on British society if it had stuck to the traditional mass meetings and petition drives. The DAC provided the methods it needed, and the moral fervor to master such methods. It also forced the Campaign to confront the thoroughgoing critique of British society embedded within the DAC's belief system. Direct actionists rejected parliamentary politics for a populist creed based on faith in the individual's ability to decide and to act and on a conviction that the Bomb resulted from the rise of a technocracy beyond the control of ordinary people. They accepted neither the reformist tactics of Labour nor the class analysis of the

31 *Peace News*, 28 Nov. 1958, p. 1; 12 Dec. 1958, pp. 9, 12; 19 Dec. 1958, p. 1; 26 Dec. 1958, p. 1; 2 Jan. 1959, p. 1; 9 Jan. 1959, p. 3. For a fictional account of the Swaffham demonstration, see Mervyn Jones, *Today the Struggle* (London: Quartet, 1978), pp. 199–212.

32 *CND Bulletin*, Dec. 1958, p. 3; Jan. 1959, p. 4. At the first National Conference of CND in the spring of 1959, the Executive treated the vote on a resolution concerning CND's support for direct action as a vote of confidence. As a result, CND remained officially opposed to the use of direct action. See *CND Bulletin*, Mar. 1959, p. 1. CND's Executive Committee Minutes bear witness to the often troublesome nature of the relationship between the Campaign's leadership and the DAC; see those of 28 Jan. 1958, 27 Feb. 1958, 18 Mar. 1958, 14 Apr. 1958, 6 May 1958, 1 June 1958, 29 June 1958, 1 Sept. 1958, 25 Sept. 1958, 15 Dec. 1958, 2 Jan. 1959, 6 Feb. 1959, 12 Apr. 1959, 5 Nov. 1960, 30 Apr. 1961 (Warwick, MSS 181).

33 E.g., demonstrators at the Swaffham missile base on 20 December named CND more than any other affiliation (*Peace News*, 9 Jan. 1959, p. 3). On 23 April 1960, the Southend CND, not the DAC, staged a vigil and sit-down at the Foulness Island Nuclear Weapons Research Establishment. As a result of this action, fifteen men and six women were sentenced to seven days' imprisonment (*Peace News*, 29 Apr. 1960, p. 1). In the summer of 1960, Pat Arrowsmith organized a summer campaign in Bristol aimed at bringing the DAC message to industrial workers. The campaign was officially backed by the Bristol CND (*Peace News*, 24 June 1960, p. 8).

34 Driver, *The Disarmers*, p. 35.

Marxists. They were individualists involved in a mass movement, individualists seeking to convert other individuals and thus to change the world.

The DAC was not, however, the only direct-action group in the nuclear disarmament campaign. In 1961, the DAC voluntarily disbanded and merged with a new anti-Bomb group, the Committee of 100.[35] Like the DAC, the Committee embraced direct action, including civil disobedience, as a means of change. The two groups were, however, quite different. The brainchild of Bertrand Russell, CND's president, the Committee of 100 at its beginnings sought not to persuade individuals but to force the government to adopt unilateralist policies by filling the British jails with protesters. It aimed at mass sit-downs in the heart of London. After a series of spectacular demonstrations in its first year of existence, the Committee entered a period of decline and disintegration. This period resulted in what Peter Cadogan, a prominent Committee member, recalled as the "great rethink,"[36] a process that led some Committee supporters to embrace a network of ideas that included a mistrust of expertise and bureaucracy, a growing suspicion of technology, a belief that vital rights and important traditions were being steadily eroded in contemporary Britain, and a realization that the solution to these woes lay in individual participation and community action, that small-scale efforts and ideas formed the basis of thoroughgoing change. This network of ideas linked segments of the later Committee of 100 not only to the earlier DAC but also to what would become the Green movement, explored in Part III, and to the romantic protest tradition.

The approach of the DAC and the later Committee of 100, but not their fundamental romanticism, contrasted with that of the third ingredient in the CND mixture: the New Left, which centered on a group of writers associated with the *New Reasoner* and the *Universities and Left Review* (merged in 1959 to form the *New Left Review*).[37] In the *New Reasoner*, E. P. Thompson, John Saville, and other ex–Communist Party members who had resigned from the party over the Soviet invasion of Hungary explored the "younger Marx" and the potential for socialist humanism in Britain. Their search for a socialism that affirmed individual choice and action and that was consonant with the traditions of British socialism led them to a concern with the question of socialist culture, and hence to links with the group around the *Universities and Left Review*. The ULR was begun at Oxford University; it expressed the horror of a number of socialist students with what they perceived as the

35 *Peace News*, 30 June 1961, p. 10. For the history of the Committee of 100, see Taylor, *Against the Bomb*, pp. 190–272.
36 Peter Cadogan, "From Civil Disobedience to Confrontation," in *Direct Action and Democratic Politics*, ed. Robert Benewick and Trevor Smith (London: Allen and Unwin, 1972), p. 169.
37 See Chapter 9.

cultural and political wasteland of postwar Britain. Unlike the Reasoners, the *ULR* group had not been shaped by the British Communist Party and was thus less interested in Marxist theory. The pivotal event for the *ULR* group was not Hungary but Suez. In the Suez debacle they perceived the bankruptcy of what became known as the "Establishment."

Although small in numbers, like the DAC, the New Left had a significant impact on CND. The New Left contributed to the CND mixture the crucial ingredients of creativity and intellectual leadership. The New Left consistently marched in the vanguard of CND, exploring difficult questions and proposing alternative policies. CND's call for British withdrawal from NATO and adoption of a stance of "positive neutralism" was to a very large degree the result of the New Left's influence. The New Left gave to CND the talents and energies of committed intellectuals, men and women engaged in sociological and historical research as part of their quest for a better Britain. It drew CND into important cultural currents: the search for an alternative socialist path, the emerging youth culture, and artistic and literary experimentation. CND became part of an ethos, part of a mood, and so more than a traditional political protest.

The National Committee for the Abolition of Nuclear Weapons Tests, the Direct Action Committee, and the New Left all helped shape CND, but the Campaign itself began with a group of well-known figures prominent in Britain's protesting establishment at the end of 1957. This leadership provided CND with the fourth essential ingredient of its success. These men and women brought prestige, experience in many protests and campaigns for reforms, and much-needed publicity. Without such leading lights, CND could not have attracted an international audience. Without such attention, it could not have attracted the number of supporters it did or sustained the interest of the nation.

The beginnings

Two key events aroused the influential founders of CND to action. The first event, the Reith Lectures of 1957, raised important questions about the assumptions governing NATO policies. George Kennan, former U.S. ambassador to the Soviet Union and one of the original architects of the containment policy that he now attacked, called for a rethinking of cold war positions.[38] He argued that nuclear weapons could not provide the basis of a constructive foreign policy and proposed the withdrawal of nuclear forces

---

38 The Reith Lectures were given annually over BBC Radio on six successive Sunday nights in November and December. Kennan's lectures were published as *Russia, the Atom Bomb and the West* (London: Oxford University Press, 1958).

from continental Europe. In essence, Kennan offered a new perspective on the cold war and the role of both NATO and nuclear weapons within it. He spoke at a pivotal time: On 18 December, just three days after Kennan's last lecture, NATO authorized the placement of tactical nuclear bombs in Western Europe.[39] His lectures received widespread publicity in both the print and the broadcast media. According to one opinion poll, 73 percent of those surveyed recognized Kennan's name by the time his six-part lecture series ended.[40] Although Kennan did not advocate total nuclear disarmament, his lectures caught the imagination of Britain's protest establishment and offered hope that alternative policies could be carried out.

A second important event in the official formation of CND was the publication of J. B. Priestley's "Britain and the Nuclear Bombs" in the *New Statesman* on 2 November 1957. Priestley's article, written in response to Aneurin Bevan's antiunilateralist speech at the Labour Party Conference of 1957 and frequently cited as the catalyst of CND's formation,[41] set forth many of the themes that were to dominate Campaign literature and speeches. Priestley argued that Britain's nuclear policy negated democratic politics and placed the crucial decisions beyond the grasp of ordinary citizens. Instead of "sensible men and women" controlling the direction of the world, "men now so conditioned by [the] atmosphere of power politics, intrigue, secrecy, insane invention, that they are more than half-barmy" stood at the top. Only "an immensely decisive gesture, a clear act of will," could break the spell. Not only would British unilateral nuclear disarmament break the spell of self-destruction and allow constructive policy-making, it would also reclaim an appropriate role for Britain. Britain had missed her great opportunity after World War II: "We ended the war high in the world's regard. We could have taken over its moral leadership, spoken and acted for what remained of its conscience; but we chose to act otherwise." By unilaterally renouncing nuclear weapons, Britain could seize again this role of moral leadership. Priestley, like many CNDers after him, viewed the Blitz as an inspirational time for the nation: "Alone, we defied Hitler; and alone we can defy this nuclear madness into which the spirit of Hitler seems to have passed, to poison the world." By unilaterally disarming, Britain would not only reclaim her leadership role, not only help bring peace in our time, but also revitalize Britain society.[42] Belief in the common sense and fundamental righteousness of "ordinary people," an appeal to morality, a vision of Britain as a leader of the smaller nations and as a mediator in the cold

---

39 Walter L. Hixson, *George F. Kennan – Cold War Iconoclast* (New York: Columbia University Press, 1989), p. 180.
40 Ibid. pp. 172–3, 176.   41 Taylor, *Against the Bomb*, p. 20.
42 "Britain and the Nuclear Bombs," *New Statesman*, 2 Nov. 1957, pp. 554–6. Priestley's article is reprinted in David Boulton, ed., *Voices from the Crowd: Against the H-Bomb* (London: Peter Owen, 1964).

war, a view of nuclear disarmament as the first step in reviving the soul and spirit of the British people – each of these themes of Priestley's would dominate CND.

Priestley's article struck a chord. At the end of 1957 a group of leading Left luminaries met at Kingsley Martin's flat in London to discuss forming a campaign against Britain's nuclear policy. Those in attendance included both Priestley and Kennan, as well as Bertrand Russell, the archeologist Jacquetta Hawkes, Professor P. M. S. Blackett, and Commander Sir Stephen King-Hall, whose newsletter advocated a national defense policy based on nonviolent resistance.[43] The group agreed on the need for an organization to fight nuclear weapons and in January 1958 officially created CND.[44] CND's first Executive, self-appointed, consisted of President Bertrand Russell, Chairman L. John Collins, Vice-Chairman Ritchie Calder, and James Cameron, Howard Davies, Michael Foot, Arthur Goss, Sheila Jones, Kingsley Martin, J. B. Priestley, and Joseph Rotblat. Peggy Duff served as secretary.[45] CND's new governing body exuded prestige. Of the nineteen members (seven more were co-opted during the first year), thirteen were in *Who's Who*, and ten were identified with the Labour Party.[46]

The combination of grass-roots protesters, direct actionists, New Leftists, and well-known leaders set CND apart from previous nuclear protests and gave it a potency and vitality in sharp contrast to the apathy engendered by

43 King-Hall published his theory of a nonnuclear national defense just before the first Aldermaston March in his *Defence in the Nuclear Age* (London: Gollancz, 1958).

44 CND Executive Committee Minutes, 21 Jan. 1958 (Warwick, MSS 181). A. J. P. Taylor gave his recollections of the founding meeting of CND twice in print – which is curious, because Taylor was not present at the first meeting. Taylor was not invited onto the CND Executive until 14 April 1958. See Taylor, "CND: The First Twenty-Five Years," *Observer Magazine*, 20 Feb. 1983, pp. 13–14; Taylor, *A Personal History* (New York: Atheneum, 1983), p. 226; CND Executive Committee Minutes, 14 Apr. 1958 (Warwick, MSS 181). See also L. John Collins, *Faith under Fire* (London: Leslie Frewin, 1966), pp. 303–6; Duff, *Left, Left, Left*, pp. 120–1; Jones, *Chances*, pp. 147–9; Bertrand Russell, *The Autobiography of Bertrand Russell, 1944–1969* (New York: Simon and Schuster, 1969), pp. 139–40.

45 CND Executive Committee Minutes, 28 Jan. 1958 (Warwick, MSS 181).

46 Driver, *The Disarmers*, pp. 42–4. Involvement in social activism and Labour politics characterized the founders of CND. Goss had been chairman and Jones the secretary of NCANWT. Collins was a canon and precentor at St. Paul's, the chairman of Christian Action, a member of the Fellowship of Reconciliation, and had been actively involved in the Campaign for the Abolition of Capital Punishment and the effort to raise funds for the South African Treason Trials Defense Fund. Calder was vice-president of the National Peace Council and a sponsor of the Labour Peace Fellowship. Davies served as the honorary treasurer of the United Nations Association. Duff had helped organize the Campaign for the Abolition of Capital Punishment and the Save Europe Now Campaign. Three on the Executive had been or would be Labour MPs: Ritchie Calder, Howard Davies, and Michael Foot. Five were connected to journalism: Cameron was a *News-Chronicle* columnist, Foot the editor of *Tribune*, Goss the proprietor of the *Hampstead and Highgate Express*, Martin the editor of the *New Statesman*, and Priestley a well-known author, broadcaster, and journalist (*Peace News*, 14 Feb. 1958, p. 3).

consensus politics and consumer affluence. In just a few years, the differences among these groups would cause the Campaign to disintegrate; until 1964, however, CND challenged British political life by offering a vision of the nation that resonated with sectors of the middle class and was rooted in the romantic tradition. In its call for participatory democracy, CND anticipated the central theme of the 1960s; the value system that shaped CND, however, looked backward to a time of greater community both among individuals and between humanity and its technological creations.

The challenge from Central Hall

CND's self-appointed leaders did not immediately second Priestley's call for immediate British unilateral nuclear disarmament. The Campaign's first policy statement challenged Britain to suspend its nuclear weapons tests, to halt the construction of missile bases on British territory, to stop patrol flights of nuclear-equipped airplanes, and to refuse to provide nuclear weapons to any country. These unilateral British actions, which did not include relinquishing the H-bomb, were intended to strengthen multilateral negotiations aimed at stopping the testing and proliferation of nuclear weapons. A less than succinct and soul-stirring statement, it was later described by CND secretary Peggy Duff as a "ghastly hotchpotch of English prose" that "might well have been accepted by Aneurin Bevan."[47] The policy of CND changed, however, and changed quickly.

The initial policy statement was issued for the first mass meeting of the Campaign, set for 17 February 1958 in Central Hall in London. This meeting transformed the Campaign's policy and outlined the pattern of protest for the next five years. The response to the first advertisements for the meeting, with Michael Foot, Stephen King-Hall, J. B. Priestley, Bertrand Russell, and A. J. P. Taylor as speakers and Collins as chairman, so exceeded expectations that five overflow halls were rented and extra speakers lined up. The speakers traveled from one packed hall to another as a kind of rotating roster. According to Duff, "The size of the response had its effect on the speakers. . . . One and all came out with a militant denunciation of nuclear weapons, and Britain's in particular."[48] Taylor recalled and Duff confirmed that Taylor received the most enthusiastic applause when he advised that pronuclear MPs be called "murderers" whenever they appeared in public:

---

47 Duff, *Left, Left, Left*, p. 123. Duff gives the text of the first policy statement in its entirety here. See also *Peace News*, 7 Feb. 1958, pp. 1, 12.
48 Duff, *Left, Left, Left*, p. 124. See also *Peace News*, 21 Feb. 1958, p. 1; 28 Feb. 1958, p. 4.

"From that moment, the campaign was unilateralist."[49] Clearly, the official policy statement had failed to meet the needs of an emotionally charged mass movement. The new policy statement called on Britain to "renounce unconditionally the use or production of nuclear weapons and refuse to allow their use by others in her defence," a clear call to unilateral nuclear disarmament, with the foundations set for CND's later demand for Britain's withdrawal from NATO.[50]

The Central Hall meeting not only made it clear that support existed in Britain for a unilateralist mass movement but also established that the Campaign was, above all, a movement of moral protest. Like Priestley's article, which had served as a catalyst, the speeches on 17 February focused on the immorality of Britain's nuclear deterrent. As Taylor pointed out so graphically with his condemnation of MPs as murderers, CND viewed a defense policy based on nuclear weapons as criminal. As one CNDer in attendance at the meeting later recalled, "Speaker after distinguished speaker hammered home the central purpose of the Campaign. . . . Britain must give up nuclear weapons to save her soul as well as her skin. The audience responded enthusiastically throughout the evening, but the loudest applause came in response to the appeals to morality and conscience."[51] Alex Comfort, for example, called the defense policy one of "civilian massacre" planned by "madmen." According to Comfort, nuclear weapons posed not only a physical threat to Britain but also a moral danger, the erosion of the very values nuclear weapons were charged with defending. He likened Britain's defense policy to "Hitler's gas chambers or Stalin's purges. . . . unworthy of sane human beings."[52]

Comfort had titled his speech "The People Must Take Over," a phrase indicative not only of his own anarchist beliefs but also of a second important theme in CND and at the Central Hall meeting. As had Priestley in his pivotal *New Statesman* article, Comfort dismissed both Britain's and the world's leaders as insane and called for leadership from ordinary people: "Much has been said about a summit conference. Sanity is always hardest to restore at the summit – the air there is rarefied. It seems to affect the brain.

49 Taylor, *A Personal History*, p. 228; Duff, *Left, Left, Left*, p. 124. See also Lomas, *Rhetoric of the British Peace Movement*, pp. 75–7.

50 See Duff, *Left, Left, Left*, p. 125, for the text of the second policy statement. For the controversy aroused by the first policy statement, see *Peace News*, 7 Feb. 1958, p. 1; 28 Feb., p. 4; 7 Mar., p. 8; 14 Mar., p. 1. See also the Executive Committee Minutes, 27 Feb. 1958 (Warwick, MSS 181).

51 George Clark, *Second Wind* (London: CND, 1963), p. 5. Clark, however, may have relied on the *Peace News* account of the Central Hall meeting. Clark's recollection used almost identical wording to the story in *Peace News*, 21 Feb. 1958, p. 1.

52 Comfort's speech is printed in Boulton, *Voices from the Crowd;* quotations from pp. 55, 56, 57.

We can reassert it at the base."[53] Although CND's leadership relied on influencing the influential to accomplish their aims, much of the Campaign's appeal and early success lay in its insistence that ordinary individuals counted, that common persons with common sense could change the world.

Not only could common individuals count but so could small nations in a world dominated by superpower rivalries, according to CND speakers in Central Hall and throughout the Campaign's history. Like Priestley, Comfort remembered "Britain's finest hour" in his call for a renewal of British greatness: "Let us make this country stand on the side of human decency and human sanity – alone if necessary. It has done so before. If it does so again I do not think we need fear the consequences."[54] Commander Sir Stephen King-Hall, too, pointed to Britain's role in World War II as part of his argument in favor of unilateral nuclear disarmament. King-Hall challenged the British government to say to the United States: "We are once again giving you a lead. We are bringing our thinking about war up to date, and we hope you will too."[55] This belief, that Britain could restore a moral balance to the world, was an integral part of CND from its very birth. At the press conference of 30 January announcing the new Campaign, Vice-Chairman Ritchie Calder said that CND wanted "to give Britain back her authority in the world." When a journalist asked, "A moral one, you mean?" Calder replied, "Yes."[56] The combination of viewing defense policy as a moral issue and of declaring that Britain still had a crucial role to play in world affairs was to give CND an enormous appeal to educated, left-leaning, middle-class men and women.

In its early years, because of a unique and short-lived combination of international and domestic crises, the movement to ban the Bomb seemed not completely quixotic, despite its unabashed summons to Britain to change the world. The meaning of CND and its direct-action allies lies not in their success or failure but in their effort to articulate a new version of an old protest. CND expressed a romantic rejection of the postwar world, but unlike Lewis and Tolkien, CNDers were optimists who trusted that the world could be made right. In order to change the world, CNDers believed the British had to change themselves. In the unbearably bright light of the nuclear age, they examined British culture and society and exposed the failures they perceived there.

53 Ibid., p. 59.   54 Ibid.   55 *Peace News*, 21 Feb. 1958, p. 2.
56 *Peace News*, 7 Feb. 1958, p. 11.

7

"Don't You Hear the H-Bomb's Thunder?"

CND originated as a single-issue campaign, an organization with only one aim: banning the Bomb. Like fallout, however, the Campaign inexorably drifted from its detonation center. In the end, CND discovered that the cry "Ban the Bomb" implied a larger critique of British culture and society. Try as CND might to stick to "the Bomb," the culture that had produced the Bomb kept intruding upon the conversation. Many CNDers found themselves at odds with this culture. Frightened by the loss of both Britain's and the individual's capacity to control events, many middle-class men and women turned to CND as a means of realizing their vision of a good society. Drawing on both the distant and the immediate past, this vision promised a world in which political and technological structures would rest on moral, rather than pragmatic, foundations. Like Tolkien's Shire and Lewis's Narnia, a Britain without the Bomb would be a world of cohesion and community.

The march toward human standards

The pivotal Aldermaston March became a ritualized form of this moral critique. It was an annual call to repentance and renewal, both a physical penance and a spiritual revival. The thousands winding their way through the English countryside in the springtime evoked such vital national myths as Chaucer's *Canterbury Tales*. One CNDer described the march as "a civilising mission, a march away from fear towards normality, towards human standards, towards the real people in the nursery rhyme whose houses are over the hill but not so far away that we will not get there by candlelight, whose hands are set to the plough and the making of things."[1] Without the march, CND would have been just another largely left-wing protest movement.

[1] From the diary of Denis Knight, secretary of Film and Television Committee for Nuclear Disarmament, later Christian CND member. Quoted in Christopher Driver, *The Disarmers: A Study in Protest* (London: Hodder and Staughton, 1964), p. 58.

With it, CND became not only a symbol of a certain moment but also a profound influence on subsequent postwar protests.

The success of the first Aldermaston March persuaded the CND Executive to abandon its misgivings about street protest and make it the key weapon in the CND arsenal. In the spring of 1958, however, the march belonged not to CND but to the DAC.[2] Because of its emphasis on symbolic actions designed to awaken individual responsibility, the DAC was particularly good at devising potent rituals of protest. Unlike the later marches organized by CND, this first march ran from London to Aldermaston, a physical expression of the DAC's belief that the decision to ban the Bomb had to be taken by those directly responsible for constructing it, rather than by the politicians in Westminster.[3] The DAC envisaged a small march of committed activists. The march, however, burst out of its creators' hands to light up the cultural landscape of postwar Britain. The committed Gandhians in the DAC found themselves joined by thousands for whom Gandhian techniques of nonviolence meant little but for whom "Ban the Bomb" meant the world. Despite horrible weather – the coldest Good Friday in forty-one years, the coldest Easter Saturday thus far in the twentieth century, the wettest Easter holiday since 1900 – participation in and publicity of the first Aldermaston March surpassed all expectations.[4] In numbers small by comparison to subsequent years but amazingly huge to participants and observers, the marchers testified that a new force was walking in Britain.[5]

What the march offered, first of all, was the experience of community. The march gathered up the diverse forces of CND and welded them into a cohesive movement. The original DAC organizers tried to prohibit the display of party or political banners because, according to Pat Arrowsmith, "we

2 The first Aldermaston March was organized by the Aldermaston March Committee of the DAC, but included non-DAC members such as Labour MP Frank Allaun. In addition to Allaun, the Aldermaston Committee included Pat Arrowsmith, Hugh Brock, Michael Randle, and Walter Wolfgang (*Peace News*, 7 Mar. 1958, p. 2; 14 Mar. 1958, p. 5; 31 May 1963, p. 10). For CND's participation, see CND Executive Committee Minutes, 28 Jan. 1958, p. 2; 18 Mar. 1958; 14 Apr. 1958; 2 Jan. 1959 (Warwick, MSS 181).

3 The reversal of the march was deliberate. Before the Aldermaston March of 1959, Canon Collins announced that the march would proceed to, rather than from, London "so that we will be marching to the center of political power" (*Peace News*, 6 Mar. 1959, p. 1).

4 *Peace News*, 11 Apr. 1958, p. 1.

5 See e.g., Alan Brien, "The Strange March," *Daily Mail*, 7 Apr. 1958, p. 4. The *Daily Mail* gave figures of 10,000 at the opening rally in London, 2,000 on the march, and 4,000 on the last day (5 and 8 Apr. 1958, p. 1). The *Christian World* put 10,000 at the opening rally, 4,000 marching the first day, 600 marching on Saturday, 3,000 on Monday, with a crowd of over 8,000 at Aldermaston (17 Apr. 1958, p. 2). *Peace News* reported that the number of marchers never fell below 540 and grew to over 1,000 on Sunday and over 4,000 on Monday (11 Apr. 1958, pp. 1, 8). See also the estimates given in n. 4 to introduction to Part II. For a fictional description of Aldermaston 1958, see Mervyn Jones, *Today the Struggle* (London: Quartet, 1976), pp. 149–62, 197–9.

want the march to represent one single united purpose."[6] Although they rescinded the order, and party and political banners became one of the colorful features of the Easter march, the sense of unity the DAC hoped for did exist, according to the testimony of marchers. One recalled "an exhilarating sense of co-operation with thousands of others for a common purpose."[7] Peggy Duff described the march as "a community for which no vows were required. All you had to do to belong was to step off the pavement and join it."[8] Not all marchers believed this community would accomplish its goals. One recalled twenty years later, "I do not really think that I actually believed that Britain would give up her Bomb, just because I and several thousand others took to the streets and the road to Aldermaston."[9] But many others believed that not only the size of the march but especially its community of purpose guaranteed its eventual success. According to A. J. P. Taylor, "As we marched along we really thought that we were bringing the good news from Ghent to Aix. And when we led this great procession into Trafalgar Square, we could not help feeling we were bound to win."[10]

The march not only became a community but also represented a call to return to a world of community spirit and human values. By marching, men and women acted out their need for such a world. An undefined era in the distant past, usually tinged with a medievalist light, appeared in CND literature as the symbol of a lost age of cultural and spiritual community. What Christopher Driver called "the sense of participation in a modern Canterbury Tale" characterized the experience of the march.[11] Participants frequently referred to it as a pilgrimage and thus rooted themselves in the past.[12]

Let Britain lead

On Easter Monday in 1958, the weary marchers slogging onto the field outside the Aldermaston research facility met a group of waiting supporters who had set up a loudspeaker from which they proclaimed, "Lift up your heads and be proud. The lead has been given to the English people. Britain must take up

---

6 Quoted by Llew Gardner, "The March of Our Time," *Tribune*, 28 Mar. 1958, p. 8.
7 John Minnion and Philip Bolsover, eds., *The CND Story: The First Twenty-Five Years of CND in the Words of the People Involved* (London: Allison and Busby, 1983), p. 16.
8 Peggy Duff, *Left, Left, Left: A Personal Account of Six Protest Campaigns, 1945–1965* (London: Allison and Busby, 1971), p. 132.
9 Ian Rodger, "Aldermaston Remembered," *Listener*, 6 Apr. 1978, p. 423.
10 A. J. P. Taylor, *A Personal History* (New York: Atheneum, 1983), p. 229.
11 Driver, *The Disarmers*, p. 58.
12 A poem written by a marcher made this connection explicit. See "Piers Plowman at Aldermaston," *Rushlight* (journal of the Christian CND) 1 (Feb. 1964): 20.

that lead in the world. 'England, arise, the long, long night is over.' "[13] In their march toward a better world, CNDers expressed their faith that Britain could once again possess international influence. As J. B. Priestley said, "We British no longer have any bright image of ourselves. And perhaps, among other things, we [in CND] went campaigning for that image."[14]

CND's vision of a better Britain reflected the nation's sense of unease after its obvious loss of world power after 1945. Neither CND nor its opposition could accept a diminished British role in the postwar world. David Marquand observed in 1960 that "the CND is to the left what the Suez expedition was to the right: the last brave hope of British nationalism." Both its opponents and CND itself clung to an outdated conception of Britain: "Even more than the right, members of the CND cannot imagine a world in which Britain's moral gestures would in fact count for very little; and if told that is the world they live in, they refuse to believe you."[15] Later, CNDers, admitted the truth of Marquand's argument. In 1983, A. J. P. Taylor reflected, "In my opinion we had a watertight case. . . . But we made one great mistake which ultimately doomed CND to futility. We thought that Great Britain was still a great power whose example would affect the rest of the world. Ironically we were the last Imperialists."[16]

The theme of "Britain as leader" dominated CND literature: "If you believe that Britain must lead, march with us, make your protest, 'do your bit.' For four days . . . let Britain lead the world!"[17] In response to the Labour Party debate over unilateralism at the Labour Party Conference in Scarborough in 1960, CND argued, "One of the least likable aspects of the controversy over nuclear disarmament . . . has been the constant underestimate of Britain's world influence, or the assumption that this influence depends on our adhering to the nuclear strategy."[18] CND preached that Britain retained its historical position as a world leader, a position threatened by its possession, rather than its renunciation, of nuclear weapons.

The conviction that Britain still played a leading role in the world was for

13 *Peace News*, 11 Apr. 1958, p. 8.   14 *New Statesman*, 19 May 1961, p. 786.
15 David Marquand, "England, the Bomb, the Marchers," *Commentary* 29 (May 1960): 384. See also David Marquand, "Bombs and Scapegoats," *Encounter*, Jan. 1961, pp. 43–8; David Marquand, "The Decline of CND," *Socialist Commentary*, 1965, pp. 25–6. For similar assertions regarding CND's imperialism, see Norman Birnbaum, "Great Britain: The Reactive Revolt," in *The Revolution in World Politics*, ed. Morton A. Kaplan (New York: Wiley, 1962), pp. 29–68; A. J. R. Groom, *British Thinking about Nuclear Weapons* (London: Frances Pinter, 1974), pp. 401–2; John Mander, *Great Britain or Little England?* (London: Secker and Warburg, 1963), chap. 5; Richard Taylor, *Against the Bomb: The British Peace Movement, 1958–1965* (Oxford: Clarendon Press, 1988), pp. 305–7; and Richard Taylor, "The Labour Party and CND," in *Campaign for Peace: British Peace Movements in the Twentieth Century*, ed. Richard Taylor and Nigel Young (Manchester: Manchester University Press, 1987), pp. 123–5.
16 A. J. P. Taylor, *A Personal History*, p. 227.   17 *Candis*, Feb. 1961, p. 1.
18 "Let Britain Lead," CND pamphlet, p. 10, BLPES/CND 10/1.

many CNDers borne out by CND itself. They viewed the Campaign as a unique creation, as the first movement in the postwar world to rebel against the nuclear order. In this assumption, CNDers were incorrect: The National Committee for a Sane Nuclear Policy (SANE) originated in the United States in 1957. SANE, however, was a traditional lobby organization. It did not, like CND, capture the imagination of the world.[19] The international publicity received by CND and the emergence of copycat movements throughout the world affirmed for CNDers their belief that they participated in a campaign that could change the course of history. The CND Executive proudly reported in 1962 that suggestions to abandon the Aldermaston March had met with protest from supporters in other countries who saw the march as the pivot point of the antinuclear movement.[20] CND literature and CNDers' writings are filled with references to CND's example and responsibility to the world. In an article in *Tribune*, for example, Arthur Greenwood, one of the Labour MPs who supported the Campaign, claimed that "all over the world peace-loving men and women are looking to us in Britain . . . as their only real hope that sanity will prevail. . . . If we fail we shall betray the future and we shall desert our friends."[21] Each year at Easter tributes and greetings poured into CND headquarters from around the world and reinforced this sense of leadership.

The surprising success of the Campaign before 1962 seemed to confirm CND's belief in the uniqueness and special moral qualities of Britain. CND had apparently restored to Britain its spiritual strength. Canon Collins recalled that "the Campaign symbol became as well known as the Union Jack and, if to some it was the mark of crankiness, to thousands the world over it became a sign of sanity and hope."[22] CNDers insisted CND had tapped into the best of Britain. In 1959, Mervyn Jones wrote that CND "has its finger on the pulse of Britain. It speaks for all that is best in the shrewd, sensible, humane, and decent people to which we belong."[23] Seventeen years later Jones described CND as "the kind of thing that happens recurrently in England. . . . CND was in the true English tradition."[24] The true English tradition, CNDers claimed, was characterized by a democratic spirit and an authority based on moral purpose.

Commander Sir Stephen King-Hall, in his proposal for the nonviolent defense of Britain, focused on the theme of British leadership. King-Hall,

---

19 For SANE, see Paul Boyer, "From Activism to Apathy: The American People and Nuclear Weapons, 1963–1980," *Journal of American History* 70/4 (Mar. 1984): 823.
20 Executive Committee Report on Easter Demonstrations 13.9.62, BLPES/CND 4/2/14.
21 Arthur Greenwood, "Why Do We Go On Marching?" *Tribune*, 29 Mar. 1963, p. 5.
22 L. John Collins, *Faith under Fire* (London: Leslie Frewin, 1966), p. 310.
23 Mervyn Jones, "Now Millions Must Make Up Their Minds," *Tribune*, 3 Apr. 1959, p. 6.
24 Mervyn Jones, "The Voice of an Era," in *Man of Christian Action: Canon John Collins, the Man and His Work*, ed. Ian Henderson (Guildford: Lutterworth Press, 1976), pp. 73–4.

who spoke frequently from CND's platforms, argued that the "British people have made notable contributions to the whole content of modern civilization. . . . They are indeed a considerable people whose general influence on human history during the past 500 years has been more significant than that of any other national group." Hence, "destiny has placed an enormous responsibility on the British people at this time." Like many other CND writers and speakers, King-Hall quoted Milton's warning that England must not forget her precedence in teaching other nations how to live.[25] King-Hall, and CND, argued that Britain's moral authority undergirded the efficacy of unilateral disarmament: Britain already had standing in the world. Other nations respected her and would follow her lead.

Moral leadership was advocated not only as a substitute for the political and economic role Britain had lost but also as part and parcel of the British tradition of benevolent reform. CND's banners, for example, pointed to Britain's leadership in ridding the world of the slave trade.[26] The nation, according to CND supporters, possessed unique endowments that would enable it to save humanity. In an argument that Southeast Asians, Irish Catholics, and both Israelis and Palestinians would find less than persuasive, Iris Murdoch insisted that "we are the people in the world who combine to the highest degree the ability to reflect and the ability to act impressively and effectively." Murdoch continued by pointing out the advantages of Britain's position in the postwar world: "We have a tradition of free and independent thinking, we can control our leaders democratically, and we are not paralysed by the responsibilities of supreme power." She concluded, "It is our duty in Great Britain to take the initiative; and if we fail it will be . . . one of our greatest moral failures as a nation."[27] In the CND vision, the true English tradition seemed to combine the virtues of a beneficent limited monarchy and the reforming, self-sacrificing civil servant. Traditions, duty, the sense of the British as a unique race – the CNDers were indeed in the British imperial line, if not, as A. J. P. Taylor thought, the very last imperialists.

Even after the Cuban missile crisis in 1962, with its clear implications that, with or without nuclear weapons, Britain had little influence on American decisions or actions, CND adhered to its belief that nuclear disarmament would provide Britain with a world role, that when "We Shall Ban the Atom Bombs" then "all the world shall live in peace."[28] Vice-Chairman Ritchie Calder summed up the CND argument in a "Memo to the Next Prime

25 Stephen King-Hall, *Defence in the Nuclear Age* (London: Gollancz, 1958), pp. 221–2; quotation from Milton on p. 223. See also King-Hall, *Power Politics in the Nuclear Age: A Policy for Britain* (London: Gollancz, 1962), p. 1.
26 "Marchers' Diary," *Sanity – the Aldermaston Daily*, Easter Saturday 1962, p. 4; Easter Sunday, p. 4.
27 Iris Murdoch, "Morality and the Bomb," in *Women Ask Why*, CND pamphlet, 1962.
28 *Candis*, Mar. 1963, p. 8.

Minister" on "our role in the modern world," first published in the *Sunday Mirror* in 1964. Calder began, "Do me a personal favour, Prime Minister, give me back my pride in my own country. Let me push out my chest, and say, 'I am British.' " Calder argued that during the week in 1962 when the world stood on the brink of nuclear war, during "the greatest crisis of all humanity, official Britain did not count."[29] Britain could count, Calder (and CND) argued, if it assumed its rightful role as moral leader.

CND deplored what it perceived to be Britain's status as a client state to the United States and campaigned to prove that their nation was "not just an appendage of the United States."[30] Certainly not all CNDers agreed with the anti-Americanism displayed by Bertrand Russell during the Cuban missile crisis,[31] nor did all CNDers share the contempt for NATO and Britain's "special relationship" with the United States that characterized both the old and the New Left. For example, many members of both the Executive and the Campaign's rank and file lamented the call by CND after 1960 for British withdrawal from NATO. The fear, however, that the special relationship relegated Britain to subordinate or even servile status permeated CND. CNDers compared Britain's position to that of the nation in the 1930s, when, they argued, weakness dictated a disastrous policy of appeasement.[32] Some of this suspicion about the special relationship, of course, resulted from simple chauvinism and leftist antagonism toward the United States. Yet, such suspicion rested as well on the conviction that American perceptions and policies in the cold war threatened the existence of the world and that Britain could show humanity a better way. In 1963 the CND weekly, *Sanity*, articulated what was a familiar argument in the Campaign after 1960: If Britain rid itself of its nuclear weapons and its allegiance to the nuclear-driven NATO, then "for the first time since 1945 Britain would have an

29 *Sanity*, 3 Oct. 1964, p. 2.
30 Alan Shuttleworth, "Tests: The Case for Unilateral Action," *Sanity*, Apr. 1963, p. 7.
31 Russell was a firm anticommunist; during the later 1950s and 1960s, however, he became convinced that the United States posed a greater threat to world peace than did the USSR. During the Cuban missile crisis, Russell argued that the U.S. protest against Soviet missiles in Cuba was illegitimate and described President Kennedy and his advisors as "American madmen." Russell sent telegrams to both Kennedy and Khrushchev. To the former, he wrote: "Your action desperate. Threat to human survival. No conceivable justification. . . . End this madness." Russell changed his tone in his telegram to Khrushchev: "I appeal to you not to be provoked by the unjustifiable action of the United States in Cuba" (Bertrand Russell, *Unarmed Victory* [London: Allen and Unwin, 1963], pp. 36, 39). In a speech given to the Midlands Region Youth CND on 15 April 1961, Russell described Kennedy and Macmillan as "much more wicked than Hitler. . . . the wickedest people that ever lived in the history of man" (Ronald Clark, *The Life of Bertrand Russell* [New York: Knopf, 1976], pp. 586–7; Clark quotes a tape recording of Russell's speech). In Russell's *Autobiography*, he amended his statement to read "Kennedy and Macmillan and others both in the East and in the West" (*The Autobiography of Bertrand Russell, 1944–1969* [New York: Simon and Schuster, 1969], p. 203).
32 Richard Gott, "25 Years After," *Sanity*, Sept. 1964, p. 3.

independent voice. For the first time she would be free to engage in the politics of peace, externally struggling to export disarmament and internally building the new society which disarmament would make possible."[33]

Events in America in the second half of the 1960s seemed to fulfill many of CND's early fears and predictions. In the eyes of those CNDers who remained in the Campaign after its heyday, the United States, morally blinded by its nuclear possessions and illusions of power, had stepped over the edge. Its violence and racism, and especially its rape of Vietnam, revealed a sick civilization and a possible future that Britain must at all costs avoid. The most important requirement for avoiding this future was the abandonment of nuclear weapons and alliances and the construction of an independent foreign policy, one based on Britain's "greatness in the moral sense."[34] "Has Britain a role?" CND asked in a broadsheet in 1973. It answered in much the same terms as it had fifteen years earlier when the Campaign began: By voluntarily withdrawing from the nuclear party, Britain would gain "real influence and prestige."[35]

The influential Britain would lead the way to a better world by joining the nonaligned and largely "undeveloped" nations both to mediate between the superpowers and to close the increasingly apparent and dangerous gap between the rich and poor nations of the world. According to this central idea of CND, described by Marquand as the " 'White Man's Burden' school of unilateralism,"[36] British nuclear disarmament would allow the nation to utilize its special relationship to the Commonwealth and thus to play a leading role in Third World development. Easter marchers in 1963 carried cans of dried milk, which were collected at the end and given to the War on Want as a symbol of "the marchers' desire to see the resources at present squandered on nuclear weapons redirected to the campaign to abolish hunger and poverty."[37] In part, such actions reflected a budding concern about the Third World as the potential spark for a nuclear world war. This theme would come to dominate CND in the years after 1965, when Vietnam claimed priority, but can be seen emerging in the years before.[38] Yet, such actions also re-

---

33 "Target Britain," *Sanity*, July 1963, p. 5.
34 The Bishop of Llandaff at a CND meeting in Central Hall, 1965; quoted in "Give Us Our Independence," *Sanity*, Oct. 1965, p. 3.
35 Broadsheet, p. 3; inserted in *Sanity*, Mar. 1973.
36 David Marquand, "Bombs and Scapegoats," *Encounter*, Jan. 1961, p. 43.
37 "Marchers Will Carry Food for Algeria," *Sanity*, Apr. 1963, p. 4.
38 E.g., CND criticized the Labour Party Conference for rejecting Stephen Yeo's amendment calling for the abolition of public schools on the grounds that the schools guaranteed the continued dominance of "the basic items of [the Establishment's] faith." These items included not only NATO and the Bomb but also the dangerous subjugation of the underdeveloped nations: "The last button may be pressed precisely because the hungry two-thirds are not going to stand it much longer" (*Focus*, 34, Labour Conference, Thursday, 3 Oct. 1963, p. 10, BLPES/CND 1/71/44).

flected CND's desire to restore British prestige. Olive Gibbs, CND chairman after 1964, told the Labour Party Conference that if a Labour government was to follow Pope Paul's plea to redirect money from arms to the relief of world poverty, "Britain as a nation, and democratic socialism as an ideal, would earn a respect and a prestige that the possession of nuclear weapons can never earn for us."[39] By abandoning the Bomb, making its scientists, technicians, and conventional armed forces available to the UN, and allying with the nonaligned nations, Britain would salvage its self-respect and save the world.

Reviving the wartime spirit

The bedrock of Britain's imperial past supplied CND with one kind of emotional nourishment, the topsoil of the British experience of World War II with another. The mythologizing of the war years, but most especially 1940, the period of the Battle of Britain and the Blitz, occurred in Britain almost immediately and was and remains crucial in fashioning Britain's postwar identity. The hard fact of British dependence on American aid disappeared beneath the tales of British pluck and ingenuity in the fight against Nazi Germany.[40] The memory of the days when "Britain stood alone" proved enduring in the postwar period. As it became increasingly clear that Britain had won the war but lost the postwar struggle for preeminence, the war days looked more and more appealing.

References to the war cropped up again and again in CND speeches and literature. *Tribune* compared the first Easter march to Dunkirk, "the turn of the tide."[41] Similarly, a CND pamphlet proclaimed in 1960 that the Campaign was "an upsurge of the spirit of the British people on a scale that recalls 'our finest hour' in 1940. . . . Now we seize another chance to win through the pressing dangers to a better future for ourselves and for mankind."[42] Commander Sir King-Hall also looked back to the Blitz for inspiration in his CND-related writing. The hope of restoring to ordinary individuals pride in Britain, a sense of purpose, and a feeling of community permeated his work. He viewed Britain's finest hour as a time when the British people knew whom they were fighting and what they were fighting for. The loss of this clarity had led to inaction and apathy, and so allowed the development of a defense policy

39 "CND's Chairman's Message to Labour," *Sanity*, Jan. 1965, p. 8.
40 For a controversial and provocative account of Britain's dependence on the United States and an indictment of Britain's productive efforts during the war, see Corelli Barnett, *The Pride and the Fall: The Dream and Illusion of Britain as a Great Nation* (New York: Free Press, 1986). This book was published in Britain as *The Audit of War*.
41 "All Out for the March!" *Tribune*, 4 Apr. 1958, p. 1.
42 "Flowing Tide," CND pamphlet, 1960, p. 1, BLPES/CND 10/1.

that King-Hall viewed as both ineffective and unethical. In his vision, even a Soviet-occupied Britain would be an improvement over the state of the nation in the late 1950s. A Soviet blockade would see "party politics forgotten and a renaissance of national purpose and unity far exceeding those stirring days . . . when Great Britain stood alone after Dunkirk."[43]

CND, its advocates argued, could awaken the spirit that had energized Britain in the 1940s and could propel the nation back onto center stage. The memory of the spirit of 1940 glowed steadily in the grayness of the postwar period. CNDers saw the Campaign as a way not only to restore Britain to its role as the world's savior but also to revive in Britain the spirit of community aroused by Hitler's bombs. Like the fuzzily medieval past, World War II and especially the time of the Blitz represented a lost age of fellowship and camaraderie. To the Tories' cry of "You Never Had It So Good," CNDers replied that Britain had it better in the Blitz.[44] To the common call, "I'm all right, Jack," CND responded that Britain had once been all right, and could be all right again, if the nation opted for nuclear disarmament.

Only you can make the choice

In order to convince people of the necessity and efficacy of moral action, CND endeavored to convince them of their responsibility for governmental actions. One of the best-known songs to emerge out of the Campaign accentuated this theme of individual responsibility:

> Don't you hear the H-Bomb's thunder
> Echo like the crack of doom?
> While they rend the skies asunder
> Fall-out makes the earth a tomb.
> Do you want your homes to tumble,
> Rise in smoke towards the sky?
> *Will you let your cities crumble,*
> *Will you see your children die?*
> CHORUS:Men and women, stand together.
> Do not heed the men of war
> Make your minds up now or never,
> Ban the bomb for evermore.
>
> Tell the leaders of the nations
> Make the whole wide world take heed

---

43 King-Hall, *Defence in the Nuclear Age*, p. 157. See also King-Hall, *Power Politics*, p. 119.
44 What Harold Macmillan actually said was, "Most of our people have never had it so good." His words, however, entered British contemporary mythology in the form indicated in the text.

Poison from the radiations
Strikes at every race and creed.
Must you put mankind in danger,
Murder folk in distant lands?
Will you bring death to a stranger,
Have his blood upon your hands?

Shall we lay the world in ruin?
Only you can make the choice.
Stop and think of what you're doing.
Join the march and raise your voice.
Time is short; we must be speedy.
We can see the hungry filled,
House the homeless, help the needy,
Shall we blast, or shall we build?[45]

The activity most associated with CND, the Aldermaston March, also drove home the message of individual responsibility. Direct action became a synonym for civil disobedience, but for many of the middle-class men and women marching at Eastertime, the experience of parading down public streets in the company of individuals they would normally avoid or ignore broke many of the social codes with which they had structured their lives. Thus, for them, even legal demonstrations and marches constituted "direct action." They became convinced that their efforts could and would make a difference, that the actions of committed individuals, joined together in a community of purpose, could save the world.

The draft for a CND leaflet entitled "Is It Any Use?" demonstrated this conviction. Written to instruct the door-to-door canvasser, the leaflet described a typical encounter: The CNDer meets the middle-aged woman who says she agrees with the Campaign, but that it is no use anyway. Against this argument, CND contended, first of all, "There are some things you have to do whether you are likely to succeed or not. . . . It is the millions who say: 'It is no use, nothing to do with me,' who are responsible for the fact that there are still nuclear weapons in the world." The abolition of the slave trade, the success of the Anti–Corn Law League, the achievement of Irish independence in 1921, and Britain's entry into World War II were held up as examples of the successes of ordinary men and women. These ordinary individuals had succeeded because they realized that the "government is not just a machine to order everyone about. . . . Sooner or later every government has to do what the people want if they want it hard enough." The nuclear disarmament of Britain would occur when ordinary individuals real-

---

45 Printed in David Widgery, ed., *The Left in Britain, 1958–1968* (Harmondsworth: Penguin, 1976), p. 99 (emphasis added). I am grateful to Mr. Widgery for permission to reprint this song.

ized their importance and began to act: "When we all get off the doorstep and into the Campaign, there won't be any Bombs."[46]

The theme, then, of what would later be called participatory democracy was central to CND's message. "Let the people decide" became a familiar cry throughout both Europe and the United States in the later 1960s.[47] CNDers recognized that the Bomb brought with it not only the danger of nuclear annihilation but also a threat to democratic decision making. No British citizen had voted to create the Bomb. The realities of nuclear strategy, of its dependency on the threat of instant retaliation, meant that no British elected body would control the use of the Bomb. Technology had seized control, CNDers argued; ordinary people must take it back. In 1959, *Peace News* urged participation in the Aldermaston March as a way of catching "something of the dynamic spirit of people bringing the foremost issues of our time into the field of consideration and action by the common man. On the road from Aldermaston we shall be marching from the tyranny of destruction to the beginnings of creative democracy."[48]

For CND's elite leadership, the concept of creative democracy was often difficult to handle. Many members of the Executive found the thing they had created rather frightening. Mervyn Jones recalled standing with Kingsley Martin and watching the columns form for the last day of the 1960 Aldermaston March. As he stared out at the thousands of people, Martin turned to Jones and asked, "What on earth are we going to do with all these people?"[49] When the political and intellectual luminaries gathered in Canon Collins's study in January of 1958 and declared *themselves* CND,[50] they saw the Campaign as a pressure group working through orthodox political channels and dependent on prestige as much as public support. The Executive decided the Campaign would have no individual members, no local committees, and no affiliated groups. It would avoid the structure, and the reality, of a democratic campaign.[51] At the first public rally at Central Hall in February, however, the Campaign took on a life of its own. It became a mass movement as local groups sprouted all across the country. Within a year the rank and file were pushing to democratize the Campaign. Such a push was bound to succeed, as it did at the

46 "Is It Any Use?" n.d., BLPES/CND 1/4.
47 See David Farber, *Chicago '68* (Chicago: University of Chicago Press, 1988), pp. 211–45; Todd Gitlin, *The Sixties: Years of Hope, Days of Rage* (New York: Bantam Books, 1987), pp. 102–3, 111–14, 134–5; Tom Hayden, *Reunion: A Memoir* (New York: Random House, 1988), pp. 73–102; and James Miller, *Democracy Is in the Streets: From Port Huron to the Siege of Chicago* (New York: Simon and Schuster, 1987), pp. 13–18, 141–54.
48 Editorial in *Peace News*, 6 Mar. 1959, p. 4.
49 Mervyn Jones, *Chances* (London: Verso, 1987), p. 161.
50 CND Executive Committee Minutes, 28 Jan. 1958 (Warwick, MSS 181).
51 CND Executive Committee Minutes, 13 Feb. 1958. See also the minutes for 6 Feb. 1959 (Warwick, MSS 181).

CND's first National Conference in 1959,[52] because it grew out of the same soil that nourished the protest against the Bomb: the belief that ordinary people, frightened by reports of strontium 90 in mothers' milk and horrified by the assumptions underlying the nuclear strategy of instant retaliation, should have a say in choosing the direction Britain traveled.

This emphasis on the right and responsibility of ordinary individuals to make the hard choices was a central tenet of the direct-action wing of the anti-Bomb movement. Direct action itself rested on the assumption that the choices and actions of individuals had political, social, and cosmic significance. To sit down in the mud outside the construction site of a rocket base could and would matter. Moreover, the theory of direct action argued that the institutions of representative democracy had failed, and that democratic decision making could occur only through direct participation. The DAC, then, based its demonstrations on the conviction that individuals such as the workers in the armaments plants and the soldiers behind the barbed wire of the bases could be persuaded to choose a different way and so help create a new world order. When the DAC merged with the newly created Committee of 100 in 1961, this idea accompanied its members into the new organization.

The Committee of 100 was a less cohesive body than the DAC. With its spectacular early successes, it quickly attracted a large group of supporters who held a variety of ideological and political convictions. Yet, within the confusing tangle of ideas and beliefs the theme of participatory democracy can be discerned, a theme that remained a constant in the Committee from its start until it disbanded in 1968. At its beginnings the Committee embodied the idea that the normal political procedures had failed, that voting and lobbying were no longer effective or adequate actions in the face of the nuclear threat. Instead, ordinary citizens were called to sit down on the pavement and confront the state directly and so participate actively in choosing the direction of Britain.

The period of mass action by the Committee ended abruptly in 1962, after which it entered its very different second phase. Yet, in this phase, even more so than in the first, the ideal of participatory democracy played an important role. According to Peter Cadogan, a member of the Committee from its beginnings, after 1962 the Committee moved in two very different directions.[53] One group within the Committee, less relevant to the argument here, aligned with the anarchist "Solidarity" group, rejected nonviolence, and sought to create a revolutionary movement of unilateralist militants and the

52 The first National Conference voted to expand the Executive to include one member from each regional council (*CND Bulletin*, Mar. 1959, p. 1).
53 Cadogan, "From Civil Disobedience to Confrontation," in *Direct Action and Democratic Politics*, ed. Robert Benewick and Trevor Smith (London: Allen and Unwin, 1972), pp. 169–70.

working class.[54] The second group headed down a different path. Retaining both its commitment to nonviolence and its rejection of parliamentary politics, it sought to create in Britain the structures of participatory democracy through the development of small-scale, decentralized organizations that addressed the needs of local communities. Committee members became involved in housing issues, protests against the Stansted site for the third London airport and traffic schemes, the construction of playgrounds, and the establishment of "Factories for Peace," an effort not only to solve the problem of unemployment in Wales and Glasgow but to develop new forms of productive and work relations.[55] While struggling to act in local contexts, they also saw themselves as part of a global community and so regarded events in Rhodesia, the Middle East, Biafra, Czechoslovakia, and Cyprus as their concern and responsibility.[56] In global as well as in local crises, this faction of the post-1962 Committee argued that the answer lay in removing the superpowers and the big bureaucracies, and instead allowing the people concerned to take control of their lives. In an argument that was to become common currency in the early Green movement, a Committee leaflet stated, "Massive aid schemes can't solve [poverty and hunger]. They upset the local pattern of life, breed corruption and often make matters worse as in India today. We need thousands of *small* schemes."[57] Only in small structures could individuals truly participate; only in small structures could democracy thrive. The Committee of 100 after 1962 had few members[58] and, like CND, after the mid-1960s had little political impact or influence. Nevertheless, the group was not insignificant. In its embrace of ideas that would later appear in E. F. Schumacher's "small is beautiful," it both foreshadowed the Green movement and echoed the romantic cultural critique.

---

54 See Taylor, *Against the Bomb*, pp. 249–54, for a discussion of Solidarity's ideology and its influence on the Committee of 100.

55 The Iona Community, discussed in Chapter 8, was also a sponsor of the Factories for Peace. The first factory was established in Glasgow in 1963 and called the Rowen (for Robert Owen) Engineering Company. Rowen manufactured electric storage heaters. The company was cooperatively owned; its profits (rarely seen) went toward various peace activities, including such community projects as the construction of a local playground. The company was also an attempt to establish a new form of industrial relations, with the distinction between management and worker less sharply drawn. A second Factory for Peace was established in South Wales shortly after the first. The Scottish factory remained in business until 1972. See NL/ML/Acc. 9084/Box 115, Box 121, Box 278; *Peace News*, 1 Feb. 1963, p. 7; *Peace News*, 13 Sept. 1963, p. 5; *Peace News*, 8 May 1964, p. 11; *Resistance*, 3, 5, 7 May 1965, p. 16; *Coracle* 47 (Dec. 1965): 19–22.

56 BLPES/CND 9/23–9/26.

57 "Our Candidate – Humanity," Committee of 100 leaflet, n.d., BLPES/CND 9/24/21.

58 In September 1963, the Committee *Bulletin* was sent to 100 subscribers; another 500 copies were distributed through the regional committees (Minutes of the National Committee, 21–22 Sept. 1963, BLPES/CND 9/23/1).

Against the postwar order

For many unilateralist campaigners, the Bomb represented not only the loss of the individual's control over the variables determining the course of his or her life but also Britain's misdirected social and cultural order. Looking back on the heyday of CND, Peggy Duff recalled, "While the bomb was its main occasion and theme, it was much more than that. It was a mass protest against the sort of society which had created the bomb, which permitted it to exist, which threatened to use it."[59] The content and aim of this protest varied enormously. For some CNDers, such as those drawn from the Labour Left, the Campaign was part of a protest against the right wing of the Labour Party and for a more truly socialist British foreign policy. Other CNDers joined the march in rejection not only of the right wing of the Labour Party but of Labour and party politics in general. Such CNDers might be apolitical and insistent that the fight against the Bomb constituted a single-issue campaign, or they might be revolutionaries who aimed for a new sort of politics entirely. For the Committee of 100, in particular after 1962, the protest against the Bomb could not be separated from the wider rejection of postwar British society. For most of the leadership in the early years, in contrast, the structures of Britain were fundamentally sound; the Bomb, however, threatened to undermine these structures and so destroy the society they believed in. These very different protesters found common ground in the belief that postwar Britain was less than it could and should be. The marches and the protests offered a way to articulate their disappointment and their dreams.

What sort of society would create the Bomb? Different Campaigners provided different answers but certain themes recur: the breakdown of community, the tyranny of expertise and bureaucracy, the loss of moral vision, the need for Britain to pursue an independent path. Some of these themes are found in the poetry of Adrian Mitchell, a longtime CND supporter. His "Song about Mary" placed the birth of Christ in contemporary Britain and narrated the results: Mary in an insane asylum, with Jesus safely bound with a mortgage to ensure he will grow up "meek and mild":

> For if Jesus came to Britain
> He would turn its dizzy head,
> You'd see him arrested at the next sit-down
> And he'd raise the poor from the dead.[60]

59 Duff, *Left, Left, Left*, p. 132.
60 I am grateful to Adrian Mitchell for permission to reprint this stanza of his poem. The lines first appeared as printed here in *Sanity*, Aug. 1963, p. 10. They are reprinted, in modified form, as part of the poem "The Liberal Christ Holds a Press Conference," in *Adrian Mitchell's Greatest Hits – The Top Forty* (Newcastle-upon-Tyne: Bloodaxe Books, 1991).

In Mitchell's poetry, the Bomb stood as the symbol of the explosion of community into alienated, hostile, and fragmented human beings who supported jingoistic, violent versions of "British greatness" such as Suez because they could no longer sustain a vision of Britain based on moral uprightness and a community of values.

For many CNDers, Britain walked the road to destruction because it had separated politics from morality. CND's simultaneous contempt for and hope in Labour lay in its view of the Labour Party as the embodiment of a movement toward a more moral, just, humane society, as not just another political party or an instrument to pile more material goods into working-class homes. Here the influence of both the Labour Left and the New Left on the Campaign was clear (see pp. 180–90). Despite the important differences between the two camps, both held to an essentially moral vision of Labour politics and both argued that Labour policies in the 1950s failed to fulfill this vision.

The question of politics provoked sharp divisions in the Campaign. Four main positions can be defined. First, for some Labour Leftists, CND's goals depended on and were subordinate to placing the Labour Party in office. The struggle over nuclear disarmament was for them part of the larger struggle to defeat the right wing of the Labour Party.[61] For some members of the Executive and many ordinary supporters, such a politically oriented vision of the Campaign failed to grasp its meaning and identity. For this second group, which included CNDers such as Canon Collins, the Campaign was a moral crusade rather than a battle in the political war. Nonetheless, Collins and many others perceived that the aims of this moral crusade could and would be achieved only through the actions of a Labour government. They believed that the British political system could be made to work and that unilateral disarmament would happen when CND captured the Labour Party and when the Labour Party won over the electorate. For the third group, the direct actionists in the DAC, such faith in the political system was misplaced. They advocated bypassing the party system entirely, as in the Voters' Veto campaign of 1959, which encouraged unilateralist voters to spoil their ballot papers and so register their rejection of Britain's political system. Such a scheme could scarcely appeal to Labour Party supporters, who, on the eve of yet another general election defeat, were being asked to countenance the loss of a large number of Labour votes.[62] The final position was that taken by most ordinary CNDers, those who were not actively involved in

61 See Frank Parkin, *Middle Class Radicalism: The Social Bases of the British Campaign for Nuclear Disarmament* (Manchester: Manchester University Press, 1968), pp. 110–39.

62 See Frank Allaun's letters to *Peace News*, 16 Jan. 1959, p. 5; 30 Jan. 1959, p. 1. See also Hugh Brock and Alan Lovell's defense of vote withholding: *Peace News*, 23 Jan. 1959, pp. 1, 8; 20 Feb. 1959, p. 2.

Labour politics, nor members of either the Executive or the DAC. To the rank and file, the political squabbles were a distraction from the key task of the Campaign. Although many were Labour voters, they were not interested in party politics and saw the Campaign, in fact, as an appealing alternative to such politics. These were the people who cried out in anger when a local Labour official at the first Aldermaston March stop in Reading in 1958 announced that the proceeds from the collection that had been taken there would be split between CND and the Labour Party. Because of the uproar, all the proceeds went to CND.[63]

What held these four main divisions together for the first three years of CND's existence was the moral protest that undergirded the Campaign. Although they disagreed on the means of achieving and on the purpose of unilateral nuclear disarmament, all four groups were convinced that Britain's nuclear policies were, quite simply, wrong. Labourite CNDers wished to cleanse the existing political system; the direct actionists and many in the rank and file thought such an aim wrongheaded and demanded instead the construction of a new political system. These opposing groups could not coexist in the same movement for long. Yet, running through their different political visions were certain shared themes, themes that indicated common romantic roots: the longing for a community in which the individual would have both place and power, the vision of Britain as uniquely endowed to save the world, and the beginnings of uneasiness about the political and social implications of advanced technology.

The problem of the technofix

During its height, CND failed to make the connections between its critique of British society and the role of technology in creating and sustaining such a society. Most CNDers seemed to believe that the Bomb represented a misdirection rather than a logical outcome of scientific and technological research. In other words, in their attitude toward science and technology, most CNDers were reformers rather than revolutionaries. They wanted to clean up rather than change this aspect of British life. Despite the Campaign's rejection of a world in which individuals possessed diminishing influence, and thus reaction against specialization and the postwar veneration of expertise, many CNDers were optimistic about the potential of science and technology to create a better world. Naive as it may seem, before the 1970s CNDers did not connect the production of nuclear energy to the construction of nuclear weapons. Therefore, a frequent CND argument was to insist

63 *News Chronicle*, 7 Apr. 1958.

that the tremendous potential of nuclear energy was being wasted on military applications. A CND exhibit, for example, was entitled "The Chance of Your Life" and contrasted photographs of the suffering victims of Hiroshima with depictions of the wonderland to be created in the "wasteland" of the world's deserts once nuclear power was freed for peaceful purposes.[64] CNDers also argued that the reduction of money spent on defense would allow for scientific development and the industrialization of the Third World.[65]

Slowly, however, CND began to question its earlier trust in technology. In 1963, for example, it rejected Wilson's equation of a technological paradise with a socialist Britain. CND accused the Labour Party statement *Labour and the Scientific Revolution* of presenting a limited vision that failed to confront the tough questions "of social values, of weariness with the life accepted as 'good' under toryism, of the relations between people and the survival of mankind."[66] All of education, not just scientific and technological education as the Labour Party statement assumed, had to be expanded if humanity was to control the "scientific revolution." The next year, CND continued on the same theme. Technology conferred tremendous power; humanity had to possess "the right kind of values from which they will make the right kind of choices." Morality, not technology, was the key: "Our moral growth, that is, the whole range of our culture which has to do with values, will in the long run determine our ability to create a peaceful world."[67] These early expressions of uneasiness about the implications of uncontrolled technology grew more pronounced in CND's later years.

Despite CND's confidence that it held the remedy to Britain's ills, CND failed either to ban the Bomb or to build the ideal Britain. Romantic protest, however, is not essentially concerned with the tallying of wins and losses. CND embodied a revulsion against the state of Britain and of Western society in the postwar period. CNDers pleaded with their nation to return to what they perceived to be its historical roots and spiritual past, and so reclaim its role as moral leader in the world. They sought an alternative society, one in which the individual mattered and yet true community existed and one in which moral and spiritual values triumphed. Although they did not make

---

64 *Peace News*, 9 Jan. 1959, p. 3.

65 See e.g., Mervyn Jones's *Freed from Fear* (London: CND Publications, 1961). Jones was not only an advocate of peaceful applications of nuclear power but also a believer in the "technofix." He wrote that the problems of the Third World would be easily solved by a massive influx of large-scale, capital-intensive, Westernized industrial development. See also Bertrand Russell and Michael Scott, *Act or Perish*, National Committee of 100 pamphlet [1961]. Russell and Scott argued that "a new Paradise" awaited if science and technology were directed toward industrial development rather than weapons construction.

66 *Focus* 32, p. 4, BLPES/CND 1/71/33.

67 *Focus*, CEWC Conference, "Education and Peace," 1964–5, 29 Dec. 1964, p. 6, BLPES/CND 1/71/80.

clear how such an alternative society could be achieved in a world increasingly shaped by technological demands, their vision of another, better Britain repeated many of the central elements of the romantic critique of industrial society.

8

Christians on the march

In CND's later years, particularly after 1962, economic and strategic arguments in favor of unilateral nuclear disarmament played an increasingly
important role in the Campaign's efforts to persuade the British public to
ban the Bomb; the moral argument, however, remained at the heart of
CND's protest. Although pragmatic arguments could be and were devised to
support CND's case, the belief that Britain would be better off without
nuclear weapons was exactly that, a belief, a faith commitment. Most
CNDers were forced onto the streets by a gut feeling that the Bomb was evil
and that this evil must be purged from their society. Such a protest would
seem to have provided the church with an important opportunity for leadership and witness. Organized Christianity, however, had little to do with
CND. Christian involvement in the Campaign was individual rather than
corporate. Many CNDers regarded the church's failure to act against the
Bomb as both evidence of its loss of vitality and a cause of the continuing
decline in Christian belief and practice in Britain. For these Christians,
CND served as an alternative source of community and commitment.

The church and the Bomb

Since A.D. 313, when Emperor Constantine embraced Christianity and declared it to be the official religion of the Roman Empire, the church has
struggled with the conflict between the citizen's obligations to the state and
the Christian's duty to be a peacemaker. In the fourth century, Augustine
formulated the concept of the just war, which was later codified by Thomas
Aquinas and subsequent medieval theologians. According to the just war
doctrine, Christians can and should fight in wars, provided that the war is
fought with the permission of the sovereign, for a just cause, and with the
intention of advancing good or avoiding evil. In addition, and most significant
for the nuclear debate, the war must be fought by proper means. It should
not result in the slaughter of noncombatants or in "disproportionate evils" to

either the combatants or the rest of the international community.[1] This final condition proved to be the point on which an increasing number of Christians, both lay and ordained, came to condemn a defense system based on the threat of annihilating total populations.

In the period immediately following the Hiroshima and Nagasaki explosions, however, few clerics realized that the Bomb had obliterated the just war doctrine. The British Council of Churches' Report of 1946, *The Era of Atomic Power*, reflected the confusion of Western Christians at the dawn of the nuclear age. The report began by recognizing that Hiroshima constituted "one of the great turning points in history" and that the church could not proceed "as though nothing revolutionary had happened."[2] It noted that the invention of the atomic bomb had profound political and social, as well as military, implications, and raised the question, "what can we hope and work for in the future if civilisation may at any moment be brought to a sudden end?"[3] Its answer to this question was less than clear. The council admitted that some of its members (no doubt future CND supporters Donald MacKinnon and George Bell, the bishop of Chichester) believed that "in no circumstances whatever should a Christian approve the use of the atomic bomb or similar weapons of wholesale slaughter." Other members, however, argued that Christians who took such a stand would weaken their government and their nation, and that a government which gave up the power to defend its people would be guilty of abandoning democratic principles.[4] The report refused to condemn the Japanese bombings, despite the condemnation issued by the Federal Council of Churches in the United States,[5] and in general accepted the validity of deterrence theory. Its writers also argued that if Britain renounced use of the atomic bomb, it would be renouncing its Great Power status, a renunciation explicitly deplored. The British Council of Churches' Report of 1946 did not accept for the church the prophetic role of condemning the new tools of technological slaughter and instead opted for general discussions and abstract principles that provided little practical guidance for Christians troubled by the nuclear age. Although hastily composed[6] and written at a time when the effects of atomic bombing, particularly the long-term consequences of radiation, re-

1 Martin Ceadel, *Pacifism in Britain, 1914–1945: The Defining of a Faith* (Oxford: Clarendon Press, 1980), p. 19; David Ormrod, "The Churches and the Nuclear Arms Race, 1945–85," in *Campaigns for Peace: British Peace Movements in the Twentieth Century*, ed. Richard Taylor and Nigel Young (New York: St. Martin's Press, 1987), p. 190.
2 British Council of Churches, *The Era of Atomic Power* (London: SCM Press, 1946), p. 7.
3 Ibid., p. 19.   4 Ibid., pp. 53–6, 40; quotation from p. 53.
5 See Federal Council of Churches of Christ in America, *Atomic Warfare and the Christian Faith: Report of the Commission on the Relation of the Church to the War in the Light of the Christian Faith* (New York, 1946).
6 The report was produced by a fifteen-man (no women) working party. The group met for discussion at three weekend meetings and submitted its completed report three months after the first meeting.

mained unknown, it set the pattern for future church responses to nuclear weapons.[7] In 1948 the Church of England Commission appointed to consider the British Council of Churches' Report confirmed the earlier report's acceptance of deterrence theory and even argued that "in certain circumstances defensive 'necessity' might justify [the] use [of nuclear weapons] against an unscrupulous aggressor."[8]

Such complacency was shattered by the advent of the hydrogen bomb, particularly after the *Lucky Dragon* accident in which fallout from an American nuclear test poisoned a Japanese fishing crew. Growing awareness of the dangers of radiation placed increasing pressure on the church to take a stand against nuclear weapons. According to Christopher Driver, the next few years witnessed a proliferation of reports issued by numerous church working and study groups, all part of the wider cultural quest to come to grips with the Bomb.[9] In 1955, the Federal Council of Free Churches, the British Council of Churches, and the World Council of Churches all passed resolutions that expressed growing unease with the Bomb. In 1957, the National Committee for the Abolition of Nuclear Weapons Tests (NCANWT) formed, with the support and participation of many Christians, including sponsors such as Bishop Bell, George MacLeod (founder of the Iona Community), and Donald Soper (a well-known pacifist and Methodist minister). The British H-bomb tests that same year ignited a storm of protest in the churches, including resolutions from both the British Council of Churches and the Federal Council of the Free Churches deploring the tests and a Methodist Church Conference declaration that the use of megaton nuclear weapons violated the conditions for a just war.[10] In 1959, the Methodist Church conference embraced unilateralism.[11]

The churches' position, however, was far from the clear and firm stance desired by CNDers. For example, the Methodist Church Conference Declaration of 1957 that condemned the concept of war fought with megaton nuclear weapons also argued that "the conditions of 'just warfare' could be

---

7 Christopher Driver and David Ormrod offer contrasting evaluations of the report. See Christopher Driver, *The Disarmers: A Study in Protest* (London: Hodder and Staughton, 1964), pp. 204–5; and Ormrod, "The Churches and the Nuclear Arms Race," pp. 195–6. See also William B. Johnston, "The Churches' Role in the Nuclear Debate," in *Ethics and Defence: Power and Responsibility in the Nuclear Age*, ed. Howard Davis (Oxford: Basil Blackwell, 1986), pp. 243–7.

8 Church of England Atomic Power Commission, *The Church and the Atom* (London: Church of England Assembly Press and Publications Board, 1948), pp. 52, 106; quotation from p. 111.

9 Driver, *The Disarmers*, p. 206.

10 Methodist Church, *Declarations of Conference on Social Questions* (London: Epworth Press, 1959), p. 44; Driver, *The Disarmers*, pp. 200–10; A. J. R. Groom, *British Thinking about Nuclear Weapons* (London: Frances Pinter, 1967), p. 201.

11 Driver, *The Disarmers*, p. 201.

observed" if the combatants agreed to "wage war with a limited range of graduated and controllable nuclear weapons."[12] That same year the General Assembly of the Church of Scotland condemned nuclear testing but defeated a motion demanding an immediate halt to the British tests, and the Unitarian and Free Church General Assembly narrowly defeated a motion calling for Britain to renounce nuclear weapons.[13] The British Council of Churches, in its Report of 1959, *Christians and Atomic War*, rejected unilateralism and, in an unfortunate phrase, suggested that Christians "live with the Bomb."[14] The report did, however, call on NATO to move away from its first-use policy and to shift toward greater reliance on conventional forces and argued that the nuclear age brought into doubt the wisdom of continuing traditional patterns of national sovereignty.[15] Two years later, in a pamphlet commissioned by the British Council of Churches to clarify and amplify the conclusions of *Christians and Atomic War*, Canon T. R. Milford argued that the policy of nuclear deterrence offered Christians the best hope of preventing war.[16]

By 1963, CND had made enough of an impact on the churches to force the British Council of Churches to charge its International Department to consider the question of whether Britain should retain its nuclear capability. The resulting document, *The British Nuclear Deterrent*, declared nuclear weapons to be "an offence to God and a denial of His purpose for man." It condemned the NATO doctrine of first use of nuclear weapons and concluded that no case could be made for independent nuclear action by Britain. The majority of the group that produced the report, however, remained far outside the CND camp: The report condemned British unilateral nuclear disarmament as "impracticable and even possibly disastrous" and presented its arguments not in moral or religious terms but rather in light of Britain's foreign relations and commitments.[17] The resulting resolution of the British Council of Churches condemned the British nuclear deterrent but not in unconditional terms and not in support of unilateralism.[18] Between 1957 and 1962, only about 12 percent of the Anglican bishops and suffragans could be considered unilateralist.[19] CND had failed to capture the churches. The

---

12 *Declarations of Conference*, p. 45.
13 Groom, *British Thinking about Nuclear Weapons*, pp. 328–9.
14 *The Church and the World: The Bulletin of the British Council of Churches*, June/July 1959, pp. 1–2; British Council of Churches, *The Search for Security: A Christian Appraisal* (London: SCM Press, 1973), pp. 9–12.
15 Ormrod, "The Churches and the Nuclear Arms Race," p. 200; John Vincent, *Christ in a Nuclear World* (Manchester: Crux Press, 1963), p. 100.
16 T. R. Milford, *The Valley of Decision* (London: British Council of Churches, 1961), p. 36.
17 British Council of Churches, *The British Nuclear Deterrent* (London: SCM Press, 1963); quotations from pp. 6, 28.
18 See British Council of Churches, *Search for Security*, p. 124.
19 Driver, *The Disarmers*, pp. 199–200.

Christian witness in and through the Campaign emerged and flourished outside institutional Christianity.

Christian CND

Christians were never in a majority in CND, but the percentage of Christian participants outweighed the percentage of churchgoers in the British population. No more than 15 to 20 percent of the population were churchgoers in 1970.[20] But in 1968, Frank Parkin's survey of former CNDers discovered 40 percent professing a Christian affiliation. Of these, 52 percent were Free Church members, 34 percent Anglicans, and 4 percent Roman Catholics.[21] In their later survey, Taylor and Pritchard found 43 percent of their sample "strongly agreed with the Christian belief system"; 41 percent actually identified themselves as practicing Christians during the period between 1958 and 1965.[22]

The Christian presence in the Campaign was further underlined by the formation in 1960 of a specifically Christian subgroup, Christian CND (CCND). CCND never grew very large,[23] but it had a flair for, as Peggy Duff recalled, "significant, small, thoughtful demonstrations."[24] The silent CCND demonstrators who converged on Chichester Cathedral in September 1963 and on Manchester Cathedral in April 1964, and especially the marchers who walked for three days from Southwark Cathedral to Canterbury every Whitsun for several years, saw themselves as consciously re-creating the pilgrim role.[25] The CCND report on the 1964 Whitsun pilgrimage began with the opening lines of the *Canterbury Tales* and throughout drew parallels between the marchers and medieval pilgrims.[26] Like the Old Testament servants of God, CCNDers utilized symbolic acts and public suffering, such as an all-night

20 In 1966, the percentages of the British population involved in the major denominations were as follows: Anglicans, 5.3% (Easter Day communicants in England and Wales, communicants in Scotland); Presbyterians, 3.6%; Methodists, 1.7%; Baptists, 0.7%; Congregationalists, 0.8%; Catholics, 9.2% (A. H. Halsey, ed., *Trends in British Society since 1900* [London: Macmillan, 1972], p. 449).

21 Frank Parkin, *Middle Class Radicalism: The Social Bases of the British Campaign for Nuclear Disarmament* (Manchester: Manchester University Press, 1968), pp. 27, 74–5.

22 Richard Taylor and Colin Pritchard, *The Protest Makers: The British Nuclear Disarmament Movement of 1958–1965, Twenty Years On* (Oxford: Pergamon Press, 1980), p. 28, p. 23.

23 Fourteen people were actively involved in 1962, and by 1967, the mailing list of *Rushlight*, the CCND journal, contained only 750 names.

24 Peggy Duff, *Left, Left, Left: A Personal Account of Six Protest Campaigns, 1945–1965* (London: Allison and Busby, 1971), p. 157.

25 Manchester pilgrimage: BLPES/CND 7/17/1; Chichester: BLPES/CND 1/26/7; Guildford: "Around the Campaign," *Sanity*, Aug. 1963, p. 3; Canterbury: BLPES/CND 7/17/5.

26 *Rushlight* 2 (Summer 1964): 19–23.

Christmas Eve prayer and fasting vigil on the steps of Wormwood Scrubs jail in support of imprisoned disarmament activists, in order to convey their message of a society on the wrong path and doomed to destruction if it refused to alter its course.[27] Members of the CCND viewed any talk of political considerations or compromise as a step off the moral path. For example, the defeat of a resolution introduced at the CND National Conference in 1963 that called for immediate unilateral disarmament by the United States was seen by the CCND as a "mess of nuclear pottage," a decision determined by practical, rather than moral or religious, principles.[28] In a pamphlet published and distributed by the group, Canon Stanley Evans went so far as to state that no Christian could support a nuclear defense policy and still lay claim to being a Christian.[29] To CCNDers, a policy based on the threat of annihilation was as much a sin as the actual act of annihilation, both contrary to the expressed will of God, and therefore to be fought by Christians.

CND saw its task as not only working for unilateral disarmament but also leading the church back to its rightful mission. Just as the larger Campaign argued that unilateralism would restore to Britain its leadership role, so CCND contended that a unilateralist church would find its pews filled once again. Most of the group's pilgrimages included some sort of appeal to the churches to take a stand against Britain's possession of nuclear weapons and thus to lead the people. The group deplored the conclusions of *The British Nuclear Deterrent*, the British Council of Churches report that gave qualified approval to deterrent theory on strategic and military grounds. The church, according to CCND, must act as a spiritual prophet and moral leader, not as a political follower.[30] The church's failure to lead in this crucial area accentuated the irrelevance of Christianity in postwar society and diminished the numbers in the sanctuaries on Sunday. Only a clear and strong call from the church for nuclear disarmament would, CCND argued, restore the church to its proper role.[31]

27 London Region CCND circular, 1962, BLPES/CND 7/17/8.
28 "Toleration Point," *Rushlight* 1 (Feb. 1964): 17–18.
29 Canon Stanley Evans, *The Nuclear Deterrent and the Christian Conscience* (London: CND, 1962?), Christian CND pamphlet, p. 2.
30 Canon Stanley Evans, "Christian CND Reply to Churches Report," *Sanity*, Jan. 1964, p. 2.
31 Frank Parkin has argued that the main agenda of the clerics in CND was not nuclear disarmament but the revival of Christianity. According to Parkin, to Christian CNDers who felt that Christianity as practiced in postwar Britain was killing the true Christian faith, CND was the perfect vehicle for church revival: "Here was an issue which raised problems vital to the Christian conscience, which could be argued in moral terms, and which was acknowledged to be one of the most serious facing mankind. If the church was to seize the initiative and place itself at the head of the growing volume of protest, it would infuse new dynamism into religious witness and provide a dramatic opportunity to

The complexities of resolving the nuclear dilemma and the church's struggle for relevance in a secular world did not trouble CCND; the group believed that the impossible became possible if the individual, and the church, dared to act on faith. A series of CCND pamphlets argued that fundamental transformation depended on the actions of each individual Christian. CCND emphasized the Christian's complicity in governmental actions and the sin of not acting on one's beliefs. In the CCND vision, human will and human faith could break the political, ideological, and technological deadlock that imprisoned the British people.

CCND looked at reality and found it wanting, in need of spiritual and moral regeneration. To effect this regeneration, it sought to widen the field of action and influence for the ordinary individual. Like Christ, CCND contended, the Christian must perform the impossible and so save the world. At the same time, it worked to rebuild the sense and reality of community missing from an industrial and secular society. Both marches and the worship services, rooted in their symbolism to an age of faith now long gone, served as reminders of and perhaps even temporary reconstructions of a world of community. CCND, like the wider Campaign, was more than a protest against Britain's defense system; it was at its heart a romantic protest against the shape and structure of British society.

Religious faith on top

CCND was also, however, a very small and relatively unknown group. The participation and leadership of public figures proved more significant in establishing the religious tone of the Campaign. Prominent religious activists often appeared on CND platforms; as part of the constellation of leftist luminaries, they helped to draw the public's attention and so establish the Campaign as a cultural phenomenon. As subsequent sections of this chapter show, the involvement of men such as L. John Collins (canon of St. Paul's), Richard Acland (the founder of the Commonwealth Party), Victor Gollancz (the publisher and one of the founders of the Left Book Club of the 1930s), and the Reverend George MacLeod (leader of the Iona Community) did not surprise too many people. They were part of the "Protesting Establishment," the type of men the British middle classes expected to see on platforms espousing radical social causes.

The uniqueness and power of CND, however, stemmed from the participation of ordinary people, the sort of people who not only never appeared on plat-

show the relevance of Christian values to contemporary problems" (*Middle Class Radicalism*, pp. 65–6).

forms but also rarely attended meetings. Moreover, a dominant issue in CND was the conflict that quickly arose between these ordinary people and the leadership. Many CNDers, particularly the youth, who joined the Easter marches by the thousands, believed CND's leaders to be tainted by their close alliance with the Labour Party and by their trust in the means and ends of orthodox party politics. In an early manifestation of the generational conflict characteristic of the social relations of the 1960s, young CNDers often spoke of their older leaders with contempt. Yet, despite the gap that existed between the leadership and the rank and file, many of the ideas articulated by the "big names" harmonized in their fundamentals with those acted out by the marchers.

The figure who represented both the religious side of CND and the Protesting Establishment to the average British observer was Canon L. John Collins, CND's chairman between 1958 and 1964. Collins used his position as canon of St. Paul's to devote himself to the causes that consumed his life: the leadership of Christian Action, a social-action group that Collins formed after World War II; the abolition of capital punishment; the fight against South African apartheid; and the unilateral disarmament of Britain.[32] For Collins, these issues fitted into his conception of what a Christian is and what a Christian ought to do. Collins saw the Incarnation as the center of the Christian belief system and argued that the Incarnate Christ had shattered the boundaries separating the physical and spiritual worlds. Addressing humanity's physical needs or working to prevent its physical destruction was to perform a spiritual deed. "Christian action" extended far beyond traditionally "religious" realms because in a religion founded on the Incarnation of Christ, on the interweaving of temporal flesh and eternal spirit, "you cannot demarcate what is spiritual and what is material, what is religious and what is secular." Hence, Collins argued, the Christian had to act: "I agree with Berdyaev that 'Bread for myself is a material thing; but bread for my neighbour is a spiritual thing.' "[33]

For Collins, the spiritual act of providing bread for his neighbor meant political activism, which, in the British context, meant participation in the politics of the Labour Party. As was suitable for a Labour Party supporter, Collins's politics were both anticapitalistic and anti-Marxist. By glorifying "competition, self-interest, prestige and privilege," Collins argued, capitalism worked to negate God's purposes on earth.[34] In much the same way, however, Marxism denied "a proper place to the spiritual dimension of life."[35] Rooted in William Morris rather than in Karl Marx, in the Methodist chapels rather than in *Das Kapital*, the Labour Party offered a vision of

32 See Ian Henderson, ed., *Man of Christian Action: Canon John Collins – The Man and His Work* (Guildford: Lutterworth Press, 1976).
33 L. John Collins, *Faith under Fire* (London: Leslie Frewin, 1966), pp. 129–30.
34 Ibid., pp. 169–71; quotation on p. 169.   35 Ibid., p. 136.

Britain that valued community over competition and self-interest, promised justice and equality rather than prestige and privilege, and asserted the need for spiritual as well as material satisfaction. Not surprisingly, Collins always viewed CND through Labour-tinted spectacles. In Collins's eyes, CND's demand for unilateral disarmament was politically expedient as well as morally right. He believed from the start that the Labour Party could and should be pressured into advocating unilateralism and that antiparliamentary activities like civil disobedience reduced the political expediency of CND's goal and so threatened its realization.[36]

In part because of his stand against civil disobedience, Collins became the leader most often vilified by the rank and file. This vilification was also a response to Collins's position as chairman and his faith in negotiation and compromise, a faith that could be and often was misinterpreted as a lack of conviction. Although much of the ridicule and many of the reproaches were undeserved, Collins's inbred respect for the power of influence and the efficacy of elite action inevitably set him against many of the Campaign's supporters, who saw CND as a rejection of elitist decision making.

Yet, Collins's fundamental vision of the Campaign harmonized with that of many CNDers. In 1966, Collins recalled the immediate post–World War II period as an era in which "as a nation we still had something, though maybe a little tarnished, of what J B Priestley had called 'a bright image of ourselves.' " That image had been lost, and the nation had disintegrated into "selfish and sectional interests."[37] A society that was truly a community, that respected other societies as fellow members of the universal community, and that accorded each individual the honor due to an eternal being would not be tempted to commit the sin of annihilating the human race. Collins viewed CND as a protest not only against nuclear weapons but also against the self-oriented, self-divided, materialist mass society that had produced these weapons and could even advocate their use against other societies.

Richard Acland: restoring the common wealth

The sight of Canon Collins heading the march from Aldermaston served as the most obvious symbol of the religious impulse behind CND, an impulse reinforced by both the residual Christian character of the British middle class and the use of speakers such as Sir Richard Acland. Born to a high social position, Acland became a Christian socialist given to courageous yet

---

36 Ibid., pp. 326–37. Collins's disagreement with Bertrand Russell over the founding of the Committee of 100 was both intense and public. See Richard Taylor, *Against the Bomb: The British Peace Movement, 1958–1965* (Oxford: Clarendon Press, 1988), pp. 62–9, 73–6.
37 *Faith under Fire*, p. 132.

quixotic gestures that bore witness to his faith in individual action. His writings testify that this individualism was linked to a longing for community and a deep, although eccentric, love for Britain. These partially romantic impulses led him naturally to CND. He became a member of CND's Executive in 1958[38] and a speaker on its platforms.

Acland is perhaps best known as the founder of the Common Wealth Party. Born in 1906 to a landed family, Acland was educated at Rugby and Balliol and in 1935 entered Parliament as Liberal member for North Devon. The following year Acland converted to socialism. The Labour Party was the natural political home for Acland but with the onset of World War II came the collapse of party politics. Convinced of the need for a genuine Opposition, even in wartime, Acland founded the Common Wealth Party. Although the Common Wealth Party dwindled to insignificance when the war ended and party politics resumed, it was intended to be more than a temporary stand-in for Labour. According to Angus Calder, the party "represented the refined essence of 'Beveridgism' – the revolutionary zeal, the millenarian dream, the unselfishness."[39] It attracted future CNDers such as J. B. Priestley and George MacLeod.[40] Common Wealth's members believed that the capitalist era was over and that a truly socialist Britain could be constructed from the bombed-out results of the war. Although the high hopes and the vision of a New Britain that it embodied were widespread in British society, the Common Wealth Party never gained more than 15,000 members. Foreshadowing CND, it drew these members from the middle classes, in particular from those in the professions.[41]

Common Wealth foundered after the war ended, and Acland became a Labour MP. Three years before CND formed, Acland resigned his parliamentary seat to protest against Britain's nuclear policies and to fight a by-election on the issue of nuclear defense. No by-election occurred, however, because of the call for a general election. Unable to campaign solely on a platform of nuclear disarmament, Acland was defeated.[42] He then became a teacher of religious education.

Acland's political beliefs were inextricably linked to his religious commitment. In 1940, he underwent a religious experience, which he described

38 He was asked to join in July 1958. See Executive Committee Minutes, 24 July 1958 (Warwick, MSS 181).
39 Angus Calder, *The People's War* (London: Cape, 1969), p. 547.
40 Angus Calder, "The Common Wealth Party, 1942–1945" (Ph.D. thesis, Sussex University, 1968), p. 215.
41 Calder, *The People's War*, pp. 548–9. See also William Harrington and Peter Young, *The 1945 Revolution* (London: Davis and Poynter, 1978), pp. 94–6, 131–3.
42 For Acland's speech announcing his decision to resign, see *Peace News*, 18 Mar. 1955, p. 1. *Peace News* followed Acland's unsuccessful campaign very closely. See the issues for 25 Mar. 1955, p. 1; 15 Apr. 1955, p. 1; 22 Apr. 1955, p. 8; 29 Apr. 1955, p. 1; 3 June 1955, p. 1; 10 June 1955, p. 1.

almost thirty years later: "The part which is incommunicable is that through such an event Someone/Something from outside has 'said': Now, as never before, you have been touched by the Truth. And it is impossible to doubt it."[43] This fundamental experience both undergirded Acland's conviction that spiritual reality transcended the material world and provided the base for his politics. Acland argued throughout his political career that socialism's strength lay in its moral core rather than in its appeal to economic self-interest. In his view, the tyranny of economics, rooted in twentieth-century materialist philosophy and its resulting moral vacuum, had weakened the Labour Party at its very center.[44]

Like C. S. Lewis, who believed that every man and woman longed for God, Acland saw "an inner core of our being which lives now and eternally towards harmony and satisfaction or towards loneliness and distress according as our lives are or are not bound up into the purposes of God."[45] He argued that individuals must cultivate "an alert open-mindedness to the Living Authority at the heart of the universe, and a determination to be used in a quest for truth."[46] He also argued that both psychology and the eternal truths of the greater religions threw into doubt the twentieth-century faith in science. Reason, according to Acland, was adequate for scientific and material progress, but not spiritual or moral. Acland believed that humanity could at least partially touch Truth, which itself was unchanging, but, unlike Lewis, he held that in order to enable fallible humanity to comprehend this unchanging Truth, organized religion, particularly in its presentation of the Christian truth, had to adapt or evolve.[47]

Acland founded his opposition to Britain's nuclear defense, like his socialism, on religious principles: No Christian could fail to resist a weapon designed to slaughter millions indiscriminately. CND was, he believed, "the central and immediate pressure-point for a movement of the spirit."[48] Such a movement of the spirit could spark the revival of British society. Acland painted a utopian future in which Britain would lead the world out of the deadlock of the cold war. Without nuclear weapons Britain would open up its scientific research and industry to both East and West. These dramatic

43 Acland, "Sleepwalking in the Desert," in *Journeys in Belief*, ed. Bernard Dixon (London: Allen and Unwin, 1968), p. 18.
44 Acland, *Public Speaking* (London: Gollancz, 1946), pt. 2.
45 Acland, *Nothing Left to Believe?* (London, Longmans, Green and Co., 1949), p. xiv.
46 Acland, *Why So Angry?* (London: Gollancz, 1958), p. 174. Acland discusses E. F. Schumacher on pp. 89–92 of this work.
47 Acland, *We Teach Them Wrong: Religion and the Young* (London: Gollancz, 1963), pp. 29–30. In his belief Acland was profoundly influenced by Teilhard de Chardin and by John Robinson, the author of the controversial *Honest to God*. See "Sleepwalking in the Desert," pp. 19–26.
48 Acland, *Waging Peace . . . The Positive Policy We Could Pursue If We Gave Up the Hydrogen Bomb* (London: Frederick Miller, 1958), p. 30.

actions would break through the cold war barriers by convincing the USSR of British good faith and allowing greater opportunity for Soviet moderates to come into positions of influence. It would also strengthen American radicalism and so increase the points of agreement between East and West.

In this new world liberated from cold war constraints, Britain would serve as the leader of an international world police force. The British would "put Mr. Krushchev in a quandary" by dropping "international teams of walkie-talkie parachutists into trouble spots to tell the world who was lying against whom." More important, "staunch citizens stolidly sitting behind their *Daily Telegraph*s as they ride to work on the 8.20. . . . would get a real thrill out of it; it would make it easier for them to put their chins up and feel proud of dear old Britain."[49] By claiming such a new world role, Britain would capture international imagination and respect, and the now-apathetic British citizen would be renewed.

In the most powerful and least quixotic part of his argument, Acland predicted that the developing nations would find communism appealing if their very real problems were not met and that these problems could not be met as long as limited resources were directed toward building nuclear arsenals. Acland insisted not only that world poverty was the problem of all humanity but, in an argument that was to grow increasingly common over the next decades but was quite prescient for 1958, that the answer was not simply advanced, large-scale technology. Peace would not come by creating mini-Americas across Africa and South America but rather by incorporating the new nations as full and independent nations into the international community. Acland, like many later developmental economists, environmentalists, and Green activists, noted the importance of working through and retaining as far as possible the corporate and religious aspects of traditional cultures, as well as fostering independent and self-sustaining local initiatives.[50]

As his problem and predictions for the Third World revealed, Acland placed a high value on community. His critique of British society rested on the belief that community had disappeared from post–World War II Britain and that the nation's social, political, and cultural life was decaying as a result. Like many CNDers, Acland believed that during the war ordinary individuals had regarded themselves as important participants in a fight for a just and humane society. Without this sense of purpose and participation, he argued, Britain was doomed to follow the path of decline marked out by Spain and Portugal in the seventeenth and eighteenth centuries.[51] Acland hoped that the Campaign would revive a spirit of community in Britain. CND could burst through the apathy that clouded the island and make

49 Ibid., p. 97   50 Ibid., chap. 10.
51 Acland, *Curriculum or Life?* (London: Gollancz, 1966), p. 23.

citizens care, as they had in 1940, about Britain's place in the world. In Acland's vision, individuals must be reconnected to their community so that they could recognize their role in saving the earth. Acland's rejection of the Bomb was part of a multifaceted, often eccentric, but quintessentially British and fundamentally romantic protest against contemporary society. He wished to restore Britain's moral vitality by reintegrating the individual and the community and by restoring the nation to its spiritual and historic roots.

Victor Gollancz: the Judeo-Christian romantic

The presence of Acland, as well as Collins, on CND's Executive came as no surprise to anyone familiar with British politics. More surprising, however, was the absence of Victor Gollancz. Gollancz, a good friend and important influence on both Collins and Acland, was a seasoned protester. He had led the Save Europe Now campaign immediately after World War II in an effort to pressure the British government to abandon any attempt to punish Germany and had also helped to shape the campaign to abolish capital punishment in Britain. Moreover, like Collins and Acland, Gollancz was a socialist who defined his political convictions in religious terms. "Efficiency" stood before him as a false idol; socialism did not deal primarily with economics. Rather, it was "morally right," "the light of the grail on the marsh," a "longing for the City of God."[52]

CND fitted very smoothly into both Gollancz's career of protest and his values. Yet, the relationship between Gollancz and the Campaign was far from smooth. By the time CND formed, Gollancz had resolved his on-again, off-again affair with pacifism by adopting an absolutist pacifist position, one that contrasted sharply with CND's carefully nonpacifist policy. Although Gollancz was insulted by his exclusion from CND's Executive,[53] he accepted the invitation to be a Campaign sponsor.[54] In demand as a CND speaker, he participated in a number of CND rallies and meetings, but his insistence that an attendance of at least 500 listeners be guaranteed caused some problems.[55] *The Devil's Repertoire*, his case against Britain's nuclear deterrent, was

---

52 Gollancz, *My Dear Timothy: An Autobiographical Letter to His Grandson* (London: Gollancz, 1952), pp. 324, 301, 387.

53 Ruth Dudley Edwards, *Victor Gollancz: A Biography* (London: Victor Gollancz, 1987), pp. 652–3. CND's leadership endeavored to keep the Campaign from being tarred with the pacifist brush in order to attract as many supporters as possible.

54 Warwick, MSS 157/3/ND/1/66, 70. Gollancz turned down his nomination to the CND National Council and was unable to attend the European Congress at Frankfurt as a CND delegate in 1958 (Warwick, MSS 157/3/ND/1/108, 109, 232).

55 Warwick, MSS 157/3/ND/1/76, 97, 116, 118, 120, 130, 134, 143, 145, 147, 150–2, 176, 180, 182, 187, 220, 241, 275, 281, 291, 295.

sold by local CND groups and so identified Gollancz with the Campaign, at least to the ordinary reader unfamiliar with the personal and ideological conflicts in the top ranks of CND.[56]

Like Collins, Gollancz was to a large degree on the wrong side of the generation gap that broke open in the Campaign. His biographer Ruth Edwards notes that he was often dismissed by young CNDers as one of the "old woolies," who were charged with sapping the Campaign's dynamism and reducing its effectiveness.[57] According to Edwards, it was Gollancz's moral argument that these young Campaigners found most offensive. The moral argument, however, permeated CND. Although there were young CNDers calling for more closely reasoned arguments based on economic, strategic, and political grounds, there were others, young and old, who found the moral arguments not only compelling but a sufficient basis for action. Gollancz's age, as well as his identification with an old leftism seemingly discredited by both its political powerlessness and its moral ambivalence, placed him at odds with the new generation of Campaigners mobilized by the Bomb. His own less-than-temperate personality further guaranteed that he played a peripheral role in CND. Yet, in his protest against the Bomb, Gollancz revealed a romantic outlook consonant with the attitudes and actions characteristic of much of the Campaign.

A longing to transcend the material world, a sense of connection to divinity, and the quest for community were recurring themes, and bear witness to the intertwining of romanticism and religiosity, in Gollancz's thought and life. Raised an Orthodox Jew, he grew up in a context of moral absolutes. He abandoned the orthodoxy, and in some senses the Judaism ("when driven into a corner I sometimes describe myself as a liberal, non-practicing Judaeo-Christian"[58]), but remained religious. In reaction against his upbringing, Gollancz saw religion not as a matter of rules or obedience to God but rather in the romantic sense as cooperation with God in the act of claiming and realizing "my birthright of unity with all things."[59]

Gollancz's religious sense, as well as his argument against Britain's nuclear deterrent, stemmed from his conviction of the existence and supremacy of the spiritual world. In one of the most unusual openings to an argument against the British H-bomb, Gollancz began *The Devil's Repertoire* by describing the transcendental effects of music, which, Gollancz argued, made the

56 *The Devil's Repertoire, or Nuclear Bombing and the Life of Man* (London: Gollancz, 1958). For CND sales of this work, see *CND Bulletin*, Nov. 1958, p. 2; Warwick, MSS 157/3/ND/1/114.
57 Edwards, *Gollancz*, pp. 653–4, 662–3.
58 Victor Gollancz and Barbara Greene, eds., *God of a Hundred Names: Prayers and Meditations from Many Faiths and Cultures* (London: Gollancz, 1985), p. 8.
59 *My Dear Timothy*, p. 108.

listener more real by allowing him or her access to the spiritual world.[60] He then described the religious and spiritual experiences of various individuals, including Evelyn Underhill, Yeats, Shelley, and Coleridge, as further evidence for the existence of the spiritual realm. For Gollancz, belief in the existence of the spiritual world was crucial because to deny it was to deny a vital part of human nature. Like C. S. Lewis and Richard Acland, Gollancz believed that the desire for unity with the spiritual existed within every human being. All human nature contained the longing "that we should become 'all beautiful within,' that we should become, no longer in part or to a degree spiritual, but spirit. The image of a return gets us nearest to the truth here."[61] With a vocabulary very similar to that of Lewis, Gollancz described human beings as "exiles from our proper home."[62]

Gollancz argued that to return home, to progress toward union with God, individuals had to live in the spirit. Such a spirit-oriented life demanded, paradoxically, focusing energy and efforts on the physical world, specifically on breaking down the barriers that divided human beings and so blocked their spiritual communion. The only way to participate in the spiritual world was through "imaginative sympathy or empathy: to love a neighbour is to feel in him, live in him, *be* in him."[63] Thus, at the heart of Gollancz's world view rested the desire for community. It is only in the context of community that individuals realize spiritual fulfillment: Individuals moved from community with fellow human beings to spiritual unity with nature, and on to a sense of unity and belonging to the world of spirit. In Gollancz's view, "It is a plain fact . . . that we have 'come into being for cooperation': we live by community, we depend for the quality and flavour of our life on community, without community we die."[64]

"Without community we die," and very likely by nuclear holocaust, because the Bomb was the product of a society that had destroyed the community of humanity by alienating itself from its spiritual foundations. Gollancz, like many CNDers, identified materialism as the central enemy. In the twentieth century, he argued, materialism had driven out the awareness of the spirit that was essential to peace and true progress. According to Gollancz, two world wars, religious decay, and scientific mastery of the material universe, especially the discovery of nuclear fission, had led to an increase in materialist influences. The result was what Gollancz perceived as the horror of postwar society: a nightmare characterized by cynicism and apathy among the young, endemic fear, obsession with the standard of living, the encroachment of the big on the small and the mass on the individual, increasing

---

60 Gollancz detailed his passionate, even rapturous, love of music in his autbiographical *My Dear Timothy.*
61 *Devil's Repertoire*, p. 93.   62 *My Dear Timothy*, p. 267.   63 *Devil's Repertoire*, p. 83.
64 Ibid., quotation from p. 32; see also pp. 43–55, 85–7.

violence, the supersession of the mechanical over the personal and creative, the growing power of television and the subsequent loss of initiative and cooperation, and increased use of drugs and other forms of artificial stimulation.[65] Materialism, however, found its greatest fulfillment in the Bomb. Gollancz saw the Bomb as both "the sovereign expression and the sovereign begetter" of materialism. The Bomb revealed "matter divorced from spirit and become wholly evil."[66]

The defeat of this evil called for a reaffirmation of the spirit and a reassertion of individual responsibility. Gollancz argued that no man or woman could evade action by trusting the experts or the government.[67] This emphasis on individual responsibility for the Bomb rested on his conviction of the reality of free will. Freedom was inherent in spirituality: The individual could choose to advance spiritually or to quench his or her spirit, but choice was necessary. If the world was to survive, individuals must choose to reject the materialism triumphant in the Bomb.[68] Like the marchers who often viewed him as part of the generation they rejected, Gollancz saw the Bomb as the product and symbol of a cultural crisis and as the betrayal of Britain's responsibility to the world.

George MacLeod: the Celtic romantic

CNDers, and sometimes CNDers such as Gollancz, rarely differentiated between the idea of Britain's and the idea of England's responsibility to the world. Many CNDers, in fact, seemed completely unaware that the two words were not synonyms. The role of Scotland in CND has yet to be studied;[69] it is clear, however, that in Scotland the Campaign resonated strongly. Scottish nationalism, in its most common form of resentment against the dictates of London, coalesced readily with CND's call for widening the sphere of decision making in British political life. In addition, Scotland's deeply rooted Labour and religious traditions made it receptive to the moral radicalism of CND. Most important, after 1960 Scotland housed the Polaris bases. Many Scots believed that the bases had been dumped on them and that their country was bearing a disproportionately large share of the nuclear load.[70] Even Scots who were not unilateral-

---

65 Ibid., pp. 99–102.   66 Ibid., p. 132.   67 Ibid., p. 21.   68 Ibid., pp. 78–9.
69 Richard Taylor's history of CND (*Against the Bomb*) does not examine the Scottish Campaign.
70 See, e.g., *The Scotsman*, 3 Nov. 1960, p. 1. In 1960, a depot was provided at Faslane, Scotland, on the Holy Loch, for American nuclear submarines equipped with Polaris missiles. In 1962, as a result of the Nassau Agreement, the British Polaris program was begun. The first British Polaris submarine was launched in September 1966. The

ists could feel outraged at the prospect of serving as Britain's nuclear wasteland.

The participation of the Reverend George MacLeod (later Lord Mac-Leod of Fuinary) in the Scottish antinuclear movement was almost a foregone conclusion. In Scotland in particular but also throughout Britain, Mac-Leod had made a name for himself as a preacher, a pacifist, and a social reformer. He functioned as a sort of gadfly to the Presbyterian Church of Scotland, year after year appearing on the floor of the General Assembly and challenging the church to make a difference in the world.[71] As befitted a Calvinist trained in John Calvin's teaching that Christ is sovereign in all spheres of life, MacLeod insisted that the church could not leave social, political, or military issues to the state. Both he and the Iona Community, a still-active experiment in a new form of ministry and worship that he originated and led until 1967, took very seriously the Christian's duty to be a peacemaker.

The founding of the Iona Community and his peace activism are inextricably linked to MacLeod's own spiritual and personal journey. His experience in World War I, in which he was awarded the Military Cross and the Croix de Guerre, shaped the rest of his life. It did not, as would be expected, make him into a pacifist – MacLeod's pacifism emerged gradually in the later 1930s. What the Great War gave MacLeod, first of all, was the experience of community. He served on the western front from 1914 through 1918 and described in the trenches as "glorious years, revealing, satisfying."[72] The glory came from the reality of community. Fifty years after the conflict, MacLeod recalled that "never since (in the Church) have I known such Fellowship and honest to goodness disregard of self."[73] He sought for the rest of his life to re-create this spirit of community in peacetime Britain, a quest that eventually resulted in the founding of the Iona Community.

The Great War also gave MacLeod a vision of a remade world. Like so many other European males, MacLeod volunteered in 1914 with high hopes and splendid ideals. From the trenches, he wrote home: "All these lives are a stepping stone to something infinitely great and are very literally the further salvation of the world."[74] In the 1930s, looking at a divided and impoverished

submarines used an American-made missile and a British warhead. CND protested against Polaris throughout the 1960s. See the Polaris file, BLPES/CND/1/68.

71 Year after year MacLeod was voted down in the General Assembly. In 1986, however, at the age of ninety-one, he finally tasted victory when the General Assembly passed his resolution declaring "that no church can accede to the use of nuclear weapons to defend any cause whatever" (Ron Ferguson, *George MacLeod – Founder of the Iona Community* [London: Collins, 1990], pp. 409–10).

72 "Or So It Seems to Me," NL/ML/Acc. 9084/Box 276.

73 "There is One Thing Mightier Than Arms," Lecture on Non-Violence to the Department of Extramural Studies, n.d. [post-1968], NL/ML/Acc. 9084/Box 113.

74 Quoted in Ferguson, *George MacLeod*, p. 36.

Britain, MacLeod recalled of the war years that "a new world did seem to lie before us resplendent for our taking." Unlike so many of his comrades, however, MacLeod refused to abandon this vision, refused to admit that millions had died for nothing: "Let us hold to the truth that they died for things worthwhile – for truth, and goodness, and beauty."[75] Just as he sought to re-create the fellowship of the trenches, so he endeavored to build the new Britain that had seemed to beckon in 1914.

The failure of the Great War to create this new Britain could not be denied in industrial Scotland in the 1930s. After almost two decades of pastoral work among both the wealthy and the unemployed, as well as a successful career as a religious broadcaster,[76] MacLeod became convinced that the conventional methods of ministering were no longer applicable to the industrial world. In 1938 he resigned his pastorate in order to build the Iona Community.[77]

Some of the impetus for MacLeod's surprising resignation came from a trip he made to Jerusalem in 1933.[78] There he attended a Russian Orthodox Easter service, where, for the first time, this Scottish Presbyterian discovered an emotionally and aesthetically satisfying form of worship. He returned to Britain convinced "that the West must learn something from the Worship of the East. . . . We too must learn putting first things first – Contemplation – God consciousness – 'All Out' pilgrimages, in which we are housed utterly, in our Religion, at least for a time."[79] For the rest of his life MacLeod struggled to infuse Western Christianity with Eastern spirituality. He insisted that in Scotland such a task was not impossible: The Celtic origins of Scottish Christianity possessed the emotional vibrancy long lost in the institutional church. Against the starkness and rationalism of Presbyterian worship, he offered Celtic poetry and Eastern beauty. He once said that "it is Poetry more than Theology that has been my mentor."[80] In the Iona Community he tried to realize his poetic vision.

For MacLeod, the individualism of contemporary society and much of contemporary Christianity contradicted the essential corporatism of the Gospel. He insisted that "the Bible is not about an individual transaction between individually atomised men and their Maker." Instead, "only in a living total fellowship can this Word of God be correctly heard."[81] The Iona Com-

---

75 Sermon at the TocH Festival Service, London, n.d.; reprinted in George Macleod, *Govan Calling* (London: Methuen, 1934), p. 121.

76 See MacLeod, *Govan Calling.*

77 For the history of the Iona Community, see Ron Ferguson, *Chasing the Wild Goose* (London: Fount Paperbacks, 1988); T. R. Morton, *The Iona Community: Personal Impressions of the Early Years* (Edinburgh: St. Andrew Press, 1977); and T. R. Morton, *What Is the Iona Community?* (Glasgow: Iona Community, 1957).

78 Ferguson, *George MacLeod,* pp. 105–6.   79 Letter, 1933, NL/ML/Acc. 9084/Box 34.

80 Untitled talk, n.d., NL/ML/Acc. 9084/Box 85.

81 George MacLeod, *Only One Way Left* (Glasgow: Iona Community, 1956), pp. 31, 58.

munity endeavored to be, although of course it never quite succeeded in being, such a fellowship. As its *Worship Book* stated, "The Iona Community sees its primary task as being the discovery and making of community in a world divided."[82] Iona's peace activism, including the involvement of its members in CND, was an extension of the idea of community: Nations, like individuals, must realize the necessity of corporate action.

MacLeod also wished to restore the ties between individuals and their work. Like other important figures in the romantic protest tradition such as Carlyle and Morris, MacLeod condemned industrial society for eliminating opportunities for good work and for making alienation the common experience of most workers.[83] The Iona Community grew out of MacLeod's effort to overcome industrial alienation. He envisaged a community comprising men in industry and men in Christian ministry, a community built on the interactions and mutual support of these two groups and aimed at both revitalizing the church and bringing Christian principles to bear on the industrial workplace.[84]

MacLeod's genius lay in the form he chose for realizing his vision: His community was not to be a monastery but a group of men living and working in the world, linked to each other by a common regime of economic and spiritual discipline. The visual focus of the community was the island site of Iona (site of Saint Columba's landing in A.D. 563 and the beginnings of Christianity in Scotland). On Iona each summer the community immersed itself not only in the construction of a spiritual community but also in the physical rebuilding of the ancient Iona Abbey.[85] Iona suited MacLeod's purposes beautifully: It was rich in imaginative significance and rooted his vision of the future church in Christianity's distant past; it provided a sheltered arena for the building of community; it gave members a concrete goal and a physical witness to work accomplished; it shattered the barriers between the religious and the industrial worlds as ministers and industrial laborers worked together.

Rebuilding the abbey was a superb tactical maneuver in MacLeod's battle against the secularization of postwar Britain; it was also a supremely romantic idea in its respect for the past. MacLeod believed the abbey was much more than a heap of weathered stones. He often described Iona as a "thin place"

---

82 *The Iona Community Worship Book* (Glasgow: Iona Community, 1984), p. 3.

83 For a discussion of Iona's industrial mission, see Penry Jones, "Men outside the Church," *Coracle* 25 (Oct. 1954): 21.

84 See the "Founding Document [1938]," reprinted in *Coracle* 36 (Mar. 1960): 1–12. The use of the word "men" is deliberate. Not until 1969 did the Iona Community admit its first female member.

85 The physical rebuilding began in 1939 and was completed in 1967. The abbey today serves as home for the small year-round resident community and as the base of the wider community's activities.

that served as "little more than tissue paper between the natural and super-natural."[86] On the island the attentive visitor could transcend the limits of time and so participate in the holiness of that ancient holy place.[87] By insisting, even in times of economic depression and world war, that the ruins of an ancient abbey had relevance in the modern world, MacLeod argued that the past could be used to help resolve the crises threatening the present. He chose to oversee not the restoration of a museum piece but the reworking of a building to be made serviceable for the needs and activities of a contemporary community. To the outrage of architectural purists, the ancient halls of the abbey were eventually lit by electric lights, serviced by modern plumbing, and even heated by solar panels. MacLeod did not call the church or the Iona Community to retreat into the past; instead, he sought to use the past to revitalize the present.

In his attitudes toward nature MacLeod reflected the same holistic perspective. A Celt as well as a Calvinist, MacLeod saw the natural world as infused with God's glory.[88] On earth as well as in heaven humanity could touch divinity if it allowed itself access to the wonders of the created world.[89] In his view of nature as in his view of the past, MacLeod stood in the tradition of the romantics. A romantic critic of his world, he used both nature and the past, as well as his own profound spirituality, to construct an alternative community that could, he believed, help redeem the present.

The present needed to be redeemed or the Bomb would destroy the possibility of a future. MacLeod, who has been described as a "tremendous sort of power in the land for CND,"[90] had been involved in the struggle against nuclear weapons before CND began. One of the original sponsors of NCANWT, MacLeod chose to focus his Moderatorial Address to the General Assembly of the Church of Scotland in 1957 on the subject "Bombs and Bishops." In an address guaranteed to raise the hackles of his many critics in the church, he declared that together with the ecumenical challenge, the hydrogen bomb must head the list of the Christian's concerns. The Bomb could not help but force Christians to confront the core doctrines of their faith.[91] MacLeod was already well known as an opponent of Britain's nuclear defense policies when he became a sponsor of CND and a speaker on its platforms, including at the final rally of the 1960 Aldermaston March. In the

---

86 "The Idea of Iona," *Christian Century*, 22 Jan. 1947, p. 109.
87 *Coracle* 27 (Nov. 1955): 4.
88 MacLeod's collection of Iona prayers is entitled *The Whole Earth Shall Cry Glory* (Glasgow: Iona Community, 1985).
89 See *Coracle* 23 (Nov. 1953): 3–5, 6–10; *Coracle* 42 (Mar. 1963): 10.
90 Rev. George Charlton, in telephone interview with the author, 1 July 1989.
91 George MacLeod, *Bombs and Bishops*, Moderatorial Address, General Assembly of the Church of Scotland, 29 May 1957, Iona Community pamphlet, 1957.

Iona Community he had helped create a base for the nuclear disarmament movement in Scotland.[92]

MacLeod's opposition to nuclear weapons grew out of his religious beliefs. Although a social radical, he was an orthodox Christian who regarded the Incarnation as the center of his theology and his life. His conviction that at a specific historical moment God had been born as a baby boy, that in Jesus the divine and the human intermingled, led him to the conclusion that any attempt to isolate the spiritual from the material would lead to disaster. The church must be involved in remedying material ills at the same time that it endeavored to heal the spiritually sick. To confine the church's sphere of operations to the "spiritual" or the "relgious" was to deny the power of the Incarnation and to make the "religious" irrelevant. In MacLeod's prophetic voice, "Beware lest you worship the Satan of Separation and not the God who came to earth to die between two thieves to save."[93] Nevertheless, to take the opposite road and thus to elevate the material above the religious – to argue that setting up clinics was more important than prayer, for example – was to effect the same disastrous separation of body and soul and hence to violate the Incarnational truth.

What did the Incarnation have to do with the Bomb? To MacLeod, everything. Because the "atom is part of the redeemed garment of God," by subordinating the atomic world to the purposes of war-making, the British, Americans, and Soviets had perverted something holy.[94] More than this, though, for MacLeod nuclear weapons served as the antithesis to the Incarnation. The Bomb had fallen on Hiroshima on 6 August, the Feast of Trans-

92 In 1960 the community had 149 full members, a figure that included 10% of the ministers and associate ministers of the Church of Scotland. Throughout the first half of the 1960s, the community's series of weeklong summer programs on the island of Iona included efforts at peace education. In addition, individual community members, many of them parish pastors, were involved in both CND and Committee of 100 protests, particularly those directed against the Polaris bases. At the same time, the community's work and youth camps on the island spread CND's message and recruited young people into its ranks. In 1966, the community adopted the "Act of Commitment in Peace" in order both to settle the controversy aroused by MacLeod's desire that the community embrace a more absolutist pacifist position and to respond to the escalation of the Vietnam conflict and CND's decline at a time when many members perceived that the world situation remained threatening and Scotland, laden with Polaris bases, especially imperiled (Charlton interview, 1 July 1989; interview with Hamish Walker, 4 Dec. 1990, London; Ferguson, *George MacLeod*, p. 355; *Coracle* 49 [Dec. 1966]: 2–19). The Act of Commitment stated that "the use of nuclear and other weapons of mass-destruction is morally indefensible . . . and politically ineffective . . . and that the attempt to maintain peace by their threat is dangerous and undesirable." More significant, the Act of Commitment went beyond condemnation to a call to action. It required community members "to work for a British policy of renunciation of all weapons of mass-destruction." The "Act of Commitment" is printed in *Coracle* 50 (Mar. 1967): 9–10.

93 *Coracle* 31 (Nov. 1957): 23. In the same sermon MacLeod condemned "you who will not muddy your hands with realist politics when they concern the H-Bomb."

94 *Bombs and Bishops*, p. 11.

figuration in the church calendar. MacLeod saw this timing as much more than coincidence. His biographer, Ron Ferguson, has argued that "the event and his interpretation of it were to play a formative role in the rest of his life."[95] On the same day on which Christians celebrated Christ's fusion of Body and Spirit, humanity had split the atom, had rent "the garment of God," without any protest from the church.[96] MacLeod perceived Christ's Incarnation as "an inherent explosion into Matter, setting up a chain reaction of igniting love that has sparked from heart to heart . . . and that one day will consume mankind in lightsomeness or burning." The language was more than metaphorical. MacLeod believed that atomic science was merely providing quantitative data for a spiritual truth: that "there is no such thing as dead matter."[97] The Incarnation had infused the physical with the divine; scientists who penetrated the mysteries of the universe in order to destroy it committed a sin against their fellow human beings and against God.

MacLeod did not believe that scientists had sinned in investigating the mysteries of the atom. Like many CNDers, MacLeod's attitude toward science was ambivalent. He abhorred the reduction of the world and humanity to their material components. To him, the physical world was God's Creation, an inherently mysterious and wonder-filled living entity. On the other hand, he believed that science, and especially atomic and nuclear science, if kept in control, could "shape [the world] into glories yet undreamed."[98] Like many CNDers, MacLeod failed to confront the problem of the peaceful atom: How was humanity to control the powers it had unleashed? In MacLeod's protest against the Bomb, as in the larger Campaign's, there rests a fundamental contradiction. Both rejected the Bomb but not the technology of the Bomb; both wished to remake the society that created the Bomb but not to rethink its technological imperatives.

MacLeod trusted that a redirected science could help make the world a better place; he placed his hopes, however, in the church. Although he supported CND, MacLeod argued that only the church could lead Britain and the world away from the brink of nuclear destruction. Today, his confidence in the church's ability to change the course of events seems naive, even astonishing.[99] In the 1950s, however, the church pews in Britain had only recently emptied, and so the possibility of refilling them seemed much less

95 Ferguson, *George MacLeod*, p. 209.   96 *Coracle* 37 (Nov. 1960): 31.
97 *Coracle* 34 (Mar. 1959): 3.
98 *Coracle* 27 (Nov. 1955): 15. See also *Coracle* 47 (Dec. 1965): 10–12.
99 Ron Ferguson also notes how dated MacLeod's trust in the institutional church now appears. Ferguson argues that at the heart of MacLeod's vision of the Iona Community lay his belief that "a reformed Church which truly lived the Gospel would draw people like a magnet." Thus for its first decades the Iona Community focused on training young men for parish ministry. See *Chasing the Wild Goose*, pp. 120–1.

farfetched that it does in today's post-Christian society. In the 1930s and 1940s, for example, London crowds still packed the vast sanctuaries of Kingsway Hall, Westminster Central Hall, and City Temple to hear Donald Soper, W. Edwin Sangster, and Leslie Weatherhead, the renowned trio of Methodist preachers.[100]

MacLeod believed that one of the reasons that fewer and fewer people filled the pews on Sunday mornings was because the church had failed to give an unequivocal lead in the fight against nuclear weapons. MacLeod saw the Bomb as "out and away the most dramatic expression of [the Church's] total bankruptcy. It is God's appointed tutor to bring us back to Christ by revealing the appalling extent of our disobedience as Christians."[101] By failing to recognize the interweaving of the spiritual and material, Christians had failed the world. Christians could save the world, however, if they jumped into the ranks of the battle against the Bomb. MacLeod declared, "Only a recovered Belief in the Power of God . . . , and *Action in the light of our Belief,* can save Civilization. It is the Church's Hour – if the Church has the courage to be true to itself."[102]

MacLeod's faith in the power of the church was shared by few CNDers. The fight against the Bomb attracted the support of a wide variety of individuals and groups with contrasting and often contradictory ideas and aims. Far from representing the average CNDer, religious peace activists such as MacLeod, Gollancz, and Acland were often condemned by the rank and file as members of an older generation increasingly perceived to be out of touch with the nascent youth culture. Yet, in their rejection of the Bomb, these men echoed the central themes of the romantic tradition, a tradition that helped shape not only CND but also many of the protests of the subsequent decade, in which the youth culture played an important role. CND's differences and divisions eventually fragmented it. But weaving through many, although not all, of its various factions can be discerned the thread of romantic protest. Neither churchgoers nor members of Christian CND, the majority of Campaigners would not have defined themselves as religious; yet, like the religious activists discussed in this chapter, they fought against a weapon and a system of international relations that they perceived as morally wrong as well as politically mistaken. More than this, many CNDers viewed the Bomb as a symbol of a fragmented society that had lost its bearings, had elevated empirical fact and expertise at the expense of truth and common sense, and had

100 Douglas Thompson, *Donald Soper: A Biography* (Nutfield, Surrey: Denholm House Press, 1971), pp. 51–3, 65–9, 85–7.

101 George MacLeod, *The New Humanity Now* (London: Fellowship of Reconciliation, 1964), p. 18.

102 Lord MacLeod of Fuinary, "The Enormity of Nuclear Warfare," Iona Community leaflet, n.d., BLPES/CND 9/19/20. Emphasis in original.

denied individuals their fundamental right to participate in the decisions that affected their lives. Although not usually phrased in religious terms, this view paralleled the romantic quest for reintegration that motivated religious figures such as Acland, Gollancz, and MacLeod.

9

E. P. Thompson and the New Left

Without the New Left, the bonfire of CND would never have flamed so high or sent off the sparks that helped ignite the protests of the 1960s and early 1970s. The New Left sought to revive in Britain a humanist socialism, a socialism faithful to the traditions of protest that, New Leftist argued, had characterized the British past and would save Britain's future. In this struggle to redirect British socialism, the New Left saw CND as a crucial ally. New Leftists formed a small group within CND and were by no means representative of the wider Campaign; nevertheless, their ideas rested on a romantic basis common to many groups and individuals in CND. One New Leftist in particular, the historian and political activist E. P. Thompson, demonstrates the link between segments of the Campaign and the romantic tradition of protest.

Origins of the New Left

The New Left's entrance onto Britain's stage preceded CND's by a matter of months. It coalesced with the groups of intellectuals associated with the journals *New Reasoner* and *Universities and Left Review*, both of which began in 1957. In their pages, New Leftists revolted against revisionism in the Labour Party and Stalinism in the Communist Party. In their view, the Communist Party of Great Britain violated the integrity and spirit of British socialism by its unquestioning commitment to Soviet-style communism and its Stalinist authoritarianism. Most New Leftists finally concluded that the Labour Party held the keys to the socialist kingdom. Labour revisionism, however, threatened to halt the coming of socialism. Associated particularly with the policies and aims of Hugh Gaitskell, revisionism was the effort to adapt the Labour Party to affluent Britain. Gaitskell's effort to abandon Clause Four of the Labour Party constitution, the clause committing the party to the principle and practice of nationalized industry, epitomized the revisionists' attempt to push Labour toward an acceptance of mixed capitalism and a less class-based social analysis and appeal. Although Gaitskell lost his battle to revoke

Clause Four, he won the war with the left wing of the party. Throughout the 1960s, Labour followed a moderate, centrist course in both its domestic and its foreign policy. Labour's commitment to consensus politics seemed to the New Left to betray the heart of British socialism. Moreover, New Leftists believed that both revisionism and Stalinism negated the essence of socialism, its fundamental humanism. Revisionists and Stalinists alike had bowed before the idol of economism and sold their souls to a mechanical materialism. Against these tendencies, the ideologically diffuse New Left stressed the reality and importance of individual agency. New Leftists painted a vision of socialism as the bedrock of a new society, as a means of transforming, not just the economic, but also the intellectual, social, and cultural relations of Britain. In their vision, CND played a crucial role as an energizing force that would hasten the transformation of British socialism.

The first important focus for the New Left, the *New Reasoner*, grew out of the *Reasoner*, a journal edited by then–Communist Party members John Saville and E. P. Thompson in 1956. Reacting to Khrushchev's "Secret Speech" against Stalinism, Thompson and Saville announced, "The first need of our movement is a re-birth of Socialist principle, ensuring that dogmatic attitudes and theoretical inertia do not return."[1] Such a rebirth of principle depended on the realization that "Socialism is not to be measured in living standards alone, but in new social relations, new values and opportunities, a new, more generous, more just, and less selfish way of life,"[2] in other words, socialism as a moral as well as a political system. Saville and Thompson saw the abandonment of its moral essence as a generating factor not only in Stalinism and the consequent misdirection of socialism in the Soviet Union but also and more immediately in the torpidity of Britain's Communist Party. The party's failure to respond adequately and vigorously to Khrushchev's speech made sense because "the weakening of the moral basis of our political life necessarily makes less vigorous our practical judgements and our practical activity."[3]

Saville and Thompson challenged the party to "win the minds of the British people for Socialism . . . in ways that take fully into account the intelligence, experience, democratic traditions and organisational maturity of the British working class."[4] Only by such a route would Britain reach the Promised Land of socialist humanism. The Communist Party failed to heed the call, however. The Yorkshire District Committee of the Communist Party passed a resolution asking Thompson and Saville to stop publication of the *Reasoner* after they issued the first number. Publication of the second issue brought the two rebels before the party Executive. In November, Thompson

---

1 *Reasoner* 1 (July 1956): 3.   2 *Reasoner* 2 (Sept. 1956): 6.
3 *Reasoner* 1 (July 1956): 4.   4 *Reasoner* 2 (Sept. 1956): 6.

and Saville produced the third and final issue of the *Reasoner* and were expelled from the party at the same time that they resigned.

By November of 1956, however, the world had changed. Thompson and Saville did not resign their party memberships because of the *Reasoner* controversy. Saville later recalled that he and Thompson "conceived our own independent journal as in no way disruptive of the Party to which we belonged, or, to be more accurate, to which we had dedicated ourselves. . . . had not the Soviet intervention in Hungary occurred, we should certainly have continued to fight for democratic rights within the Party."[5] The Soviet military suppression of the Hungarian reform movement revealed that despite Khrushchev's repudiation of Stalin, Stalinist authoritarianism flourished in the Soviet Union. To the Reasoners, Hungary affirmed their evaluation of the sorry state of communism both in Britain and in the Soviet Union.

In 1957, Saville and Thompson issued the *New Reasoner*. The new journal continued to develop the themes introduced by the *Reasoner:* the need, especially in the wake of Stalinism, to insist that the individual can act and is responsible; the search for a socialism suited to the unique history and current political and social conditions of Britain; the quest for a role for intellectuals in the making of this socialism. The ex–Communist Party members who edited and contributed to the *New Reasoner* sought not to turn away from Marx but to emphasize the more humanist-oriented writings of his earlier period, and thus to avoid the reduction of Marxism to an authoritarian and mechanical political doctrine.

The *New Reasoner* argued that socialism entailed an entire way of life, that socialism transcended economics. The liberation of people required moving beyond concern for standard-of-living statistics to addressing such problems as the role of technology in reducing the ordinary person's feeling of responsibility and sense of control, the devaluation of culture and the ugliness of modern society, and the political apathy triumphant in Britain.

In its concern to define socialism as more than increasing the flow of refrigerators into working-class homes, the Reasoners found themselves converging with a group of Oxford graduate students who, in 1957, began publishing the *Universities and Left Review*. Unlike the Reasoners, the *ULR* group was not concerned with revitalizing British Marxism. In 1957 its editors – Stuart Hall, Gabriel Pearson, Raphael Samuel, and Charles Taylor – ranged in age from twenty-two to twenty-seven years old. Coming of age in the postwar

---

5 John Saville, "The Twentieth Congress and the British Communist Party," in *Socialist Register, 1976*, ed. Ralph Miliband and John Saville (London: Merlin Press, 1976), pp. 7, 14. See also Eric Hobsbawm, "The Historians' Group of the Communist Party," *Rebels and Their Causes*, ed. Maurice Cornforth (London: Lawrence and Wishart, 1978), pp. 21–47.

period rather than the 1930s or the war years led this younger generation to focus its energies not on Marxism but on the spiritual failure of the welfare state. The decay of the Labour Party rather than the bankruptcy of the Communist Party occupied the group's attention. Socialist, but less politically experienced and more Labour-oriented than the Reasoners, *ULR*'s writers focused on questions of culture and community. In tandem with Labour revisionists such as Gaitskell, the *ULR* group recognized that the changing economic conditions and relations in Britain demanded a redefinition of socialism's aims to ensure its relevance in the welfare state. The group's aims, however, contrasted sharply with the revisionist program. It defined socialist society as a cooperative community "in which men and women can find a meaning for their lives through a greater control over their work and leisure."[6] The *ULR* devoted its pages to a multifaceted critique of the culture and politics of the welfare state and to the effort to define socialist humanism and explore its potential for realization in postwar Britain.

The two key figures in shaping the *ULR* perspective were Richard Hoggart and Raymond Williams.[7] Hoggart's *The Uses of Literacy*, published in 1957, is an extraordinarily evocative personal memoir combined with acute literacy analysis.[8] In it, Hoggart contrasted his recollections of the vibrant culture of the prewar working class with the stagnant, mass-produced, commercialized culture of the welfare state. Although open to serious criticism because of its historical methodology,[9] Hoggart's work resonated among educated, left-leaning young persons dissatisfied with the cultural parameters of postwar Britain.[10] Hoggart's concern with Britain's cultural vitality blended well with Raymond Williams's more scholarly *Culture and Society* (1958). In this still-influential work, Williams argued that "the idea of culture, and the word itself in its general modern uses, came into English thinking in the period which we commonly describe as that of the Industrial Revolution."[11] Williams traced the origins, development, and permutation of the idea of culture as a defense against industrialism and laissez-faire ideology. He succeeded in placing individuals as diverse as Edmund

6 "Editorial," *ULR* 4 (Summer 1958): 3.
7 The editorial to the special issue on culture and community, which contained articles by both Hoggart and Williams, specifically acknowledged the journal's debt to these two writers (*ULR* 5 [Autumn 1958]: 3).
8 Richard Hoggart, *The Uses of Literacy* (London: Chatto and Windus, 1957).
9 E. P. Thompson offered a critical analysis of Hoggart, and the *ULR* group's use of him, in the *ULR* itself. See his "Commitment in Politics," *ULR* 6 (Spring 1959): 50–5.
10 The second issue of *ULR* included a special section entitled "The Uses of Literacy," comprising Raymond Williams's "Working Class Culture," Alan Lovell's "Scholarship Boy," John McLeish's "Variant Readings," and Gwyn Illtyd Lewis's "Candy Flossing the Celtic Fringe" (*ULR* 2 [Summer 1957]: 29–41).
11 Raymond Williams, *Culture and Society* (1958; New York: Columbia University Press, 1983), p. vii.

Burke, William Blake, John Stuart Mill, Charles Dickens, Matthew Arnold, William Morris, R. H. Tawney, and F. R. Leavis within a single coherent cultural tradition. In his concluding chapter, Williams offered his own cultural critique, which focused on the postwar problems of mass culture and the loss of a sense of community, and thus added his own contribution to the cultural tradition he outlined.

The *ULR* group's concern with what it perceived as the destructive potential of mass-produced commercial culture was heightened by its belief that the welfare state was destroying the traditional and central strength of the working class: its sense of community. New sociological studies, such as Peter Willmott and Michael Young's examination of working-class family patterns, provided the group with the ammunition it needed for its fight for a revival of community.[12] These studies reported that urban development programs and the new housing estates, although they provided workers with cleaner and safer housing, undermined the family and community support systems that served not only as a means of survival but also as sources of alternative values in a capitalist society. For the *ULR* group, redefining socialism meant exploring the ways in which it should be directed toward revitalizing the people's culture and re-creating a genuine socialist community.

In its discontent with the welfare state and with the postwar Labour Party, the *ULR* group provided a center for the unfocused anger that began to erupt, particularly among the educated young, in Britain in the second half of the 1950s. Although to a large extent the creation of the media, the "Angry Young Men" explosion of this period revealed widespread dissatisfaction with the status quo.[13] Discontented and angry young men like then–Oxford undergraduate Dennis Potter, whose *Glittering Coffin* is a self-indulgent and passionate indictment of Britain in the 1950s, rejected the equation of socialism with the existing welfare state. Potter fumed that "with idealism dwindling into a ritual cant, the Welfare State being corroded into a grey purposelessness . . . one could claim that this was a time of crisis, and make clear the need for revolt. But against what, for what?"[14] The *ULR* group sought to answer such questions: against the dehumanizing currents running through postwar Britain, and for the powerful torrent of a humanist socialism. It

---

12 Peter Wilmott and Michael Young, *Family and Kinship in East London* (London: Routledge and Kegan Paul, 1957).

13 The key texts of the "Angry Young Men" explosion of the era include John Osborne's *Look Back in Anger*, John Braine's *Hurry on Down*, Alan Sillitoe's *Saturday Night and Sunday Morning*, and Kingsley Amis's *Lucky Jim*. The *ULR* dealt directly with the Angry Young Man in articles such as David Marquand's "Lucky Jim and the Labour Party" (*ULR* 1 [Spring 1957]: 57), W. I. Carr's "Mr. Osborne and an Indifferent Society" (*ULR* 4 [Summer 1958]: 32), and Stuart Hall's "The Politics of Adolescence" (*ULR* 6 [Spring 1959]: 2).

14 Dennis Potter, *The Glittering Coffin* (London: Gollancz, 1960), p. 16.

never, however, explained how to translate the rejection of the first and affirmation of the second into concrete action.

Despite the differences in political enthusiasms and emphases, the *New Reasoner* and *ULR* groups quickly recognized each other as the core elements of the New Left. Both rejected the postwar political consensus; both sought to revitalize British socialism and to move beyond an exclusively economic analysis and perspective. Both fluctuated between rejecting and endeavoring to reshape the Labour Party. Such commonalities made it almost inevitable that the two journals would coalesce.[15] They shared many of the same contributors; the first issue of the *ULR*, in fact, included an article by E. P. Thompson.[16] With the sixth number of the *New Reasoner*, the two journals began offering joint subscriptions. They exchanged writers and finally, at the end of 1959, merged to form the *New Left Review*, which Stuart Hall edited. Unlike the *New Reasoner*, the *New Left Review* did not see itself as a forum for international communism; nevertheless, until 1962, it continued along the lines established by its parent journals. Labour politics took up a good deal of space but so, too, did issues of "socialism-as-a-way-of-life." The *New Left Review* delved into "the question of what it is for man to live well, both as an individual and as a social and political animal."[17]

A prerequisite for living well, the New Left argued, was banning the Bomb. From 1958 on, the New Left and CND existed in a symbiotic relationship.[18] The pages of the New Left journals reveal this mutual nourishing. Their editors assumed that their readers would be CND supporters and that CND activity constituted New Left activity. In both the *New Reasoner* and the *Universities and Left Review*, agitation against Britain's official nuclear policy predated the formation of CND. In the summer of 1957, the *ULR* called for Britain to stop the manufacture and testing of the H-bomb as a way forward

---

15 The *ULR* was, however, always more successful. According to G. L. Arnold, "*ULR's* circulation steadily topped 8,000 almost from the first, while *NR* never got much above 2,500" ("Britain: The New Reasoners," in *Revisionism: Essays on the History of Marxist Ideas*, ed. Leopold Labedz [New York: Praeger, 1962], p. 304).

16 "Socialism and the Intellectuals," *ULR* 1 (Spring 1957): 31–7.

17 J. M. Cameron, "New Left in Britain – II," *Listener*, 15 Feb. 1960, p. 407.

18 Perry Anderson highlighted this symbiosis as one of the reasons for the New Left split. He described the New Left as "centrally focused around the Campaign for Nuclear Disarmament." When the Campaign faltered, so did the New Left. By 1962, "the political basis on which the journal had been launched was giving way, and no new one was readily discernible" (*Arguments within English Marxism* [London: New Left Books, 1980], p. 136). According to Peggy Duff, "CND did them [the New Left] no good. It swallowed them up as a political force in Britain" (*Left, Left, Left: A Personal Account of Six Protest Campaigns, 1945–1965* [London: Allison and Busby, 1971], p. 128). See also David R. Holden, "The First New Left in Britain, 1956–1962" (Ph.D. diss., University of Wisconsin at Madison, 1976), pp. 222–3, for the interpenetration of the New Left and CND.

out of cold war positions.[19] The *New Reasoner* went further in the winter of that year and demanded a reconsideration of the NATO alliance.[20] When CND emerged in 1958, the New Left welcomed it as a challenge to the foreign policy consensus. The *New Left Review* continued to publicize, support, and offer insider critiques of the Campaign.

The symbiosis of CND and the New Left is most clearly seen in the pattern of their mutual decline. Both found themselves in 1962 divided by internal controversies and rapidly losing purpose and power. In the case of the New Left, the end came in concrete form: a change in the editorship of the *New Left Review*. In 1962 and 1963, the familiar names from both the *New Reasoner* and the *Universities and Left Review* disappeared, to be replaced by a younger editorial team headed by Perry Anderson, the former editor of the *New University*. According to Thompson, the *new* New Left had pulled off an editorial coup and then had proceeded to deny and undermine the values and ideals he and his associates had labored to establish and realize. Under Anderson, the *Review* became much less lively, more theoretical, and more oriented toward Continental Marxism.[21] It also ceased to concern itself with CND. By 1964, however, CND had ceased to concern many people.

Positive neutralism and a new kind of politics

In the years before CND's decline, the New Left played a central role in shaping the Campaign's stand against British involvement in NATO. CND first clearly declared its opposition to the Western alliance in 1960. Although withdrawal from NATO had been one of the aims of Operation Gandhi (the DAC's parent organization) when it was established in 1951, few of the protest-establishment figures who founded the CND and made up its leadership followed through their anti-Bomb argument to its anti-NATO conclusion. The CND National Conference resolution in 1960

19 "Hungary, H-Bomb, Germany," *ULR* 2 (Summer 1957): 4.
20 "Editorial," *New Reasoner* 1/3 (Winter 1957–8): 3.
21 For a more detailed account of the "coup" and the debate between Thompson and Anderson, see Michael Bess, "Rebels against the Cold War: Four Intellectuals Who Campaigned to Recast World Politics, 1945–1985" (Ph.D. diss., University of California at Berkeley, 1989), pp. 268–70, 278–89. Bess's work has been published in a revised version as *Realism, Utopia, and the Mushroom Cloud* (Chicago: University of Chicago Press, 1993). Perry Anderson insisted that "the notion of an editorial coup is a legend" and that his accession to the *NLR* editorship was the result of an "abdication" rather than a "usurpation" (*Arguments within English Marxism*, pp. 135–6). For the ideological dispute between Thompson and Anderson, see also Thompson, "The Peculiarities of the English," in *Socialist Register, 1965*, ed. Ralph Miliband and John Saville (London: Merlin Press, 1965), pp. 311–62; Thompson, *Poverty of Theory and Other Essays* (New York: Monthly Review Press, 1978); Anderson, "Socialism and Pseudo-empiricism," *New Left Review* 35 (Jan.–Feb. 1966): 2–42.

calling for withdrawal from NATO did not, in fact, meet with the unanimous approval of the Executive.[22] These Labour-oriented leaders recognized that the Campaign's assumption of an anti-NATO stance moved CND beyond the simple moral protest cry of "ban the Bomb." In Michael Gordon's words, CND's espousal of neutralism meant "the repudiation of the entire edifice of Labour's foreign policy over the past fifteen years – NATO, Anglo–American relations, armed balancing of the Soviet Union, multilateral East–West disarmament."[23] Yet, the Executive could not stand against the rising tide of anti-NATO sentiment in CND,[24] nor could it deny that neutralism stemmed quite logically from CND's call for British unilateral nuclear disarmament. As opponents of unilateralism like Bevan and Gaitskell were quick to point out, the moral argument lost its righteousness if Britain banned the Bomb in order to shelter under America's nuclear force.

The logic of the case, coupled with the anti-American sentiment characteristic of the Labour Left, would probably have pushed CND to its anti-NATO stance eventually. Neutralism and Labour leftism were natural partners, a marriage rooted in the soon-shattered dream of a social democratic Europe emerging out of the ruins of the Second World War. This vision of Britain uniting with the rest of Europe to form a "Third Force" as a counterweight to and mediator between the hostile superpowers inspired much of the Labour Left's hostility to its own party's foreign policy in the second half of the 1940s and the 1950s.[25] No supporter of NATO, the Labour Left quickly linked unilateral nuclear disarmament to abandonment of the American alliance. Leftist Labour MPs in 1958 called for replacing NATO, SEATO, and the Baghdad Pact with regional agreements and a strengthened United Nations.[26]

22 Nicholas Sims, "Notes on Neutralism," Factsheet no. 4 – "Neutralism in CND Policy and Literature," BLPES/CND 9/17/20.

23 Michael R. Gordon, *Conflict and Consensus in Labour's Foreign Policy, 1914–1965* (Stanford: Stanford University Press, 1969), p. 276.

24 By the end of 1959, e.g., the demand that Britain leave NATO was common in the Oxford CND (see *Isis*, 11 Nov. 1959, p. 8). In January 1960, both the Southern Region CND Policy Conference and the Combined Universities CND Conference passed resolutions calling on the Campaign to advocate British withdrawal from NATO (*Peace News*, 22 Jan. 1960, p. 8; *Guardian* 4 Jan. 1960, p. 1).

25 According to Michael Gordon, Bevan's resignation from the cabinet in 1951 should be set in the context of a resurgence of neutralist sentiment and anti-Americanism (*Conflict and Consensus*, pp. 240–2). Gordon argues that Bevan's resignation cleared the way for the emergence of a clear and influential Labour Left faction (the Bevanites) and thus "the disintegration of Labour's fragile consensus in foreign policy that had been eroding since autumn, 1950" (p. 247). See also Jonathan Schneer, *Labour's Conscience: The Labour Left, 1945–1951* (Boston: Allen and Unwin, 1988), pp. 52–60, 90–4.

26 *Tribune*, 7 Nov. 1958, p. 5. The MPs who signed this article were Frank Allaun, John Baird, Fenner Brockway, George Craddock, Harold Davies, Bob Edwards, Sir Fred

It was the *New* Left, however, that served as the catalyst, the intellectual prod, even the hyperactive moral conscience, to drive the Campaign into neutralism. The New Left espoused a neutralist stance before CND began and developed its position in subsequent years through its interaction with the Campaign. After the defeat of a nuclear disarmament resolution at the Labour Party Conference in Brighton in 1957 (the occasion of Bevan's "naked in the conference chamber" speech; see p. 124), Thompson and Saville urged the Left to prepare "a blue-print showing how Britain might break with the whole NATO complex of diplomacy and strategy, and take the lead [in forming a neutralist Europe]. . . . If Mr. Bevan finds himself naked, we must make him some clothes, and ask him, in the name of decency, to put them on."[27]

Making some clothes for Mr. Bevan meant developing a socialist foreign policy that the New Left termed positive neutralism. After Aldermaston 1958, Thompson and Saville issued a challenge to CND: "The uncompromising 'Aldermaston mood' of moral protest . . . must be matched by a growing internationalist outlook which comprehends the weight of responsibility which events have placed upon the British people and which anticipates . . . active neutralist diplomacy."[28] Although New Leftists argued that both official Britain's pro-American and the hard Left's pro-Soviet stances must be abandoned to enable Britain to break the logjam of the cold war, they focused on the American alliance. This emphasis on the United States stemmed from more than traditional leftist anti-Americanism. New Leftists believed, first of all, that the American presence in Europe escalated tensions; its removal, then, was a prerequisite for peace.[29] Second, and more important, New Leftists perceived that British action would have a greater impact on American than on Soviet policy. British unilateral action could, in fact, effect the breakup of NATO. Neutralism and, specifically, withdrawal from NATO would guarantee that Britain could once again play an influential role in the world.[30]

Britain's influence could extend far beyond the European continent. New Leftists held that a neutral Britain would be less tainted by cold war power politics and therefore more palatable as a leader to Third World nations. Whereas the postwar Left had envisaged a social democratic Europe standing between the superpowers after World War II ended, the New Left's

---

Messer, Ian Mikardo, Walter Monslow, Maurice Orbach, John Rankin, Julius Silverman, Sydney Silverman, Leslie Sprigg, Stephen Swingler, William Warbey, and Konni Ziliacus.

27 "Editorial," *New Reasoner* 3 (Winter 1957–8): 3.
28 "Editorial," *New Reasoner* 5 (Summer 1958): 2.
29 "Can We Have a Neutral Britain?" *New Reasoner* 1/4 (Spring 1958): 3–10.
30 See, e.g., "Beyond the Bomb," *New Reasoner* 1/4 (Spring 1958): 2.

vision extended beyond Europe to embrace the developing nations as well.[31] E. P. Thompson argued that its "Natopolitan ideology" blocked Britain from looking "in the one direction where real hope lies for the world." He defined "the place of positive hope" as the "growing world – the world of India, Brazil, Ghana, Mali, Yugoslavia, Indonesia, Cuba, Egypt."[32] Without the Bomb, Britain would take its place in the front ranks of these neutral nations and so lead the world out of the darkness of the nuclear night.

Neutralism in the New Left vision meant more than reducing the chances of nuclear annihilation, however. By breaking the cold war deadlock, neutralism would lead to a revival of democratic politics in Britain and abroad. New Leftists argued that CND represented a reaction against not just the Bomb but the kind of politics that produced the Bomb, a politics that above all denied the responsibility and agency of ordinary people.[33] In Thompson's words, "As [the cold war] drags on the half-frozen antagonists become more sluggish in their reactions. Political and economic life is constricted . . . reaction and the subordination of the individual to the State is intensified, and the crooked ceremonies of destructive power permeate our cultural and intellectual life."[34] By renouncing both the Bomb and the American alliance, Britain would make the first crack in the frozen positions of the cold war era. In a world dominated by the seemingly unmovable superpowers, the individual felt paralyzed. But once movement occurred, people would realize that their actions could make a difference and so would begin to take action, to make choices, to effect change.

New Leftists welcomed CND as the beginning of the democratic revitalization of Britain, as "the expression of the growing belief amongst ordinary people that, if they are to save themselves, they must take matters into their own hands. . . . There is no mistaking the shift of the current towards personal involvement and direct action."[35] For a year the *New Reasoner* and the *Universities and Left Review* had called for a moral awakening within Britain and had sought to revive within the nation the desire for what they perceived as true socialism, for a way of life that would affirm the responsibility and agency of every individual. CND's sudden blossoming seemed to answer the New Left's call. Here was a movement that broke the mold of parliamentary

---

31 In 1959, e.g., Frances Kaldor and John Gittings called for CND to advocate withdrawal from NATO and its replacement by "a 'Third Bloc,' composed of as much of the Commonwealth as would join us, and the so-called 'uncommitted' countries from the Middle East, South-East Asia, and elsewhere" ("A New Look at CND," *Isis*, 2 Dec. 1959, p. 31).

32 E. P. Thompson, "The Metaphysic of NATO," *Isis*, 2 Mar. 1960, p. 17.

33 See, e.g., D. G. Arnott, "Ammunition for the Campaign," *New Reasoner* 1/5 (Summer 1958): 25.

34 E. P. Thompson, "NATO, Neutralism , and Survival," *ULR* 4 (Summer 1958): 51. See also E. P. Thompson, "The New Left," *New Reasoner* 9 (Summer 1959): 1–17.

35 D. G. Arnott, "Ammunition for the Campaign," *New Reasoner* 5 (Summer 1958): 25–6.

politics. The thousands tramping between Aldermaston and London demonstrated that they had overcome the political alienation New Leftists feared was engulfing Britain. Within the ranks of CND marchers, the New Left identified the core of a revolutionary force that could shatter the barriers confining Britain within the boundaries of welfare capitalism and thus open the way to a more socialist Britain.

In the New Left vision, CND was about much more than banning the Bomb. New Leftists viewed the Campaign as part of their struggle to break through both the deadlock of international affairs and the stagnation of domestic politics. They saw CND as an embodiment of individual agency, a concrete realization of their faith that the actions of ordinary people could change the world. By affirming the importance of individual choice, CND appeared to be an important step on the road to a new sort of socialism, a socialism defined not by nationalization or a more efficient management of the recalcitrant British economy but rather by its creation of a cultured and vibrant community that fostered opportunities for meaningful work: socialism in the Morrisian rather than the Fabian tradition.

Their support of CND and their rejection of the post–World War II status quo place many New Leftists within the romantic tradition of protest. The search for a more humanist socialism was primarily a quest for reintegration, an effort to reconnect individuals in a community shaped by the traditions and values of a preindustrial world. It is not surprising that a number of leading New Leftists were also sociologists and historians who endeavored in their professional lives to identify the sources of that community life which they believed needed to be rebuilt in contemporary Britain.

E. P. Thompson and the Morrisist message

Although not directly linked to CND, E. P. Thompson's historical works reveal the main themes of the New Leftists' interpretation of Britain's past, an interpretation that colored their hopes for Britain's future as well as their understanding of CND's role in that future. Perhaps more than any other single individual, Thompson helped shape the New Left critique of industrial society. Through his political and historical writings, he added his voice to CND's cry of moral protest against the society Britain had become. Although one of the most important British historians in the postwar period, Thompson is, as T. W. Heyck has argued, "best seen not in the line of academic historians ranging from Bury to Namier to Elton, but in the traditions of sages beginning with Blake and Shelley, and extending to Carlyle, Ruskin, Morris, and Leavis. Thompson is the moralist as Marxist historian."[36] He is also a romantic whose battle against the structures and shape of industrial Britain places him within the tradition of protest.

The central themes of the New Left and CND critique – the reality of individual agency, the importance of moral choice, the necessity of political engagement and activism – defined the world in which Thompson grew up. His older brother, Frank, was executed at age twenty-four by Nazi sympathizers while serving with a Bulgarian partisan unit. Active liberals and antifascists, Thompson's parents were shaped by a decade in India (they lived on the subcontinent from 1912 to 1923) and their close involvement in the Indian independence movement.[37] Thompson's parents had gone to India as Methodist educational missionaries; instead, India educated them. Thompson's father, Edward John Thompson, began to study and write about the Bengali poets, and eventually left the Methodist church.

Thompson became a Marxist while in his early years at Cambridge and has remained one ever since, albeit a Marxist within the tradition of romantic protest.[38] He resisted the economism of socialists who reduced both humanity and Marxism to mechanical entities. Thompson believed that these Marxists committed the very sin that lies at the core of capitalism: the definition of "human relations as being primarily economic. . . . the injury is in defining man as 'economic' at all."[39] Economics is not the base for all human action, Thompson argued. He regarded the base–superstructure model as simply a metaphor used by Marx, not a historical or objective reality. Thompson admitted that Marx himself fell prey to the delusion of treating the human individual as "economic man" when he posed "revolutionary economic man . . . as the antithesis to exploited economic man."[40] But implicit in the

36 T. W. Heyck, "E. P. Thompson: Moralist as Marxist Historian," in *Recent Historians of Great Britain: Essays on the Post-1945 Generation*, ed. Walter L. Arnstein (Ames: Iowa State University Press, 1990), p. 122. For other interpretations of Thompson's political and historiographical significance, see Fred Inglis, *Radical Earnestness: English Social Theory, 1880–1980* (Oxford: Martin Robertson, 1982), pp. 185–204; Harvey J. Kaye, *The British Marxist Historians* (Cambridge: Polity Press, 1984), pp. 167–220; Harvey J. Kaye, *The Education of Desire: Marxists and the Writing of History* (New York: Routledge, 1992), chap. 4; Bryan Palmer, *The Making of E. P. Thompson* (Toronto: New Hogtown Press, 1981). See also the interview with Thompson in the *Radical History Review*, (Fall 1976); and Henry Abelove, "Review Essay on 'The Poverty of Theory,' " *History and Theory* 21/1 (1982): 132–42.

37 E. P. Thompson, "The Nehru Tradition," in *Writing by Candlelight* (London: Merlin Press, 1980), pp. 137–45.

38 In interviews with Michael Bess in 1986, Thompson described himself as a "dissident Communist" and as a "libertarian Communist." As Bess argues, however, "this tenacious adherence to the political label of 'Communist' was arguably due more to a sense of loyalty and tradition than to any substantive correspondence with contemporary ideological alignments" ("Rebels against the Cold War," p. 272). Thompson joined the Labour Party in 1962.

39 Henry Abelove, ed., *Visions of History* (New York: Pantheon Books, 1983), p. 22.

40 Thompson, "The Peculiarities of the English," p. 355.

early Marx, Thompson contended, was the assertion that exploitation was cultural and moral as well as economic.

Without abandoning or compromising his own sense of himself as a Marxist, Thompson sought throughout both his historical and his political work to develop and add to the Marxist critique of industrial capitalism. In 1976, when asked to identify the connecting thread in all his work, Thompson admitted that he had a "preoccupation" with "a real silence in Marx, which lies in the area that anthropologists would call value systems." In place of Marx's economic base/cultural superstructure model, Thompson examined "the dialectic of interaction, the dialectic between 'economics' and 'values,' " and, in the process, fought to retain in Marxism a vocabulary of agency and moral choice.[41]

A lover of poetry, particularly that of William Blake, Thompson turned to the English Romantics in his attempt to fill the silences of Marx.[42] For Thompson, poetry was not an ornament, an attribute of the good life, but rather a necessity, an integral part of politics. In the early 1980s, for example, in the heat of the campaign to block the establishment of cruise missile bases in Britain, Thompson called for a revival of the national political discourse. For him, such a revival depended in part on an infusion of poetry: "Langland, Chaucer, Marlowe, Milton, Marvell, Pope, Wordsworth, Blake, Shelley, Byron. . . . They weren't interior decorators who made the place more pretty. They were part of what life was about, they asked where society was going."[43]

Thompson believed that Marxism and Romanticism stemmed from the same soil and that these two traditions needed to be grafted together for English socialism to bear abundant fruit. He concluded *The Making of the English Working Class*, his most famous and influential work, by mourning the failure of English Romanticism to merge with working-class radicalism in the early nineteenth century: "After William Blake, no mind was at home in both cultures, nor had the genius to interpret the two traditions to each other. . . . In the failure of the two traditions to come to a point of junction, something was

---

41 Abelove, *Visions of History*, pp. 21–2.

42 Quotations and references to Blake are common in Thompson's writings. In Thompson's science fiction novel *The Sykaos Papers*, e.g., Helen faces the question of what to bring with her on her space voyage to Oitar, a doomed quest to save Earth from nuclear destruction. She says to herself, "Books? . . . I want my Blake." In the end, Helen is killed by the Oitarians. In her final moments, she recalls fragments of Blake's poetry. (*The Sykaos Papers* [London: Bloomsbury, 1988], pp. 426, 459)

Thompson is himself a poet. See, e.g., the poems collected in *Infant and Emperor* (London: Merlin Press, 1983). This collection makes explicit the link between poetry and politics in Thompson's world view. As Thompson notes in the introduction, "Mother and Child" is his poetic response to Suez and Hungary; "Lamentation in Rama" and "Visitors at the Inn" are both rooted in his CND experience.

43 Thompson, *The Heavy Dancers* (London: Merlin Press, 1985), p. 4.

lost. How much we cannot be sure, for we are among the losers."[44] Much of Thompson's historical writing and political action sought to remedy this loss, to unite once again the English working class and English Romanticism.

The key to Thompson's efforts at such a fusion lay in the work of William Morris. According to Thompson, "the moral critique of capitalist process was pressing forward to conclusions consonant with Marx's critique, and it was Morris's particular genius to think through this transformation, effect this juncture, and seal it with action."[45] In his first major historical study, the 800-page *William Morris* written in 1955, Thompson succeeded in establishing Morris's Marxism. The theme of the tome centered, however, not on Marxism but on Romanticism: the work traced "the trajectory" of Romanticism in English history. From its Wordsworthian, revolutionary, and hope-filled beginnings, Romanticism descended into the escapism characteristic of the mid-Victorian Pre-Raphaelite Brotherhood. In this later form, Romanticism so much ceased to be a threat to industrial society that it was even eagerly welcomed by industrialists. The Pre-Raphaelite Brotherhood, including Morris, "desired to paint Visions; but the result was 'dream,' a world of compensation."[46] After dreaming came despair. Thompson viewed Morris's *Earthly Paradise* as an embodiment of Romantic degeneration in which rebellion gave way to escapism.[47]

According to Thompson, Romanticism foundered in the abyss of escapism until Morris's conversion to Marxism. Strengthened by the spiritual vitality of the Icelandic sagas and goaded into public action by both the aesthetic horrors of Victorian architectural "restoration" (actually the destruction of ancient buildings) and the human horrors denounced by the Bulgarian Atrocities Campaign,[48] Morris passed "the River of Fire" into Marxist socialism. Marx's theory of class struggle unified all Morris's previous activities and thought and replaced his despair with hope: "Blake's Jerusalem might yet be built in earnest, and Shelley's Phantoms and Sages be given flesh and blood. The long romantic breach between aspiration and action was healed."[49] The result was personal, poetic, and political regeneration. Morris aroused himself from his personal despair and became a leading

44 Thompson, *The Making of the English Working Class* (New York: Vintage Books, 1966), p. 832.
45 Thompson, *William Morris: Romantic to Revolutionary*, rev. ed. (New York: Pantheon Books, 1977), p. 779. This revised edition is hereafter cited as *Morris II*.
46 Thompson, *William Morris: Romantic to Revolutionary* (London: Lawrence and Wishart, 1955), p. 88. Hereafter cited as *Morris*.
47 *Morris*, pt. II, chaps. 2 and 3.
48 Led by Gladstone, the Bulgarian Atrocities Campaign was a moral protest against the Disraeli government's support of Turkey after the Turkish massacre of 12,000 men, women, and children.
49 *Morris*, pp. 310, 311.

British socialist. Romanticism emerged from the emptiness of escapism, and socialism found a voice to fill Marx's silences.

Thompson's own voice articulated a "Morrisist" world view. Morris reconciled Thompson's Marxism and his romanticism and shaped the way he approached both the historical past and the political present. As Thompson explained, "Morris, by 1955, had claimed me. . . . The Morrix/Marx argument has worked inside me ever since. . . . I have no license to act as [Morris's] interpreter. But at least I can now say that this is what I've been trying, for twenty years, to do."[50]

A romantic vision of the past

Like the man he attempted to interpret, Thompson articulated a romantic vision of Britain's past. Thompson's histories may seem to have little to do with either his New Leftist activism or his CND campaigning.[51] But just as Morris's painting, poetry, crafts work, bookbinding, and revolutionary socialism all expressed his rejection of capitalist industrialism, so also the varied aspects of Thompson's career form a coherent whole. His histories place him in the romantic protest tradition and reveal the assumptions and ideals that lay behind his support for CND.

To Thompson, being a historian "is like being a painter or poet. A poet loves words, a painter loves paint. I found a fascination in getting to the bottom of everything, in the sources themselves. I got this fascination with the archives."[52] Like a poet or a painter, the historian must work under inspiration. Thompson recalled that when writing *William Morris*, "Morris seized me. I took no decision. Morris took the decision that I would have to present him."[53] In Thompson's view, the historian becomes the vessel by which the past speaks, just as a poet or a painter is the instrument by which art finds embodiment.[54] The historian must commune with the past: He or she "has got to be listening all the time. . . . The material itself has got to speak to him. If he listens, then the material itself will begin to speak through him."[55] When Thompson wrote that Morris believed that "the imagination, when working upon the records of the past, was able to apprehend truths

---

50 *Morris II*, p. 810.
51 In 1958, Thompson and his wife, Dorothy (also a leading historian of nineteenth-century Britain), organized the CND group in Halifax (Bess, "Rebels against the Cold War," p. 264).
52 Abelove, *Visions of History*, p. 13.   53 Ibid.
54 For this observation, I am indebted to T. W. Heyck.
55 Abelove, *Visions of History*, p. 14.

which the Gradgrinds, for all their measuring-rods and calculating tables, overlooked," he expressed his own approach to history as well.[56]

For Thompson, the economic historian is the Son-of-Gradgrind. The *Making of the English Working Class* served as a double-barreled blast against both the "abbreviated economistic notations of Marxism" and "the extremely firm, intellectually very well-based discipline of economic history that has (with notable exceptions) been a continuous tradition from Adam Smith and the orthodox political economists through to the present day. It is a tradition largely contaminated with capitalist ideology."[57] Thompson deplored the Cliometrician's obsession with quantification, which, he charged, rested on the assumption that counting something reveals its significance. Quantification, according to Thompson, "is of course the mumbo-jumbo of those latter-day astrologers who stem from Conjurer Bentham, whose spells are woven each quarter in the *Economic History Review*, and who for two hundred years have been trying to persuade us that nothing is real that cannot be counted."[58]

Thompson's foray into the battle over whether the British workers' standard of living rose or fell as a result of the Industrial Revolution, a skirmish that occupied much of *The Making of the English Working Class*, struck hard against these latter-day Benthamites and contemporary Gradgrinds. After rehearsing and giving due credit and criticism to both sides of the debate, Thompson concluded that for the crucial decades between 1780 and 1840, the ordinary British people suffered a fall in their standard of living. For Thompson, this conclusion was based on more than tallying up wage and price levels. "Standard of living" included "the total life-experience, the manifold satisfactions or deprivations, cultural as well as material, of the people concerned." Such a holistic perspective, sharply at odds with the economist approach, led to an indictment of capitalist industrialism, "the source of that 'ugliness' which, D. H. Lawrence wrote, 'betrayed the spirit of man in the nineteenth century.' "[59] This ugliness, the betrayal of the spirit, resisted quantification; yet, for Thompson, it was as much "fact" as statistics on the production of cotton. Numbers easily deceive, and almost always minimize. As a result, Thompson argued, the historian must rely on subjective evidence, must recount stories, in order to be sure that he or she deals with the past as it was experienced by human beings: "It is quite possible for

56 *Morris*, p. 27.

57 Abelove, *Visions of History*, pp. 6–7. See also Thompson's remarks on the ideology of Adam Smith in "The Moral Economy Revisited," in *Customs in Common: Studies in Traditional Popular Culture* (New York: New Press, 1991), pp. 268–85.

58 Thompson, "Anthropology and the Discipline of Historical Context," *Midland History* 1/3 (Spring 1972): 48.

59 *Making of the English Working Class*, pp. 444–5, 446–7. Quotation from D. H. Lawrence, *Selected Essays*, Penguin ed., pp. 119, 122.

statistical averages and human experiences to run in opposite directions."[60] Numbers cannot reveal the human experience in its totality.

Thompson's concern for the totality of human experience weaves through all his historical work. Morris, of course, had refused to confine the human experience to strictly economic matters. His arts and crafts, his literature, and his efforts to preserve ancient buildings demonstrated a more holistic approach to the problems of human experience and eventually to socialism. Thompson, too, approached both his political and his historical work holistically; he condemned the quantifiers for dropping such crucial concepts as culture and community from their vocabulary. Although the debasement of culture cannot be quantified, it can and does affect human experience. The existence, decline, or lack of community, too, eludes the numbers but shapes the way individual men and women perceive their world. The quantifiers, however, fail to see the human experience as a whole. Thompson argued, "The objection to the reigning academic orthodoxy [re the Industrial Revolution] is not to empirical studies per se, but to the fragmentation of our comprehension of the full historical process."[61]

Moreover, after breaking history into fragments, the quantifiers and empiricists put the fragments together into "a model of the historical process made up from a multiplicity of interlocking inevitabilities. . . . [Thus] we arrive at a post facto determinism."[62] Like culture and community, human agency drops from the vocabulary. In *The Making of the English Working Class*, Thompson endeavored to restore human agency to English history by asserting that the working class made itself.

By ascribing a certain inevitability to the course of British history, the quantifiers not only buttressed a dehumanizing determinism but also ignored the question of values. In this area where Marx had kept silent, Thompson spoke loudly. Throughout *The Making of the English Working Class* runs the theme that "it did not have to happen this way," that the suffering undergone by the laborers of England was caused not by the inevitable process of industrialization but by the values of the ruling class, by a capitalist ideology allowed to operate without any checks and strengthened by the counterrevolutionary spirit of the early decades of the nineteenth century. The plight of the handloom weavers, usually dismissed by historians as exceptional, unfortunate, and unavoidable, was seen by Thompson as "a paradigm case of the operation of a repressive and exploitive system upon a section of workers without trade union defences."[63] Industrialization as carried out in early-nineteenth-century England resulted from human choice and human action, and therefore could and should be condemned. Thompson rejected both

---

60 *Making of the English Working Class*, p. 211.   61 Ibid., p. 204.   62 Ibid., p. 205.
63 Ibid., p. 312.

Marxist and anti-Marxist visions of history as a relentless march toward a predetermined future. Human beings act, he insisted, to shape their destinies.

Thompson's later studies in eighteenth-century history also emphasized the reality of human agency and Thompson's concern with the question of values. He rejected the orthodox view of the century as one of consensus, paternalism, and deference. The working class had not yet made itself, but the "plebs," as Thompson called them, did not defer to either paternalist rulers or the imposition of the new market economy. By the use of traditional forms of revolt, such as anonymous action, crowd riots, and countertheater, the plebs restrained the actions of both elites and fellow plebs and shaped their own world. With this "rebellious traditional culture," the plebs protested against and resisted such manifestations of the market economy as enclosures and unrestricted grain prices.[64] Against this new form of economy, against this set of values, the plebs posed their own value system, that of the moral economy: "a consistent traditional view of social norms and obligations, of the proper economic functions of several parties within the community" – hence, the just price and a fair day's work for a fair day's pay over against the free market and open competition.[65]

The ongoing struggle

By refusing to reduce historical reality to the quantifiable, by insisting on a holistic approach to history, and by affirming the role of human choice and action, Thompson echoed the central themes of romantic protest. For Thompson, the writing of history constituted part of the battle against the dehumanizing and reductionist forces of empiricism and industrialism. In Thompson's view, the past shaped the future. He sought to introduce English workers and socialists to their past in order to move forward into a better Britain. He addressed his historical works to others besides historians. Like Tolkien and especially Lewis, Thompson stepped outside the boundaries of academia in an effort to communicate his message to a wider public. From the 1950s on, Thompson's historical work informed and inspired his

---

64 Quotation from "Eighteenth-Century Society: Class Struggle Without Class?" *Social History*, May 1978, p. 154. (This essay is partially reprinted in Thompson's *Customs in Common.*) See also "Crime of Anonymity," in *Albion's Fatal Tree: Crime and Society in Eighteenth-Century England*, by Douglas Hay et al. (New York: Pantheon, 1975), pp. 255–308; "The Moral Economy of the English Crowd in the Eighteenth Century," *Past and Present* 50 (1971): 76–136; "Rough Music: Le Charivari Anglais," *Annales* 27/2 (Mar.–Apr. 1972): 285–312; "Patrician Society, Plebeian Culture," *Journal of Social History* 7 (Summer 1974): 382–405; and *Whigs and Hunters: The Origins of the Black Act* (New York: Pantheon Books, 1978).

65 "Moral Economy," p. 79.

political activism. Fred Inglis has noted that "the history he has written backwards is the ground for political moves forwards."[66] What Thompson perceived as he surveyed the centuries of British history was the existence of "the alternative nation," a culture of resistance against official Britain and the forces of authoritarianism and oppression.[67] The faces and names changed, but the issues remained the same.[68] In an ongoing argument with his successors at the *New Left Review*, Thompson denied Perry Anderson's and Tom Nairn's description of the British working class as politically backward and contended that they had misread British history. Thompson saw in Britain's past a peculiar and potent form of socialism.[69] It was "foolish . . . to underestimate the long and tenacious revolutionary tradition of the British commoner. . . . From the Chartist camp meeting to the docker's picket line, it has expressed itself most naturally in the language of moral revolt."[70]

For Thompson, CND continued this moral revolt, despite its lack of working-class support. It articulated the voices of ordinary citizens, who found their right of self-determination threatened by the antidemocratic process of decision-making that produced and was fostered by the Bomb. More than this, CND recognized the Bomb as the symbol of the postwar status quo, which had to be rejected for humanist socialism to triumph. Thompson, like so many on the Left, had dreamt that the horrors of World War II would be redeemed by the building of a genuinely democratic and socialist Europe in the postwar era. Instead, the cold war had locked both sides of the conflict into antiprogressive positions.

The characteristic British nostalgia for the purpose-filled war period had for Thompson distinctly political and personal overtones. He looked back to the war years and their immediate aftermath as a time of unique, and tragically wasted, opportunity. The sense of a dream deferred possessed immense power for Thompson because of the wartime death of his brother, Frank. Edward and Frank Thompson had been close; like his younger brother, Frank was an extraordinarily intelligent man who loved books and poetry. His decision to join the Communist Party in 1939 clearly played a role in shaping his younger brother's communist allegiance. More significant, Frank's dream of a better Europe arising from the ruins of World War II remained a

---

66 Inglis, *Radical Earnestness*, p. 203.   67 *Heavy Dancers*, pp. 4, 75; see also pp. 100–4.
68 See, e.g., E. P. Thompson, ed., *Warwick University Ltd . . .* (Harmondsworth: Penguin, 1970), pp. 17, 93.
69 See Anderson, *Arguments within English Marxism;* and the following articles: Anderson, "Origins of the Present Crisis," *New Left Review* 23 (Jan.–Feb. 1964): 26–53; Anderson, "Socialism and Pseudo-empiricism," *NLR* 35 (Jan.–Feb. 1966): 2–42; Tom Nairn, "The English Working Class," *NLR* 24 (Mar.–Apr. 1964): 43–57; Nairn, "The Nature of the Labour Party – I," *NLR* 27 (Sept.–Oct. 1964): 38–65; Nairn, "The Nature of the Labour Party – II," *NLR* 28 (Nov.–Dec. 1964): 33–62.
70 Thompson, "Revolution," *New Left Review* 3 (May–June 1960): 9.

crucial part of E. P. Thompson's political thought. Thompson wrote of his brother: "The war meant far more to him than an interruption in his life. He understood it as a critical turning point in the history of human society, the logical climax of past history and the threshold of a new civilisation."[71] Frank's letters reveal his tremendous confidence in the future.[72] On his last Christmas, Frank wrote to his parents and brother, "There is a spirit abroad in Europe which is finer and braver than anything that tired continent has known for centuries, and which cannot be withstood."[73] To Frank's younger brother, the cold war had violated and threatened to destroy this spirit.[74]

Thompson saw CND as a resurgence of the democratic socialist spirit his brother had died for, as an uprising against not only the Bomb but also the postwar political divide that threatened to engulf British, and European, socialism. In the early 1980s, he recalled that in 1944, "all of Europe, from the Urals to the Atlantic, was moved by a consensual expectation of a democratic and peaceful post-war continent. We supposed that the old gangs of money, privilege and militarism would go." Instead, the cold war divided Europe and "turned those famous victories into a pile of shit."[75] In Thompson's vision, CND's counterpart of the 1980s, the European Nuclear Disarmament (END) campaign, offered the chance both to step off the path to nuclear annihilation and to retrace the route to a more truly democratic Europe and to reclaim Britain's democratic tradition.

Thompson must be seen, like most CNDers, as very much a patriot. Concern for the integrity and independence of British culture, and a mistrust of American hegemony, recur as important themes in his writings. In Thompson's view, just as individual agency was restricted in postwar British society, so too was Britain's capacity for action and influence as a nation. With the New Left, and with CND, he called for Britain to break the bonds of NATO and assert her independence. Only when independent could Britain become the Morrisist society Thompson envisaged, a society free not only of nuclear weapons but also of the narrowly materialist culture that so idolized technology that it tolerated the construction and possible utilization of the Bomb.

Although re-creating Britain to fulfill Morris's socialist vision proved impossible in the postwar period, in the mid-1970s Thompson took heart that "in one area one may detect the first signs of a 'thaw' in the icy resistance to Morris: a generation nourished upon Tolkien and C. S. Lewis . . . is now

---

71 Thompson, *There Is a Spirit in Europe: A Memoir of Frank Thompson* (London: Gollancz, 1947), pp. 15–16.
72 See, e.g., his letters of 22 Oct. 1943 and 13 Jan. 1944, in ibid., pp. 141, 170–1.
73 Letter, 25 Dec. 1943, in ibid., p. 169.
74 For Thompson's postwar dream of a social democratic Europe, see also his essay in E. P. Thompson, ed., *The Railway: An Adventure in Construction* (London: British–Yugoslav Association, 1948).
75 *Heavy Dancers*, pp. 199–200.

willing to read with more complaisance the later prose romances."[76] In the pages of Morris's romances, Tolkien lovers found what they had discovered in Middle-earth: the evocation of another world that served as a powerful critique of the economism and materialism of postwar society. Thompson's histories, too, create an alternative reality that protects against the present world in fundamentally romantic terms. Moreover, in his later nonhistorical writings, Thompson revealed a sympathy with the emerging Green movement, a sympathy that is not surprising given the romantic assumptions that lay at the heart of both Thompson's work and the Green critique of industrial society.[77]

Thompson's role in END in the 1980s was much more significant than his position in the earlier CND.[78] Nevertheless, both Thompson and the first British New Left played an important part in shaping CND's ideas. New Leftists forced CND to confront the anti-NATO implications of its call for nuclear disarmament and offered the option – never clearly defined and always several removes from reality – of positive neutralism. More significant, the New Left effort to look at the total human experience, to look beyond politics and economics and define socialism in cultural, social, and moral terms, revealed the wider social critique embedded in the call to ban the Bomb. The strong influence of historians in the New Left emphasized the links between this critique and the British tradition of romantic protest. Their interpretations of the past became weapons in the struggle to re-create the present and restore community, purpose, and independence to the British people.

76 *Morris* II, p. 764. The "Pen Friends" listings of *Amon Hen*, the British Tolkien Society journal, confirm this identity of interest. Individuals who belonged to the Tolkien Society were often members of the William Morris Society as well.

77 See *The Sykaos Papers*, pp. 197–8; *Exterminism and Cold War*, ed. New Left Review (London: NLR, 1982), p. 347; *Heavy Dancers*, p. 3; *Customs in Common*, pp. 14–15. See also Michael Bess's interview with Thompson in 1986. When asked to articulate his vision of a free Europe, Thompson painted a picture in the colors of *Small Is Beautiful*: "The nation-state begins to decline in importance, giving way to a heightened sense of regional and cultural identities. . . . One would hope to see what used to be called workers' control or greater autonomy, smaller units of control; public industry being cooperative, or corporations municipally owned, and so on. And that would underpin, perhaps, a growth in local and regional consciousness. But for larger economic, cultural and legal arrangements you would have bridging institutions" (Bess, "Rebels against the Cold War," p. 313).

78 Thompson was one of the seven leading figures in END. His involvement made him one of the four most well known people in British public life in the early 1980s – along with the Queen Mother, Margaret Thatcher, and Queen Elizabeth II! See Abelove, *Visions of History*, p. 6; see also Bess, "Rebels against the Cold War," pp. 293–355.

Conclusion:
CND as romantic protest

In their survey of former CNDers, Richard Taylor and Colin Pritchard concluded that participation in CND worked "to alienate and disillusion a substantial section of a generation from orthodox politics of both the traditional Liberal Left and the Marxist Left." This generation turned instead to a new style of populist politics. Although 41 percent of Taylor and Pritchard's sample had decreased their political activity in the two decades after CND began, 43 percent had become involved in community politics, 57 percent in single-issue campaigns, and 37 percent in environmental groups. Taylor and Pritchard rightly concluded that CND "was the precursor of a whole range of very important protests against the growth of an uncontrolled, super-technological society."[1] CND did not change Labour Party politics, as its founders had hoped; instead, it offered an alternative way of thinking about and practicing politics.

Behind all the divisions and debates in the Campaign stood the concept of participatory democracy. In differing ways, the leadership, the DAC, the New Left, the Committee of 100, and the Aldermaston marchers expressed their conviction that the Bomb represented a denial of democratic decision making and that the only hope for Britain lay in the revival of political participation. Fundamentally a movement of moral protest, CND viewed the Bomb as immoral not only because of its potential for destruction but also because it violated democratic principles. In the decision to make the Bomb, democratic processes had played no role. In any decision to use the Bomb, such processes would be ignored. The Bomb threatened to destroy the very democracy that it was designed to protect. To respond to this threat, CND called on ordinary people to act and so reclaim their right to determine their own and their nation's future.

The call for participatory democracy that became the rallying cry of protest movements across the world later in the 1960s was at its heart a rejection of the alienating effects of technological development and the corresponding

---

1 Richard Taylor and Colin Pritchard, *The Protest Makers: The British Nuclear Disarmament Movement of 1958–1965, Twenty Years On* (Oxford: Pergamon Press, 1980), pp. 111, 32, 131.

institutional structures that were emerging in the postwar world. To some CNDers, the Bomb represented the elevation of the expert and the triumph of technology at the expense of ordinary people. CND saw that one of its central missions was to convince ordinary individuals that they knew better than the experts, that the almost instinctive emotional revulsion against the idea of nuclear war should be trusted as much as or more so than any strategic calculations. Britain's nuclear policies had come into being because its structures of decision making were no longer built to human scale. CND's cry for participatory politics was, then, a demand that politics be brought down to the human level.

In the CND vision, such a return to human scale would revive the spirit and reality of community in postwar Britain. Participatory democracy was more than a demand for individual action; it rested on the belief that only when individuals were involved in and responsible for the governing structures of society would a true community be built. The community spirit that arose in the first Aldermaston Marches appeared to validate this faith. Tens of thousands of disparate individuals, drawn together in action, created a world of their own during those cold, wet Easter weekends.

The crowds of Aldermaston marchers both inspired and frightened CND's leaders. These protest elites never really undertood the force they had unleashed. They called for greater participation in British politics but they were at heart establishment individuals, conservative souls unable to abandon a lifetime of allegiance to the Labour Party. CND, however, challenged such a traditionalist approach. The internal conflicts that tore apart the CND resulted from not only exhaustion and extremism but also the disquieting implications of the call to ban the Bomb. The CNDers who marched on from the Aldermaston road to the community and environmentalist campaigns of the 1960s and 1970s rejected the parliamentary route of change and opted for a locally based activism much more consonant with the ideal of participatory democracy.

As Paul Boyer has shown, fears concerning the loss of individual autonomy and the triumph of the technocracy were powerful forces in the American reaction against the atomic bomb in the 1940s.[2] In Britain in the late 1950s such fears coalesced with the anxiety produced by the sense of national decline and impotence. Nationalism and imperialist nostalgia played an important role in shaping the Campaign's protest and in strengthening its anti-Americanism. In calling for a British lead in the struggle to save the world from nuclear holocaust, however, CNDers were doing more than endeavoring to revive Britain's imperial role. They were also responding to a

---

2 Paul Boyer, *By the Bomb's Early Light: American Thought and Culture at the Dawn of the Atomic Age* (New York: Pantheon Press, 1985), chap. 13.

fundamentally romantic vision of British history and character. Much of CND's power came from its ability to tap into what many of its middle-class supporters believed about themselves and their nation's past. Whether it was E. P. Thompson's alternative version of history with its stress on the antiauthoritarian tradition of the freeborn Englishman or the more familiar orthodoxy of the Whig interpretation of the steady unfolding of democratic rights within a stable democratic system, the British, or at least the English, past could be and was used to criticize and challenge the nuclear present. The British were supposed to be different, CNDers claimed. The British were supposed to be better.

In its criticism of postwar Britain, CND took its place within the romantic tradition of protest. Its use of the past, its stress on the efficiency of individual action in changing the world, its effort to reconstruct a true community in the face of industrial and technological atomization, and its willingness to give credence to routes of truth beyond or apart from the rational echo the themes of romantic protest. So, too, does its failure. Romanticism originated as a protest against the dominant intellectual and economic structures of British life. A strong undercurrent in modern British history, it was nonetheless an *under*current that pulled against the more visible stream of British industry and political economy. CND constituted the protest of a minority. At no time during its heyday did a majority of the population support unilateralist nuclear disarmament. CND's minority status, however, does not nullify its significance. It succeeded in mobilizing a large segment of the middle class and thus in breaking through the "Great Apathy" of the 1950s. The fact that CND struck a chord in the middle class, that its call to action resonated throughout British offices, detached houses, and university classrooms, suggests that the ideas and themes detailed above had taken root in middle-class Britain. The essential romanticism at the core of this very diverse and internally divided movement was not confined to a small group of disengaged intellectuals or alienated artists. This romanticism did not characterize all of postwar British society and did not, evidently, penetrate the ranks of the working class. Yet, CND's success, like the surprisingly large readership of Lewis's and Tolkien's fantasies, indicates the power of romanticism in British middle-class culture after 1945.

What was missing from CND's protest in terms of the romantic tradition was a holistic perspective. Essential to the romantic vision is the dismissal of analysis as a limited tool and the insistence that the whole transcends the parts, and thus that science, although useful, cannot save the world. CNDers often argued that the call to ban the Bomb was a demand for a new politics and a new society; they also frequently painted the Bomb as the logical culmination of technology out of control and experts out of order. Yet, many in CND still had great faith in the scientific promise of a new age: hence the stress on releasing resources for the massive industrialization of the Third World and the advocacy of civilian nuclear power. The later, less influential CND moved away from this technofix stance and in the 1970s joined the anti-nuclear-power movement. As early as 1963, CND's future chairman Malcolm Caldwell pointed out the complexities of Third World industrialization in the form of soil erosion, destruction of tropical forests, pollution, and the reckless use of nonrenewable resources. Caldwell called for the West to reconsider its "present wanton improvidence."[3] Caldwell's argument was to become quite familiar later in the decade, but CND at its height rarely questioned the growth orientation of either Britain or the Western world. The members of the DAC came the closest of the various groups within the Campaign to achieving a holistic outlook: The DAC emphasized changing attitudes as well as actions, processes as well as parties, ways of living as well as weapons.

Ex-CNDers began to make some of these connections as well. Taylor and Pritchard have argued that their survey of ex-CNDers showed that the Campaign had "its true heirs in a variety of local and national movements – from tenants' associations to the Ecology Movement – which are concerned with decentralising and humanising society, curbing the unbridled growth of the technological society at the expense of the world's resources, and putting power into the hands of ordinary people."[4] These endeavors coalesced in the Green movement, which Part III explores. Like CND, the Green movement articulated a critique of society already embedded in the cultural and intellectual soil of contemporary Britain.

3 Malcolm Caldwell, "The Desperate Race to Feed the World," *Peace News*, 12 Apr. 1963, p. 6.
4 Taylor and Pritchard, *The Protest Makers*, p. 131.

PART III

Economics, ecology, and E. F. Schumacher: painting Britain green

In May 1971, approximately one hundred men and women, most of them young, dumped 1,500 throwaway bottles on the doorsteps of the headquarters of Cadbury Schweppes. With this publicity coup, Friends of the Earth U.K. (FoE) signaled its arrival onto the British cultural scene. Almost immediately FoE captured the leading role in British environmentalism, a position it retained into and through the 1980s. The Schweppes bottle dump was significant not only in establishing FoE's presence in British environmental politics but also in its illustration of a new kind of environmentalist action. Unlike such long-standing environmentalist organizations as the Royal Society for the Protection of Birds and the Commons, Open Spaces, and Footpaths Preservation Society, both dating from the nineteenth century, FoE saw environmental problems such as pollution or the extinction of plant and animal species as part of the larger failure of modern society and called for thoroughgoing social, economic and political change. As in CND, then, rejection of one aspect of modern society became part of a wider critique of industrial civilization.

This radical form of environmentalism, a constellation of ideas and activities labeled "Green" since the electoral success of *die Grünen* in Germany in the early 1980s, involved far more than concern for the environment; it rested on the effort to apply ecological principles to society's structures in order to create new and sustainable patterns of life.[1] Although clearly aware of and concerned about environmental degradation, the supporters of the early Green movement differed from "environmentalists" in linking environ-

---

1 Like "radical environmentalism," "Green" is a misleading label. It is popularly understood to mean "environmental," even though environmentalism is only one thread in the Green tapestry. Moreover, "Green" is a label of the 1980s; as will be seen in Chapters 10–12, many of the threads that weave together to give the later movement its peculiar pattern figured much less clearly in the earlier period. Feminism, a strong egalitarian impulse, and a sharp focus on unilateral nuclear disarmament – integral elements of the Green movement of the 1980s – were frequently absent in the earlier period. To *not* use the Green label for the movement of the 1960s and 1970s, however, would be to obscure the direct links between this earlier phase and its later form. Thus, "Green" is used (although with some misgivings) throughout the study below.

mental problems to economic structures, industrial relations, and cultural and religious attitudes. In 1971, Michael Allaby called the new protesters eco-activists.[2] This term, which indicates the centrality of both an *eco*logical perspective and an *eco*nomic analysis in the movement, as well as the characteristic stress on activism, will be used interchangeably with the label "Green" in the following pages. Like CND, the Green movement can be seen as a form of romantic protest, a call to British society to change its modern course, to remake the world by reviving what these environmental activists believed to be Britain's historic strengths.

Before the emergence of Green parties as significant forces in European politics, eco-activism was often viewed as more American than British or European,[3] in part because of the influential role of American writers in shaping the concerns of the new movement. In 1962, the publication of Rachel Carson's *Silent Spring*, a passionate indictment of the use of pesticides because of their devastating consequences for wildlife, made first an American and then a British public aware of the ecological concept of the food chain and its implications. The work aroused a great deal of controversy; its publication is often marked as the starting point of eco-activism.[4] Six years later, Paul Ehrlich placed the focus for environmental problems on the population explosion. Ehrlich met strong opposition from another American, Barry Commoner, who viewed technology, not overpopulation, as the main culprit for environmental degradation.[5] Both Ehrlich and Commoner became leading activists in the new movement. The publicity surrounding their debate, particularly when it received international attention at the United Nations Conference on the Human Environment in Stockholm in 1972, and their leadership roles painted eco-activism in American colors. Yet, as the next several chapters show, Green ideas had already taken root in Britain by the time of the Stockholm conference.

One of the most important texts in the early Green movement in Britain was *Small Is Beautiful: Economics As If People Mattered*, by the German-born E. F. Schumacher, economic adviser and statistician for the National Coal Board.[6] Released one year after the Stockholm conference, *Small Is Beautiful* made Schumacher into a cult figure and one of the apostles of the new

---

2 Michael Allaby, *The Eco-activists: Youth Fights for a Human Environment* (London: Charles Knight, 1971).
3 See, e.g., "Sons of the Earth," *New Statesman*, 3 Aug. 1973, p. 146.
4 Rachel Carson, *Silent Spring* (Boston: Houghton Mifflin, 1962); Frank Graham, Jr., *Since "Silent Spring"* (Boston: Houghton Mifflin, 1970).
5 Barry Commoner, *The Closing Circle* (New York: Bantam, 1971); Paul Ehrlich, *The Population Bomb* (New York: Ballantine, 1968). See also Ehrlich's later work, with Anne H. Ehrlich, *The Population Explosion* (New York: Simon and Schuster, 1990).
6 E. F. Schumacher, *Small Is Beautiful: Economics As If People Mattered* (New York: Harper and Row, 1973).

movement. In this best-seller, Schumacher showed how the environmental crisis constituted only one branch of a three-pronged crisis facing industrial society. Impending energy shortages and the breakdown of human relations under the impact of large-scale industrialization and heedless commitment to endless economic growth also threatened humanity with disaster. Hence, Schumacher argued, the problem of pollution could not be separated from the economic, cultural, and technological framework of Western industrial society. In *Small Is Beautiful,* he articulated a comprehensive critique of the modern world.

Schumacher popularized ideas that had emerged in Britain in the 1950s and 1960s. As one of the best-known and most-influential of the early Greens, or eco-activists, Schumacher and his work will be closely examined in Chapter 12. He must, however, be set in the context of the wider movement. Demands for political and economic decentralization, a no-growth or steady-state economy, environmental preservation, alternative technologies, and the conservation of energy resources coalesced in the first phase of Green awareness in Britain in the 1960s and 1970s. What many eco-activists called for was a radical reorientation of British society. Their vision of a better Britain blended elements of the fantasy world of Lewis and Tolkien – its medievalism, fear of science and technology, conservatism, and religiosity – with CND's political activism, humanist socialism, and nonviolent credo. This synthesis spotlights the commonalities between these movements, illumines the common cultural context from which they emerged, and demonstrates the continuing impact of, and the serious limits upon, the romantic protest tradition in Britain.

10

The greening of Britain

The late 1960s and early 1970s witnessed an upsurge of environmental concern in Britain and throughout the Western world. Membership in environmentalist organizations escalated in response to doomsday predictions of the imminent collapse of industrial society, forecasts that seemed believable in a world in which rivers caught on fire and cancer-causing chemicals laced the food supply. This environmental awareness coalesced with calls for limits to population and economic growth and demands for political decentralization to produce the early Green movement. As an examination of some of the key organizations, events, and publications that shaped the new movement reveals, British eco-activists broke quite sharply with the conservationism of earlier decades to challenge the assumptions and structures of the postwar world. Chapter 11 will explore the romantic nature of this challenge; this chapter will focus on drawing the parameters of the new movement.

From conservationism to eco-activism

Conservationism, the impulse to conserve flora, fauna, and habitat, first emerged in Britain in the nineteenth century. As industrialization transformed England's social and political structures, so it redesigned its landscape. Already in 1865 the Commons, Open Spaces, and Footpaths Preservation Society was formed to limit encroachments of industry and urbanization on the countryside. The late Victorian years saw an explosion in the numbers of similar organizations such as the Society for the Protection of Birds (later the Royal Society), founded in 1889; the Society for the Preservation of the Fauna of the Empire (later the Fauna Preservation Society), founded in 1903; and the British Vegetation Committee, founded in 1904, which in 1913 gave birth to the British Ecological Society.[1] The Coal Smoke Abatement Society, the National Trust, the Metropolitan and Public Gardens

---

1 Edward M. Nicholson, *The Environmental Revolution* (Harmondsworth: Penguin, 1972), chap. 7.

Association, and the Camping Club were also all formed in the two decades after 1880.[2]

After World War I, environmental concern abated, but in the second half on the 1920s, as Philip Lowe and Jane Goyder have charted, it surged forward again. In 1926, the formation of the Council for the Preservation of Rural England constituted an early attempt to coordinate the various voluntary preservationist and conservationist societies. In the next decade, the Ancient Monuments Society, the Ramblers' Association, the Council for the Preservation of Rural England, the Pedestrians' Association for Road Safety, the Youth Hostels Association, the National Trust for Scotland, the Pure Rivers Society, and the Central Council for River Protection were born.[3] This second era of conservationism ended with the outbreak of World War II, but in 1949 the formation of the Nature Conservancy signaled a revival of conservationist action. The Nature Conservancy was an official governmental agency with the responsibility for conserving plant and animal wildlife through both research efforts and reserve management.[4] The end of the 1950s witnessed the beginning of a third phase in the conservationist movement, marked by the establishment of local amenity and planning organizations and county naturalists' trusts. By 1957 approximately two hundred societies concerned with townscape beauty and amenity existed in Britain.[5] This later period also saw the formation of the Civic Trust, the Council for Nature, the Victorian Society, the Noise Abatement Society, and the British Trust for Conservation Volunteers.[6]

During the decade after 1965 conservationism continued to prosper, boosted by newer, more holistic, more radical forms of environmental concern, the beginnings of *eco-activism*. By 1973 the number of amenity organizations in Britain had risen to one thousand. The membership lists in these groups also expanded dramatically. Between 1962 and 1972, for example, membership in the Ramblers' Association doubled.[7] Both a cause and a result of this rise in environmental awareness was the expansion of media attention: Coverage of environmental issues in the *Times* increased by 281 percent between 1965 and 1973.[8] The number of specialist journals focusing on conservation and the environment rose as well: In 1976 the *Environmental*

2 Philip Lowe and Jane Goyder, *Environmental Groups in Politics* (London: Allen and Unwin, 1983), p. 16.
3 Ibid., pp. 16–17.   4 Nicholson, *Environmental Revolution*, pp. 158–60.
5 S. K. Brooks and J. J. Richardson, "The Environmental Lobby in Britain," *Parliamentary Affairs* 28/3 (1975): 312.
6 Lowe and Goyder, *Environmental Groups*, pp. 16–17.
7 Brookes and Richardson, "Environmental Lobby," p. 314.
8 S. K. Brookes et al., "The Growth of the Environment as a Political Issue in Britain," *British Journal of Political Science* 6 (Apr. 1976): 245–55. For a critical analysis of this survey, see Francis Sandbach, *Environment, Ideology, and Policy* (Montclair: Allanheld, Osmun, 1980), p. 2.

Periodicals Bibliography listed fifteen journals, only two of which had begun before 1967 and eleven of which had been formed between 1967 and 1970.[9]

The upsurge of environmentalist concern and action at the end of the 1960s can be seen as a consequence and a continuation of postwar conservationism.[10] Such an interpretation, however, tends to minimize the very real difference between these conservationist organizations and the eco-activist groups that emerged in the 1960s. The new groups were more likely to link environmental problems to the economic structures of society and to adopt activist political stances. They were also more inclined to use radical tactics such as public protests and civil disobedience to achieve their ends. The ends themselves also differed. The eco-activists wanted not only to preserve certain animal species and woodland habitats but also to redirect Britain along paths of development that would be more in harmony with the needs and limitations of the natural environment. One survey found that although most eco-activists, like most conservationists, were largely middle class, the eco-activists were more likely to be employed in the professions, the arts, and education. Operating outside the market, the early Greens tended to reject market-oriented values and instead placed a high value on participation and community.[11]

The important change in environmentalism in the 1960s and 1970s was not quantitative but qualitative: It involved not simply an increase in conversationist organizations but the emergence of new types of groups. The traditional environmentalists or conservationists were concerned with protecting amenities and preserving wildlife but had no interest in social and political change. They worked to protect this bird species or block that highway, but they did not view their world in ecological terms: They were not holists who believed in the interrelatedness of all creatures in the world's ecosystem. They did not perceive a major, all-embracing environmental crisis. In the 1960s and 1970s, however, new groups emerged in Britain that possessed this holistic vision. Unlike the conservationists, they argued that correcting environmental abuses demanded far-reaching social, economic, and political change. They condemned not only environmental degradation but also the society that did the degrading.

9 Sandbach, *Environment, Ideology, and Policy*, p. 4.
10 This is the interpretation given by Philip Lowe and Jane Goyder in their excellent *Environmental Groups in Politics*. David Evans distinguishes what he calls "nature conservationists" from the "new conservationists" of the 1960s. See his *A History of Nature Conservation in Britain* (London: Routledge, 1992), pp. 112–14.
11 Stephen Cotgrove, *Catastrophe or Cornucopia: The Environment, Politics, and the Future* (New York: Wiley, 1982), pp. 18–19, 35; Stephen Cotgrove and A. Duff, "Environmentalism, Middle-Class Radicalism, and Politics," *Sociological Review*, May 1980, 340–2; Stephen Cotgrove and A. Duff, "Environmentalism, Values, and Social Change," *British Journal of Sociology*, Mar. 1981, pp. 98–103.

Barbara Ward and the vision of a small planet

In 1966, Barbara Ward (later Baroness Jackson of Lodsworth), the respected economist and writer, published *Spaceship Earth* and placed herself at the forefront of the fledgling Green movement.[12] An examination of Ward's ecological writings reveals the major themes of early eco-activism, as well as the key points of contention within the movement. Moreover, the evolution within Ward's work of a more comprehensive social critique, of an eco-activist rather than conservationist perspective, illustrates the important distinctions between these two forms of environmentalism.

In *Spaceship Earth* Ward drew on a powerful postwar image. In the 1960s, the United States surged ahead in the space race. The space capsule became a familiar concept: a total but limited environment on whose scanty resources human lives depended. Rather suddenly, the idea that the earth was itself a form of space capsule emerged. In the pictures taken by the *Apollo* space teams, the earth hung like a ball suspended in a vast abyss of darkness. To a generation increasingly oriented to visual images, the *Apollo* photographs were stunning and unsettling. The earth seemed limited, and fragile, hardly larger than the spaceship in which the astronauts traveled.

In *Spaceship Earth* and in its sequels *Only One Earth* (1972) and *Progress for a Small Planet* (1979), Ward set out her influential vision of the interconnections among economic and political structures and of the environmental degradation of the planet. Ward was not the only observer, or the first, to adopt the imagery of Spaceship Earth. One year earlier, Adlai Stevenson had compared the earth to a spaceship in a speech in the United Nations.[13] In the same year that *Spaceship Earth* appeared, the economist Kenneth Boulding published a formative essay that also relied on the evocative power of the spaceship imagery. Boulding described the earth as "a single spaceship, without unlimited reservoirs of anything . . . and in which, therefore, man must find his place in a cyclical ecological system." Instead of a "spaceman" economy, however, human society pressed ahead with the economics of the "cowboy," characterized by "reckless, exploitative, romantic, and violent behavior" and the view of production and consumption as limitless goods. The

---

12 Barbara Ward, *Spaceship Earth* (New York: Columbia University Press, 1966).
13 Adlai Stevenson, speech to the Nineteenth Session of the United Nations Assembly, 1323d Plenary Meeting, *Official Records of the General Assembly* (New York: United Nations, 1966), p. 15. Ward credited Buckminster Fuller with the concept of Spaceship Earth (Ward, *Spaceship Earth*, p. 15). In 1969, Fuller published his *Operating Manual for Spaceship Earth* (Carbondale and Edwardsville: Southern Illinois University Press, 1969).

result was environmental degradation, in the form of spreading pollution, and the wasting of precious resources.[14]

In *Spaceship Earth* Ward sketched a picture of human society at a point of crisis. Three interrelated scientific and technological developments – worldwide communications, economic modernization, and the potential to destroy the earth with nuclear weapons – had drawn the world together into a "single, vulnerable, human community." As a result, the "most rational way of considering the whole human race today is to see it as the ship's crew of a single spaceship. . . . This space voyage is totally precarious. We depend upon a little envelope of soil and a rather large envelope of atmosphere for life itself. And both can be contaminated and destroyed." The most serious threat of destruction came from the worldwide imbalance of power and wealth seen in the divide between North and South. The developing nations' demands for economic justice would have to be met, and quickly, before the population growth of these countries made economic development under moderate leaders an impossibility.[15]

Ward believed that the solution to the crisis lay within humanity's grasp, but only if it overcame the outmoded barriers of the nation-state. Although the world had become a single economic and technological community, its political structures had failed to keep pace; this failure now threatened the security of the human race. Ward advocated the abandonment of the idea of national sovereignty and the development of organizational structures that matched the effective interdependence of the world's nations. Shaped by the experience of the Second World War, and convinced that nazism was the product of nationalism, Ward believed that only the cultivation of a sense of world citizenry could save the human race and its planet from destruction.

In this argument, Ward articulated a number of the key themes of the early Green movement. First, she called for a radical rerouting of the direction of postwar international politics. Her conviction that the nation-state was a dated and dangerous form of organization became a central premise of Green ideology, which, like Ward, called for the fostering of supranational loyalties and recognized that environmental crises demanded international solutions. Ward's stress on the fundamental unity of the world and its peoples and her vision of the earth as a spaceship reflected an ecological understanding of the relationships between humanity and its environment and a perception that ecology could be ignored only at humanity's peril.

14 Kenneth Boulding, "The Economics of the Coming Spaceship Earth," in *Toward a Steady-State Economy*, ed. Herman Daly (San Francisco: W. H. Freeman, 1973). First published in *Environmental Quality in a Growing Economy* (Baltimore: Johns Hopkins University Press, for Resources for the Future, Inc., 1966). Also published in Herman Daly ed., *Economics, Ecology, Ethics: Essays toward a Steady-State Economy* (San Francisco: W. H. Freeman, 1980), with a follow-up essay, "Spaceship Earth Revisited."

15 *Spaceship Earth*, p. 139; quotations from pp. 1, 15.

Ward's analysis also coalesced with that of the Greens in her interpretation of the era of England's Industrial Revolution. Looking back one hundred years, she condemned the first industrialists and their economist cheerleaders for sins against humanity. A fervent anti-Marxist, Ward argued that much of Marx's power came from his stand as a Jewish prophet who "could not, any more than a Jeremiah or an Ezekiel, tolerate the serious, complacent faces of the bourgeois around him, congratulating themselves on doing God's work while little children fell to their death in the machinery in the cotton mills."[16] Ward, a devout Roman Catholic, argued that the first generations of factory workers were sacrificed for an economic principle that made a mockery of England's profession of Christianity.[17] She also stressed that industrialization, even in its more humane later phases, did not guarantee an improvement in the quality of life. In the industrial cities, especially, human beings encountered structures that were "bleak, uncreative, obstructive, and even antihuman."[18] The idea that industrialization in some senses violated the spiritual sanctity of humanity was a strong undercurrent in the early Green movement.

Another significant current in Green thought that appeared in *Spaceship Earth* was the fear that humanity lacked the wisdom to match its technological capabilities. Ward wrote the book to answer the question, "Can we prevent the sheer inventions and pressures of our society from running so far beyond our political, social, and moral wisdom?"[19] A distinctly Green question, it drew a line between knowledge and wisdom, and demanded that technology be subjected to a moral calculus.

Ward, however, at first answered the question in distinctly non-Green ways. She argued that the wisdom needed to guide humanity through the crisis would come through science and, more specifically, through economic growth. Ward did not believe it "too audacious to hope that if, in the next decades, most of mankind can be set, by way of new technologies, on the path of growth, then human conquest . . . may now become the conquest of things of the mind. . . . If the triumphs and contests of abundance take the place of the old grinding enmities bred of scarcity, then, perhaps, we shall not destroy ourselves." The necessary expansion of abundance, according to Ward, would only come if national boundaries were transcended and a planetary consciousness developed, so that the North realized that its own survival rested on sharing its wealth with the South. Ward dared to hope for such a political and intellectual revolution because of her faith in science. She argued that in the

---

16 Ibid., p. 63.
17 See also Barbara Ward, *The West at Bay* (New York: Norton, 1948), pp. 61–3, 277–9; *Five Ideas that Change the World* (New York: Norton, 1959), p. 62; *Progress for a Small Planet* (New York: Norton, 1979), pp. 116–23.
18 *Spaceship Earth*, p. 71.   19 Ibid., p. 16.

past it "required great vision, great holiness, great wisdom to keep alive and vivid the sense of the unity of man." In the second half of the twentieth century, however, this vision of "the saints, the poets, the philosophers" had become scientific fact.[20] Equipped with the force of fact, scientists, economists, and the world's leaders could save Spaceship Earth from destroying itself. As Ward explained in a later work, "since this reality comes to us with all the weight of scientific proof and cogency, we can hope that it will be more convincing than was the earlier, less scientifically substained knowledge."[21]

Ward's faith in the power of science and technology to save the earth contrasted with the strong antiscientist current in the early Green movement. Yet, as we will see, the romantic condemnation of the scientific outlook intermingled in the early movement with more positive evaluations of the role of science in finding a path out of the industrial wasteland. More important was Ward's trust that economic growth contained the keys to the kingdom. Ward's early works revealed her liberal faith in the beneficent effects of the spread of Western ideas and structures, including Western patterns of industrialization. She advocated wealth creation through mechanization and capital investment, to be stimulated by the outpouring of aid from the industrial nations.[22] In *Spaceship Earth* she noted the importance of matching aid to local conditions, but she lacked both the mistrust of capital-intensive industrial schemes and the deeper resistance to the idea of economic growth that lay at the heart of early Green ideology.

Ward's later works, however, reveal the evolution of a more eco-activist perspective in her increasingly critical stance toward orthodox schemes of economic development. In 1972 Ward joined with René DuBois to write *Only One Earth*, a report on the state of the environment commissioned by Maurice Strong, secretary general of the United Nations Conference on the Human Environment, held in Stockholm. Written just six years after *Spaceship Earth*, this later book devotes much more attention to the fact of environmental degradation and so reflects the upsurge in environmental awareness that swept Europe and the United States at the end of the 1960s. *Only One Earth* carried forward the theme of Ward's earlier book: that supranational structures were needed to address the problem of Third World development and that the population explosion made the task urgent. But it added to this theme by emphasizing the ecological fragility of the earth and, especially, the need to conserve its limited resources. Ward remained committed to the aim of economic growth, but she qualified this aim more carefully in 1972 than she had six years earlier. She argued that the measure of growth must be made more

20 Ibid., pp. 50–1, 148.
21 Barbara Ward and Rene DuBois, *Only One Earth* (London: Andre Deutsch, 1972), p. 86. See also Ward, *Progress for a Small Planet*, pp. 265–6.
22 See, e.g., *Policy for the West* (New York: Norton, 1951), pp. 40–1, 135, 148–9, 304–7.

accurate, more environmentally sound. The quantitative indicators of national welfare, which failed to count environmental costs of production, were inadequate, and technologies that degraded the environment were inappropriate. But, she insisted, "growth and environment are not in necessary opposition. If population becomes stabilized, basic injustices are redressed, effluent charges imposed, new systems of non-polluting technologies evolved . . . societies can still 'grow,' yet still preserve and enhance their environments."[23] Seven years later, in *Progress for a Small Planet*, Ward reiterated her belief that economic growth and environmental preservation could be partners, but only if the measures and types of growth were adapted to the demands of a fragile ecosystem. She insisted that she was not seeking a return to the preindustrial era but rather the abandonment "of perpetual pursuit of 'more' which is the root of inflation, the core of boredom, the rungs of a meaningless treadmill."[24] In this later work, she was, however, less confident that the will existed in the developing nations to tackle the task at hand.

The more deeply Green tone of *Only One Earth* demonstrates the reevaluation of the development process that emerged from the economic failures of the Third World. By 1972, it was becoming increasingly apparent that despite the aid programs and the transfer of industrialized agricultural techniques, the developing nations had not yet "taken off" into continuous economic growth. Slowly, planners and politicians began to question the orthodox patterns of aid. In 1971, Ward helped found the International Institute for Environment and Development, which proved significant in introducing the concept of "sustainable development,"[25] a key Green idea and one that was central to *Only One Earth*. In this work, DuBois and Ward cautioned that substituting capital-intensive technologies for labor-intensive systems could and did upset the ecological and economic balance of traditional societies. They called for a more locally oriented approach to development, one that utilized the developing world's vast resources of labor without overtaxing its scarce supply of capital.[26] In *Progress for a Small Planet* Ward repeated this call and emphasized much more clearly and strongly the need to build a sound agricultural base in the developing nations before embarking on large-scale industrialization. In agriculture, as in industry, aid efforts would have to be locally based, labor-intensive, and reliant on cheaper, smaller-scale technologies to succeed.[27]

This demand for a more gradualist, smaller-scale, locally oriented development process would be heard more and more loudly in the 1970s and 1980s as

23 *Only One Earth*, pp. 35–48, 76–87, 171–205; quotation from pp. 202–3.
24 *Progress for a Small Planet*, p. 169.
25 Jonathon Porritt and David Winner, *The Coming of the Greens* (London: Fontana, 1988), p. 229.
26 *Only One Earth*, pp. 221–50.   27 *Progress for a Small Planet*, pp. 171–89, 198–227.

the development failures, and the starving bodies, piled up in the Third World. It reflected, however, more than a pragmatic approach to a world problem. It indicated a willingness to retreat from the "Bigger – Better – More – Now" ethos of industrialized society and to insist upon a valuation of success based on more than statistics. It indicated an ecological world view that recognized the interdependence of technological choices, environmental health, and human choices. It indicated a resistance to the abstraction and quantification of modern scientific thought. Hence, it cohered with the Green critique of modern industrial society.

Only One Earth and Progress for a Small Planet reveal a tempering of Ward's technocratic faith. Instead of relying on the experts and on development from the top down, Ward stressed the need to involve the local community and to make room for independent initiative.[28] In Ward's view, the "most basic of all basic needs turns out to be the right to participate in the adventure of change and to see the advantage of the work." She insisted on the importance of participation not only at the level of the developing nations but within the industrialized world as well. In 1979, as she surveyed the environmental successes and failures of the last decade, Ward concluded that the key to saving the environment and creating a stable economy lay not in governmental action but in the involvement of ordinary citizens. She called for a "grand assize" of the government, unions, management, and consumer representatives to forecast the scale of resources and production needed to meet every citizen's right to satisfying work and a sufficient income. Decentralization of economic power through the encouragement of small businesses and the establishment of co-management structures would, Ward argued, "dissolve perhaps the worst aspects of traditional industrialism, the alienation of the mass of workers from their community of work."[29] It would also re-create the sense of community among men and women at the local levels and so make possible the emergence of the sense of global community without which no resolution to the linked environmental and development crises was possible. This stress on participation and community, and on the interconnections between local action and global consciousness, flowed as a strong current in the Green stream.

In Ward's work, the central themes of the Green critique can be discerned. Suspicious of conventional political structures, she called for the creation of new structures that would be more suitable to the requirements of Spaceship Earth, to the ecological needs of the earth and its inhabitants. One of the demands of Spaceship Earth was a reevaluation of the definition and aims of economic growth: In her later writings she displayed a mistrust of

28 Only One Earth, p. 236; Progress for a Small Planet, pp. 188, 239–40, 262, 273.
29 Progress for a Small Planet, pp. 75–81, 136–7; quotations from pp. 197, 149.

conventional growth economics and focused on the need for ecologically sustainable development, a concept based on an entirely different hierarchy of values than that which undergirded orthodox economic growth.

The Conservation Society

One of the most important early Green organizations in Britain, the Conservation Society, was formed in 1966 in response to what it perceived as clear environmental constraints on growth. At its beginnings, it focused on the strains placed on the earth by a growing population; by 1970, it embraced the arguments against economic growth as well. Its history illustrates the centrality of the challenge to growth, both economic and demographic, in the ideas and actions of the early Green movement.

In challenging the ideal of growth, the Conservation Society confronted one of the basic assumptions of postwar industrial society. The horrors of the Second World War had given way to an era of unprecedented economic expansion in Europe. Europe's "economic miracle," together with the seemingly unstoppable growth of the U.S. economy and the supposed success of industrialization in the Soviet Union, shifted the focus of economic thinking. In the interwar years, with unemployment the key issue, the problem of distribution consumed economists' thoughts. After 1950, however, economic growth moved to center stage. According to H. W. Arndt, governments began to view growth as the remedy for all economic woes, including balance-of-payments problems, underemployment, and inflation.[30] The construction of tables comparing rates of growth in different countries heightened awareness of inequalities and made growth an important standard by which to judge national, political, and personal performance. The cold war elevated this economic competition by making economic performance a testing ground for the merits of capitalist and communist ideologies.[31]

Decolonization added further impetus to growth-oriented economics: The development of the Third World became a central economic and political problem. The 1950s and 1960s witnessed the painful and protracted process of decolonization as imperial powers such as Britain and France resisted and then acceded to the inevitable in Africa and Asia. For the newly formed nations, economic success proved to be even more difficult to

30 H. W. Arndt, *The Rise and Fall of Economic Growth* (London: Cheshire, 1978), p. 43. See also Arndt's *Economic Development: The History of an Idea* (Chicago: University of Chicago Press, 1987).
31 T. Wilson, "The Price of Growth," *Economic Journal* 73 (Dec. 1973): 604–7; J. R. Hicks, "Growth and Anti-growth," *Oxford Economic Papers* 18 (Nov. 1966): 263–5; Nicholas Kaldor, "Economic Growth and the Problem of Inflation," *Economica*, Aug. 1959, p. 212.

achieve than political independence. As more and more Europeans moved into the ranks of the Haves, concern grew over burgeoning numbers of Have-Nots in the Southern Hemisphere. The answer appeared to be economic growth: the rapid industrial development of the South through the injection of capital, technology, and other forms of financial assistance from the North. In 1960, Eugene Black, head of the World Bank, christened the postwar era the Age of Economic Development.[32] For most economists, planners, and politicians, the task looked immense but straightforward; in Barbara Ward's critical paraphrase, "the now increasingly emancipated ex-colonial South would industrialize, modernize, and expand by 'stages of growth' comparable to those achieved in the North. . . . until all, North and South, rich and poor together, would hasten forward to the felicity of the high-consumption economy."[33]

The Conservation Society emerged in the context of widespread faith in the gospel of growth; its formation, however, revealed a growing uneasiness in Britain about the effects of postwar development. For many people, development became linked to environmental degradation. Demographic predictions heightened the perception of crisis. In 1964, experts predicted that by 2001 the United Kingdom would have a population of 74.7 million. With a population of 54 million in 1965 and with many Britons already feeling the pressure of these numbers, especially middle-class Britons who found their favorite holiday spots invaded by newly affluent workers, people began to wonder where 20 million extra bodies would fit. At the same time, the population numbers of the former colonial regions were booming, with no cessation in sight.

This vague sense of crisis gave birth to the Conservation Society. At the end of 1964, the *Observer* published a letter from Edith Freeman, who wrote about her disenchantment with the current political system.[34] This letter, together with an article by Nigel Calder in *New Scientist* that argued that the division of politics along a Left–Right line no longer accorded with reality and that the real division lay in attitudes toward technology,[35] impelled Dr. Douglas M. C. MacEwan to call for a new organization. Convinced that the growth of the world's population had reached the point where it threatened to disrupt both rural and urban communities, to overtax natural resources, and to eliminate "wild and unsettled regions," MacEwan demanded the

32 Eugene Black, "The Age of Economic Development," *Economic Journal*, June 1960, p. 268.

33 Ward, *Progress for a Small Planet*, pp. 5–6.

34 "The Uncommitted," letter from Edith Freeman, Sudbury, published in *Observer*, 11 Oct. 1964, p. 28. Freeman wrote, "The election is being fought on the standard of life; what ought to concern us is the quality of living." She contended that the population explosion rather than nuclear war posed the greatest threat for humanity.

35 Nigel Calder, "Means in Search of Ends," *New Scientist*, 8 Oct. 1964, p. 86.

creation of a politically oriented group that would refuse to settle for piece-meal measures but would instead focus on the root causes of the modern crisis.[36] Encouraged by Freeman and others to whom he distributed his outline, MacEwan announced the formation of the Conservation Society in the *Observer* in March 1966. MacEwan explained that this new society would fight "against the menace of decreasing standards of life due to population pressure." He described this erosion of living standards in environmental terms: "the threat to wildlife, interference with existing areas of unspoilt coastline, the spoiling of historic cities, pressure to apply chemical methods of food production and control before they are properly tested."[37] At the founding meeting of the Conservation Society, MacEwan urged the group to "see the problem of conservation as a whole" and to focus on "fundamental objectives." The group agreed that "the expansion of population was . . . the fundamental factor" in the crisis they perceived.[38]

Despite its focus on the population question, the Conservation Society was not a single-issue campaign. An early division between those who saw the organization as a population stabilization pressure group and those who believed the society should adopt "a more comprehensive approach . . . in-volving a general concern about conservation, . . . resources and the pres-sures upon them" was decided in favor of the more comprehensive perspec-tive.[39] The society saw itself as distinct from conservationist organizations in that it did not seek to address the symptoms but rather the cause of the environmental crisis: a human population too big for the environment to bear. Continued population growth would degrade the natural and human environments to such a degree that the quality of life would suffer. To the members of the Conservation Society, protecting the environment and stabi-lizing the world's population were two sides of the same coin. Hence, the society *Newsletter* contained articles on not only population policy and related issues such as the family-planning bill and abortion law reform but also environmental concerns such as water conservation, the preservation of wil-derness areas and national parks, opposition to a third London airport and the Concorde project, the problems of derelict land and hedge destruction, the maintenance of footpaths, and the importance of recycling.[40]

The society worked to educate the British public about the population

36 Douglas M. C. MacEwan, "Some Recollections of the Formation of the Society," *Conser-vation News* 61 (June 1976).
37 *Observer*, 17 Mar. 1966, p. 31.
38 Minutes of the founding meeting of the Conservation Society, 22 July 1966.
39 *Newsletter* 2/10 (Dec. 1968): 7
40 I am grateful to John Davoll, director of the Conservation Society from 1970 to 1987, for allowing me access to the society's *Newsletter*s at what was, in 1986, the society's head-quarters in Chertsey, Surrey. The society no longer exists; I have not been able to track down the new location of its papers.

crisis and to pressure the British government to formulate a population policy. Although during this first phase it experienced steady growth, with a doubling of membership every year, by the beginning of 1970 it still had only one thousand members.[41] It was a very active group, however, with a sense of mission, the task of stabilizing Britain's population. The society recognized the demographic crisis in the Third World but argued that only if developed nations such as Britain moved forward with population policies would the developing nations be given incentive to do the same. It saw population as the key to a worldwide problem but focused its efforts on Britain. The family-planning bill, which became law on 26 June 1967, served as the centerpiece of much of its earliest actions.[42] During its first years the society also worked on behalf of abortion law reform, agitated for the maintenance of immigration controls, and opposed blanket increases in family allowances, a policy it defined as "pronatalist." It regarded these measures as pieces of a larger effort, the endeavor to persuade the government to establish and effect a population policy. Only a population policy aimed at educating the public about the social consequences of their individual reproductive choices would stabilize Britain's population and so safeguard the nation's quality of life.[43]

By the end of the 1960s the society had succeeded in presenting its case to both the government and the public. In February 1968, 323 MPs called on the government to review Britain's population trends and their implications. In November 1969 the House of Commons Select Committee on Science and Technology began its inquiry into the consequences of population growth in the United Kingdom. The society's submission to the committee, "Why Britain Needs a Population Policy," received a great deal of press attention.[44] The committee's report, published in May 1971, noted the society's recommendations.[45] That year, the establishment of an official Population Panel demonstrated that the government recognized the existence of a population problem.[46]

By 1971, however, Britain's demographic patterns had confounded the experts. After 1964, the annual number of births began to fall, with the first actual reduction in population achieved in 1974–5. By 1969, the predicted

---

41 *Newsletter* 67 (Nov.–Jan. 1977/8): 3.
42 This legislation was in some ways a defeat for the Conservation Society. It granted local authorities the right to set up family-planning facilities through the National Health Service – but did not require or provide funds for them to do so. It did, however, have a positive impact on the society: Local branches began to press their local authorities to set up and expand family-planning facilities – and so found a clear and concrete focus for activism.
43 Conservation Society, "Why Britain Needs a Population Policy" (1969); Conservation Society, "A Population Policy for Britain" (1972).
44 *Newsletter* 4/2 (Mar.–Apr. 1970).
45 Conservation Society, "Annual Report for 1971," p. 2.
46 Lowe and Goyder, *Environmental Groups*, p. 67.

population of the United Kingdom in 2001 was lowered from 74.7 to 66.5 million.[47] By the end of the 1970s, the Conservation Society faced the task of convincing the British public that demographic decline did not constitute a cause for worry.[48]

As it became evident that British population growth was not the problem they had perceived it to be, members of the society began to widen the focus of their analyses of the crisis facing modern society. Although in the 1970s the group continued to extol the benefits of a stable population, economic, rather than population, growth became its main enemy. In 1969 in an article for the society *Newsletter* that was intended to outline the society's aims and philosophy, Chairman John Davoll argued that "continuous growth in either field [demographic or economic] cannot be a permanent feature on a planet which is limited in its space, its irreplaceable resources, and its capacity to absorb pollution and exploitation without ecological collapse."[49] This shift of emphasis encountered resistance from some society members who viewed the challenge to economic growth as a leftist product, but by 1970 anti-economic-growth ideas were firmly established in the society.[50]

In 1970 the society's membership rose from approximately 1,000 to 4,500.[51] That same year, John Davoll accepted the position of Conservation Society director and became the first full-time paid employee of the organization. Widely read, Davoll had studied the antigrowth works of Edward Mishan, Kenneth Boulding, Herman Daly, and Garrett Hardin, and became convinced that economic growth posed as great a threat to modern humanity as overpopulation.[52] Under his leadership the Conservation Society played an important role in the first phase of the Green movement in Britain. During 1971 Davoll and Sam Lawrence, the society's honorary secretary, worked with a team of editors from the journal *Ecologist* to produce *A Blueprint for Survival*, one of the key documents of eco-activism. It was released on 13 January 1972 in a blizzard of media attention (see pp. 230–36). In the spring, the society's submission of three papers to the working parties set up

---

47 *Newsletter* 4/5 (Sept.–Oct. 1970): 2.
48 See Conservation Society, "The Twilight of Parenthood: The Elderly in a Stationary or Declining Population" (June 1975); Conservation Society, "Good News about Britain's Population" (1979?).
49 *Newsletter* 3/5 (June–July 1969): 3.
50 Interview with John Davoll, 18 Mar. 1986. The *Newsletters* during 1971 and 1972 contain letters both for and against the shift in focus to economic growth. For the Conversation Society's argument against economic growth, see "Why Britain Needs a Conservation Policy for the Environment" (1970), pp. 5, 7, 11; "The Decade of Decision" (1971), p. 11; "A Population Policy for Britain" (1972), p. 7; "The Economics of Conservation: An Outline Plan for the United Kingdom" (1973), pp. 6–9; Margaret Laws Smith, *Towards the Creation of a Sustainable Economy* (Chertsey: Conservation Society, 1975).
51 *Newsletter*, Nov.–Jan. 1977/8, p. 3.   52 Davoll interview, 18 Mar. 1986.

by Peter Walker to prepare for the United Nations Conference on the Human Environment in Stockholm led to Davoll's membership on the Working Party on Pollution and to his substantial contribution to its report, *Pollution: Nuisance or Nemesis?*[53] That same year, the society's exposure of cyanide dumping in Warwickshire resulted in not only extensive press coverage but also the Deposit of Poisonous Waste Act of 1972.[54]

By the beginning of 1973, the society's membership had grown to 8,320.[55] Membership numbers, however, peaked in 1973–4, at 8,734, and then began a steady decline until the Conservation Society finally closed shop in 1987.[56] The society never fulfilled its early promise, although it played a crucial role in the Windscale Inquiry of 1977.[57] Davoll, director until the society's end, became convinced that short-term actions could not save the world. The result was institutional paralysis and the loss of initiative to other organizations, such as Friends of the Earth, which combined the society's concerns with a more effective program of action. During the second half of the 1960s and the early 1970s, however, the Conservation Society helped set the agenda of eco-activist concerns, demonstrated that the challenge to growth stood at the center of the Green critique, and offered an alternative vision of what Britain should become.

Friends of the Earth

The Conservation Society illustrates the fundamentally radical nature of the Green critique; it did not succeed, however, in communicating its message to the British public. It adopted a far-reaching social and cultural protest but failed to adapt its techniques to its message. In contrast, Friends of the Earth (FoE), the leading eco-activist campaigning organization in Britain during the 1970s and 1980s, packaged its protest in fresh and provocative ways.[58]

53 *Newsletter*, Sept. 1972, p. 11; "Annual Report for 1972," pp. 1–2, 5–6; Davoll interview, 18 Mar. 1986.
54 "Annual Report for 1972," p. 5; Lowe and Goyder, *Environmental Groups*, p. 78.
55 *Newsletter*, Nov.–Jan. 1977/8, p. 3.   56 See *Conservation News* 97 (Mar./June 1987).
57 Ian Breach, *Windscale Fallout* (Harmondsworth: Penguin, 1978), pp. 95, 142–55. Breach reprints Davoll's testimony before the Inquiry in full and describes Davoll as "one of the most respected and authoritative observers on the environmental scene" (p. 142).
58 "But what about Greenpeace?" may be the reaction of many readers at this point. Greenpeace has undoubtedly grabbed the lion's share of press coverage in the last decade. It was not, however, established in the United Kingdom until fairly late – in 1977 by members of FoE who were unhappy with the group's emphasis on research and its refusal to engage in civil disobedience. Moreover, Greenpeace is much less of a British organization than is FoE. It is part of an international structure run on fairly undemocratic lines. Its individual members and local groups are asked to give financial contributions but little else; they are not, in fact, allowed to conduct Greenpeace campaigns on their own.

FoE began in the United States when David Brower, forced to resign as executive director of the Sierra Club because of his confrontational approach, formed an organization more suited to his vision and style. Like Brower, the new organization was iconoclastic, given to dramatic demonstrations, and imbued with a sense of urgency.[59] In 1970 Brower met with Graham Searle, then vice-president of the National Union of Students (NUS).[60] The year before, Searle, a geology student, had examined the question of resource sustainability for the NUS's contribution to the "Countryside in 1970" Conference[61] and had concluded that industrial societies could not continue in the direction they were heading. Searle convinced Brower that FoE in Britain should not be a branch of its U.S. parent but rather an autonomous organization.[62] It was a wise decision; it freed FoE to place itself in a British context and appeal to a British constituency. A second wise decision was to forgo the substantial tax advantage offered by charity status; by not registering as a charity, FoE left itself free to agitate for political change.

Searle and a small group of activists set up shop in Covent Garden in 1970. Ballantine Books, for whom Searle worked as an editor of fantasy literature, lent the group office space and commissioned it to write a British version of *The Environmental Handbook*, a successful American publication.[63] FoE began its endeavor to save the earth with three specific and potentially winnable campaigns: the battle to ban imports of whale and endangered-species products, as well as the fight against the fur trade; the fight against mining in national parks, specifically the struggle to block Rio Tinto Zinc's plan to open copper mines in Snowdonia National Park; and the effort to focus British public attention on packaging and recycling through the campaign against Schweppes's nonreturnable bottles.[64] The organization soon expanded its efforts to include a focus on renewable resources. Amory Lovins, an American with expertise in the energy field, resigned his research fellowship at Oxford's Merton College to join the FoE staff as energy special-

59 See Michael P. Cohen, *The History of the Sierra Club, 1892–1970* (San Francisco: Sierra Club Books, 1988), pp. 333–434; John McPhee, *Encounters with the Archdruid* (New York: Farrar, Straus and Giroux, 1971), pp. 208–20.

60 For a history of FoE U.K., see Chris Church, *Coming of Age – The First Twenty Years of Friends of the Earth in Britain* (London: Gollancz, 1992).

61 Under the patronage of the Duke of Edinburgh, the "Countryside in 1970" Conference was the culmination of several years of coordinated effort by hundreds of environmentalist and conservationist organizations. It was held at the Guildhall in London.

62 Interview with Graham Searle, 10 July 1989.

63 Searle interview, 10 July 1989; Walt Patterson, "A Decade of Friendship: The First Ten Years," in *The Environmental Crisis*, ed. Des Wilson (London: Heinemann, 1984), p. 141.

64 See *Ecologist* 1/18 (Dec. 1971): 33; *Ecologist* 2/7 (June 1972): 33. For the Snowdonia campaign, see "Mining in Snowdonia," *Ecologist* 1/12 (June 1971): 4–8. For the Schweppes battle, see "Ecology Action," *Ecologist* 1/13 (July 1971): 34.

ist. Lovins's renewable resources campaign ensured that FoE played a crucial role in arousing opposition to the nuclear power industry in Britain.[65]

It was, however, the brilliantly engineered Schweppes bottle dump that propelled FoE into the headlines and the British consciousness. FoE deplored Cadbury Schweppes's decision to switch from returnable to throwaway bottles. Realizing that it did not possess the resources or the clout to confront Schweppes head on, FoE decided to attack the enemy with humor, always the powerful weapon of the underdog.[66] The group used Schweppes's own advertising campaign, a series of billboards playing with the "sch" sound a screwtop bottle makes when opened, to call attention to the industry's decision to shift to nonreturnable bottles. It set up an unforgettable photo of a line of glass bottles forming the shape of the British Isles, headed with the slogan "Don't let them Sch . . . on Britain." It then punctuated this campaign by dumping more than a thousand bottles on the steps of Schweppes headquarters in May 1971, followed by bottle dumps across the nation in October.

The bottle dump appealed to large numbers of Britons concerned about the environmental degradation they perceived around them and inspired the formation of local FoE groups throughout the United Kingdom.[67] The number of groups grew quickly, and FoE eventually became one of the largest British environmentalist organizations. From 8 local groups in 1971, the organization expanded to 140 in 1976 and 250 by 1981. Registered supporters numbered 1,000 in 1971, 5,000 in 1976, and 17,000 by 1981. By 1980 it was one of the highest-earning environmentalist organizations in Britain (with a turnover in 1979/80 of £250,000).[68] It attracted frequent mention in the press. Twice in the 1970s over 300 press articles featuring FoE appeared in a single month: in June 1977, during the public inquiry into British Nuclear Fuel's plans to extend its nuclear reprocessing facilities at Windscale, and in July 1979, when the International Whaling Commission met in London.[69]

From its beginnings, FoE gave the local groups a great deal of freedom. Some were started independently; others colonized from London. All, how-

---

65 Lovins coined the term "soft energy," now widely used to refer to forms of energy that are, in Lovins's words, "flexible, resilient, sustainable, and benign" – e.g., hydraulic and solar energy. See Lovins, "Soft Energy Technologies," in *Thinking Green: An Anthology of Essential Ecological Writing*, ed. Michael Allaby (London: Barrie and Jenkins, 1989), pp. 149–55.

66 Searle interview, 10 July 1989; interview with Colin Blythe, 12 July 1989. In a published interview in 1974, Searle said, "I hope that one of the things we've added [to the environmental movement] is a bit of humour" (Patrick Rivers, *Politics by Pressure* [London: Harrap, 1974], p. 125).

67 Patterson, "A Decade of Friendship," p. 141.

68 Lowe and Goyder, *Environmental Groups*, pp. 127, 133. See also David White, "Friends or FOE?" *New Society*, 16 June 1977, pp. 353–4.

69 Lowe and Goyder, *Environmental Groups*, p. 130.

ever, were independent campaigning organizations (although FoE in London retained the right to withdraw use of its name, a power it never had to exercise).[70] FoE U.K. provided information and suggestions for action that local groups used in developing their own projects. Although a network of regional coordinators was in place by the end of FoE's first year of existence, frequent conflicts broke out between the London office and the local groups, with some groups charging that the office did not provide enough guidance and direction and others viewing the center as dictatorial and antidemocratic.[71] Because both the FoE staff and board members were appointed rather than elected, and because no formal mechanisms existed for local groups to determine or influence the choice of direction of national campaigns, resentment grew. In 1981, a more democratic structure was established.[72]

Although an ad hoc response to the needs of the moment, FOE's organizational setup illustrated one of the most important principles of the early Green movement: the need to convince and enable ordinary persons to act to change the world. FoE's publications demonstrate its conviction that given accurate information, ordinary Davids could defeat the industrial Goliaths. For example, FoE Aberdeen's *A Promise to Move Mountains* (1977) endeavored to alert the general public to the issue of uranium mining; Mick Hamer's *Wheels within Wheels* (1974) explained how the road lobby worked and how it could be fought; *Polluters Pay* informed individuals how to use the Pollution Control Act of 1974 against industry and government; the *Whale Campaign Manual* (1974) set out the facts about the whaling industry and offered suggestions for protest. This stress on individual action remained constant in FoE past the 1970s. Its *Handbook*s, published in 1971, 1981, and 1987, insisted that "the world is there for saving, and it's up to you."[73]

FoE's success in saving the world was rather limited in the 1970s.[74] The Schweppes campaign won it considerable attention but did not result in banning nonreturnable bottles from Britain. The group won some noticeable victories, however, including the prevention of copper mining in Snowdonia and a series of bans on the importation of products made from endangered species, culminating in the Endangered Species Act of 1976. In addition,

70 Blythe interview, 12 July 1989.
71 Blythe interview, 12 July 1989; Lowe and Goyder, *Environmental Groups*, pp. 136–7. The FoE Norwich newsletters, deposited in the British Library, reveal ongoing resentment against the London office.
72 In 1981 FoE overhauled its organizational structure; under the new setup, local groups elected representatives to the FoE Board, which formulated policy and staffed the central office. See Walt Patterson, "A Decade of Friendship," pp. 153–4.
73 *FoE Handbook* (London: FoE, 1981), p. 11. See also John Barr, ed., *The Environmental Handbook: Action Guide for the U.K.* (London: Ballantine and FoE, 1971), pp. 217–18; Jonathon Porritt, ed., *FoE Handbook* (London: Optima Press, 1987), p. 30.
74 Chris Church gives a more optimistic assessment of FoE's accomplishments in his history of the group. See his *Coming of Age*.

FoE's efforts helped to spark a national debate over the issue of nuclear energy and to mobilize opposition to the official oil policy of both Labour and Conservative governments. It can be argued that because of its agitation, at least in part, the amount of land protected under the national park system was expanded and, at the local level, environmental consideration won a place on planning agendas. Certainly throughout the 1970s, FoE raised public awareness about ecological issues and established its own credibility on these issues. Its opposition in 1977 to British Nuclear Fuel's plans to add an oxide reprocessing plant to its Windscale operations was instrumental in forcing Peter Shore, secretary of state for the environment, to call for a public inquiry into the plans and enhanced FoE's reputation for careful preparation and attention to detail. FoE and Windscale's other opponents, however, lost their battle against construction of the plant.[75]

FoE's ultimate failure during the 1970s on issues such as returnable glass bottles and Windscale should not be allowed to obscure its significance. FoE was an eco-activist, not a conservationist, organization. It sought fundamental change. Influenced by the writings of Paul Ehrlich, among others, it questioned the sustainability of continued industrial and population growth.[76] Its publications in the 1970s advocated such eco-activist policies as restricted use of mineral and energy resources, political and economic decentralization, and greater national, regional, and individual self-sufficiency.[77] FoE restricted its

75 For Windscale and FoE, see Malcolm Pithers's report in *Guardian*, 20 Oct. 1977, p. 13; Godfrey Boyle, *Nuclear Power: The Windscale Controversy* (Milton Keynes: Open University Press, 1978), pp. 20–1, 24–6; Friends of the Earth, *Nuclear Times*, Summer 1978, pp. 4–5; Jeremy Bugler, "Friends of the Earth Is 10 Years Old," *New Scientist*, 30 Apr. 1981, pp. 295–6; Brian Wynne, *Rationality and Ritual: The Windscale Inquiry and Nuclear Decisions in Britain* (Chalfont St. Giles, Bucks: British Society for the History of Science, 1982), pp. 98–100, 105–11; Sandbach, *Environment, Ideology, and Policy*, pp. 123–4. See also Walter C. Patterson and Czech Conroy, *The Parker Inquiry* (London: FoE, 1978); Czech Conroy, *What Choice Windscale?* (London: Conservation Society and FoE, 1978); "The Windscale Inquiry," report by the Honourable Mr. Justice Parker, presented to the Secretary of State for the Environment, 26 Jan. 1978 (London: HMSO, 1978); Mark Southgate, comp., *Index to the Transcripts of the Hearings held before Mr. Justice Parker* (London: Department of Energy, 1978). For additional studies of Windscale, see Breach, *Windscale Fallout;* David Pearce et al., *Decision Making for Energy Futures: A Case Study of the Windscale Inquiry* (London: Macmillan, 1979), pp. 111–82, 236–73. Over fifteen years later, FoE and the other critics of the Windscale (renamed Sellafield) reprocessing plant appear to have been right all along. As of May 1993, the plant had yet to begin operation. It is now regarded by many officials as redundant, as well as potentially dangerous. See "Secret N-waste White Elephant," *Observer*, 7 Mar. 1993. See also *Independent*, 1 Mar. 1993, p. 12; *Independent*, 12 May 1993, p. 7.

76 Blythe interview, 12 July 1989.

77 E.g., Michael Allaby, Colin Blythe, Colin Hines, and Christopher Wardle, *Losing Ground* (London: FoE, 1975); FoE Wandsworth, *Windfall* ([Wandsworth]: FoE, 1979); FoE, *Evidence Submitted by Friends of the Earth Ltd. to the Committee on Minerals Planning Control, 2 Jan. 1973* (London: FoE, 1973); Christopher Wardle, *Britain and the World Food Crisis* (London: FoE, 1974, 1977); FoE, *Eco Cookbook* ([London?]: FoE, 1975); *FoE*

activities and limited resources to a small number of campaigns but saw these issues, and those the group could not tackle, as part of an interrelated ecological crisis. Colin Blythe, FoE's director in 1972, articulated this perception when he recalled why he joined FoE: "I just had a feeling that the world was ... wounded in a way from which it might not recover." This general sense of a wounded world, of "a feeling of global malaise," propelled FoE into its specific actions.[78]

FoE practiced what later Greens would preach: Think globally, act locally. Its first director, Graham Searle, believed in the persuasiveness of winning: "By winning, you teach."[79] He set up an organization built around specific campaigns with concrete goals. Unlike the Conservation Society, for example, FoE did not focus on the population question. Despite its adherence to the eco-activist goal of stabilizing Britain's and the world's population, it stressed more attainable goals such as banning the importation of products made from endangered species. Its literature reveals this practical approach: *Food Co-ops: How to Save Money by Getting Together and Buying in Bulk* (1976), *The Allotments Campaign Manual* (1977), *Economic Growth: The Allotments Campaign Guide* (1979), *Back on the Right Rack* (n.d.; obtaining village bicycle racks), *The Great Heat Escape* (1975; household energy efficiency), *Many Happy Returns* (n.d.; recycling). The "can-do" emphasis of these publications, however, did not place FoE within the camp of ameliorist conservationism. Behind the specific and local concerns lay the perception of a wounded world, the conviction that a global ecological breakdown would occur if humanity failed to change its course.

The Ecologist and *A Blueprint for Survival*

The impending global breakdown served as an important theme in the *Ecologist*, the leading eco-activist journal in the early 1970s. The *Ecologist* was significant in the early Green movement for a number of reasons. First, it analyzed the extent of environmental degradation in both the industrialized and the developing nations. A slick, well-produced, and expensive publication, it brought an air of professionalism to a movement often beset by amateurism. Second, the *Ecologist* was a forum for debate; in its pages crucial issues were aired and ideological battles fought. For example, in 1976, the

Cookbook ([London?]: FoE, 1980); FoE Plymouth, *Towards 2001: The Future of the Plymouth Subregion: Some Observations*, submission to Devon and Cornwall County Councils (FoE Plymouth, 1976). Part of FoE's case against nuclear energy stemmed from its advocacy of decentralization; see FoE Norwich, "Broadsheet No. 1. Energy," p. 4; Michael Flood, *Torness: Keep it Green* (London: FoE, 1979).
78 Blythe interview, 12 July 1989.   79 Searle interview, 10 July 1989.

question of the efficacy and desirability of aid to overpopulated Third World countries became the center of a heated argument that continued through three issues of the journal.[80] Third, the journal outlined the perimeters of early Green concern. As its tables of contents attest, issues such as pollution constituted only part of the Green agenda. From its beginnings the *Ecologist* rejected economic growth and questioned the exportation of advanced technology to the Third World. It also focused from the start on the problems of overpopulation and limited energy resources. It thus belonged in the eco-activist, rather than the conservationist, camp: It rejected the fundamental assumptions of industrial society and challenged the very idea of progress. Finally, the *Ecologist* played a significant role in the early Green movement by producing one of its key texts: In 1972 its editors published *A Blueprint for Survival*, a manifesto that in its demands for social, political, and economic change articulated the ideals of eco-activism.

The originating and guiding spirit of the *Ecologist* was Edward Goldsmith, the older brother of Sir James Goldsmith, the financial tycoon and corporate raider.[81] Born in Paris in 1928, Edward Goldsmith grew up in both France and England and was educated at Millfield and Magdalen (Oxford). In the 1960s, he traveled fairly frequently with James Aspinall, a successful gambler whose hobby was the study and protection of wildlife. Goldsmith's interests focused less on animal life and more on tribal societies. During trips to Africa, Goldsmith witnessed what he perceived as the destruction of these traditional societies and came to conclude that the spread of industrialization, far from being a sign of progress, was instead an environmental and cultural disaster.

He found support for his views in what would become Survival International, then the Primitive People's Fund. Begun by Robin Hanbury-Tenison in 1969, Survival International emerged in response to the plight of the Amazonian Indians in Brazil. Its aim throughout the 1970s and 1980s was the protection of the rights of aboriginal peoples worldwide.[82] Two members of Survival International, Jean Lliedloff, the American explorer, and Robert Allen, its treasurer, joined Goldsmith when he started the *Ecologist* in 1970. According to Goldsmith, "we suddenly realized that primitive people had no future. . . . and nothing else that one cherished had any chance at all." The problem, he and Allen concluded, was economic development: "Develop-

80 See the May, July, and Aug./Sept. issues for 1976.
81 For Sir James Goldsmith, see Robert Preston, "Goldsmith Goes in to BAT," *Independent*, 12 July 1989, p. 21; and "Goldfinger Is Back," *Newsweek*, 24 July 1989, pp. 48–9.
82 "A Philosophy for Survival International," *News of Survival International*, Apr. 1974, p. 2; Survival International, *Annual Review, 1988;* "Ten Years of Survival," *Ecologist* 9/4–5 (July–Aug. 1979): 168–70.

ment, period, is wrong."[83] Goldsmith and Allen both came to an ecological awareness via anthropological interests. They were joined on the journal by Peter Bunyard, a writer for *World Medicine*, who, like them, came from a background in the sciences and, like them, came to eco-activism through anger at the fate of tribal societies.[84]

The anthropological interests of the editorial group helped shape the *Ecologist*'s approach, at the heart of which lay what can be called the "hunter–gatherer ideal." Goldsmith, like many social critics, argued that society, to effect the political and economic transformation he deemed necessary, needed a picture of what it should be moving toward, an ideal that would highlight the wrongs of the present. For him, as for Allen, this ideal was the hunter–gatherer and tribal societies. He argued that instead of devising imaginary utopias, humanity should look to the actual experience of actual peoples. If they looked at tribal societies, they would find a people supremely adapted to their environment. Nicholas Hildyard, a later editor of the *Ecologist*, explained that "traditional societies are the only groups in existence which can provide us with a working model of social and ecological stability."[85] In Goldsmith's view, "to postulate an ideal society for which there is no precedent within the human experience, as many of our political theorists, including Karl Marx, have done, is very much like postulating an alternative biology without reference to the sort of biological structures that have so far proved viable."[86] For Goldsmith, tribal societies were "the normal units of social organizations"; all other social modes were aberrations.[87] Allen argued that "natural man" was the hunter–gatherer; hence, tribal societies "can help us answer some of the most vexing questions troubling us today. Are we innately violent and greedy? What do we mean by good health and a sound

83 Interview with Edward Goldsmith, 15 June 1989. For the founding of the *Ecologist*, see also the *Journal of the Soil Association*, Jan. 1972, p. 2.

84 Interview with Peter Bunyard, 19 June 1989. Like Goldsmith, Bunyard remained closely involved with the *Ecologist* through the 1970s and 1980s. Allen (since his marriage called Robert Prescott Allen) left the journal in 1973 to take a position with the International Union for Conservation of Nature and Natural Resources (IUCN). Established in 1948, the IUCN is "the principal nongovernmental international organization for environmental protection in which governments, nevertheless, have been participants" (Lynton Caldwell, *International Environmental Policy: Emergence and Dimensions* [Durham: Duke University Press, 1984], p. 37). Allen played an important role in writing the IUCN's World Conservation Strategy (1980). Bunyard and Goldsmith were soon joined by Nicholas Hildyard, who remains one of the *Ecologist*'s editors.

85 Nicholas Hildyard, Foreward to Edward Goldsmith, *The Great U-Turn: De-industrializing Society* (Bideford, Devon: Green Books, 1988).

86 Goldsmith, Introduction to *The Great U-Turn*.

87 *The Great U-Turn*, p. 155. The chapters in this work were all previously published in the *Ecologist* between Jan. 1974 and July 1980.

diet? What is the best way to bring up our children? Are we capable of living in harmony with our environment?"[88]

According to the *Ecologist*, traditional societies intuitively recognized the limits of the environment. Their activities were organized to promote stability rather than change and so interfered with the natural environment as little as possible. Even such seemingly destructive activities as slash-and-burn agricultural techniques worked with, rather than against, ecological processes. It was only when industrialization penned traditional societies into too small a space that such techniques caused environmental degradation.

The hunter–gatherer ideal offered the *Ecologist* editors an example of what they perceived to be the good society: an environmentally sustainable, coherent culture. This ideal could and did lead them onto some morally shaky ground. In 1975, Robert Allen defended the Khmer Rouge in the pages of the journal as an embodiment of a decentralized, rural society. Allen acknowledged that thousands had died on forced marches out of the cities (he did not then know that the actual numbers were much higher), but he argued that such losses were a price that had to be paid in order for the Khmer Rouge to free themselves from the bourgeois, industrial world.[89] Somewhat ironically, a theory that arose out of horror at the disappearance of ancient cultures led, in this instance, to an inability to recognize attempted genocide.

The hunter–gatherer ideal shaped the main ideas of *A Blueprint for Survival*, one of the key texts of the early Green movement.[90] First released as a special issue of the *Ecologist* (January 1972) and then published separately, the *Blueprint* listed as its authors *Ecologist* editors Goldsmith, Allen, and Michael Allaby, and two of the leading members of the Conservation Society, John Davoll and Sam Lawrence. All five men participated in planning the document, but it was written by Goldsmith and Allen, strongly reflected their ideas, and should be seen as their work.[91] The *Blueprint*, like the *Ecologist*, shows that what the early Greens sought was not environmental reform but revolution, a radical alteration in the structures, values, and assumptions of modern society.

88 Robert Allen, *Man and Nature – Natural Man* (Madrid: Danbury Press, 1975), p. 7.
89 Robert Allen, "Editorial: The City Is Dead," *Ecologist* 5/6 (July 1975): 186–8. It must be noted that Allen later repudiated his support of the regime.
90 Edward Goldsmith, Robert Allen, Michael Allaby, John Davoll, and Sam Lawrence, *A Blueprint for Survival* (New York: New American Library, 1974). First published as vol. 2, no. 1 (Jan. 1972) of the *Ecologist*, and in book form by Penguin in 1972.
91 Goldsmith wrote the introduction and most of the appendixes; Allen wrote the central part of the document, "Strategy for Change." Michael Allaby gave the *Blueprint* its title, and John Davoll suggested its actual shape: on his recommendation, the work was divided into an argument plus theoretical appendixes. Allaby and Goldsmith disagree on which of them wrote the sections on agriculture (interview with Michael Allaby, 14 Apr. 1986; Goldsmith interview, 15 June 1989; Goldsmith letter to author, 2 May 1992; Davoll's comments, 22 Nov. 1971, in *Blueprint for Survival* file, Conservation Society).

The *Blueprint* consisted of a short discussion explaining the need for change and proposals to guide that change, as well as a series of appendixes documenting the extent of the environmental, energy, and food crises that threatened modern society. A doomsayers' document, the *Blueprint* predicted severe food shortages "within the next 30 years," the exhaustion of "present reserves of but a few metals . . . within 50 years," and "the breakdown of society and the irreversible disruption of the life-support systems on this planet . . . within the lifetimes of our children."[92] In its message of doom, it fitted the prevailing eco-activist mood. In 1971, for example, the *Yorkshire Post* had named G. R. Taylor's *The Doomsday Book* as its Nonfiction Book of the Year. Taylor predicted systematic breakdown of industrial society in thirty years.[93] Similarly, Kenneth Allsop introduced the FoE *Environmental Handbook* of 1971 by arguing that an environmental holocaust was imminent.[94]

The *Blueprint* offered an escape route from the future of doom: "If . . . we can respond to this unprecedented challenge with informed and constructive action, the rewards will be as great as the penalties for failure."[95] The answer lay in the creation of a stable society, defined as one characterized by minimum disruption of ecological processes, maximum conservation of materials and energy, and zero population growth. The model in the *Blueprint*, as in other issues of the *Ecologist*, was the hunter–gatherer society, perceived by Goldsmith as the climax of evolution and environmental adaptation.[96] To bring about this stable society, the *Blueprint* demanded backpedaling from the aim of economic growth, development of alternative technologies, and, most important, political and economic decentralization. It envisaged a new Britain, consisting of neighborhoods of 500, communities of 5,000, and regions of 500,000, between 1975 and 2075.[97]

Just how such a remarkable and comprehensive transition was to occur was not made clear; like most utopian literature, the *Blueprint* depicted a new society but failed to offer instructions for building this new society. In two ominous sentences that were to haunt Goldsmith for the next decade (although they were actually written by Robert Allen), the *Blueprint* warned that "there is no doubt that the long transitional stage that we and our children must go through will impose a heavy burden on our moral courage and will require great restraint. Legislation and the operations of police forces and the courts will be necessary to reinforce this restraint." This warning led some eco-watchers to assume Goldsmith was a fascist or at least a proponent

---

92 *Blueprint*, pp. 11, vii.
93 G. R. Taylor, *The Doomsday Book* (London: Thames and Hudson, 1970).
94 Kenneth Allsop, Introduction to Barr, *Environmental Handbook*, p. xiv.
95 *Blueprint*, p. 15.
96 See ibid., chap. 4, pp. 77–100 (Appendix B, "Social Systems and Their Disruptions" in the original edition).
97 Ibid., p. 41.

of political authoritarianism. Yet, the warning continued: "but we believe that such external controls can never be so subtle nor so effective as internal controls. It would therefore be sensible to promote the social conditions in which *public opinion and full public participation in decision-making* become as far as possible the means whereby communities are ordered."[98] Rather than being drawn to fascism, both Goldsmith and Allen believed that only in small, self-sufficient communities could authoritarianism be avoided. They also, however, believed that industrial society stood on the brink of a crisis so cataclysmic that authoritarian measures could very well become a necessity. As in CND, urgent prophecies of doom mingled with visions of utopia, and with the belief that to this generation had been given the task of saving the world.

The *Blueprint* received a remarkable amount of attention. The special *Blueprint* issue of the *Ecologist* sold out immediately, was published by Tom Stacey, and then picked up by Penguin. The success of the *Blueprint* stemmed in part from brilliant publicity techniques. Before its publication Robert Allen asked a number of "establishment" scientists and academics for their signatures on the document. As a result, thirty-six eminent names, including Sir Frank Fraser Darling, Sir Julian Huxley, the Marquess of Queensberry, Peter Scott, Professor W. A. Robson, and Professor C. H. Waddington, appeared on the inside front cover of the *Blueprint* and were mistakenly regarded by some reporters as its authors.[99] This gave the publication a respectability it would never have been accorded if it were simply viewed as a publication of the *Ecologist*. Allen scored a second coup when he engineered a press conference on 13 January 1972 to announce the release of the *Blueprint*. Sir Frank Fraser Darling, a member of the Royal Commission on Environmental Pollution and an eminently respectable scientist whose Reith Lectures in 1969 had focused public attention on environmental issues, chaired the conference and described the *Blueprint* as "the sanest popular statement" of the crisis he had yet seen.[100]

Perhaps misled by the scientists' signatures, on 13 January the press flocked

98 Ibid., pp. 37–8 (emphasis added).

99 E.g., the *New York Times* quotation of the day for 14 Jan. came from the *Blueprint* but was credited to "A report by 33 leading scientists in Britain, warning against a world environmental catastrophe." See also Andrew Weintraub et al., *The Economic Growth Controversy* (White Plains, N.Y.: International Arts and Sciences Press, 1973). At least two of the essayists in this volume believed that the scientist signatories of the *Blueprint* had actually written the work; see pp. 40, 64. In *The Rise and Fall of Economic Growth* (1978), Arndt presented the *Blueprint* as the scientists' work (p. 130).

100 Fraser Darling's assessment of the *Blueprint* was quoted on the front page of the *New York Times* (14 Jan.) and in the *Daily Mail* (14 Jan., p. 14), the *Guardian* (14 Jan., p. 12), and "Mandrake's" column in the *Daily Telegraph* (16 Jan.). For Fraser Darling's Reith Lectures, see Sir Frank Fraser Darling, *Wilderness and Plenty: The 1969 Reith Lectures* (London: BBC, 1970).

to hear the *Blueprint's* warning of imminent doom.[101] The following day, reports on the *Blueprint* appeared on the front page of the *Times* (and the *New York Times*) and in the *Daily Telegraph*, the *Daily Mirror*, the *Daily Mail*, and the *Guardian*. The *Times* and the *Daily Mail* also both discussed the *Blueprint* in their leaders for 14 January. During the next week, the *Observer* (16 January), the *Sunday Times* (16 January), the *Evening Standard* (17 January), and the *Economist* (22 January) all reported on the *Blueprint*, as did the *Washington Post* (19 January), *Time* (24 January), and *Newsweek* (January 24). Letters to the editor of the *Times* joined in the discussion on 18, 20, 21, 24, and 25 January. Goldsmith found himself a guest on television and radio programs.[102]

Although clever publicity guaranteed the *Blueprint* press attention, it could not ensure a positive response. Yet, for a document that called for the systematic disassembling of industrial society, the *Blueprint* received remarkably favorable reviews. Articles presented its main points accurately and fairly and treated it as a credible document that deserved close attention. In the *Observer*, for example, Gerald Leach noted that "some of the facts are a little wild and its analysis . . . is often naive." He concluded, however, that the *Blueprint* could not be ignored and that the problems it outlined were urgent.[103] The comments of John Stevenson in the *Daily Mail* were more critical: "While it brilliantly outlines social and environmental problems confronting an ever-industrialised [*sic*] society like Britain, its solutions are too frequently vague and too often meaningless."[104] Nevertheless, the *Daily Mail's* leader on the same day argued that *"The Ecologist's* prophecy of a world blindly careening towards self-destruction remains profoundly disturbing. . . . surely, the prophets of doom deserve to be heard with as much respect as those who continue to worship the Gross National Product." In the *Guardian*, Anthony Tucker compared the *Blueprint* to the Communist Manifesto.[105] Lewis Chester in the *Sunday Times* admitted, "The Blueprint, for me, is nightmarishly convincing. . . . it is mind blowing. After reading it nothing seems quite the same any more."[106] In a leader entitled "The Prophets May Be Right," the *Times* con-

---

101 Allaby interviews, 14 Apr. 1986, 19 June 1989; Goldsmith interview, 15 June 1989. Allen's press release began, "Five Fellows of the Royal Society, three Professors of Biology . . . [and twenty-eight] other distinguished scientists have publicly stated their support."

102 I am grateful to Edward Goldsmith for access to his file of press cuttings regarding *A Blueprint for Survival*.

103 "The Alternative Future," *Observer*, 16 Jan. 1972. Leach, it should be noted, was himself an environmentalist. He participated in a weekend conference in 1971 that tried, unsuccessfully, to set up a British version of the Club of Rome (see n. 117). Other participants included Michael Allaby, Robert Allen, John Davoll, Edward Goldsmith, and Sam Lawrence ("Minutes of Meeting Held on 30th/31th October 1971 at Orsett Hall," in *Blueprint for Survival* file, Conservation Society).

104 *Daily Mail*, 14 Jan. 1972, p. 17.   105 *Guardian*, 14 Jan. 1972, p. 12.

106 "A Manifesto for Man," *Sunday Times*, 16 Jan. 1972.

cluded that "the thesis is too plausible to be dismissed." It commended the writers of the *Blueprint* for arguing this thesis in "a convenient and cogent form which firmly fixes its political relevance."[107]

The *Blueprint* received further backing on 25 January, when a letter from 187 scientists appeared in the *Times*. These signatories, including nine fellows of the Royal Society and twenty university professors, stated that although they were unable to sign the *Blueprint* because it contained "scientifically questionable statements of fact and highly debatable short and long term policy proposals," they welcomed it "as a major contribution to current debate" and with it affirmed that a serious and inescapable ecological crisis existed, one that could only be met by a population policy, conservation and recycling of resources, and "the transition to industrial and agricultural techniques which do not threaten the stability of the environment." A report on this letter appeared on the front page of the *Times* and on page 3 of the *New York Times*.[108]

Given the amount of attention it received, the *Blueprint* was bound to cause a few ripples on the political sea. Peter Walker, secretary of state for the environment, realized quickly that political capital could be gained by responding favorably to the document. In a meeting in February that included Allen, Goldsmith, and Davoll, as well as the antigrowth economist E. J. Mishan (who had signed the *Blueprint*), Walker and senior officials discussed the *Blueprint*'s analyses and asked its authors to produce proposals for discussion with government advisors.[109] The next month the *Blueprint* provoked questions in both Houses, to which the government replied that it was meeting with the authors.[110]

The favorable response to what was a rather unorthodox publication based on some dubious calculations[111] can only be explained if the *Blueprint* is set in

---

107 *Times*, 14 Jan. 1972.
108 *Times*, 25 Jan. 1972; *New York Times*, 26 Jan. 1972. An article on the letter also appeared in the *New York Herald Tribune* for 26 Jan.
109 *Times*, 1 Mar. 1972; Conservation Society Annual Report for 1972, pp. 5–6.
110 Viscount Thurso in the House of Lords, 21 Mar. 1972 (*Hansard*, 5th ser., pt. 2, vol. 329 [7–30 Mar. 1972] col. 670); Sir David Renton, Conservative member for Huntingdon, in the Commons, 14 Mar. 1972 (*Hansard*, 5th ser., pt. 1, vol. 833 [13–24 Mar. 1971–2], col. 85). On 28 Apr., Bruce Douglas-Mann, member for Kensington North, made a sixteen-minute speech in favor of the no-growth position. In his reply, Eldon Griffiths, under-secretary of state for the environment, displayed a detailed knowledge of the *Blueprint*, which he described as "a quite remarkable document." This was, however, a Friday afternoon debate in front of a nearly empty House, which adjourned with Griffiths still speaking (*Hansard*, 5th ser., pt. 1, vol. 835 [17–28 Apr. 1971–2] cols. 2018–30.) This debate was reprinted in *Ecologist* 2/9 (Sept. 1972): 4–7.
111 See the "Comments" on the *Blueprint* published in subsequent issues of the *Ecologist* for criticism of its quantitative work: *Ecologist* 2/3 (Mar. 1972): 20–2; 2/4 (Apr. 1972): 23–5; 2/5, (May 1972): 27–9; 2/7 (July 1972): 22–5; 2/9 (Sept. 1972): 23–5; 3/1 (Jan. 1973):39.

its immediate context. It had been some time in the making (Goldsmith conceived of the *Blueprint* in 1970, and by July of 1971 was meeting with Davoll and Lawrence[112]), but its release on 13 January was a stroke of good fortune. That month witnessed an upsurge in environmentalist concern, with particular focus on the question of overpopulation. First, five days before the *Blueprint*'s release, a letter on the population problem signed by fifty-five doctors appeared in both the *Lancet* and the *British Medical Journal*, neither publication a hotbed of environmental radicalism. The letter, which declared that overpopulation posed an urgent world crisis and demanded dramatic measures to meet the problem, provoked intense public response, including articles in the *Times* on 12 and 13 January.[113] Second, on the same day that reports on the *Blueprint* appeared in the daily papers, Paul Ehrlich, the American writer who had first outlined the population problem for the general public, spoke to a capacity crowd at Westminster's Central Hall when he gave his Presidential Address for the Conservation Society. Ehrlich declared to a receptive audience that "Britain may hold a key, maybe the key, to the entire problem. . . . England is still looked to as standard setter in the world. . . . educated people look a great deal to England to lead the way."[114] Thus, the *Blueprint*, with its demands for a rapid reduction in Britain's population and drastic decentralization, appeared at the precise moment when its proposals seemed, if not necessary, at least worthy of discussion. Fourteen years later, John Davoll recalled that during a triumphant dinner with Ehrlich after his speech in Central Hall, "we felt we could do it all." It was, according to *Ecologist* editor Michael Allaby, a period of "high euphoria."[115]

The controversy sparked by the *Blueprint* continued into the spring when *The Limits to Growth* was published.[116] This book, the end result of a four-year project sponsored by the Club of Rome,[117] depended heavily on the work of

112 Davoll interview, 10 Apr. 1986; Davoll to Goldsmith, 3 Aug. 1971, in *Blueprint for Survival* file, Conservation Society.

113 *Lancet* 1/7741 (8 Jan. 1972): 89–90; *British Medical Journal* 1/5792 (8 Jan. 1972): 108.

114 Paul Ehrlich, *The Population, Resources, Environment Crisis – Where Do We Stand Now?* Presidential Address delivered to the Conservation Society, 14 Jan. 1972, at Central Hall, Westminster ([Chertsey?]: Conservation Society, 1972), p. 5. Ehrlich's speech was heard by 2,600 people; 500 individuals had to be turned away. For reports on the speech, see Anthony Tucker, "Britain Should Give a Lead," *Guardian*, 15 Jan. 1972; Donald Gould, "Have We Woken Up at Last?" *New Statesman*, 21 Jan. 1972, pp. 67–8.

115 Davoll interview, 10 Apr. 1986; Allaby interview, 14 Apr. 1986.

116 D. H. Meadows et al., *The Limits to Growth: A Report for the Club of Rome's Project on the Predicament of Mankind* (Washington, D.C.: Potomac Association, 1972). See also *Towards Global Equilibrium: Collected Papers*, ed. Dennis H. Meadows and Donella H. Meadows (Cambridge: Wright and Allen Press, 1972).

117 The Club of Rome was founded in 1968 by Aurelio Peccei, an Italian economist and businessman. He invited approximately fifty scientists, humanists, economists, planners, educators, and industrialists to study the problems and possibilities of the future. *The Limits of Growth* was funded by the Volkswagen Foundation. See U.S. Congress Commit-

Professor Jay Forrester, a systems-dynamics analyst with the Massachussetts Institute of Technology who had devised a computer model of the workings of the environment.[118] The authors of *Limits to Growth*, led by Dennis Meadows, also associated with MIT, developed a more complex model that, like Forrester's, looked at factors such as population, natural resources, industrial and agricultural production, and pollution, and concluded that human society faced serious limits to its economic growth. Goldsmith obtained an advance draft of the *Limits to Growth* in late 1971 and concluded that Meadows and his colleagues' work provided scientific and mathematical backing for conclusions he had already reached.[119] Like the *Blueprint*, *Limits to Growth* predicted the depletion of environmental and energy resources within a century. Described as the "best popularly known book on ecology since *Silent Spring*,"[120] the work provoked great controversy and helped keep public attention focused on the issues raised in the Blueprint.[121]

The Stockholm conference

By the summer of 1972, the early Green movement had made its presence known. Through eco-activist organizations such as the Conservation Society and Friends of the Earth, and through publications such as the *Ecologist* and *A Blueprint for Survival*, the Green critique of industrial society had reached the front pages of Britain's leading newspapers. The stage was set for the

tee on Merchant Marine and Fisheries, Subcommittee on Fisheries and Wildlife Conservation and the Environment, *Growth and Its Implications for the Future* (Washington: GPO, 1973), pp. v–vi.

118 Jay Forrester, *World Dynamics* (Cambridge: Wright-Allen, 1971).

119 Goldsmith and Meadows had met at a scientific conference in the fall of 1971. Meadows then sent a draft of his work to Goldsmith (Goldsmith interview, 15 June 1989; Allaby interview, 19 June 1989; Bunyard interview, 19 June 1989; Davoll interview, 10 Apr. 1986).

120 Donn Block, *Environmental Aspects of Economic Growth in Less Developed Countries: An Annotated Bibliography* ([Paris]: Development Centre of the Organisation for Economic Co-operation and Development, [1973?]), p. 16; Lester Brown, *Building a Sustainable Society* (New York: Norton, 1981), p. 345.

121 For a more extended discussion of *Limits of Growth*, see Wade Rowland, *The Plot to Save the World: The Life and Times of the Stockholm Conference on the Human Environment* (Toronto: Clarke, Irwin and Co., 1973), pp. 9–19; David Elliott and Ruth Elliott, *The Control of Technology* (London: Wykeham, 1976), pp. 17–29. For reactions to the work, see *Economist*, 11 Mar. 1972, p. 20; *Science* 175 (1972): 1088; "A Sober Look at Doomsday," *Guardian*, 6 Mar. 1972, p. 10; Allen Kneese and Ronald Ridker, "Predicament of Mankind," *Washington Post*, 2 Mar. 1972, p. 81; "Another Whiff of Doomsday," *Nature*, 10 Mar. 1972; Rudolf Klein, "Growth and Its Enemies," *Commentary*, June 1972; Kenneth Mellanby, "Ecologists Who Ignore Technology's Successes," (London) *Times*, 3 Mar. 1972; John Maddox, *The Doomsday Syndrome* (New York: McGraw-Hill, 1972), pp. 283–7; Wilfred Beckerman, *In Defence of Economic Growth* (London: Jonathan Cape, 1974), pp. 113–15. See also the essays in Weintraub, *Economic Growth Controversy*.

United Nations Conference on the Human Environment at Stockholm. Stockholm revealed both the contents and the limits of the early Green critique. It also marked the culmination of this first period of eco-activism in Britain.

The Stockholm conference was officially initiated in May 1968, when the permanent representative of Sweden, in a letter to the secretary general of the United Nations, requested the convening of an international environmental conference. The next four years witnessed an immense amount of preparation, in the form of preliminary papers, meetings, specialized conferences, and negotiations. The preparation for Stockholm was itself one factor in the raising of environmental consciousness that occurred throughout the Western world in the late 1960s.[122]

These preparations resulted in one of the more productive and efficient international conferences ever held under UN auspices, not of course a very high standard.[123] The conference established an international convention on marine dumping, set up a global environmental monitoring system called Earthwatch, and established the United Nations Environment Programme (UNEP). Despite these achievements, Stockholm illustrated the limits of international action. Although the conference condemned nuclear weapons tests, the French continued atmospheric tests in the Pacific. The conference also called for a ten-year moratorium on whaling, a plea that went unheeded for another ten years.[124] In 1982, a UN Special Session concluded that Stockholm's "Action Plan has only been partially implemented and the results cannot be considered as satisfactory."[125]

For this study, however, Stockholm's significance lies less in its achievements than in the ideas it embodied. The Stockholm conference represented

122 Caldwell, *International Environmental Policy*, p. 47.
123 See United Nations, *Report of the United Nations Conference on the Human Environment, Stockholm, 5–16 June 1972* (New York, 1973); United Nations Centre for Economic and Social Information, *Environment Stockholm: Declaration, Plan of Action, Recommendations, Resolutions, Papers Relating to the U.N. Conference on the Human Environment, held at Stockholm, Sweden, June 5–16, 1972* (Geneva, 1972).
124 Caldwell, *International Environmental Policy*, pp. 33, 43–7, 54–81; Nigel Hawkes, "Stockholm: Politicking, Confusion, but Some Agreements Reached," *Science* 176 (23 June 1972): 1308–10; "A Special Report: What Happened at Stockholm," *Bulletin of the Atomic Scientists*, Sept. 1972, pp. 17–20, 22–23; Rowland, *Plot to Save the World*, pp. 2–5, 33–42, 105–17. See also John McCormick, *Reclaiming Paradise: A History of the Global Environmental Movement* (Bloomington: Indiana University Press, 1989), pp. 88–105, 149–151.
125 Quoted in Caldwell, *International Environmental Policy*, p. 77. For the *Ecologist*'s response to Stockholm, see the special Stockholm issue: 2/6 (June 1972). See also Robert Allen, "Can Stockholm Survive New York?" *Ecologist* 2/10 (Oct. 1972): 4–9; "United Nations Declaration of the Human Environment: Principles," *Ecologist* 2/10 (Oct. 1972): 10–11; Edward Goldsmith, "The United Nations Environment Programme Ten Years after Stockholm," *Ecologist* 12/2 (Mar./Apr. 1982): 50–1; Edward Goldsmith, "The Retreat from Stockholm," *Ecologist* 12/3 (May/June 1982): 98–100.

an important turning point in environment consciousness. As Lynton Caldwell has explained, Stockholm both symbolized and realized a change in paradigm "from the view of an earth unlimited in abundance and created for man's exclusive use to a concept of the earth as a domain of life or biosphere for which mankind is the temporary resident custodian."[126] Caldwell contrasts two previous international environmental conferences with Stockholm. In 1949, the United Nations Conservation Conference at Lake Success, New York, devised policies and action plans that treated the earth as a resource bank and embodied the spirit of technological optimism.[127] The United Nations Conference on the Application of Science and Technology for the Benefit of Less Developed Areas, held in Geneva in 1963, was, according to Caldwell, "in many ways a replay, with elaborations and refinements, of the Lake Success conference." Stockholm broke with this mold; its Action Plan, both in its realized and in its ignored clauses, rested on a new paradigm, an ecological perspective that focused on the health not of individual streams or species but of the biosphere, "an evolved, integrated, planetary, life-supporting system."[128]

In addition to demonstrating this paradigm shift, Stockholm bore witness to the inextricable ties between ecological issues and Third World development. Eco-activism cannot be understood if it is equated with environmentalism. At the heart of early Green ideas lay the question of economic growth and the tragedy of the underdeveloped areas of the world. The representatives of these areas grabbed the microphone at Stockholm and kept a firm grip on it. A panel of Third World scientists and economists insisted in a preliminary report to the conference that "the current concern with environmental issues has emerged out of the problems experienced by the industrially advanced countries. . . . the major environmental problems of developing countries . . . are predominantly problems that reflect the poverty and very lack of development of their societies. . . . [These problems] can be overcome by the process of development itself."[129] Third World nations feared that environmental concerns would dilute Western aid and undermine their already-fragile economies. They pointed out that the industrialized areas consumed a disproportionate share of the world's resources and demanded compensation for those developing nations whose exports suffered from the imposition of stricter environmental standards.[130] The central position of development issues at the Stockholm conference thus clearly revealed, first

126 Caldwell, *International Environmental Policy*, p. 19.
127 For a different evaluation of the Lake Success Conference, see McCormick, *Reclaiming Paradise*, pp. 36–8.
128 Caldwell, *International Environmental Policy*, pp. 39, 25.
129 Founex Report, June 1971, quoted in Rowland, *Plot to Save the World*, p. 49.
130 Ibid., pp. 47–58.

of all, that ecological concern could not be separated from economic and political factors and, second, that Third World opposition to Green ideas would have to be overcome before any eco-activist plan for saving the world could be implemented.[131]

Stockholm occurred at a time when environmental concern was at its highest point since the century began. Held just after the publication of *A Blueprint for Survival* and *The Limits to Growth*, the conference contributed to the tremendous excitement felt by those who thought they might be able to change the world. For leading British eco-activists, it was a heady time. At Stockholm the *Ecologist* team joined with representatives from Friends of the Earth to produce the *Stockholm Conference Eco*, an unofficial daily newspaper. Maurice Strong, the conference secretary general, allowed the paper inside the conference buildings despite its lack of official standing. In an extraordinary coup, *Eco* scooped the world's press by being the first paper to print a report on China's stand on the conference's Declaration on the Human Environment, a document that proved the subject of intense controversy.[132] (Because China had been only recently admitted to the UN, its position was unknown and a matter of considerable speculation.) Despite revealing that the Third World's desire for industrial development threatened the Greens' chances of success, Stockholm was a high point in early British eco-activism. The conference indicated a change in environmental awareness and seemed to prefigure changes in actions. Buoyed by their perception of success in Stockholm, after their return the *Ecologist* team moved from London to Cornwall, in an effort to put their ideals of decentralization and rural revival into practice.[133]

The Ecology/Green Party

The same combination of despair over the future of industrial society and high hopes for revolutionary change that led the *Ecologist* team to relocate prompted another small environmentally aware group to form a new political party, which would become Britain's Green Party. Its formation revealed that although eco-activism called for thoroughgoing political and economic change, many early Greens believed such changes could occur by working through the existing political system. Moreover, the failure of the Ecology

---

131 See Peter Stone, *Did We Save the Earth at Stockholm?* (London: Earth Island, 1973), pp. 100–21.
132 Allaby interview, 14 Apr. 1986; Rowland, *Plot to Save the World*, pp. 92–3. For the important role played by *Eco* at Stockholm, see Stone, *Did We Save the Earth?* pp. 55–6. *Eco* was such a success that "the UN took it over and institutionalised it" (Patterson, "A Decade of Friendship," p. 142).
133 Peter Bunyard, "Ecological Living: Dream or Reality?" *Ecologist* 5/1 (Jan. 1975): 16.

Party to gain a significant following during the 1970s, even among eco-activists, indicates that no Green political consensus existed: Many more Greens than those who supported the new party retained their faith not only in party politics but in the two-party system, whereas others withdrew from political activity of any color, whether green, red, or blue.

Born in 1973, the Ecology Party waited sixteen years for a significant electoral win. In the elections for the European Parliament held in June 1989, the now-renamed Green Party won 15 percent of the votes cast in Britain – more than two million votes and the highest percentage of votes ever cast for a Green party anywhere in Europe. Because of Britain's lack of a system of proportional representation, the Greens did not, however, win a seat in Parliament.[134] The Greens' success in 1989, if failing to win a single seat can be considered a success, was a sharp break in the party's history. During the 1970s and into the 1980s, the Ecology/Green Party remained small and powerless. Its early history demands study, however, both because it formed part of the early Green landscape and because its failure indicates the resistance of the British political system to the eco-activist agenda and hence the limitations of the eco-activist critique.

The Green Party began in Coventry, in the heart of industrial decline. As Wolfgang Rudig and Philip Lowe have explained, a group of people who "were witnessing the breakdown of the world around them" were brought together in 1972 by the task of placing a major manufacturing company in receivership.[135] They began to discuss what had gone wrong in their world, and to read. Both Paul Ehrlich and *A Blueprint for Survival* proved to be important influences. In 1973, four members of this group – Tony and Lesley Whittaker, both solicitors, and Michael Benfield and Freda Saunders, an estate agent and his assistant – decided the only path to survival lay in the creation of an independent political party. They decided to call this party "People."[136]

134 The British Greens' victory was part of a Europe-wide Green surge: Greens won 39 seats in Brussels, and together with the Communists and Socialists held a small left-of-center majority (260 seats in the 518-seat assembly). The Green Party argued that under a system of proportional representation, twelve British Green Euro-MPs would have been elected in 1989 (*Econews* 46 [Aug./Sept. 1989]). The Greens performed the weakest in Labour strongholds: They won just 7.3% of the vote in Scotland and 10.3% in northern England. But in the southeast, Greens captured 20.3% of the vote; in Sussex West they came in at 25% (*Economist*, 24 June 1989, pp. 11–12, p. 56; *Observer*, 2 July 1989, pp. 18–22).

135 Wolfgang Rudig and Philip Lowe, "The Withered 'Greening' of British Politics: A Study of the Ecology Party," *Political Studies* 34 (1986): 269.

136 *Coventry Evening Telegraph*, 31 Jan. 1973, Classified Section, p. 1; "Britain's Ecological Party," *Ecologist* 4/2 (Feb. 1974): 42–3; Goldsmith interview, 15 July 1989. See also Sara Parkin, *Green Parties: An International Guide* (London: Heretic Books, 1989), pp. 217–19; and Lesley Whittaker, "Too Nice to Turn People Green," *Independent*, 11 Mar. 1993, p. 29.

At the same time that People was being born, the Movement for Survival, another effort to color British politics green, was dying. The movement was intended to be an environmental coalition working to convince the British government to take measures consistent with the aims of the *Blueprint for Survival.*[137] Edward Goldsmith envisaged the movement as a form of political pressure group, one that would ignore partisan politics "to ensure that the majority of the Members of the next Parliament . . . are committed to implementation of the "Blueprint for Survival."[138] The *Blueprint* itself, however, declared that the time had come for a "national movement to act at a national level, and if need be to assume political status and contest the next general election."[139] The Movement for Survival never really materialized. Political activities would have threatened the charitable status of many environmentalist organizations called on to participate, and the editors of the *Ecologist* found their attention diverted by the Stockholm conference, the move to Cornwall, and the task of getting a journal out every month; more important, the purpose of the movement never became clear. Contacted by the founders of People, Goldsmith passed on to them the "mountains of mail" he had received in connection with the Movement for Survival. He also became a member of the new party, served on its national executive, and ran as its candidate twice.[140] In the pages of the *Ecologist*, the party received continuous publicity and support throughout the 1970s.

In 1975, People changed its name to the Ecology Party and, again in 1985, to the Green Party. No matter what its name, the organization had little impact on British politics until the end of the 1980s. The party fought its first national election in February 1974. Its candidates in five constituencies won an average of 1.8 percent of the vote. In the October election of that year, the four Ecology candidates did even worse, with an average vote of 0.7 percent. For the May 1979 election, the party decided to stand candidates in at least fifty constituencies, the minimum needed to receive five minutes of broadcast time on television and radio. For a party with only 550 members, fielding 53 candidates was a remarkable achievement. Even though these candidates average only 1.5 percent of the vote, for the first time the party received a significant level of national publicity. Membership rose to 5,000, and hopes

---

137 *Ecologist* 2/1 (Jan. 1972): 23.
138 Goldsmith to Davoll, Lawrence, Allaby, and Searle, 11 Apr. 1972, in *Blueprint for Survival* file, Conservation Society.
139 *Ecologist* 2/1 (Jan. 1972): 1; *Times,* 14 Jan. 1972, p. 1.
140 Goldsmith interview, 15 June 1989; Goldsmith, open letter headlined "Movement for Survival," 11 Feb. 1974, in *Blueprint for Survival* file, Conservation Society. See also Michael Schwab, ed., *Teach-in for Survival* (London: Robinson and Watkin Books, 1972). This work is an account of a weekend seminar at Queen Elizabeth College, London, that was set up in May 1972 in response to *A Blueprint for Survival.* For the Movement for Survival, see pp. 63 and 120, n. B.

soared even higher.[141] The 1980s failed to fulfill these hopes; until its surprising performance in the European elections of 1989, the party was ignored in national elections. At the local level, the picture looked somewhat brighter. By 1987, the party had elected fifty-five local councillors.[142]

Argument between those who wanted to reshape the Ecology Party to fit a more conventional political mold and those who believed such pragmatic politics violated the principles that the party proclaimed reveals that even for many of its members, the Ecology Party was an embodiment of moral protest rather than a means to effect political change. Issues such as electing a leader, establishing a central London office, and proposing specific and short-term policies potentially at odds with the party's conviction that the industrial system had to be radically reoriented raised the question of the purpose and identity of a Green party.[143] Despite its growing professionalism, and the opening of headquarters in London, the Ecology Party throughout the 1970s and into the 1980s refused to act as just another political party. Jonathon Porritt, one of the party's national spokespersons in the early 1980s and its most well known and charismatic member throughout the decade, admitted that "the Green Party's unique role is as 'defenders of the faith.' "[144]

Throughout the party's almost two decades of existence, the faith defended by the party was eco-activism. It rejected conventional short-term politicking for a long-range vision of a reconstructed Britain. Economically naive and secure from the threat of ever actually having to govern, the party painted a picture of a decentralized, demographically stable, self-sufficient Britain. From its very beginnings the party embraced no-growth economics and called for the radical economic restructuring of British society by means of a National Incomes scheme. It also demanded population limitation, a result of the identification of overpopulation as a central threat to human survival.[145] By restructuring Britain, the party hoped to revive the community spirit that it believed had disappeared from industrial society. Decentraliza-

---

141 "The First Decade," *Econews* 16 (Feb. 1983). See also Jonathon Porritt, "Gearing Up for the General Election," *New Ecologist*, Jan./Feb. 1979, pp. 20–2.

142 *Econews* 16 (Feb. 1983); *Econews* 18 (July 1983); *Econews* 35 ([June/July 1987]). See also Parkin, *Green Parties*, pp. 219–26.

143 See, e.g., the report "The Ecology Party Conference, 1979," *Ecologist* 9/7 (Oct./Nov. 1979): 247.

144 Porritt and Winner, *Coming of the Greens*, p. 78.

145 At the Green Party conference of 1989, faced with unprecedented publicity, the Greens dropped their aim of reducing Britain's population to thirty or forty million and made clear that the party did not support coercive population control measures (*Guardian*, 23 Sept. 1989; *Daily Telegraph*, 23 Sept. 1989, p. 8). Contrast the policy adopted in 1975: "No [population] policy should disparage childbearing or create negative feelings towards children or the family. It should avoid coercion *until voluntary measures have been tried and failed*" (Ecology Party, *Manifesto for a Sustainable Society*, 1975, p. 17, Warwick, MSS 50; emphasis added).

tion, self-management, and participatory politics remained central to its vision. It attacked the alienation it believed integral to the industrial system and
argued that social as well as economic limits to growth demanded radical
changes in British society. The Ecology Party was never a single-issue or
"environmentalist" party. From its beginnings the party stood for a rejection
of the assumptions and values of contemporary British society.

Affluence and awareness

The new politics proposed by the Ecology Party, the criticism of industrialism in the pages of the *Ecologist* and *A Blueprint for Survival* (which conflicted
with some of the more orthodox economic assumptions aired at the Stockholm conference), and the proposals for ecologically motivated reform offered by Friends of the Earth and the Conservation Society all helped define
the early Green movement as it emerged in Britain in the 1960s and early
1970s. Various forces promoted the perception of a global ecological crisis
and instigated this new movement of moral protest. The first, the postwar
population boom, has already been discussed. Perhaps the most basic factor
was the postwar affluence of the Western world. Affluence led to eco-
activism in two ways. First, postwar affluence rested on environmentally
destructive industrial expansion. The most environmentally devastating form
of industrial expansion occurred in agriculture, with the arrival after World
War II of heavily mechanized, chemically dependent agribusinesses. In the
decades after 1945, Norfolk lost 45 percent of its hedges; Devon, 20 percent
of its native woodlands; Suffolk, 73 percent of its heathland; Bedfordshire,
70 percent of its wetlands.[146] A growing number of British men and women
began to react against the transformation and degradation of Britain, changes
that seemed an inevitable by-product of industrial activity and economic
growth.

Affluence led to eco-activism in a second way: by creating not only the
conditions for an eco-activist movement but also a constituency. A certain
degree of prosperity is, in general, a necessary precondition for concern
about ecological issues – hence the middle-class makeup of environmentalist
organizations. In his study of the history of environmentalism in the United
States, Samuel Hays has argued that the postwar movement must be set in
the context of an affluent society geared to consumption. Hays views environmentalism as a form of, rather than a reaction against, consumption. In his
analysis, consumers began to demand clean air and untouched wilderness in
the same way that they began to expect affordable refrigerators and automo-

146 Des Wilson, ed., *The Environmental Crisis* (London: Heinemann, 1984), pp. 41, 43.

biles. Affluence allowed environmentalists to raise their expectations and to consider "quality of life" issues in their assessments of their standard of living.[147] Although the British did not enjoy the same levels of affluence as did their American counterparts, after the 1950s more British men and women than ever before possessed the material foundations to awaken ecological concern.

A second, more tangible propelling force behind eco-activism was the accumulation and publication of disturbing data about various forms of pollution and their consequences for human health. Certainly Britons had been aware of pollution before the 1960s. The National Smoke Abatement Society (later the National Society for Clean Air) was formed in 1929 to combat what later generations would know as smog. During the late 1950s and early 1960s, however, new dangers became apparent. After the publication of Carson's *Silent Spring* in Britain in 1963, controversy over pesticides sparked a debate in the House of Commons in which Carson or her book were mentioned twenty-three times.[148] By the mid-1960s, a significant portion of the population had been alerted to the dangers of chemical pollutants. Perhaps even more frightening was the growing realization of the effects of radiation on human beings, even those yet unborn. Here CND played a crucial role in informing the public about the health hazards of nuclear weapons testing and in forcing governments to come to grips with the scientific and medical data pointing to the insidious effects of overexposure to radiation. Gradually, large numbers of people began to realize that the wonders of science and technology could also be viewed as unparalleled horrors, particularly in an environmental context.

This reaction against the technological optimism of the 1950s and early 1960s served as a third reason for the emergence of eco-activism. Francis Sandbach has argued that not only growing awareness of the extent of environmental pollution but also such factors as the skyrocketing financial costs of high-tech toys like the Concorde and, most especially, the escalating moral costs of the Vietnam War worked to sour the hopes for technology embodied in Harold Wilson's promise of the "white hot" technological revolution and Tony Benn's dream of a Ministry of Technology. Sandbach points out that the Vietnam conflict demonstrated in unforgettable ways the destructive potential of modern science; not surprisingly, eco-activism emerged at the same time as the protests against the Vietnam War.[149]

---

147 Samuel Hays, "From Conservation to Environment: Environmental Politics in the United States since World War II," *Environmental Review*, Fall 1982, pp. 20–3; Samuel Hays, *Beauty, Health, and Permanence: Environmental Politics in the U.S., 1955–1985* (New York: Cambridge University Press, 1987).
148 Frank Graham, Jr., *Since "Silent Spring"* (Boston: Houghton Mifflin, 1970), pp. 81–2.
149 Sandbach, *Environment, Ideology, and Policy*, pp. 36, 138.

The next chapter explores the romantic impulse that colored much of the early eco-activist critique. Not all Greens were romantics, just as not all CNDers battled the Bomb because of a romantic impulse and not all fantasy readers participated in Lewis's and Tolkien's romantic world view. Chapter 11 shows that in the early Green movement a romantic rejection of the scientific method and human reason as paths to truth battled a belief that through science the world could be saved, if science were reformed. Faith in and skepticism about science clashed in an unresolved conflict within the eco-activist protest. This conflict illustrates the complexity of the early Green movement; it should not, however, obscure its often romantic tone. Eco-activism emerged in the context of a world in which the detritus of industrial affluence threatened to engulf the values and structures by which individuals made sense of their lives. It was a movement of the postwar years. Its fundamental romanticism, however, enabled it to draw on a long-established tradition of protest in middle-class Britain.

11

The romantic challenge to postwar affluence

Like CND, the early Green movement consisted of a number of different groups and individuals, often espousing fundamentally contradictory aims and ideologies. The conviction that the world stood on the brink of ecological disaster and that politics-as-usual could not resolve the crisis threw libertarians, protofascists, socialists, conservatives, and the apolitical together into an uneasy alliance. The assumptions that led to such a conviction also varied. Although not all the early Greens can or should be considered romantics, the romantic current within the movement was more than a tributary; the romantic critique flowed through the center of the movement and helped dictate its course. Appalled by the present and fearful of the future, many eco-activists challenged postwar Britain with a protest rooted in romanticism: They looked to nature and the past for guidance in their effort to build in Britain a society that would suit not only the demands of ecology but also the spiritual and communal needs of humanity.

The small state: Leopold Kohr

The critique of bigness lay at the heart of the Green protest. Greens perceived that the economic and political structures of modern industrial society had grown beyond the limits of human comprehension or comfort. They argued that only when these structures were rebuilt to human scale could individuals truly participate in the decisions that shaped their lives, and only then could true community emerge. The restoration of right relationships between and among individuals, as well as between humanity and nature, and humanity and the spiritual realm, depended on a re-creation of proper size.

An Austrian immigrant, Leopold Kohr, articulated one of the earliest arguments in favor of a rescaling of political structures. Kohr immigrated to Britain after living and working in the United States and Puerto Rico. Although he was an economist, his work focused on the need for political decentralization. Beginning in 1941, he called persistently for the renunciation of the nation for smaller and, he contended, more manageable political units. Looking ahead to peacetime reconstruction, Kohr anticipated and rejected the arguments that would lead to the creation of the European Economic Community. He contended that true European unity would be achieved not through national and international integration, through creating bigger units, but rather through the cantonization of Europe, the construction of small states that could unify under a federal system and form "a mosaic with fascinating variations and diversity, but also with the harmony of the organic and living whole."[1]

Kohr's most well known work, *The Breakdown of Nations* (1957), presented the basic "political no-growth" argument. A libertarian, Kohr believed that socialism, as realized in postwar Europe, exacerbated the loss of the individual's ability to control the shape and course of his or her life. Kohr's desire to safeguard this freedom led him to condemn the increasing size of nations. Kohr argued that overly large nations demanded socialist structures; once nations passed a certain size, the potential for chaos became so great that government regulations had to multiply to ensure the continued functioning of the social mechanism. According to Kohr, society was too big when "problems are caused by proportions rather than by institutional or human shortcomings."[2] The typical nation-state of the postwar world had already reached this "critical size"; political or economic remedies to problems such as rising crime rates, urban decay, and worsening quality of life were doomed to fail because these societies has passed the limits of a viable community. Kohr argued that to restore individualism to modern life, society must opt for political decentralization.

Kohr rested his demand for political decentralization on the maxim that function should determine size. Human beings formed themselves into communities for companionship, prosperity, security, and cultural interaction. These functions required a human community of at least 200,000 members, according to Kohr's calculations; although with the aid of modern technology, education, and advanced organization, societies could contain a population of fifteen million and still perform their convivial, economic, political, and cultural functions.[3] Once a society passed this limit, it reached critical

---

1 "Disunion Now," *Commonweal*, 26 Sept. 1941, p. 542. Kohr submitted this article under his brother's (Hans) name. See also Leopold Kohr, "The Aspirin Standard – or How to Measure Living Standards," *Business Quarterly* (London, Ontario School of Business Administration, University of Western Ontario), Summer 1956/7, pp. 91–105.

2 *The Overdeveloped Nations: The Diseconomies of Scale* (New York: Schocken Books, 1978), p. 9.

3 Kohr, *The Breakdown of Nations* (New York: E. P. Dutton, 1978 [reprint of 1957 edition]), pp. 106–8; Kohr, *Overdeveloped Nations*, chap. 2. See also Kohr, "Appropriate Technology," in *The Schumacher Lectures*, ed. Satish Kumar (London: Blond and Briggs, 1980), pp. 182–92.

size and began to undermine the very qualities of life it was supposed to ensure.[4]

In order to decentralize and save the future, humanity had to look to the past. Although Kohr viewed the medieval era as a golden age during which small communities achieved intellectual and cultural greatness,[5] he turned to the Renaissance for specific guidelines on political organization. The Italian city-state served as Kohr's model for the future, particularly in regard to the Third World. Kohr believed that aid efforts that ignored the principle of human scale, both in size and in speed (the need for gradual evolution of political and economic structures), threatened to destroy the viability and integrity of Third World regions. He called for "development without aid," defined as village-oriented, gradual development based on self-help. Such development would require disciplined leadership after the Renaissance model: The Third World "generalissimo" would function as the Renaissance prince in fostering community development.[6] Democracy could only be evolved; premature establishment of democratic political systems would destroy the Third World and democracy itself.[7]

Kohr's naive belief that the "generalissimo" would lead the new Third World city-state to democracy reflected his reduction of the complexities of world history to the question of size. He admitted that he offered "an essentially new interpretation of history in which the chief influence on historic change . . . is assigned to change in social size."[8] Bigness was the bogeyman in Kohr's work. Reduce the size of nations, and most of the problems of modern life would dwindle. In part because of this overly simplified vision of both past and future, Kohr's work remained largely unknown. A second factor in Kohr's obscurity was, no doubt, timing: In 1957, the future looked bright for the West, and Kohr's call for a radical rerouting of society found few receptive listeners.

Nevertheless, Kohr was an important influence on Green thinkers, particularly E. F. Schumacher, and on the political decentralization movement of the late 1960s and 1970s.[9] Moreover, Kohr's work was fundamentally romantic. He looked to the past and perceived there a true community in which individuals could participate and thus find for themselves genuine significance. He saw the present as spiritually unsatisfying as well as ecologically unsound, a world that had lost its proper perspective and so could not foster

---

4 *Breakdown of Nations*, pp. 106–8; *Overdeveloped Nations*, chaps. 3, 7.
5 *Breakdown of Nations*, pp. 48, 62.
6 *Development without Aid: The Translucent Society* (Llandybie: C. Davies, 1973), p. 87.
7 *Breakdown of Nations*, chap. 6; *Development without Aid*, p. 93.
8 *Overdeveloped Nations*, p. 70.
9 George McRobie described Leopold Kohr and R. H. Tawney as "Schumacher's gurus." John Papworth also noted the importance of Kohr in shaping Schumacher's ideas (interview with George McRobie, 29 Apr. 1986; interview with John Papworth, 16 Apr. 1986).

genuine relationships among human beings and the natural and spiritual realms.

The call to decentralization: John Papworth

A second important figure in the political decentralization movement was John Papworth, whose journal *Resurgence* featured regular contributions by Schumacher and became one of the voices of early eco-activism. The significance of Papworth's work, like Kohr's, does not rest on the numbers of readers it influenced; neither man gained a large following, but they served as an influence upon and provided a context for better-known writers such as Schumacher. Papworth, like Kohr, looked to the past for guidance out of the soulless present into a more satisfying future. He called for a renewal of the ties that bound individuals to each other and to their environments through the scaling back of industrial, urban society and hence the revival of both participatory democracy and vital community.

Papworth's career also illustrates the direct links between CND and the Green movement. Papworth was a CND supporter who joined the Committee of 100 because he believed that the urgency of nuclear disarmament justified and demanded civil disobedience. In 1961, he was sentenced to one month in prison for the Committee sit-down outside the Soviet embassy on 31 August. He found himself in some rather exalted company: Robert Bolt, Arnold Wesker, Michael Scott, and Bertrand Russell were also sentenced to prison for their part in the demonstration. Papworth remained in the committee of 100 until its end in 1968, but he became convinced long before the Committee's demise of the necessity for a new approach to the creation of a nonviolent society.

Like a number of Committee members, Papworth's protest against the Bomb led him to a wide-ranging critique of the society that had produced the Bomb. As early as 1961 he began to connect the large-scale technological and economic structures of industrialized society with both the problem of alienation and the threat of energy shortages. He warned the nuclear disarmament movement that it would achieve its goals only "inside communities which are small and which are run on a scale appropriate to human beings rather than machines. . . . Democracy in fact, is *impossible* in mass societies." Ordinary individuals had been deprived of power by the growth of political and economic bureaucracies. To regain that power, individuals must change their lifestyles, shift from consumption to conservation, and thereby regain control over the economic structures of their lives. A society without such participation would not only fail to satisfy its citizens but also fail the test of sustainability. One decade before concerns about energy conservation became widespread, Papworth warned that industrial society was pressing against the limits of its material resources. Like many CNDers, he concluded that the "Bomb is not like some poisonous almond nut topping a macaroon. It is in every way a reflection of the kind of society which has produced it."[10] Like Kohr, Papworth concluded that modern civilization's illness was rooted in its size: in large-scale political and economic organizations and the concentration of real power in the hands of a few individuals.

As was the case in the work of Kohr, the question of development and the fate of the Third World stood at the center of Papworth's ideas. During the early 1960s Papworth worked as a correspondent for *Peace News* in Africa. He became a close friend of Kenneth Kaunda (president of Zambia since 1964) and, at times in the 1970s, served as his economic advisor. Papworth's work in Africa convinced him that the importation of large-scale technologies threatened the viability of the newly independent African nations. He called for human-scale structures that allowed for participation and the construction of community.[11] His belief that an alternative path of development existed led him, in 1967, to formulate the concept of the Fourth World: "the province of those countries which are small enough to enable democratic procedures to prevail without being subverted by the mechanics of mass politics which are brought into play when overgrowth takes place."[12]

Like Kohr, Papworth believed that because overgrowth was at the root of the contemporary crisis, political solutions that did not mandate a change in scale would effect little improvement. Political allegiances mattered little in a world dominated by overgrown political structures. Voting for this or that party or plotting the overthrow of this or that government failed to address the "powerlessness of people which is the key to the war situation, a powerlessness which springs directly from the acceptance of a machine-scale of organisation in defiance of human considerations.... on such a scale *all* power becomes oligarchic."[13] In an overly large society, the individual's freedom to decide was increasingly encroached upon by the "expert," the powerlessness of ordinary people increased, and the modern industrial world accelerated toward its final destruction.

Humanity's only hope lay in the creation of small, relatively independent, self-governing communities designed to human, rather than machine, scale. Such radical change depended on the cumulative impact of individual endeavors and on a reassertion of the primacy of religious values. Papworth

---

10 "Centralised Government: How Do We Break Out?" *Peace News*, 15 Dec. 1961, p. 5.
11 See, e.g., *Peace News*, 24 Apr. 1964, p. 8.
12 *Economic Aspects of the Humanist Revolution of Our Time* (Lusaka: National Educational Company of Zambia, 1973), p. xiv. One of the sponsors of the Fourth World was Lord MacLeod (see Chapter 8).
13 *Resurgence* 1/1 (1966): 2.

argued that the individual must act, must set a creative example, and must become involved in education, in local government, and in community organizations. He or she must first, however, concentrate on internal regeneration, a rediscovery of the spiritual basis of life. Papworth believed that small-scale communities of the past had fostered such a spiritual foundation. In the historic skyline, the steeple towered over all other buildings as "the general acknowledgement that the font of all this gregarious bustle and activity is an ineluctable mystery of which only the most shadowy intimations are revealed to human perception." By contrast, the modern skyline dominated by the corporate skyscraper "does not express a particular order or complex of values so much as the collapse of all order and value in man's interior world."[14] As Papworth's interpretation of the "historic skyline" reveals, he viewed the past, particularly the Middle Ages, as a golden age in which "medieval man was engaged in a quest for harmony and beauty as a matter of course."[15] Decentralization was, for Papworth, not only a means to save the world from nuclear holocaust and from a debilitating shortage of natural resources but also a way to restore the souls of individual men and women, and so heal humanity of the modern disease of giantism and its corollary, ugliness.

Papworth placed his main emphasis on the need for smaller political structures but argued against the modern stress on bigness in economics as well. An economist trained at the London School of Economics, he saw the theory of efficiency of scale as flawed because "any scheme of economics which places man himself on the same footing as inanimate aggregates of capital or reaches of land, will, whatever its incidental advantages, conspire to defeat his true interests."[16] Orthodox economic theory led inexorably to large-scale economic practice, and so to the tragedy of industrial alienation and the defeat of the true interests of humanity.

Papworth articulated his critique of industrial society in romantic terms. Frightened and enraged by the alienation he perceived in the large-scale, increasingly technological and bureaucratic world about him, he worked for a return to smaller organizational structures designed to foster rather than deny the participation of ordinary individuals. He called for spiritual as well as economic and political change, and believed that human beings must look to the past if they wished to alter the present and improve the future. Reintegration, the central theme of the romantic protest, weaves its way through Papworth's work: the reintegration of individuals and their work, history, and God through a return to smallness.

14 *Economic Aspects*, pp. 124–5.
15 "The Economics of Non-violence," in *The School for Non-violence*, ed. Satish Kumar (London: Christian Action, 1969), p. 53.
16 *Prerequisites of Peace* (London: Housman's, 1966), p. 8.

The challenge to economic growth: E. J. Mishan

Papworth, like Kohr, focused most closely on political structures. Their call for decentralization was, however, echoed in the economic sphere with the emergence of the no-growth movement. Doubts about the beneficence of an industrial economy devoted to growth were not new: John Stuart Mill had called for a stationary state over a century earlier.[17] In the post–World War II period, however, such a call sounded like heresy. Nevertheless, as H. W. Arndt has shown, although the assumption that economic growth is intrinsically good undergirded the economic and political agenda of both the industrial and the industrializing nations after World War II, murmurs of doubt about the wisdom of allegiance to the ideal of an ever-rising gross national product began to be heard as early as 1950.[18] By 1955, W. A. Lewis found it necessary to include in his *Theory of Economic Growth* an appendix that dismissed growth-doubters as reactionary elitists.[19]

The publication of the American economist J. K. Galbraith's *The Affluent Society* in 1958 highlighted some crucial issues sidestepped by Lewis and most economists and marked a significant challenge to the "conventional wisdom" (a term coined by Galbraith). Galbraith dared to question what he called "the central economic tradition," the production-oriented economics that characterized both the Right and the Left, both pre- and post-Keynesians. In anticipation of many of the key ideas of E. F. Schumacher's *Small Is Beautiful*, Galbraith depicted conventional economists as "a respected secular priesthood whose function it has been to rise above questions of religious ethics, kindness, and compassion and show how these might have to be sacrificed on the altar of the larger good. That larger good, invariably, was more efficient production." The morality of such sacrifice became increasingly dubious in a world focused on "the more efficient production of goods for the satisfaction of wants of which people are not yet aware" and for which desire had to be manufactured. Striking at a central pillar in the growth-obsessed structure, Galbraith raised doubts

17 John Stuart Mill, *The Principles of Political Economy* (1848). See the excerpt reprinted in Michael Allaby, ed., *Thinking Green: An Anthology of Essential Ecological Writing* (London: Barrie and Jenkins, 1989), pp. 131–2.

18 See, e.g., Karl William Kapp, *The Social Costs of Private Enterprise* (Cambridge: Harvard University Press, 1950). Revised and extended as *The Social Costs of Business Enterprise* (Nottingham: Spokesman, 1978). Kapp argued that the pursuit of economic growth resulted in environmental losses not accounted for in the free market. Kapp is discussed in H. W. Arndt, *The Rise and Fall of Economic Growth* (London: Cheshire, 1978), pp. 84–99. I have relied heavily on Arndt's work in this section.

19 W. Arthur Lewis, *The Theory of Economic Growth* (London: Allen and Unwin, 1955).

about both the means and the ends of conventionally measured economic growth.[20]

By the end of the 1960s, the continuing human tragedy of the Third World made antigrowth sentiments much more common. The failure of growth-oriented development schemes led some development economists to reject the focus on economic growth as a priority in planning and development programs. According to Arndt, by the early 1970s, the development literature was dominated by demands for abandoning the quest for an ever-rising gross national product and searching instead for ways to address the real needs of real people.[21] Many of these doubters remained convinced that orthodox economic analysis would present the needed solution; the Green critique of growth was, however, more thorough and much less complacent about traditional economic and social structures.

The "father of modern antigrowthmen" in Britain was the economist E. J. Mishan.[22] Mishan, a much-published welfare economist, received his Ph.D. in economics from the University of Chicago in 1951 and four years later accepted an appointment at the London School of Economics, where he remained until he resigned his chair in 1977. *The Costs of Economic Growth* (1967) was Mishan's first attempt to present in a systematic way his "doubts about the value for human welfare of the growing tide of postwar economic expansion."[23] As early as 1960, however, Mishan had questioned "the basic unwritten premise of economic science . . . that economic development is a good thing." He noted then that the "precondition of sustained growth is sustained discontent" and warned the developing nations that "the thorny path to industrialisation leads, after all, only to the waste land of Subtopia."[24] In *The Costs of Economic Growth* and later writings, Mishan expanded on this basic argument.

A libertarian, Mishan defined a good society as one in which the individual was free to make the choices directing his or her own life.[25] He argued that

20 J. K. Galbraith, *The Affluent Society* (Boston: Houghton Mifflin, 1958). Quotations from pp. 24, 290–1. See also "*The Affluent Society* Revisited," in J. K. Galbraith, *The Affluent Society*, 4th ed. (Boston: Houghton Mifflin, 1984), pp. xi–xxxvii.

21 H. W. Arndt, *Economic Development: The History of an Idea* (Chicago: University of Chicago Press, 1987), pp. 91–113.

22 *Daedalus* 102 (Fall 1973): 235. Michael Allaby, an associate editor of the *Ecologist* in the 1970s, and John Davoll, director of the Conservation Society, stressed Mishan's central role in the no-growth movement during discussions with the author (interview with Michael Allaby, 14 Apr. 1986; interview with John Davoll, 18 Mar. 1986).

23 *The Costs of Economic Growth* (London: Staples Press, 1967).

24 "Review of *The Economics of Underdevelopment*," *Economica* 27 (May 1960): 194.

25 In 1978 Mishan wrote that he was committed to "a decentralized and institutionally pluralistic order" on the grounds that such an order would keep governmental growth in check. See "Whatever Happened to Progress?" *Journal of Economic Issues* 12 (June 1978): 408. Mishan's concern with political liberty translated into a rejection of socialism. He was convinced of "the historical and logical connections between capitalism

the technocrats' and economists' obsession with economic growth made the ordinary citizen see only imperatives where there were, in fact, choices. Mishan asserted that "in a civilisation that is being shaped by the apparently irresistible forces of technology and commerce there are, still, vital options open to society, other than just 'forward' or 'back,' if only we could break away from imaginary pressures to 'keep up.' "[26] If a society's laws made pollution easy and legal, this was the consequence of a choice, not of necessity. Mishan warned, however, that economic growth was rapidly reducing the range of individual choice. Increasing economic growth brought with it widening government intervention, in such forms as laws regulating traffic and zoning and through state involvement in problems like the storage of information and the disposal of chemicals and nuclear waste.[27] Mishan believed that if economic growth was allowed to continue unchecked, then the resulting technological structures would require the growth of government as well, and thus the individual would be pressed to a position of helplessness by both economic and political forces.

The economists who served as cheerleaders for economic growth failed to see the limits of quantification, according to Mishan. Economists pretended to be operating within a value-free environment and so blinkered their eyes from the value-laden effects of their decisions. Mishan insisted that "if we are genuinely interested in the welfare, and the character, of society, we should be unwilling to reconcile ourselves to this restriction on our judgment – to accept that the smooth operation of competitive markets, and the level and distribution of outputs, are the only critieria to be respected."[28] Mishan regarded the quantitative bias of economics as wrongheaded. He noted of his own work, "My observations do not derive from painstaking statistical studies but, in the main, from casual observation and unbounded conjecture – for which I never apologize."[29]

Mishan mounted an unapologetic onslaught against the world he perceived science and technology to be creating, a world in which quantities increased, quality declined, and human needs remained unfilled.[30] He charged, first of all, that in the modern world the relationship between workers and their work had been marred. In Mishan's view, industrialization

and freedom, both political and personal" (*Economic Myths and the Mythology of Economics* [Atlantic Highlands, N.J.: Humanities Press International, 1986], p. 203; see also p. 133).

26 *Making the World Safe for Pornography and Other Intellectual Fashions* (London: Alcove Press, 1973), p. 160.

27 "On the Road to Repression and Control," *Encounter* 47 (July 1976): 5–17.

28 *The Economic Growth Debate: An Assessment* (London: Allen and Unwin, 1977), p. 35.

29 "What Monsters Hath Technology Wrought," *Business and Society Review* 26 (Summer 1978): 5.

30 "Ills, Bads, and Disamenities: The Wages of Growth," *Daedalus* 102 (Fall 1973): 86.

transformed workers "from artisans and craftsmen to machine-hands and dial-watchers."[31] The numbers indicated a rising standard of living as a complement to increasing economic growth, but numbers could not comprehend the relationship between the maker and the made. Mishan also accused the growth-oriented modern world of shattering the bonds that made lasting and meaningful relationships between human beings possible.

A key problem, according to Mishan, lay in the breakdown of hierarchical social structures in modern civilization. Economic equality was not, in Mishan's eyes, a laudable ideal: "It is enough that no one should starve while others eat well. . . . To hold it to be indecent that some men have incomes which are ten times, nay fifty times, as large as some others, when, in fact, nobody in the community suffers any deprivation, strikes me as being no more than a political posture for which no persuasive moral arguments can be mustered." Class tensions, according to Mishan, arose to a large degree from the stimulation of greed and envy by economic growth and its henchman, mass advertising. Such tensions would not exist if people "learned to accept differences in inherited wealth and talent as the capricious decrees of fate; and for the rest turned their eyes from self-inflicted temptations, striving instead to live their lives joyously within the limits of their capacity." In Mishan's view, industrialization had severely restricted those limits. The common people did not know, could not know, their own best interests because their "values and pursuits and tastes have been shaped from birth by the technological society."[32] The "masses" (a term frequently used by Mishan) could not be trusted.

Economic growth corroded the social structure not only by leveling society and so increasing class tensions but also by weakening the roles of the sexes and thus hastening social collapse, according to Mishan. Economic growth demanded a "unisex meritocracy" that clashed with the social order centered on the family. Women were needed in the workplace to help feed the insatiable hunger for material goods; in the process, the human craving for mutual dependency and separate sexual roles was left unsatisfied. In contrast to the feminist picture of the traditional oppression of women, Mishan pointed to the centuries-old "belief that it needed a man and a woman to make a home together; the belief that while a man went out into the world as the family breadwinner, the woman kept the home tidy and attractive, kept it warm and cosy, looked after the children, . . . welcomed her husband's return with a good meal on the table, and, withal, took pride in, and derived satisfaction from, this role."[33] What Mishan saw as the modern illusion of woman's oppression was created, he believed, by the

31 "To Grow or Not to Grow," *Encounter* 40/5 (May 1973): 24.
32 *Economic Growth Debate*, quotations from pp. 127–8, 128, 99.   33 Ibid., p. 193.

distorting haze of individualism and quantification. For example, feminists tabulated work hours and wage rates but could not quantify the "instinctual satisfaction" provided by homemaking.[34]

Mishan's glorification of the traditional home reflected his sentimental-ized view of the past. The reality that many homes were not and could not be tidy and attractive, or that the husband's return could and often did occur in an atmosphere of violence rather than familial love, had no place in Mishan's golden past. He regarded the past as not only a repository of wisdom, not only a teacher for the present, but also as quite simply better. Mishan's preindustrial England was a world of "small towns, wood fires, mansions and cottages, a close-knit society of privileges and obligations," an idyll in sharp contrast to the "highly competitive post-industrial world of congested high-ways, unquiet skies, metropolitan overspill, of increasing pace and pressure, of corrosive envy, and of endless jockeying for status." To Mishan, the modern world was thoroughly diseased, "a stricken society, a sick society, a dissolving society."[35]

At the root of this disease lay a malignant irreligiosity. Mishan believed that in the battle between science and religion, religion had lost, with humanity the victim. In the modern world, "there is no mystery, no source of exaltation, no beatific vision, through which men may hope to communi-cate with God that science cannot turn to ashes."[36] The scientific inceneration of the lines between God and humanity will ultimately lead to the death of community. Acquisition of material goods could not give the indi-vidual the sense of belonging granted by belief in God, nor could economic growth stop the decay of civilization's moral code. In the acquisitive society, distinctions "between good and bad, truth and falsehood, vice and virtue, and sickness and health" were left with "an unending succession of savants and specialists, themselves victims of the current erosion of the moral, aesthetic and intellectual consensus on which Western civilisation was raised." These experts, like the masses, could not be trusted. Chaos awaited: "The liberal West may be passing through a twilight state, its social cohesion shored up only by the crumbling remains of its moral capital."[37]

Mishan's aversion to the visions of past and future painted by the growthmen and those he perceived as their allies underlay his fury at the constant warnings about Britain's economic decline. Mishan denied that "the problem of Britain" was economic in nature. The constant "national self-castigation, in all economic matters" reflected the triumph of the mis-taken ideal of quantitative economic growth and the resulting loss of perspec-

---

34 "To Grow or Not to Grow," p. 28.   35 *Making the World Safe*, pp. 215, 146.
36 Ibid., p. 218.   37 *Economic Growth Debate*, pp. 139, 202.

tive.[38] Because of this obsession with economic growth, all the best of Britain was ignored and undermined. Mishan warned that "this new economic assessment of the worth of a nation" threatened the survival of Britain.[39] The nation lay vulnerable because of economic growth, not because the economy was growing too slowly, according to Mishan. Britain's environmental problems were ignored because economic problems claimed first priority, and social cohesion was destroyed by the constant stress on individual gain. Moreover, Britain's leaders had failed to capitalize on the transforming experience of World War II. Like so many of the CNDers, Mishan looked back with longing to the Blitz. He argued that by focusing on the "English Disease," joining the European Economic Community and failing to halt Commonwealth immigration quickly enough, Britain's leaders had squandered its wartime inheritance of unity and purpose, and so had undermined the nation's greatness.[40]

As in CND, the demand that Britain be seen as great accompanied strong anti-American sentiments in Mishan's work. To Mishan, the United States presented a horrifying glimpse into Britain's future. He argued that Britain's leaders had visited the United States and learned the wrong lessons: "They have been impressed by the efficient organisation of industry, the high productivity, the extent of automation, and the new one-plane, two-yacht, three-car, four-television-set family." But they did not learn the lessons taught by "the spreading suburban wilderness, the near traffic paralysis, the mixture of pandemonium and desolation in the cities, a sense of spiritual despair scarcely concealed by the frantic pace of life."[41] The lesson of the United States, Mishan insisted, was that ceaseless economic growth and a commitment to material acquisition, combined with the lack of any historic community, led to disaster. He called on Britain to recant its faith in the ever-rising gross national product and to concentrate on reviving and sustaining its community.

Mishan, together with Kohr and Papworth, articulated many of the basic ideas within the Green movement; a mistrust of political and economic orthodoxies, a respect for the lessons and institutions of the preindustrial past, a desire to overcome the alienating effects of technology and mass society through the restoration of small-scale communities, and a perception that the natural world could not sustain the burden of "bigness" indefinitely. Their works rested on a romantic foundation: They believed that the twin victories of industrialization and empirical science threatened the soul and heart of humanity. For many Greens, the environmental crisis merely af-

38 *Technology and Growth: The Price We Pay* (New York: Praeger, 1973), p. 11.
39 *Economic Growth Debate*, pp. 26–7.
40 "The New Inflation: Its Theory and Practice," *Encounter* 42 (May 1974): 20.
41 *Technology and Growth*, p. 8.

firmed what romantic critics had argued over a century earlier: Affluence would not usher in the abundant life if communities disintegrated and spiritual values disappeared.

The dictates of nature: the Soil Association

The history of the Soil Association, an important player on the eco-activist stage during the 1960s, also reveals the extent to which the romantic protest underlay the Green critique. The association has been described as probably the first environmentalist group in Britain with a holistic world view.[42] Although the association had only 4,500 members in the mid-1960s,[43] it helped define and articulate important elements of the Green outlook. The Soil Association represented a way of perceiving the land and its uses that challenged the assumptions of industrial society and offered an alternative vision of Britain's future.

The Soil Association officially began in 1946, but its roots extend back into the interwar years and the emergence of the organic and rural revival movements. Confronted with the apparent failure of capitalism during this period of economic depression, many British men and women began to explore alternative ideologies, including communism and fascism. One group of interconnected individuals, labeled High Tory by Anna Bramwell in her history of twentieth-century ecology,[44] became convinced that the solution to Britain's woes lay in the revival of the British countryside and a return to traditional (nonchemical) methods of food production. They saw agriculture as the heart of civilized society and argued that a healthy society depended on a healthy agriculture, which in turn depended on a healthy rural community.[45]

The Soil Association belonged within the context of this interwar rural revival movement. It originated with the work of Lady Eve Balfour, a niece of the prime minister and a Suffolk farmer. In 1938, Balfour first encountered the work of Sir Robert McCarrison. Intrigued by the differing physiques of the peoples he observed while in India, McCarrison designed a series of

42 Interviews with Michael Allaby, 14 Apr. 1986, 19 June 1989.
43 Virginia Payne, "A History of the Soil Association" (master's thesis, Victoria University of Manchester, 1971).
44 Anna Bramwell, *Ecology in the Twentieth Century: A History* (New Haven: Yale University Press, 1989), p. 104.
45 See ibid., pp. 104–5, 112–22, 128; Philip Conford, ed., *The Organic Tradition* (Bideford, Devon: Green Books, 1988), pp. 1–15; Richard Griffiths, *Fellow Travellers of the Right: British Enthusiasts for Nazi Germany, 1933–1939* (London: Constable, 1980), pp. 142–6, 317–29; Richard Thurlow, *Fascism in Britain: A History, 1918–1985* (Oxford: Basil Blackwell, 1987), pp. 172, 185; James Webb, *The Occult Establishment* (La Salle, Ill.: Open Court, 1976), pp. 95–9, 102–3.

experiments using rats in order to test the links between diet and health. He concluded that a diet heavily dependent on processed foods and refined flour, the diet common to industrialized nations, was the primary cause of illness. Although his methodology was criticized by the medical profession, McCarrison's work became a key text in the organic foods movement. Balfour was an immediate convert; confronted at the same time with what she called humus theory, the basic agricultural and ecological principles of natural (or organic) farming, she concluded that modern, chemical-dependent methods of farming deprived the soil of fertility and produced less healthful foods and therefore less healthy people.[46]

In 1938, Balfour and Alice Debenham formed the Haughley Trust. Through the trust, Balfour aimed to provide scientific confirmation for what she already knew to be true. To prove the links among methods of cultivation, soil fertility, and nutritional value of food, Balfour and Debenham combined their Suffolk farms to serve as the data base of a massive agricultural experiment. They divided the land into three sections: the first a stockbearing farm run on organic principles and techniques, the second a mixed farm that carried livestock but utilized chemical fertilizers as well, and the third a modern, stockless farm fertilized with chemicals.[47] The coming of World War II halted the Haughley Experiment, and by 1947 lack of funds seemed to ensure its failure. In 1943, however, Balfour had published *The Living Soil*, a readable argument on behalf of organic agricultural principles and aims.[48] The favorable response to that work led to the creation of the Soil Association in 1946, a group organized to serve as the link among individuals interested in organic cultivation, to carry out biological and ecological research, and to educate public opinion on the environmental and health benefits of organic foods and farming.[49] The Soil Association assumed control of the Haughley Experiment in 1948.

Balfour hoped that both the experiment and the Soil Association would spark an organically based agricultural revolution that would lead to a national "spiritual and moral revival." In her view, soil fertility could not be separated from national "vigour." Written during World War II, *The Living Soil* depicted Britain at a turning point. Despite all the talk of national reconstruction, the genuine rebuilding of Britain depended, Balfour argued, on restoring health to its soil.[50] This restoration would transform not only the

46 E. B. Balfour, *The Living Soil*, rev. ed. (London: Faber and Faber, 1949), pp. 28–30, 34–41, 143.

47 Ibid., pp. 170–1.

48 Lady Eve Balfour, *The Living Soil* (London: Faber and Faber, 1943).

49 Balfour, *The Living Soil* (1949), 174–5; E. B. Balfour, "Why It Happened," *Mother Earth* 1/1 (1946): 1.

50 *Living Soil* (1949), quotations from pp. 214, 50, 191. See also p. 9.

way Britain organized its food production but also its economic and social structures. The abandonment of chemical and mechanized agricultural processes in favor of more natural methods would require the return of large numbers of laborers to the land, as well as the decentralization of production and political life.

The Haughley Experiment stood at the heart of the association's activities until 1970 and revealed at its core a conflict between the romantic world view and faith in the scientific method. The experiment represented a commitment to scientific research and methodology, although according to one close observer, the scientific results it obtained "were always of a curious quality."[51] Rather poorly designed, it was a massive and enormously complex undertaking with an impossibly large number of variables. As a result, it failed to convince the unbelieving scientists that it set out to persuade.[52] The fact that the attempt was made, however, reveals the association's trust in a scientific approach as a means of indicating and verifying truth.

To find truth, however, science would have to be reformed. Association literature emphasized that science had failed in the realm of modern agriculture because science was out of balance. Chemistry had usurped the throne and must be forced to abdicate to the less reductive discipline of biology. Such faith in biology merged easily in the 1960s with high hopes for *ecology:*

51 Allaby interview, 19 June 1989.
52 The organic section was treated as a closed system: Nothing was to be added to the soil that did not come from the soil. Thus, for example, manure from animals other than those raised on the section could not be imported, nor could the animals on the section be given feed not produced within the organic section. Since milk and agricultural products were taken off the farm rather than plowed back into the soil, the cycle was not, however, truly "closed."

   The data from the Haughley Experiment did produce a number of intriguing results. The experiment found that the levels of nitrate, phosphates, and potash in the soil varied considerably by season, and thus brought into question the practice of fertilizer treatment based on spot analysis. The experiment also showed that the humus content on the organic section rose, whereas it remained stable on the mixed section and fell on the stockless – an affirmation of the Soil Association's assertion that chemicals robbed the soil of its vitality. A more surprising result was the fact that the cows on the organic section, although fed less because the crop yields on the organic section were lower, produced more milk than the better-fed cows on the mixed section – a possible indication that more could be produced from less, provided the less was of higher quality. See Mary Langman, "A Short History of the Soil Association," *Living Earth* (journal of the Soil Association), Jan./Mar. 1989, p. 19. See also Soil Association, *The First Twenty-five Years, 1938–1962* ([Stowmarket?]: Soil Association, 1962); E. B. Balfour, *The Living Soil and the Haughley Experiment* (1973; New York: Universe Books, 1976), pt. 2; D. B. Long, "Preliminary Considerations and the Methods Used in the Investigations of Nutritional Values at the Soil Association Research Farms," in *Just Consequences,* ed. Robert Waller (London: Charles Knight, 1971), pp. 176–90. Research at Haughley continued after the Soil Association severed its links with the farm. See Colin Fisher, "The Pye Research Centre," *Soil Association* 2/9 (Nov./Dec. 1974): 13–14; "Farming for Better Food – The Work of the Pye Research Centre," *Soil Association,* Sept. 1976, pp. 4–8.

This new discipline was perceived as a means of restoring a holistic perspective to science. With ecology at its center, a reformed, holistic science would highlight the dangers of modern methods of agriculture and would vindicate the Soil Association's approach.[53]

The Soil Association's faith in science, even a reformed science, clashed with its fundamental romanticism. For many association members, ecology represented a world view rather than a scientific discipline. In 1965, L. T. C. Rolt defined "ecology" in the pages of *Mother Earth* as "the study of our earthly home, not as an empty mansion of dead sticks and stones but as a temple. . . . Earth and sky become for [the ecologist] one manifestation of that mysterious and abundant life and creative purpose of which he is himself a part."[54] Rolt's definition of ecology reflected the strong romantic strand that wove through the Soil Association and became tangled with its scientific aims. Ecology was seen as a path to reintegration, as a means of overcoming the alienation of industrialized humanity, as much as a method of evaluating agricultural techniques. Because the Soil Association viewed organic agriculture as more than a matter of farming, as, rather, one means of reincorporating humanity into the biological and spiritual web of relationships that undergirded the universe, the results from the Haughley Experiment were meant to verify what many association members already knew to be true. It is not unfair to say that many association members, although certainly not all, embraced organic farming and gardening not primarily because of the existence of scientific proof establishing the inferiority of modern agricultural methods but because of an emotional, aesthetic, moral, or religious rejection of such methods.[55]

For Balfour and the association that emerged in response to her work, organic cultivation clearly meant more than manure. During the 1950s, the editor of *Mother Earth*, the appropriately named association journal, explained that the organic movement was "concerned with much more than so-called agricultural techniques. It seeks to re-awaken the creative and cooperative spirit in men, and to cultivate healthier and happier relationships between them and the living environment in which they are set."[56] Organic farming was a way to revitalize society as well as the soil. The first issue of

53 Such faith in ecology was perhaps misplaced. As Donald Worster traced in his masterful *Nature's Economy*, after World War II scientific ecology became dominated by models drawn from economics and thermodynamic physics. In their quest for scientific respectability and validity, ecologists abandoned the holistic approach that so appealed to members of the Soil Association. See Donald Worster, *Nature's Economy: A History of Ecological Ideas* (San Francisco: Sierra Club Books, 1977), pp. 291–315.

54 L. T. C. Rolt, "Ecology," *Mother Earth*, Jan. 1965, p. 415.

55 I wish to make it clear that I am *not* arguing that such scientific data did not exist, or that the scientific case for the greater nutritional value of organically produced food is not compelling.

56 Jorian Jenks, *Mother Earth*, Summer 1951, p. 3.

Mother Earth declared, "The population of our earth is in decline and decay, and the son takes after the soil. So the problem before the Association is this: how is life to be put into the soil? . . . That in a nutshell is the object of the Association – to put life into the soil and the sons of the soil."[57]

In a post-Nazi world, phrases like "sons of the soil" sound somewhat suspect, and they should. Links between the association, the wider interwar agricultural revival movement, and the darker side of right-wing politics do exist. The editor of *Mother Earth*, Jorian Jenks, went to prison during World War II for his fascist activities, and a second prominent association member, Rolf Gardiner, sought throughout the interwar decades to strengthen the ties between England and Germany. Gardiner backed the Nazis after their take-over in Germany and visited and corresponded with R. W. Darre, the Nazi agricultural minister who espoused the ideal of a peasant-led Germany. Gardiner saw in the Nazi movement a powerful ally in his battle against the debilitating effects of industrial capitalism until 1940, when he condemned the Nazis for corrupting the ideal of organic farming.[58]

The links between the organic movement and the Nazis can be over-sensationalized: Few members of the Soil Association were fascists or Nazi sympathizers.[59] The connections between the movement and nazism rested on the fundamental romanticism at the root of both. Nazism was, of course, a complex and contradictory ideology; its glorification of the peasant contended with and eventually was defeated by a proindustrial, technocratic emphasis. But some of its elements, and particularly the visions and policies associated with Darre, reveal a romantic rejection of urban, industrial society.[60] Although the British rural revival movements shared this rejection, they did not, on the whole, embrace a foreign import. Links with the Nazis can be used to dismiss the organic and rural revival movements as far-right-wing fringe groups essentially alien to British political and cultural traditions. They were not. In their belief in the superiority of the natural over the man-made and their formation of organizations that promised to combat the evils of industrial society, these movements placed themselves within the native tradition of British romanticism. The Soil Association belonged to this tradition. Its romanticism linked it far more firmly to the centuries-old British protest against industrialism and empiricism than to extremist political ideologies.

---

57 [Jorian Jenks], *Mother Earth* 1/1 (1946): p. 6.
58 Anna Bramwell, *Blood and Soil – Richard Walther Darre and Hitler's "Green Party"* (Bourne End: Kensal Press, 1985), pp. 171–80.
59 Both Michael Allaby and Robert Waller recall, however, that the post frequently brought far-right-wing propaganda to the offices of the Soil Association (Allaby interview, 19 June 1989; interview with Robert Waller, 27 June 1989).
60 See Jeffrey Herf, *Reactionary Modernism: Technology, Culture, and Politics in Weimar and the Third Reich* (Cambridge: Cambridge University Press, 1984), chap. 1, esp. pp. 14–15.

The Soil Association assumed that questions of land use, farming methods, and food production were not simply economic or scientific matters but were, in fact, moral issues. Scientific analysis could reduce a soil sample down to its chemical components, but it could not thus comprehend the reality of that soil and its role in agriculture. Such comprehension could only come through a holistic approach that recognized spirit as well as matter. The association refused to let reductionist scientific techniques set the boundaries of reality.[61] Its literature expressed an essentially romantic revulsion against the structures and products of an industrial society. The land was more than a factor in production; its cultivators, more than employees. To treat agriculture as industry was to misunderstand the complexity and the significance of the natural world.

61 See, e.g., Jorian Jenks, "Editorial Notes," *Mother Earth*, Summer 1949, pp. 2–3; G. Scott Williamson, "What Is Science?" *Mother Earth*, Oct. 1952, pp. 41–42.
  An interesting aspect of Eve Balfour's refusal to accept the limits of reality set by empirical science is her respect for Rudolf Steiner's agricultural theories. Balfour regarded Steiner as one of the "pioneers" of organic cultivation (*Towards a Sustainable Agriculture: The Living Soil* [Stowmarket: Soil Association, 1977?]; the British Library gives [1982?] as the date of publication, but the work is the text of a talk given in 1977). Steiner taught that "all transformations in the substances of the earth planet are manifestations of spiritual forces lying behind these substances" (Rudolf Steiner, *An Outline of Occult Science* [Spring Valley: Anthroposophic Press, 1972], p. 103). Plants and animals comprise spiritual forces as well as physical matter. Agriculture cannot, then, operate on an exclusively material plane. It must instead treat the earth as "a living organism, with its own life-forces, which, in the plants springing from its surface, rise up to meet the downpouring life-forces of the Cosmos" (A. P. Shepherd, *Scientist of the Invisible: Spiritual Science, the Life and Work of Rudolf Steiner* [1954; New York: Inner Traditions International, 1983], p. 201). In the words of Eve Balfour, the nutritive cycle consists of "a flow of *vitalised* materials and forces from the soil through plant, animal, and man, and back to the soil" ("The Soil Association," *Mother Earth*, July 1952, p. 43; emphasis in original). The Steinerite echoes in the Soil Association serve to accentuate the romantic themes in the organic movement. Both Steinerism and the Soil Association rejected many of the basic assumptions of industrial society and sought to widen the boundaries of reality beyond those set by empirical science.
  It is important to note, however, that no official ties between the Soil Association and anthroposophy existed, and few association members were anthroposophists. Michael Allaby, one of the editors of the association's journal during the 1960s, described the Steiner link as "always slightly embarrassing" and pointed out that the Steiner movement was never discussed by the association's council or executive committee (correspondence with the author, 20 Jan. 1992). In addition, Ruth Harrison, a member of the council from 1966 through 1972, had no idea that anthroposophy played a role in the ideas or practices of the organization (interview with the author, 17 July 1989).
  Two of the Inklings, Cecil Harwood and Owen Barfield, were leading Steinerites in England. C. S. Lewis, however, always rejected Steiner's teachings. In West Germany, Steinerites formed a clearly identifiable sector in the ecological movement of the 1970s, the soil out of which the German Green Party grew. About 60,000 anthroposophists, knit together by a network of hospitals, kindergartens, schools, publishing centers, and societies, lived in West Germany (Werner Hulsberg, *The German Greens: A Social and Political Profile* [London: Verso, 1988], pp. 66 and 230, n. 5).

The poetry of ecology: Robert Waller

In 1964 Robert Waller succeeded Jorian Jenks as editor of the Soil Association's journal. Unlike Jenks, Waller was no fascist but rather a freethinking,
philosophically inclined poet who had hovered on the fringes of Bloomsbury.[62] Waller came to the association from the BBC, where he had become
interested in agricultural and environmental issues. He and Michael Allaby,
his assistant editor after 1966, pressed the association to link its agricultural
concerns with the related issues of environmental degradation and economic
growth. The association's very early awareness of the need for resource
conservation and of the dangers of soil and water pollution, food contamination, and overmechanization gave it a Green outlook long before the early
Green movement emerged. During the 1960s, the association helped shape
the new protest against industrial Britain. Although after 1972 the association returned to a narrower focus on food production and land issues, it had
by then a recognized place in the eco-activist movement, one that was consistent with its long-term refusal to march in step with industrial society.

Waller's ecological interests were clear from the start of his tenure at the
Soil Association. Under his editorship the journal remained focused on
agricultural and food matters; Waller sought, however, to integrate these
matters more thoroughly with the larger philosphical and environmental
questions that they raised.[63] The first issue that he edited contained his
article on the problem of overpopulation.[64] As early as October 1964 an
entire issue of the journal was devoted to the emerging ecological crisis, with
the feature article a study of environmental contamination.[65] By 1969, the
early Green movement was establishing itself in Britain, and Waller endeavored to make sure that the Soil Association joined the eco-activist march. He
argued that "the Soil Association stands for making society have second
thoughts about many of the profitable things it has not the moral courage to
resist – the pollution of the air, soil and water by car exhausts, fertilisers,
nuclear reactors, sewage and many industrial processes that could destroy
our environment beyond redemption in the next fifty years." Waller believed
that the association could fulfill this aim by an ecological approach, by exploring and explaining the connections among pollution, industrial processes,

---

62 Waller was a close friend of Graham Bell and Colin MacInnes, both of whom were
    associated with the Euston Road School during the late 1930s. See Bruce Laughton,
    The Euston Road School (Aldershot, England: Scolar Press, 1986), pp. 265–7; Colin
    MacInnes, *Absolute MacInnes*, ed. Peter Gould (London: Allison and Busby, 1985),
    pp. 220–2.
63 Waller changed the name of the journal from *Mother Earth* to the more prosaic *Journal of
    the Soil Association* in April 1968.
64 "The Vermin Society," *Mother Earth*, Apr. 1964, pp. 105–7.
65 *Mother Earth*, Oct. 1964.

and the Western way of living and thinking.[66] By 1970, he was making these connections in editorials calling for a rejection of the ideal of quantitative economic growth.[67]

Waller's efforts to widen the focus of the Soil Association did not meet with unanimous approval. He left as editor at the end of 1972, in the midst of a major reorganization and reorientation of the association.[68] His departure signaled the return of the journal to a narrower focus, one that reflected the association's commitment to concentrate on issues related to the soil, rather than on becoming a more generalist eco-activist or environmentalist organization.[69]

After Waller left the Soil Association, he continued to write and think about ecological issues. Never a public figure like Schumacher, he nonetheless became well known within the Green movement and stood squarely in the romantic tradition.[70] For Waller, a poet, environmental concerns were inextricably linked to the question of culture. He connected modern methods of agriculture to what he perceived as the contemporary cultural crisis: "Good husbandry always creates beauty. . . . Only a people living with a full, diverse, many sided well rotated character will cultivate a land with all its character at work for them as well. Bored people produce a flavourless culture and bored land produces flavourless food."[71] The severing of ties with the land resulted, he argued, in the loss of a poetic sense.[72] Waller had come to his ecological perspective via Shakespeare. He recalled that when he first saw *Hamlet* performed, it worked on him "like a religious conversion."[73] What Waller discovered in Shakespeare, as well as in Dante and other late medieval and early modern writers, was an organic world view, a holistic

---

66 "Editorial: The Aims of the Soil Association," *Journal of the Soil Association* 15/8 (Oct. 1969): 430.

67 *Journal of the Social Association*, Apr. 1970, July 1970.

68 The Oct. 1972 issue was the last Waller edited.

69 In this rethinking of the association's path and purpose, the association's new president, E. F. Schumacher, played an important role. See "Taking Stock," *Soil Association*, Apr. 1973, pp. 2–3; E. F. Schumacher, "The Future of the Soil Association," *Journal of the Soil Association*, Oct. 1971, pp. 313–16; Waller interview, 27 June 1989.

70 In correspondence with the author, Waller described himself as a "critical Romantic" (letter dated 11 June 1991, in possession of the author).

71 "Introduction to Discussion," in Soil Association, *Man's Place in Agriculture – The Attingham Conference, 1968* (Stowmarket, Suffolk: New Bells Press, 1969), pp. 91–2.

72 See Robert Waller, "Culture and Nature," *New Society* 23/7 (Mar. 1963): 27; see also "It Is Not Natural" and "An Apology for My Own Poems," in *The Two Natures – Poems in Pamphlet: A New Anthology for 1951* (Aldington, Kent: Hand and Flower Press, 1951), pp. 118–19, 122–3.

73 Waller interview, 27 June 1989. In an unpublished manuscript, Waller explained that he "arrived at ecology through culture and gave up writing about literature to write about the devastation done to the human soul and reason by the way we managed industrial progress" ("Ecology and Culture," manuscript in possession of the author, p. 12).

outlook fundamentally opposed to the mechanism dominant in the modern world.[74]

Waller criticized modern science for what he believed was its central philosophical failure: It took methods and explanations appropriate only for inorganic areas of life and misapplied them to the intellectual and spiritual realms of existence. Waller absorbed his epistemological vision from the philosopher John Macmurray, his teacher in the early 1930s, who taught that it was reductionism to explain the higher dimensions of reality in terms of the lower.[75] An undogmatic Christian and a deeply spiritual man, Waller rejected the materialism and empiricism of twentieth-century British society. In his view, the atrophying of a sense of reality beyond the confines or comprehension of the scientific method had devastating environmental and cultural consequences. He called not just for changes in legislation and in business practices to take into account environmental concerns but also for a new world view that recognized the limits of science and of human reason.

Waller argued that the need for a new world view was most apparent in Britain, where the "British disease" warned of impending societal breakdown. With Papworth and Mishan, he thought the answer lay not in more economic growth but rather in a stable-state economy that recognized the environmental limits of natural and human resources. Here Britain could lead the way: "In many ways the ideal circumstance for creative renewal and religious and philosophic depth of experience is provided by the rich civilisation with an inherited culture that is falling into hard times and losing confidence in mere material power."[76] Britain's weakness could become its strength; its loss of influence could be transfigured into real authority as the Western world floundered in an environmental and spiritual crisis of its own making.

To resolve the crisis, Britain and all of twentieth-century society needed to turn to the past for instruction and guidance. Waller contended that the "teaching of the wise people of the past has always been in conformity with human ecology. They have taught men their unity with God, nature and neighbour: they have talked of the 'chain of being.' "[77] Although he did not want to turn the clock back, Waller insisted on the necessity of recognizing the coherence and validity of the cultures destroyed by industrialism. Past societies, such as Shakespeare's England, had intuitively understood ecologi-

---

74 Robert Waller, "Critique of the Organic Conception of Society," manuscript in possession of the author, pp. 1–14; "Ecology and Culture," manuscript in possession of the author, pp. 11–14.

75 For Macmurray's influence on Waller, see Robert Waller, *Be Human or Die* (London: Charles Knight, 1973), pp. 66–111. See also John Macmurray, *Interpreting the Universe* (London: Faber, 1933); John Macmurray, *Religion, Art, and Science* (Liverpool: Liverpool University Press, 1961); John Macmurray, *Persons in Relation* (London: Faber, 1961).

76 *Be Human or Die,* pp. 216–37; quotation from p. 260.   77 Ibid., p. 55.

cal realities; they had realized that human beings and the natural environment coexisted in a delicate balance. Such an ecological understanding had to be revived, in Waller's view, in order for industrial society to avoid environmental, spiritual, and cultural breakdown.

The antiromantic current:
Edward Goldsmith's systems theory

His respect for the past, together with his organic outlook, his anti-materialism and antiempiricism, and his fundamentally poetic view of the natural world linked Waller to the tradition of romantic protest against industrial society. His romanticism led him, and through him the Soil Association, to take an active role in the early Green movement. This movement, however, like CND, constituted a large quilt in which the threads holding together the separate pieces often seemed quite thin. The romanticism seen in the works of Waller, Mishan, Papworth, and Kohr clashed with a strong antiromantic impulse in the work and writings of other leading eco-activists, even though the individuals themselves often worked in harmony and mutual respect and even though their tactics and goals often converged. Graham Searle, the motivating force behind the establishment of Friends of the Earth in Britain, and John Davoll, the longtime director of the Conservation Society, would both fall into the antiromantic camp: from scientific backgrounds, both men regarded eco-activism as the logical conclusion of empirical observation. Barbara Ward, too, viewed the ecological crisis as the product of poor science and faulty reasoning and thus capable of resolution through improved scientific research and more rigorous application of logic. However, the extensive writings of Edward Goldsmith, the editor of the *Ecologist* and an influential figure in the movement, provide the clearest illustration of the antiromantic thread in eco-activism.

Elements of the romantic critique are evident in the pages of the *Ecologist* in the 1970s. Because it carried articles by a wide variety of individuals within the movement (including, for example, Robert Waller), and, more important, because at several points the romantic and the antiromantic critique of industrial society converged, the *Ecologist*'s pages reverberate with familiar notes: respect for the sanctity of nature and humanity's place in it, insistence on the significance and efficacy of individual action, the quest for community, belief in the necessity of a religious framework for life, and looking backward for answers and guidance. The *Ecologist*'s editors, however, proceeded from fundamentally antiromantic assumptions. Unlike romantic thinkers such as Waller, they did not believe that realms of being existed that could not be penetrated by scientific enquiry. They saw science as it was practiced as limited, but if science could be reformed, if it could be set back on track, then it and it alone would lead humanity into a safer, more sustainable future. Opposed to the framework and methodology of contemporary science, they sought to create a new scientific framework and methodology.[78]

The work of Edward Goldsmith centered on this quest for a new science. Independently wealthy from the mid-1960s, Goldsmith pursued the life of a scholar and developed his own theory of general systems. He argued that "living entities" such as organisms, ecosystems, and human societies "are, at a certain level of generality, very similar, and that, at such a level, their behaviour can be shown to be governed by the same basic laws."[79] From the perspective of systems theory, tribal societies were highly developed organisms that had evolved to suit their natural environment. Tribal family patterns, gender roles, religious beliefs, structures of authority, and hunting and gardening techniques were all components of a stable system. Industrial society, too, was a system but a maladapted one, on its way toward breakdown.[80]

In contrast to industrial society, tribal societies were stable because of their social organization. Goldsmith argued that carefully defined roles, evolved in accordance with biological and environmental constraints, enabled the family to work as an economic and social unit. Family-based clans, tribes, and kinship networks meant that traditional societies were essentially self-regulating: There was no need for a state or a bureaucratic apparatus because the people shared the same values, traditions, and interests. According to Goldsmith, "Self-government is only possible among a people displaying great discipline and whose cultural pattern ensures the subordination of the aberrant interests of the individual to those of the family and the society as a whole."[81] Self-government did not mean democracy, but in the hierarchy of traditional society tyranny was not possible either, because of the force of community control. Duties, responsibilities, and a sense of place meant the subordination of the individual to the good of the whole and thus a guarantee of the continued stability of the community.

Unlike tribal communities, industrial society acted in violation of the environmental and biological limits of humanity. It promoted change rather than stability and thus, in Goldsmith's argument, increased the vulnerability of

---

78 The discussion that follows concerns Goldsmith's ideas in the 1970s. Many of his ideas have changed considerably since then; see Edward Goldsmith, *The Way: An Ecological World View* (London: Rider, 1992).

79 *The Great U-Turn: De-industrializing Society* (Bideford, Devon: Green Books, 1988), pp. 74–5.

80 See Edward Goldsmith, ed., *Can Britain Survive?* (London: Tom Stacey, 1971), pp. 44–55; and Edward Goldsmith, *The Stable Society* (Wadebridge, Cornwall: Wadebridge Press, 1978), pp. 1–13, for a detailed explanation of Goldsmith's application of systems theory to human society.

81 *The Great U-Turn*, p. 7.

human society to ecological disaster. By exalting the individual and encouraging the disintegration of the family, industrialization guaranteed the decay of communal values and an increase in social and political alienation, as well as a rise in criminal and antisocial acts. The end result would be social and economic breakdown; but, with a rather surprising degree of optimism, Goldsmith predicted that "out of the ruins of our industrial society, we can hope to see emerge smaller, more decentralized societies that might eventually develop the capacity for cultural self-regulation."[82]

In Goldsmith's view, modern science could not address the impending systemic breakdown of industrial society, because it was itself a product of that society. Because the very nature of scientific activity was reductionist, the analysis of the parts rather than the whole, it could not see the way environmental, economic, social, and political factors interacted. Like many Greens, Goldsmith condemned modern science for its approach and achievements. He viewed scientists as the "priesthood of industrial society," whose faith in the scientific method blinded them to the environmental crisis.[83] He also attacked the scientific obsession with quantification, pointing out that although numbers were convenient tools, the complexity of the natural world often limited the effectiveness of a quantitative approach.[84]

Goldsmith argued that the reductionism inherent in modern science resulted in the removal of humanity from its natural context. Because of this distortion, modern scientists, and the society they dominated, failed to see that human behavior, like that of any system, could be precisely predicted. Concepts or entities like the soul, mind, free will, or culture were merely illusions.[85] Different cultures, for example, were simply adaptive responses to environmental conditions. Therefore, "human behaviour can be predicted like that of ants, and . . . the dogma of man's intelligent and rational behaviour [should be put] in the proper place, as anthropocentric myths."[86] In order to understand humanity's place in the ecosystem, science would have to abandon what Goldsmith called "our fatal illusions," the ideas that lead us to believe that human beings were more than or different from animals.[87]

Goldsmith seemed to enjoy shocking people; he also had the courage, buttressed, to be sure, by his independent wealth, to take his ideas to their logical conclusions. The environmentally aware tend to line up on the Left; Goldsmith's views placed him on the other side of the political spectrum. His belief that only a culturally cohesive society could be stable led him to label both racial tolerance and social permissiveness as warning signals of systemic breakdown. Goldsmith never suggested one ethnic or racial group was superior to another; he insisted, however, that the differences between these

82 Ibid., p. 95.   83 *Ecologist* 2/10 (Oct. 1972): 3.
84 *The Stable Society*, pp. 78–9.   85 *Ecologist* 1/7 (Jan. 1971): 3.
86 *Ecologist* 1/11 (May 1971): 3.   87 *The Stable Society*, pp. 86–97.

groups must be accommodated rather than denied. He argued, "What is today regarded as prejudice against people of different ethnic groups is a normal and necessary feature of human cultural behaviour, and is absent only among members of a cultural system already far along the road to disintegration." Stable systems developed mechanisms to exclude foreign bodies that might threaten their integrity.[88] As a result of his belief in the unstable nature of a racially mixed society, Goldsmith advocated the halting of all immigration into Britain. Goldsmith himself is what he called a "half-breed": French and English, Jewish and Christian. "People like me . . . have no identity," he noted.[89] Identity came from community; without community, a society would fail. Social permissiveness, too, indicated that the mechanisms to maintain communal values, to maintain a system's integrity, had failed to function in modern society.[90]

Another outcome of Goldsmith's systems approach was his condemnation of both aid to the Third World and social-welfare programs in Britain. Goldsmith argued that "natural controls" like infant mortality constituted part of the system's self-regulation. By interfering with the process of natural selection, humanity threatened to destroy itself. In Goldsmith's view, the population explosion in the Third World resulted from the disintegration of traditional cultural patterns that had worked to regulate population growth.[91] Aid was bound to worsen the situation. According to Goldsmith, the introduction of modern medicine had "reduced the 'order' or 'negative entropy' " of Third World populations. As a result, "instead of allowing the less adapted among us to be slowly eliminated by the normal operation of natural selection, it has created a situation in which they will simply be eliminated in much larger batches at a slightly later date by famine, epidemics and other disasters."[92] In Goldsmith's view, aid programs to the Third World did not demonstrate society's compassion, only its stupidity. He urged that they be halted, along with domestic welfare programs. The need for social welfare signaled the disintegration of a community and thus served as an asystemic response to crisis guaranteed to make the crisis worse.[93]

Goldsmith also rejected what was then the woman's liberation movement. He regarded human beings as components of a system, with specific and necessary functions. Failure to perform these functions could only result in disaster. Women had been adapted by evolution for a certain biological role; he believed that some feminists pretended such biological realities did not exist. Moreover, the move of women to jobs outside the home led to the

---

88 *Can Britain Survive?* p. 51.   89 Interview with Edward Goldsmith, 15 June 1989.
90 *Can Britain Survive?* p. 48.
91 "Population," unpublished manuscript, June 1989, pp. 46–50.
92 *Ecologist* 5/9 (Nov. 1975): 326–7.
93 *Can Britain Survive?* pp. 227–9; *The Great U-Turn*, pp. 16–17.

further disintegration of the family. With this basic unit of society under attack, systemic instability increased.[94]

Goldsmith's stress on the subordination of the individual for the stability of the whole, as well as his belief that different races and cultures should not mix, led opponents to describe him as an "eco-fascist."[95] Such a label is, however, inaccurate. Goldsmith described himself as an anarchist; the call for decentralization and a strong antiauthoritarian sentiment dominate his writings. Goldsmith viewed the state as the product of a move away from an ecological existence, as an asystemic control unnecessary in a stable and self-regulating society.[96] He opposed industrialization in part because he believed that in a mass society without cultural cohesion, discipline will be imposed by those with the power to do so.

Goldsmith was not a fascist; he was also not a romantic. Like the romantics he looked backward for inspiration and guidance. Like the romantics he attacked industrialization for destroying the natural world. Like the romantics he called for the re-creation of community. Like the romantics he viewed modern science as reductionist. But Goldsmith proceeded from different assumptions and toward different ends. No romantic could have written the following:

> The concept of "happiness" can only be taken into account in a scientific theory of society once it is shown to be something other than a sensation, something in fact that can be measured and related to the other variables made use of in this science. . . . I shall equate "happiness" with adaptability and "unhappiness" with redundancy.[97]

For Goldsmith, science, if it were reconstituted, could describe and account for reality. For the romantics, reality extended far beyond the reach of science, even an ecologically oriented, holistic science. Goldsmith denied those very levels of reality that the romantics sought to affirm. He also denied the capacity of the individual to influence and determine events. In his theory,

---

94 *Can Britain Survive?* pp. 229–30.
95 Wolfgang Rudig, "In the Wings," *New Statesman* 106 (5 Aug. 1983): 10. See also Brian Johnson, "Eco-Fascists or Nuclear Ostriches?" *Ecologist* 6/6 (July 1976): 200–2; and Michael Allaby and Peter Bunyard, *The Politics of Self-Sufficiency* (Oxford: Oxford University Press, 1980), pp. 18–19, 32. Peter Hillmore called Goldsmith "the Enoch Powell of the Ecology Party" (*Guardian*, 19 Apr. 1979, p. 15).
    In the dissertation that served as an early draft of this study, I failed to grasp the complexity of Goldsmith's ideas and did not clearly distinguish those ideas from fascism. I welcome the opportunity to apologize to readers of the dissertation and to Mr. Goldsmith for oversimplifying and thereby misinterpreting his views.
96 Goldsmith interview, 15 June 1989; "Thermodynamics or Ecodynamics," *Ecologist* 11/4 (July/Aug. 1981): 195; *The Stable Society*, p. 28; *The Great U-Turn*, pp. 6–9, 13–14.
97 "The Stable Society: Can We Achieve It?" *Ecologist* 1/6 (Dec. 1970): 8.

individual human beings did not and could not matter much; the general system was what counted.

Goldsmith's ideas indicate that the entire early Green movement cannot be classified as romantic; British eco-activism proceeded from contending world views. It can be argued that as the decade progressed, the movement became more ideologically coherent. The Ecology Party, for example, embraced a "Goldsmithian" perspective at its beginnings but had rejected this radical conservatism by 1979 and espoused feminism, the goal of a multicultural, racially mixed society, and an expanded role for the state in some areas.[98] Throughout the 1980s, however, contrasting and conflicting assumptions intermingled in the Green movement. Individuals who regarded the movement as intrinsically egalitarian, feminist, and rationalist frequently cited the writings of Schumacher as important texts, although, as the next chapter argues, Schumacher's world view centered upon hierarchy and viewed human reason as severely limited.

Amidst this patchwork of contradictions and complexities, the thread of romanticism wove its way through the early Green movement. Although not present in all the squares, it colored the eco-activist quilt. Kohr's and Papworth's call for political decentralization, Mishan's antigrowth writings, the Soil Association's program for rural revival, and Waller's ecologically oriented poetry belong on the same shelf with the poems of the eighteenth-century Romantics, Morris's *News from Nowhere*, and Tolkien's *The Lord of the Rings*. Whether they make for practical politics or desirable economic policies is not at issue here; regardless of their political and economic impact, they reflected and furthered the deeply rooted cultural tradition of romanticism. Embedded in an aversion to industrialization and its products, these critics called for a renewal of the connections that, they believed, had once united humanity to nature and to divinity, and human beings to each other. They sought, whether successfully or no, to view society in holistic terms and to break through conventional ideas and solutions to what promised to be a richer, more satisfying, and more sustainable future.

98 The publications of People, the precursor to the Ecology Party, reflected Goldsmith's influence. Like the *Blueprint*, these publications can be classified as "radically conservative." See, e.g., People handout, hand-dated 2/73; "A Future for Our Children: An Environment fit for PEOPLE, A Political Statement by PEOPLE," [1974] (Warwick, MSS 50). In 1975, People became the Ecology Party, a name change that signaled a change in ideas and activists as well. Younger, more left-leaning individuals came into the party and challenged its more conservative ideas (Wolfgang Rudig and Philip Lowe, "The Withered 'Greening' of British Politics: A Study of the Ecology Party," *Political Studies* 34 (1986): pp. 271–2). The contrast between People's early publications and the manifestos of 1975 and 1979 illustrate the movement of the party from Right to Left. See "Manifesto for a Sustainable Society," 1975 (Warwick, MSS 50); "The Real Alternative," 1979 (Warwick, MSS 50X).

12

Schumacher's romantic quest

In the early 1970s the phrase "black is beautiful" resonated in Western consciousness as a call to action and an affirmation of a new social order. Anthony Blond, of the publishing company Blond and Briggs, recognized the potency of this battler cry and so retitled a manuscript on economics by the National Coal Board's director of statistics, E. F. Schumacher. The *Homecomers* became *Small Is Beautiful: Economics As If People Matter*, and both a best-seller and a cliché were born. "Small is beautiful" grew into a catchphrase of the early Green movement. It not only summed up and oversimplified the Green appeal for a more ecologically sustainable society, it also introduced a wide audience to the Green critique of industrialism. In the pages of *Small Is Beautiful*, this audience encountered a reformulation of the romantic protest against industrial society.

Schumacher's journey from mind to spirit

The author of *Small is Beautiful* bore the Christian name of his paternal uncle, Ernst Friedrich, an architect and city planner whose rebuilding of much of Cologne and Hamburg after World War II reflected a hatred of "Megalopolis" and a concern that architecture not contribute to the alienation of human beings and the destruction of nature.[1] Uncle and nephew were close, and the elder's ideals may have lodged themselves deeply within the younger's soul. But, in his early years, Fritz Schumacher embraced the modern world's love affair with bigness and passion for numbers. Born in 1911 in Bonn, Germany, the third child of Hermann Schumacher, a professor of economics, and Edith Zitelmann, a mathematician,[2] Schumacher was an empiricist-turned-romantic, an atheist who journeyed via Buddhism to Roman Catholicism. He derived his perception of the beauty of smallness

---

1 Rolf Rosner, "Fritz Schumacher's Hamburg," *Architectural Review* 167 (Mar. 1980): 166–9.
2 E. F. Schumacher was the brother-in-law of Werner Heisenberg, the physicist.

from his religious quest. As he discovered a new direction for his own life, he began to draw a map for modern society as well.

Schumacher chose his father's profession and very quickly established himself as a skilled economist.[3] In 1930, following one year at the University of Bonn, he went to England as a Rhodes Scholar. After two years at Oxford, during which he earned a diploma in economic and political science (his only formal educational qualification), he went on to Columbia University to study the New York money market. As always, he did well academically. Seven months after arriving in the United States, only twenty-two years old and with no degree, he was given the position of lecturer at the School of Banking at Columbia. He supplemented his income by preparing briefing papers for Congress on the New York Stock market and with a job at the Chase Bank.

An opponent of Hitler and National Socialism, Schumacher returned to Germany in 1934 to explore whether or not he could "lead a moral life within an immoral system without compromise."[4] He decided he could not and, in 1937, emigrated with his new wife to England. As an enemy alien during the war, Schumacher was at first unable to use the intellectual skills he valued so highly in himself. In 1940, his friend David Astor, later the editor of the *Observer*, found him a position as a farm laborer in Northampshire, where, it was hoped, Schumacher could wait out the war without danger. But shortly after moving to the farm, Schumacher was placed in an internment camp for enemy aliens near Wales. His imprisonment lasted only three months, but these months were crucial. During this period, Schumacher, raised a liberal, embraced Marxism.

In 1942 Schumacher returned to the life of a professional economist when he received a prestigious position with the Oxford Institute of Statistics. He also worked in journalism, with articles and leaders in the *Observer, Times, Tribune,* and other papers. With publicity came some power, as MPs began to solicit his advice. He joined Joan Robinson and Nicholas Kaldor in shaping William Beveridge's *Full Employment in a Free Society* and wrote three plays for the BBC to explore the issues dealt with more academically in that report. In 1945 he participated in J. K. Galbraith's American Bombing Survey of Germany, and in 1946, now a British citizen, he took the post of economic advisor to the Economic Sub-commission of the British Control Commission in Germany. In 1950, he returned to England as economic advisor to the National Coal Board. During the following decades he served as one of the chief economic advisors to the Labour Party. He was a close friend of Beveridge and

---

3 This section relies heavily on Barbara Wood, *Alias Papa: A Life of Fritz Schumacher* (1984; Oxford: Oxford University Press, 1985).
4 Ibid., p. 65.

Richard Titmuss and was well respected. Joan Robinson, for example, was said to have regarded him as one of Britain's foremost economists.[5]

As Schumacher's fame as an economist grew during the decades before 1950, so did his reputation for intellectual arrogance and heartlessness. From early childhood, Schumacher had displayed intellectual precocity, as well as utter contempt for those he considered his intellectual inferiors. Throughout his school and university years, academic success marched hand in hand with frustration and impatience with teachers he considered unworthy of him. He became known as sharp-witted and sharp-tongued, all mind and no heart. A companion on a trip across the United States in 1933 recalled that Schumacher "rejected every kind of reflection, basically his nature was not contemplative. His scale of values was based on speed and efficiency."[6] One acquaintance of Schumacher's while he was at the Oxford Institute of Statistics said of him, "I don't believe that man was born. I think he came out of a bottle."[7]

Schumacher's coldness stemmed from the combination of his unqualified materialist philosophy and self-confidence. Truth lay in what the senses discerned and the mind analyzed. Because he believed his own senses and mind to be especially acute, he had immense faith in his own abilities and judgments, and a hearty impatience for all who disagreed. As his daughter and biographer explained, "He believed that he possessed resources necessary to find the key to mastering the problems that he saw."[8] He judged reality to comprise mind and matter alone and dismissed appeals to emotion or to belief in any sort of spiritual existence as irrelevant or dangerous. He not only excluded religion from his own life but, after he embraced Marxism, fought to eliminate it from his wife's as well. He condemned her Christianity for its failure to stand up to scientific examination and its outmoded concept of an absolute reality.

During these years Schumacher's faith in the ability of the human mind to discover truth and improve the world through study of the material facts underlay his "big is beautiful" approach to the world. As economic advisor in Germany he declared that the future of Germany, and all of Europe, lay in large-scale state monopolies geared toward standardization and mass production.[9] He designed all-encompassing world improvement plans and had no doubts that they would succeed if implemented.

Schumacher's faith in himself and his materialist world view was shaken, however, by his experience in Germany. His plan for rebuilding the devastated nation on the basis of English democratic politics and Marxist economics was rejected. In the late 1940s, as he became increasingly frustrated with

5 According to George McRobie (interview with George McRobie, 29 Apr. 1986).
6 Wood, *Alias Papa*, p. 49.   7 Wood, *Alias Papa*, p. 152.   8 Ibid., p. 142.
9 Ibid., p. 139.

his position in Germany, he began to reexamine his belief that logic and scientific fact formed the only path to truth and progress. After his return to England in 1950, he continued to question and explore. He had gone to Germany confident he could help create a better world. He left believing that he had failed.

Career-oriented frustration continued after Schumacher took up his position with the National Coal Board. Until Lord (Alfred) Robens took over the chairmanship in 1961, Schumacher had little influence and no clear role to play on the board.[10] Instead, he poured his energies into his reexamination of the assumptions on which he had based his life and career. His daughter explained that Schumacher's failure in Germany led him to believe that his education had failed him in the fundamentals.[11] Rethinking the fundamentals led Schumacher to reject his materialism and to explore religious and spiritualist beliefs. The logic-oriented, numbers-minded economist set off on a spiritual quest; Mr. Gradgrind went looking for God. His spiritual journey in many ways anticipated that of the counterculture over a decade later. Astrology, yoga, organic foods, Eastern religions, and Western mysticism all played their part in leading Schumacher away from an empiricist outlook to a romantic world view.

One of the more interesting way stations along Schumacher's journey was that of the Soil Association. After the move back to England in 1950, Schumacher bought a house on four acres of land in the Surrey countryside. There he began to garden and, as with everything he did, he gardened with energy and passion. He rapidly rejected the orthodox, chemical-dependent methods of cultivation and instead took up organic techniques. In the early 1950s, Schumacher's rejection of the wonders of the chemical culture was rather unusual. The Soil Association, however, existed to aid those gardeners and farmers who chose the nonchemical route. Schumacher joined the association and received the gardening assistance he needed; he also was put into contact with one of the heartier forms of antimaterialism in Britain.

Schumacher became the president of the Soil Association in 1970. This position was for the most part honorary, but he attended council meetings

10 After the death of Sir Arthur Street, the board's deputy chairman, in 1951, Schumacher was left without a receptive listener on the board. The decade that followed was one full of frustration for Schumacher, who felt he was underutilized. The situation changed when Robens became chairman in early 1961. Robens agreed with Schumacher that the board must fight the European trend toward phasing out the coal industry. Schumacher worked closely with Robens throughout the 1960s. (See ibid., pp. 226, 268, 275–7, 290, 300–11.) George McRobie recalled the mid-1960s as a time of great excitement and hope on the board. He and other associates of Schumacher were energized by their belief that as a public corporation the board could break new pathways in Britain (McRobie interview, 29 Apr. 1986).

11 Barbara Wood to Caroline Moorehead, "Growing Stuggle against Arrogance," *Times*, 14 May 1984, p. 20.

and played a role in determining association policy.[12] It is unclear how important the association was in shaping Schumacher's ideas. It would be surprising, however, if Schumacher did not absorb a great deal of mystery at the same time that he was learning about muck. Schumacher himself credited organic gardening with his conversion. It shattered his loyalty to the intellect and opened him up to the spiritual world.[13]

The Surrey soil provided spiritual nourishment of one sort to Schumacher; another kind of enrichment came from study of Eastern philosophy and religion. Schumacher's failure in Germany convinced him of a lack in his education, and so, during his eighty-minute commute each day between his home in Caterham and the National Coal Board headquarters at Hobart House in London, he began to reeducate himself by reading Eastern philosophy, history, and religion. By 1952 this reeducation program produced results. In a letter to his parents Schumacher admitted that his "whole way of thinking has come into motion."[14] The spiritual dimension that he had once dismissed as an illusion now appeared to be the ultimate reality. Even more disturbing was the discovery that his most prized possession, his intellect, could not penetrate this higher realm. Having turned in a new direction, Schumacher ran down this new road with the same energy and overconfidence with which he had embraced atheism. He joined the Society of Psychical Research as a means to explore the existence of spiritual forces, began to practice astrology and yoga, and, through an acquaintance at the National Coal Board, joined a group of disciples of the spiritual master G. I. Gurdjieff.[15] With his mother, he translated into German *The New Man*, a work by Maurice Nicoll that linked Gurdjieff's teachings to Christianity.[16]

It was Buddhism, however, that spoke most clearly to Schumacher. In 1955 the National Coal Board seconded Schumacher to the Burmese government as economic advisor. Schumacher welcomed this opportunity to learn Buddhist meditation, or *sattipatthana*. By weekday an economist, on weekends he retreated to a monastery as a Buddhist novice. In Burma, his quest ended; he found his Holy Grail. As Schumacher explained, "I came to Burma as a thirsty wanderer, and there I found living water." He returned from Burma declaring, "I am a Buddhist."[17] In fact, Schumacher continued his explorations in religious philosophy and in 1971 was received into the Roman Catholic church. He regarded the step from Buddhism to

12 Interview with Michael Allaby, 19 June 1989; interview with Robert Waller, 27 June 1989.
13 Wood, *Alias Papa*, 236–7.   14 Ibid., p. 230.
15 See Colin Wilson, *G. I. Gurdjieff, the War against Sleep* (Wellingborough, Northamptonshire: Aquarian Press, 1986).
16 Maurice Nicoll, *The New Man: An Interpretation of Some Parables and Miracles of Christ* (Baltimore: Penguin Books, 1972).
17 Wood, *Alias Papa*, pp. 252, 254.

Christianity as quite small, because he believed that religious truth was not confined to Christianity alone.[18] He finally chose the Christian path when he became convinced that "it was better to follow Gandhi's advice . . . 'and stay at home.' "[19]

For Schumacher, staying at home did not mean passivity or inaction. His journey from mind to spirit turned him into a romantic crusader battling the forces of materialism. Convinced that both the natural and spiritual environments faced serious threats, he sought to redirect Britain along a more ecologically sustainable and spiritually satisfying path. In his vision, most twentieth-century Western individuals existed in "a wasteland in which there is no meaning or purpose, in which man's consciousness is an unfortunate cosmic accident, in which anguish and despair are the only final realities."[20] The modern individual lacked an accurate map out of this wasteland. The twentieth-century map provided faulty guidance because it left out crucial realms and routes. It omitted not only religious experience but also unorthodox theory in medicine, agriculture, and psychology, and the possibility of art as anything but self-expression or escapism. As a result, "the entire map from right to left and from top to bottom was drawn in utilitarian colours: hardly anything was shown as existing unless it could be interpreted as profitable for man's comfort or useful in the universal battle for survival."[21] The map also magnified the scientific, technological, and quantitative regions at the expense of all others. Sense impressions and reason were marked as the only paths to truth. Those areas of knowledge and being that resisted quantification were outlined as inferior, stigmatized as "subjective," or simply left out altogether. The modern map indicated that humanity's hope for the future lay in extending the scientific and technological realms even further. As the borders of these regions had widened, so, too, had humanity's standard of living. Therefore, progress was assured if individuals and societies kept to the indicated route and silenced the reactionary voices who posited alternative pathways. Schumacher, however, insisted that *unless* these alternative paths were highlighted and taken, humanity would destroy itself.

18 Schumacher, *Good Work* (London: Abacus, 1980; first published in 1979 by Jonathan Cape), p. 122.

19 "E. F. Schumacher: Making a Viable Future Visible in the Present," *Spiral*, Winter 1977, pp. 19–20. According to one of his colleagues, Schumacher joined the Roman Catholic church for the sake of his wife and for the sake of his work. He believed fewer people would dismiss him as a "crank" if he spoke as a Roman Catholic rather than a Buddhist (personal communication with the author).

20 Schumacher, *Small Is Beautiful: Economics As If People Mattered* (New York: Harper and Row, 1973), pp. 90–1.

21 Schumacher, *A Guide for the Perplexed* (London: Abacus, 1978; first published in 1977 by Jonathan Cape), p. 12.

The failure of orthodox economics

Schumacher indicted the discipline of economics for promising escape from the wasteland but instead drawing humanity further into the wilderness. The central mistake of orthodox economics was its effort to be a "science" like physics and chemistry.[22] Unlike the physical sciences, economics concerned human choices and actions, which by their very nature eluded exact quantification. Economists' ambition to be recognized as scientists obscured a vital religious truth, the existence of free will, and led to the economic idolatry of quantification. Schumacher, a renowed statistician, believed numbers could be misleading, particularly in reference to human beings. He insisted that "my theory has always been that figures don't mean anything if you can't make them sing."[23] Numbers had no meaning, no melody, in and of themselves. Counting alone could not establish significance. For example, "the substance of man cannot be measured by Gross National Product. Perhaps it cannot be measured at all, except for certain symptoms of loss." Like E. P. Thompson in his conclusion to the standard-of-living debate (see pp. 195–96), Schumacher argued that numbers and human experience can diverge: "The Gross National Product may rise rapidly: as measured by statisticians but not as experienced by actual people, who find themselves oppressed by increasing frustration, alienation, insecurity." Most economists failed to see this divergence because they refused to look at the individual in his or her totality and refused to recognize that the human being was more than a factor in production or a consumer to be manipulated. They pursued "the absurd ideal of making their 'science' as scientific and precise as physics, as if there were not qualitative difference between mindless atoms and men made in the image of God."[24]

By elevating the adjective "economic" to the ultimate value, economists threatened society with destruction. Schumacher argued that in the industrialized world, one could "call a thing immoral or ugly, soul-destroying or a degradation of man, a peril to the peace of the world or to the well-being of future generations; as long as you have not shown it to be 'uneconomic' you have not really questioned its right to exist, grow and prosper." But "economic" meant only the ability to earn an adequate short-term profit in terms of money. Because the practice of environmental conservation, for example, usually lowers short-term monetary profits, "it has therefore no acknowledged place in a society under the dictatorship of economics. When it is occasionally introduced into the discussion, it tends to be treated not merely as a stranger but as an undesirable alien, probably dishonest and almost

22 *Small*, p. 239.   23 *Good Work*, p. 125.   24 *Small*, pp. 20, 31, 49.

certainly immoral."[25] The result of economics' narrow set of values could only be, according to Schumacher, despair and destruction.[26]

The failure of Britain

Schumacher argued that the history of Britain in the twentieth century revealed the disastrous results of deifying the economic calculus. The nation's betrayal of the socialist ideal, its nuclear policies, and its economic difficulties all indicated that its spiritual strength had atrophied. Like the New Left, active during the period Schumacher's ideas were taking shape although not associated with him, Schumacher refused to accept socialism as primarily a means for getting more goods for the workers. He saw it as "a religious issue, a battle for the soul of man." At its beginnings, British socialism had been a moral protest not just against the economic workings of capitalist society but against the very nature of that society.[27] In the postwar period, however, "British socialism has lost its bearings and presents itself merely as a device to raise the standard of living of the less affluent classes faster than could be done by private enterprise."[28] Schumacher insisted that what was at stake was "not the standard of living but the quality of life."[29] Like E. P. Thompson and the New Left, Schumacher preached a humanist socialism that would revive British culture, create opportunities for soul-satisfying work, give each individual a sense of worth, and foster true community.

Also like Thompson and the New Left, Schumacher believed that the possession of the Bomb undermined Britain's strength and threatened the realization of a humanist socialism. During the war, even while interned as an alien, Schumacher had believed England held the key to the future. He wrote to his wife from the detention camp, "Let us hold to England whatever happens to us. . . . I can see my tasks more clearly than ever: Europe, a new Europe: Coming from England." The Labour victory in 1945 seemed to confirm his faith in England as a new world leader: "What a chance for Britain and for Europe!" By the mid-1950s, however, his hopes had dissipated. With his new spiritual orientation, he saw signs of decay in affluent Britain. In addition, the fruitlessness of Schumacher's first decade on the

---

25 Schumacher, "Clean Air and Future Energy," Does Voeux Memorial Lecture to the National Society for Clean Air, Blackpool, 19 Aug. 1967. Reprinted in *Schumacher on Energy: Speeches and Writings of E. F. Schumacher*, ed. Geoffrey Kirk (London: Cape, 1982), pp. 17, 19.
26 *Good Work*, p. 128.
27 Schumacher, "Socialisation in Britain," 1961, in Wood, *Alias Papa*, p. 293.
28 *Good Work*, p. 26.   29 *Small*, p. 260.

Coal Board and the Conservative victories in the 1950s surely tainted Britain's great socialist experiment for him. The most direct factor in making Schumacher turn elsewhere for hope, however, was Britain's development of atomic weapons. Buddhism had taught Schumacher the importance of non-violence in terms of the individual's relationship both to other people and to nature. Therefore, in his eyes, Britain had disqualified itself as a spiritual or moral leader by opting for the Bomb. Schumacher became a CND supporter at the end of the 1950s, but he had abandoned his belief in Britain as the hope for the future some years ealier, when he came to see the issue of nuclear arms through a spiritual prism. Like the New Left that was to emerge a few years later, he declared in 1955 that he had placed his hopes in the newly independent and nonaligned nations because they "might introduce something new into the deadlock, a spiritual force. . . . The fact that Britain and France are now also producing H Bombs is a clear demonstration to me that they cannot do it."[30]

In Schumacher's view, Britain also revealed its spiritual lethargy in its notoriously poor industrial relations, and its consequent economic decline. He saw Britain's economic crisis as primarily a spiritual failure, as the inevitable result of an economic system that eliminated opportunities for satisfying work in order to maximize production of unnecessary and often environmentally destructive material goods. He blamed Britain's productivity problem not on technological backwardness but on "a creeping paralysis of non-cooperation." In Schumacher's analysis, this paralysis was a cause of hope, not despair. It indicated that despite almost two centuries of industrialization, the British worker refused to be reduced to a mechanical appendage. Schumacher's answer to the problem of Britain was not to seek to heighten production levels or to increase wages but to widen opportunities for men and women to engage in work that promoted the spiritual values of beauty, simplicity, and nonviolence. He insisted that British workers wanted something more than material goods, that "in their heart of hearts . . . [they] understand that their real interests lie somewhere quite different." Like Jesus, they understood that "Man shall not live by bread alone but by every word of God."[31] The word of God pointed to a way out of the wasteland of alienation and apathy into which Britain, and modern society, had fallen by reaffirming the significance of individual human beings otherwise nullified by the quantitative bias of orthodox economics. In lectures Schumacher often turned to the Old Testament story of King David and the census (II Samuel 24). In the story, David is punished for the sin of counting because, in Schumacher's interpretation, "there was something wrong in having a census which treats people as if they were units, whereas they are not. Each is a universe."[32]

30 Wood, *Alias Papa*, pp. 109, 182, 291.   31 *Small*, p. 32.   32 *Good Work*, p. 145.

Guidance from nature

Schumacher believed that for British industry and British socialism to treat individual men and women as each a universe, British society would have to discard the materialist map it had been using and look to other sources for guidance. To find its way out of the wasteland, humanity must respect the teachings of nature, history, and religion.

Like the fantasy writers who created other worlds to enable their readers to see anew the wonders of this world, Schumacher responded to nature with awe and delight. He cautioned that "man must never lose his sense of the marvellousness of the world around and inside him."[33] An enthusiastic organic gardener, Schumacher found great personal sustenance in the soil and saw nature as a source of not only physical and emotional refreshment but also spiritual wisdom. In 1976 Schumacher testified that "all my life has been a journey of discovery of the *generosity of nature*. . . . I discovered that everything will be done for us, provided only that we realise our 'nothingness' and thereupon start to search for a way of fitting-in with the great processes of Nature."[34] By losing touch with these processes, humanity had deprived itself of an important teacher.[35] The consequence was not only alienation from nature and loss of wonder but ultimately humanity's self-destruction as it trespassed beyond nature's, and therefore its own, limits. By conquering nature, humanity conquered itself.

Humanity's attempts to conquer, rather than cooperate with, nature left behind devastation everywhere. In *Small Is Beautiful* Schumacher pointed to the practices of industrial agriculture and factory farming as one manifestation of this tragedy. Schumacher believed that by treating agriculture as an industry modern society denied the sanctity of nature, the holiness of a world beyond human capacity to create. He saw agriculture as essentially the husbandry of living beings, whether organisms in the soil or cows in the barn. In contrast, industry sought "to eliminate the living factor, even including the human factor, and to turn the productive process over to machines."[36] As a result of this effort to mechanize a living system, modern agricultural practices threatened humanity's survival. The dependence of industrial agriculture on chemicals and oil squandered limited energy resources while the heavy machinery used by industrial farmers and the practice of monoculture added to the pollution of land and water. Moreover, monoculture violated

33 Schumacher, *The Age of Plenty: A Christian View* (Edinburgh: St. Andrew's Press, 1974), p. 17. Reprinted in Herman Daly, ed., *Economics, Ecology, and Ethics: Essays toward a Steady-State Economy* (San Francisco: Freeman, 1980).
34 Schumacher, "The Generosity of Nature," *Soil Association Quarterly Review* 2/4 (Dec. 1976): 2 (emphasis in original).
35 *Good Work*, p. 140.   36 *Small*, p. 110.

nature's lessons on the necessity of balance and variety for stability and thus left food supplies increasingly vulnerable to ecological upset. Monoculture also threatened the economic and social stability of Third World societies by turning entire nations into producers of specialty crops for export while their peoples went hungry. Humanity with its chemicals and combines had nearly conquered nature and, in the process, threatened to destroy itself.

In his approach to the problem of energy resources, too, Schumacher sought guidance from nature. He condemned nuclear energy because not only did the technology involved in its production epitomize the worst of the modern age in its expense, violence, and potential for irredeemable damage, but also the interlocking complexity of the ecosystem ensured that radiation pollution would work its way throughout the food chain. More generally, nature taught the importance of variety and balance for stability and sustainability; overdependence on any one energy source violated this teaching and thereby weakened modern society. With its cyclical processes and its continual recycling of waste into nutrient matter, nature also exemplified renewability and conservation, both keystones in Schumacher's attempts to construct a workable solution to the energy crisis.[37]

Guidance from the past

Nature served as one guide to lead humanity out of the modern wasteland; the past offered a complementary map to a better future. In Schumacher's analysis, the great modern failing was the belief that humanity had emerged from "a history of error" and that the past had nothing to offer.[38] Rather than error and obscurantism, the past offered spiritual wisdom in the religious and philosophical teachings of humanity, stored in great literature and art as well as in the scriptures of the great world religions and the works of philosophers. This traditional wisdom would meet the "most urgent need of our time . . . the need for *metaphysical reconstruction,* a supreme effort to bring clarity into our deepest convictions with regard to the questions What is man? Where does he come from? and What is the purpose of his life?"[39] To answer these questions, modern society had to resurrect the wisdom of past centuries.

In Schumacher's interpretation, traditional wisdom taught, first of all, the reality and necessity of hierarchy. The medieval Great Chain of Being depicted a spiritual truth: "Everything, everywhere, can be understood only when its *Level of Being* is fully taken into account." Minerals, plants, animals, and human beings occupy different levels of being. Life distinguishes

---

37 Ibid., pp. 134–45.　38 *Guide,* p. 10.　39 *Good Work,* p. 123 (emphasis in original).

plant from mineral; consciousness, animal from plant; self-awareness, human beings from animals. With each ascending level, complexity, uncertainty, and importance increase. Each level can be defined in terms of those lower, but it cannot be adequately understood thereby. For example, Schumacher argued that "to describe an animal as a physico-chemical system of extreme complexity is no doubt perfectly correct, except that it misses out on the 'animalness' of the animal." Humanity, too, could be described and studied in terms of the lower levels, but such a method would fall short of describing humanness. Traditional wisdom taught that to understand that which makes an individual human, the totality of the individual had to be considered: body (matter and life) and soul (consciousness) and spirit (self-awareness).[40] Failure to treat the whole man or woman, the attempt to reduce his or her level of being, led to the sort of metaphysical confusion epitomized by the orthodox economic view of the human individual as merely a factor in production.

Such metaphysical confusion could also lead to the excesses of the violent animal rights movement, with its insistence that the death of a human being matters no more than the death of an animal. In his embrace of the idea of hierarchy, Schumacher differed from many later Greens, who based their ecological concerns on egalitarianism. In contrast, Schumacher viewed the medieval concept of the Great Chain of Being as a religious as well as an ecological truth, crucial for the formulation of value and policy priorities. This insistence on the truth of hierarchy meant that Schumacher would have rejected the feminism and biocentrism of the later Green movement. In the feminist rejection of patriarchy Schumacher would have perceived the renunciation of much of traditional wisdom that granted women a specific and separate role to play from that of men. In the biocentric assertion that all beings, whether human or animal, sensate or insensate, are of equal value, he would have discerned a dangerous abnegation of responsibility, of the noblesse oblige that should govern human relationships with what Schumacher regarded as the lower orders.[41]

A second important truth revealed in traditional wisdom, according to Schumacher, was the reality of the spiritual world. The Great Chain of Being reached upward beyond humanity. To recognize the existence of a higher spiritual reality, the individual must acknowledge the limitations of both the senses and the intellect. Neither empirical nor rational processes could lead a person to God. Instead, through religious training and practices such as yoga and meditation, individuals must cultivate the "Eye of the Heart" rather than

40 *Guide*, pp. 23, 29, 47.
41 For the principle of noblesse oblige, see E. F. Schumacher, "Modern Pressures and the Environment," *Soil Association* 1/9 (Dec. 1973): 3.

the intellect, and so achieve insight.[42] Truth lay at the end of a romantic quest, not of a rational effort.

Schumacher's insistence on the limitations of both reason and observation undergirded what he perceived to be a third crucial teaching of traditional wisdom: the distinction between "convergent" and "divergent" problems. Convergent problems are those to which the sciences could and should be trusted to find solutions: "The more intelligently you study them, the more – whoever you are – the answers converge." The construction of a workable internal combustion engine, landing people on the moon, and splitting the atom were convergent problems, open to quantification and observation, capable of rational solution. Schumacher explained that "convergent problems relate to the dead aspect of the Universe, where manipulation can proceed without let or hindrance." Divergent problems, in contrast, are those for which no single solution emerges, for which, in fact, opposite answers develop. Divergent problems are the genuinely human issues, the difficulties that demand the very best and highest of human beings. In education, for example, teachers struggle with the polarities of freedom and discipline. Divergent problems such as this cannot be solved "in the sense of establishing the 'correct formula.' " Such polarities had to be reconciled, and reconciliation demanded spiritual understanding as well as compassion and empathy.[43]

Great art and great literature dealt with divergent problems, according to Schumacher. He rejected most of twentieth-century art as symptomatic of modern society's disease and saw the Middle Ages as the period of humanity's highest artistic development, the period before materialism corroded the link between humanity and divinity. In Schumacher's evaluation, "all great works of art are 'about God' in the sense of showing to the perplexed human being the path, the way up the mountain, providing a guide for the perplexed."[44] To argue that a work of Shakespeare and the second law of thermodynamics are equivalent, as C. P. Snow did in the *The Two Cultures*, was to display metaphysical confusion.[45] The second law of thermodynamics deals with a convergent problem, with dead matter; Shakespeare, on the other hand, grappled with the divergency of human existence. Challenging Snow, Schumacher asked, "What do I miss . . . if I have never heard of the Second Law of Thermodynamics? The answer is: Nothing. And what do I miss by not knowing Shakespeare? Unless I get my understanding from another source, I simply miss my life. . . . Science cannot produce ideas by which we could live."[46]

In fact, Schumacher argued, science could very well produce the ideas by

42 *Guide*, pp. 35, 58.   43 Ibid., pp. 140, 144, 145.   44 Ibid., p. 149.
45 C. P. Snow, *The Two Cultures and the Scientific Revolution* (Cambridge: Cambridge University Press, 1959), pp. 14–15.
46 *Small*, p. 87.

which humanity will die if society refused to recognize that its task was not in devising fail-safe technological solutions but in reconciling the opposites. The never-ending effort of reconciliation was what made human beings human. Scientific materialism deepened the modern crisis by treating all problems as convergent and thereby dehumanizing individuals. To avoid self-destruction, humanity had to reassert its humanness and turn again to religious truth. Schumacher based all of his work on this central theme: "*The modern experiment to live without religion has failed.*"[47]

Buddhist economics

Living with religion meant recognizing that religious wisdom, whether drawn from Buddhism or Christianity or some other tradition, must serve as the foundation for economic thought and policy in a sustainable society. Schumacher regarded orthodox economics, despite its claims to scientific objectivity, as the by-product of a materialist world view. What were usually held to be economic "facts" were, rather, materialist assumptions. Change the world view, and you would change economic practice and policy. In his important essay entitled "Economics in a Buddhist Country," Schumacher sought to do exactly that. The subjection of the economic calculus to the traditional wisdom of Buddhism involved a rejection of the GNP-obsessed approach to development, and, Schumacher asserted, the promotion of a more sustainable way of life. Both in the Third World and in the industrialized nations, the Buddhist view of work and consumption would aid economists in "finding the right path of development, the Middle Way between materialist heedlessness and traditionalist immobility."[48]

In Schumacher's vision, Buddhist economics treated work as essential for the happiness and development of each human being. It condemned the modern view of work as a wicked necessity, as something to be curtailed to the smallest amount of time possible in order to leave an individual free for the real life of leisure. Buddhism recognized "one of the basic truths of human existence, namely that work and leisure are complementary parts of the same living process and cannot be separated without destroying the joy of work and the bliss of leisure." Moreover, Buddhist economics viewed work in terms of what it meant for humanity rather than in terms of production. Whereas Western economics countenanced, even advocated, certain levels of unemployment so long as production was maintained, Buddhist economics saw unemployment as an evil because it denied persons a necessity for a good life. Without work, an individual could not fulfill his or her human potential:

47 *Guide*, pp. 147, 159 (emphasis in original).   48 *Small*, p. 62.

"The Buddhist sees the essence of civilisation not in a multiplication of wants but in the purification of human character. Character . . . is formed primarily by a man's work."[49]

Buddhist economics, however, did not view all work as good. Buddhism gave work a threefold function: "to give a man a chance to utilise and develop his faculties; to enable him to overcome his ego-centredness by joining with other people in a common task; and to bring forth the goods and services needed for a becoming existence." A Buddhist system of economics endeavored to expand opportunities for good work and to eliminate labor that failed to fulfill these functions. Similarly, not all technology was bad. Rather, a Buddhist economics would subject technology to a rigorous set of criteria. Machinery "that enhances a man's skill and power" was to be utilized; but technology "that turns the work of man over to a mechanical slave, leaving man in a position of having to serve the slave," must be rejected as unworthy of human beings.[50] The producer, not the level of production, claimed the highest priority.

Buddhist economics did not ignore the problem of production but viewed it in terms of the central Buddhist values of nonviolence and simplicity. For the Buddhist, struggling to live up to the ideal of nonviolence, the wasteful use of natural resources constituted a violent act against the living world. Moreover, the Buddhist virtue of simplicity called for sufficiency rather than surfeit. A high standard of living depended not on maximizing consumption but on "the maximum of well-being with the minimum of consumption." Such a goal reduced not only the violence inflicted by society on the environment but also the violence inflicted by peoples on one another, because it decreased the level of competition for scarce resources.[51] Subjecting economics to the standards of Buddhism rather than materialism demonstrated, according to Schumacher, the necessity as well as the beauty of smallness.

Small Is Beautiful

Although written in 1955 during Schumacher's stint as economic advisor in Burma, "Economics in a Buddhist Country" was not published until 1966. Seven years later Schumacher included it in *Small Is Beautiful*, the book that established Schumacher as a Green prophet and communicated his romantic protest to a large audience. *Small Is Beautiful* was an odd book to find on the best-seller list, although its author never doubted the appropriateness of such a position. Confident that the work would sell well and ensure a healthy

---

49 Ibid., p. 55.   50 Ibid., pp. 54–5.   51 Ibid., pp. 58–60; quotation from p. 57.

income for his family, Schumacher called it his *Goldregen,* or golden rain.[52] Since the book consisted of a diverse assortment of essays and lectures, written years apart and for different audiences, and cobbled together by new material, his confidence appeared misplaced. Nevertheless, as Schumacher predicted, *Small Is Beautiful* showered a fair income as well as fame down on him. Through a series of discussions on topics ranging from energy re- sources to education, from organizational structures of large corporations to the meaning of socialism, from futurology to factory farming, Schumacher convinced thousands of his many readers that although a crisis threatened the survival of humanity, salvation lay within reach.

Small Is Beautiful begins with a diagnosis of the crisis threatening the indus- trialized world: The West faced a shortage of the materials on which its existence depended. Schumacher insisted that the economic and social struc- tures of the advanced nations had overtaxed three crucial resources and so stood in danger of imminent breakdown: Without adequate energy, environ- mental, and human resources, the advanced nations would founder. At the same time, the nations of the Third World confronted a crisis of development. Without effective aid, these emerging nations were doomed to disintegration.

Schumacher's predictions in *Small Is Beautiful* of an impending energy shortage rested on over two decades of work and worry about this problem. His position with the National Coal Board drew Schumacher's attention to the question of energy resources. As the economic advisor of the Coal Board during the 1950s and 1960s, he participated in a period of dramatic change in the industry. In the first half of the 1950s, the Coal Board found itself in a situation of steadily rising demand. Until 1957 oil was used in Britain only to fill the gaps where coal did not exist in adequate supplies to meet demand. The peak year for the home consumption of coal in the twentieth century came in 1956. Very suddenly, however, the situation changed. After 1957 consumers began to turn to oil and natural gas, and the coal industry found itself struggling to survive. By 1973, coal, which had supplied 91 percent of the United Kingdom's energy consumption needs in 1948, accounted for only 37.6 percent of the energy consumed in the United Kingdom.[53]

Until the end of the 1950s, Schumacher, like the rest of the members and employees of the Coal Board, failed to perceive that the coal industry would shortly be fighting for its life as it contended with the new and stronger oil

52 Wood, *Alias Papa,* p. 348.
53 William Ashworth, *The History of the British Coal Industry,* vol. 5, *1946–1982: The Nation- alized Industry* (Oxford: Clarendon Press, 1986), pp. 38–9, 235–43. After 1973 the rising cost of oil made coal more competitive. In 1981–2, coal regained its position as the primary source of energy in Britain. At that time 36.7% of the nation's energy needs were supplied by coal; 35.5% by oil; 22.8% by natural gas; 4.3% by nuclear power; and 0.7% by hydroelectric power (Ashworth, p. 39).

and natural gas industries.[54] But even during the 1950s, in the short-lived period of prosperity, Schumacher warned of the energy resource problems facing the industrialized nations. Two themes began to appear in his writings and speeches for the Coal Board: first, the unreliability of oil and nuclear power; and second, the need to conserve nonrenewable energy resources. In a period in which economists and industrialists were placing great faith in nuclear power as a source of almost limitless energy, Schumacher expressed skepticism about the nuclear industry's ability to become a chief energy supplier in Britain in the twentieth century.[55] (His skepticism was well founded: By 1981–2, only 4.3 percent of the energy consumed in Britain was from nuclear power.)[56] Faith in oil, too, was misplaced. He pointed out a number of times, including in a talk given as early as 1952, that reliance on oil would mean dependence on one of the most volatile regions of the world, the Middle East.[57]

As an employee of the Coal Board, Schumacher not surprisingly struggled to keep coal at the center of British industry. There was, however, more than industrial self-interest at work. Schumacher's position made him acutely aware of the nonrenewability of fossil fuels and the need for conservation long before an energy shortage became the bogeyman of the industrialized world. Throughout the 1950s he urged the Coal Board to think in the long term and to adopt a policy of conservation.[58] In 1958 he argued that economists had a responsibility "to open people's eyes to the fact that the problem of resources is in no way solved and that the way we are carrying on exposes our children to totally insoluble problems."[59] The problem lay, Schumacher believed, in what he perceived as Western Europe's "addiction to a purely

54 In an address to the National Association of Colliery Managers in 1952, Schumacher predicted that in "the 1970s and probably already in the 1960s . . . coal will increasingly have to replace oil and natural gas" ("Coal Prospects," 22 Nov. 1952, p. 2 [NCB]). See also "The Place of Coal in the National Economy," National Coal Board Oxford Summer School, July 1952, p. 2 (NCB). For the Coal Board in the 1950s, see Ashworth, *British Coal Industry*, pp. 155–235.

55 Schumacher, "Investment in Coal," National Coal Board Summer School, Oxford, September 1955, p. 2 (NCB); "Coal, Oil, and the Atom," notes for a lecture given at the National Coal Board Summer School, 11 Sept. 1956 (NCB); "Nuclear Energy and the World's Fuel and Power Requirements," FBI Conference on Nuclear Energy, 10 Apr. 1958 (NCB).

56 Ashworth, *British Coal Industry*, p. 39. The discovery of North Sea oil, of course, limited the appeal of nuclear energy.

57 "The Place of Coal in the National Economy," July 1952, p. 3 (NCB). See also "Coal, Oil, and the Atom," and "Nuclear Energy and the World's Fuel and Power Requirements," p. 9.

58 "Coal, Oil, and the Atom"; "Coal – The Next 50 Years," paper read at the NUM Study Conference, London, 25–26 Mar. 1960, pp. 6, 19 (NCB). See also Ashworth, *British Coal Industry*, p. 57.

59 "Long-Term Demands for Fuel," 21 May 1958, p. 5 (NCB). See also "Nuclear Energy and the World's Fuel and Power Requirements," pp. 11–12.

quantitative concept of economic growth."[60] In a talk given in Germany in 1954, Schumacher became one of the first economists to warn that Western civilization, by escalating its consumption of nonrenewable fossil fuels, was living off its capital instead of its income.[61] In 1960, Schumacher offered this idea to a larger audience with an article in the *Observer* entitled "Non-violent Economics: Next Task for Mankind."[62] Schumacher reiterated in *Small Is Beautiful* what had been his constant theme for two decades: The earth's limited fuel supplies demanded the replacement of the Western lifestyle of consumption with one of conservation. Failure to effect such a substitution would result in a devastating energy crisis.

According to Schumacher, profligate use of natural capital also brought on the second, and most dangerous, aspect of the crisis in resources: the crisis of the environment. In *Small Is Beautiful* Schumacher argued that although the energy crisis could threaten the survival of industrial civilization, the environmental crisis threatened to destroy the very earth.[63] The quantitative leap in industrial production since World War II and the qualitative shift involved in the development of synthetic compounds had placed an enormous strain on the environment, had, in fact, pushed to the limits nature's tolerance margins, her capacity to absorb the various shocks imposed by industrialization.

Schumacher saw the environmental crisis as primarily a religious, rather than a technical, problem. The tragedy of environmental pollution, the loss of ecological habitats, and the disappearance of species all stemmed from misplaced priorities and mistaken values. In a lecture given at about the time *Small Is Beautiful* was released, Schumacher argued that the "environment crisis is the glass, the mirror, showing us *what manner of men we are.*" He went on to state that the teaching of Christianity, with its call to the four cardinal virtues of *prudentia, justitia, fortitudo,* and *temperantia,* "shows us what manner of men we could and should be." Had humanity been temperate and heeded the Christian call to self-control, nature would not be straining under the burden of human excess. Even more important, the cultivation of prudence, "a clear-eyed recognition of reality," would have enabled men and women to perceive both the viciousness of the status quo and the means to victory over it.[64] Not only Christianity but all traditional religious systems demanded that humans show restraint and humility in their relationships with the natural world and with each other. By throwing off this restraint, humanity threatened to destroy the natural world and eliminate the best of human civilization.

---

60 "Nuclear Energy and the World's Fuel and Power Requirements," p. 11.
61 Wood, *Alias Papa*, p. 241.   62 *Observer*, 21 Aug. 1960, p. 17.   63 *Small*, p. 17.
64 "Modern Pressures and the Environment," *Soil Association* 1/9 (Dec. 1973): 3. This article is the printed version of a talk given by Schumacher in Canterbury Cathedral on 8 Nov. 1972.

In the process of pushing nature to its limits, industrialization threatened to use up the tolerance margins of humanity itself. According to Schumacher, current methods of production were not only swallowing up fossil fuels and corroding the environment but also "eating into the very substance of industrial man." Schumacher identified what he perceived as rising rates of "crime, drug addiction, vandalism, mental breakdown, rebellion, and so forth" as symptoms of this abuse of human resources.[65] Industrialization had brought to the West the goods but not necessarily the Good Life.

The human crisis of the West indicated that individuals in the industrial nations had lost the tools by which to live. The Third World faced an even more deadly version of the human crisis. During the 1950s and 1960s, his work on problems of development in both Burma and India convinced Schumacher that Western aid efforts exacerbated, rather than alleviated, the problems of debt and famine. Western aid to the Third World had created the economic and human tragedy of the "dual economy." In the developing nations a Westernized and urban elite lived in comfort while most of the population existed in a state of misery. Factories possessing the most advanced technological equipment abutted extremely primitive workshops, with no middle ground. The modern and Westernized sector of the developing nations, about 15 percent of the population, survived as "small ultramodern islands in a pre-industrial society." Such pernicious patterns of growth led to what Schumacher labeled the " 'process of mutual poisoning,' whereby successful industrial development in the cities destroys the economic structure of the hinterland, and the hinterland takes its revenge by mass migration into the cities, poisoning them and making them utterly unmanageable."[66]

Schumacher linked the problem of the dual economy to what he perceived as the peculiarly modern horror of "immiseration." He argued that the impoverished men, women, and children clustered in cardboard shacks outside cities like Buenos Aires and Calcutta were in a state of not only poverty but also misery, more degraded than their poor ancestors because of their loss of structures for survival. Misery was a psychological and spiritual condition as much as physical fact. Apathy and paralysis exacerbated age-old problems of hunger and lack of shelter. Poverty characterized preindustrial societies, but misery, "associated with and promoted by the twin evils of unemployment and limitless urbanisation – this is a new phenomenon in the history of mankind, the direct result of modern technology thoughtlessly applied."[67] Modern aid, in its efforts to catapult Third World societies into

65 *Small*, p. 20.   66 Ibid., pp. 166, 167.
67 "Industrialisation through Intermediate Technology," *Resurgence* 1/2 (July 1966). Reprinted in Michael North, ed., *Time Running Out: The Best of "Resurgence"* (Chelmington: Prism Press, 1976), p. 9.

industrialization, had destroyed centuries-old traditions and techniques that had enabled the poor to live, without offering adequate alternatives. Western methods of production, distribution, and administration were often inappropriate for all but a small minority of these societies. Aid efforts ignored the historical experience of England's industrial revolution, with its lessons of gradualism and organic growth, and attempted instead to graft branches of advanced technology on a preindustrial cultural and social trunk. The result was the sickening of the entire tree, as the immiseration of the majority infected the industrial achievements of the minority.[68]

Despite his emphasis on the severity of the triple crisis in the West and the specter of famine in the Third World, Schumacher proclaimed more than doom in *Small Is Beautiful*. The affirmation expressed in the title rang loudly throughout the work's pages: Crisis served as one theme, but resolution provided the counterpoint. An optimist, Schumacher believed humanity could not only survive the crises he outlined but actually use them to construct a better world. In *Small Is Beautiful* he offered what he perceived as workable guidelines for the creation of this alternative future.

To make a better world, humanity had to realize that "man is small, and therefore, small is beautiful."[69] Continued insistence on large-scale, indiscriminate, quantitative growth (as measured by the gross national product) would exacerbate the crisis undermining human society. The modern belief that "bigger is better" needed to be challenged and refuted if humanity was to have a future worth welcoming. Big was not always bad, Schumacher admitted.[70] To resolve the modern crisis, however, humanity had to see that political and economic organization must be brought down to "human scale," which was, in most cases, small, decentralized, and gradual.

The most important area in which humanity needed to implement "smallness" was that of technology. In *Small Is Beautiful* Schumacher placed technology on center stage by arguing that it determined the structures and aims of modern civilization. He refused, however, to acknowledge it as hero. Technological advance did not always guarantee progress. According to Schumacher, the needs of technology and the needs of human beings could be and increasingly were at odds with each other. Whereas incessant growth is a sign of disease, a cancer that will kill, both in human beings and in the natural environment, "technology recognises no self-limiting principle – in terms, for instance, of size, speed, or violence."[71] As a result of the lack of technological limits, the maker had to adapt to the made, and industrial society grew into a world scaled to machines rather than to people.

68 Schumacher, "A Humanistic Guide to Foreign Aid," paper given at the Congress for Freedom and Gokhale Institute of Politics and Economics International Seminar, India, 1961 (ITDG).
69 *Small*, p. 159.   70 Ibid., p. 66.   71 Ibid., p. 147.

This distortion of scale had its most tragic consequences in the developing nations. Schumacher, who rejected calls for reproductive limits even before he embraced Roman Catholicism, could not accept the argument that the predominant problem of the Third World was overpopulation and that the preeminent need was the implementation of population controls. Not only did Schumacher view birth control as one more example of the worship of technique at the expense of human and religious values, he also believed that the overpopulation of the Third World was not a problem that could be solved by Western nations. Perceiving the paternalism and "Westocentrism" that lay beneath much of the outcry against population growth, Schumacher argued that the key crisis of the age was not overpopulation in the developing nations but instead overconsumption of resources by the developed world. He believed that the demographic focus of many early Greens, such as the Conservation Society and the authors of *A Blueprint for Survival,* was wrong and counterproductive. In his analysis, population control advocates over-generalized from specific problem areas to the world at large and failed to empathize with the Third World peasant, for whom a brood of children was necessary provision for old age.[72] Most important, this emphasis on the seemingly insoluble problem of overpopulation led to apathy and inaction on the part of the West.[73]

Schumacher saw that the impoverished peoples in the Third World needed action. They required the tools that would enable them to help themselves. The need to adapt technology to the scale of impoverished individuals in Third World societies led Schumacher to devise the concept of intermediate technology, which he defined as a "£100 technology" in a world divided into "£1,000 technologies" and "£1 technologies." Stagnating and starving with a £1 technology, Third World nations received a £1,000 technology from aid programs. Such expensive and complex machinery increased their dependency on the industrialized world while destroying indigenous social and economic structures. In other words, the £1,000 technology killed off the £1 technology and left the poor worse off than before. Schumacher proposed an alternative that was more productive than traditional technology but less expensive and complicated than that supplied by the industrialized nations, and therefore within reach of ordinary

72 McRobie interview, 29 Apr. 1986; "Why Small Is Beautiful: A Conversation with E. F. Schumacher," *Annual Series of Authoritative Commentaries in Current Social and Economic Problems That Affect Business and Individual Investment Strategies,* 3, Inter-regional Financial Group, Minneapolis, n.d.; E. F. Schumacher, "Message from the Universe," *Ecologist* 4/9 (Nov. 1974): 318; E. F. Schumacher, "An Economist's Look at Farming," *Soil Association* 2/9 (Nov./Dec. 1974): 3.

73 E. F. Schumacher, "The World Crisis and the Wholeness of Life," Findhorn Foundation Lecture Series, Oct. 1976. (I am grateful to Barbara Wood for allowing me to borrow her tape of this lecture.)

people.[74] The introduction of intermediate technology would provide work opportunities in the rural areas and thus address the problem of unemployment, halt the process of rural decay, stabilize the base of these developing nations, and create a solid foundation for healthy growth. In *Small Is Beautiful* Schumacher advocated an aid and development program with employment and regional development as the central aim and with the provision of simple, affordable, and workable technologies as the means.

Intermediate technology exemplified the "small is beautiful" principle not only by meeting the needs of small, ordinary people but also by promoting gradual development that would not overwhelm individuals with sudden, large-scale change. Because the central failure of aid efforts lay in their ahistoricism, Schumacher urged policymakers to learn from the record of the past. There they would see that industrial development was an evolutionary process. Quite simply, people needed to walk before they could run. Successful development depended on far more than the construction of large factories or the provision of tractors to peasants. A successful development policy would foster the educational and organizational structures needed for the evolution of an economically prosperous and spiritually sound civilization.

Intermediate technology, or "technology with a human face," provided tools suited to human needs, rather than machines to which humans must adapt. Intermediate technology did not mean simply "labor-intensive." As his exercise in Buddhist economics demonstrated, Schumacher valued technology in the form of tools to eliminate degrading, backbreaking, dangerous, dulling labor. Most modern technology, however, failed this test. The capital-intensive technology of the advanced nations either put laborers out of work or condemned them to the assembly line. Rather than eliminating mind-numbing labor, modern technology tended to increase it. In contrast, Schumacher argued, a genuine tool, a human-scale technology, "instead of making human hands and brains redundant, helps them to become far more productive than they have ever been before."[75]

Schumacher designed intermediate technology to meet the needs of the underdeveloped nations such as he had encountered in Burma and India, but he soon found that the concept had relevance as well as to the resolution of the triple crisis besetting the industrialized world. His work in development led him to perceive a link between modern technology and the creation of an essentially dehumanizing system that ignored the nonrenewability of energy resources and abused the environment. No Luddite, he did not propose that the modern world scrap technology. Instead, he called for "a revolution in technology to give us inventions and machines which reverse the destructive trends now threatening us all."[76] Intermediate

74 *Small*, pp. 179–81.   75 Ibid., pp. 148, 149, 153.   76 Ibid., p. 34.

technology could be part of the technological revolution that would rescue the industrialized world from its energy shortage, environmental problems, and social ills. Intermediate technology was energy-efficient, environmentally gentle, and designed to meet the needs of human beings rather than to force people to adapt to the demands of a machine. In the industrial nations, just as in the Third World, Schumacher concluded that "small is beautiful."

His faith in the potential of individual human beings gave Schumacher a message in striking contrast to the "doom and gloom, woe is upon us" cry of many eco-activists. Just as he regarded small scale as a goal, so he regarded it as an appropriate means. Individual action counted; individual endeavor could make a difference; individuals joined together could change the world. He placed great trust in the common sense of common people. In many ways a populist, Schumacher declared over and over again that the experts and the technocrats did not possess the answers; they were more often part of the problem, "people of the forward stampede" hurling themselves and all of humanity into the abyss. He believed that the "case for hope rests on the fact that ordinary people are often able to take a wider view, and a more 'humanistic' view, than is normally being taken by experts."[77]

Like C. S. Lewis and J. R. R. Tolkien, Schumacher proclaimed the necessity of individual spiritual regeneration, but, unlike the fantasy writers, he believed this personal revitalization would lead to the renewal of the larger society. Schumacher's optimism contrasted vividly with the despairing outlook of Lewis and Tolkien, who counseled a retreat to communities of friends and to the refreshment of fantasy. The contrast between the quiet cloisters of Oxford, which sheltered Lewis and Tolkien, and the clamorous conference rooms of the Coal Board, where Schumacher worked, is telling. Instead of withdrawing from modern society into a dream of a better world, Schumacher used the dream in order to change that society. Like the CNDers marching every Easter, Schumacher believed that the actions of individuals could remake the world. Schumacher was a rare mix of the contemplative and the activist, both a monk and a missionary. The combination gave him great confidence. When rooted in the spiritual world, human beings could change the structures of their everyday universe. Schumacher admitted he preached "a romantic, a utopian, vision. . . . We jolly well have to have the courage to dream if we want to survive and give our children a chance of survival."[78] For Schumacher, the crisis of modern society made the romantic vision a realistic guide for the future.

77 Ibid., pp. 155, 158.   78 Ibid., p. 152.

Schumacher's influence

In Martin Stott's *Spilling the Beans* (1986), a satirical guide to the alternative lifestyle in the same genre as the American *Preppie Handbook*, the vegetable-munching, natural-fiber-wearing, bearded eco-activist described by Stott was a disciple of E. F. Schumacher.[79] As Stott's stereotype revealed, in the public mind the Green movement and Schumacher were firmly linked. Although this perception of Schumacher as *the* Green prophet was somewhat skewed, Schumacher's ideas had enormous impact. Described as "one of the most influential writers in the development of green politics," Schumacher played an important role in British eco-activism, both during the early 1970s and in the decade following his death in 1977.[80]

Schumacher's importance is illustrated in the way in which his name became synonymous with the ideas he presented in *Small Is Beautiful*. Both Britain and the United States had Schumacher societies and Schumacher lecture series by the 1980s.[81] In an address at St. James' Church, Piccadilly, in 1987, the bishop of Durham praised "the Schumacher suggestions" for their practicality.[82] Like the bishop, Green writers often referred to the "Schumacherian ideal," the "Schumacherian message," the "Schumacherian thesis."[83] Greens warned against oversimplifying Schumacher's ideas and

79 Martin Stott, *Spilling the Beans* (London: Fontana, 1986), p. 30. According to Stott, Schumacher tops the Green pantheon, ahead even of Gandhi and Martin Luther King, Jr.

80 Joe Weston, ed., *Red and Green: The New Politics of the Environment* (London: Pluto Press, 1986), p. 25. Eminent British and American Greens such as Jonathon Porritt, Hazel Henderson, Fritjof Capra, and Kirkpatrick Sale acknowledged Schumacher's importance. For Porritt, see the account of Porritt's talk at the Schumacher Lectures in *Resurgence* 109 (Mar./Apr. 1985): 42; see also Jonathon Porritt and David Winner, *The Coming of the Greens* (London: Fontana, 1988), pp. 233–4; and Porritt's essay "Beyond Environmentalism," in *Green Britain or Industrial Wasteland*, ed. Edward Goldsmith and Nicholas Hildyard (Cambridge: Polity Press, 1986). For Henderson, see Fritjof Capra, *Uncommon Wisdom: Conversations with Remarkable People* (New York: Simon and Schuster, 1988), pp. 232–3. Schumacher wrote the preface for Henderson's *Creating Alternative Futures: The End of Economics* (New York: Berkley Publications Corp., 1978). For Capra, see *Uncommon Wisdom*, pp. 206ff. For Sale, see *Resurgence* 114 (Jan./Feb. 1986): 17.

   Prince Charles has also explicitly acknowledged Schumacher as an intellectual and spiritual mentor and has become a champion of Schumacher's work. The prince's advocacy of alternative medicine and intermediate technology, conversion of his Gloucestershire farm to organic methods of cultivation, concern with revitalizing inner-city communities, abhorrence of modern architecture, and interest in yoga and meditation all place him within the Green camp. See Andrew Stephen, "The Man Behind the Images," *Sunday Times Review*, 18 Aug. 1985, pp. 33–4.

81 See Satish Kumar, ed., *The Schumacher Lectures* (London: Blond and Briggs, 1980); and Kirkpatrick Sale, "Letter from America," *Resurgence* 108 (Jan./Feb. 1985): 31.

82 Quoted in Porritt, *Coming of the Greens*, pp. 244–5.

83 Godfrey Boyle, "Letter," *Resurgence* 122 (May/June 1987): 5; Kirkpatrick Sale, "Letter from America," *Resurgence* 108 (Jan./Feb. 1985): 31; Donald D. Evans, *Appropriate*

pointed out that the works of nineteenth- and twentieth-century thinkers such as Ruskin, Morris, Galbraith, and Jacques Ellul "mirrored those of Schumacher."[84] Lists of recommended books on Green issues almost invariably included *Small Is Beautiful*.[85]

Schumacher's influence is also clear in the movement to reshape the discipline of economics. In 1984, impatience with the failure of the international economic summits since 1975 to deal adequately with the immiseration of the Third World and the environmental crisis led a group of 170 people from sixteen countries to gather as The *Other* Economic Summit (TOES). The aim of the first and subsequent annual summits was to construct "a whole new economic framework incorporating the collective wisdom and insights of what might loosely be termed the Schumacher school of economics – 'economics as if people mattered.' "[86] Out of the summits came an organizational, research, and publishing structure intended to turn ideas into action. TOES condemned conventional economics for its policy of giving priority to short-term benefits over long-term needs, its blindness to factors beyond the reach of the pricing mechanism, its concentration on macroeconomics, and its tendency to ignore the wider implications of economic policy.[87] In the second half of the 1980s, the approach basic to TOES remained unorthodox. As the inadequacies of the gross national product as a measure of economic and social welfare became increasingly obvious, however, even "establishment economists" became involved in trying to find more accurate analytical tools.

Schumacher played his most significant role in the area of alternative technologies.[88] Although it was not until the Ethiopian famine in the summer

Technology for Development, quoted in Marilyn Carr, ed., *The AT Reader: Theory and Practice in Appropriate Technology* (New York: Intermediate Technology Publications, 1985), p. 45. See also Maurice Ash, *Green Politics: The New Paradigm* (London: Green Alliance, 1980), pp. 4, 8, 15, 18.

84 Quotation from Carr, *AT Reader,* p. 5. See also Maurice Ash, "After Schumacher," *Resurgence* 111 (July/Aug. 1985); Jonathon Porritt, excerpt from talk given at the Schumacher Lectures, 1984, *Resurgence* 109 (Mar./Apr. 1985): 42.

85 E.g., Peter Bunyard and Fern Morgan-Grenville, eds., *The Green Alternative Guide to Good Living* (London: Methuen, 1987), list *Small Is Beautiful* as a recommended reading in "Ecophilosophy and Politics." According to Jonathon Porritt, the chapter on Buddhist economics "remains one of the classics for budding Greens" (*Coming of the Greens,* pp. 233–4).

86 The Other Economic Summit, *Report and Summary,* 1985, p. 39.

87 The Other Economic Summit, 6–10 June 1984, *Report and Summary,* pp. 6–7.

88 Schumacher's intermediate technology is one kind of alternative technology. Similar concepts include "appropriate technology," "soft technology," "community technology," and "liberatory technology." See Francis Sandbach, *Environment, Ideology, and Policy* (Monclair: Allanheld, Osmun, 1980), pp. 167–8; Nicolas Jequier, *Appropriate Technology: Problems and Promises* (Paris: OECD, 1976), pp. 25, 32; Langdon Winner, *The Whale and the Reactor: A Search for Limits in an Age of High Technology* (Chicago: University of Chicago Press, 1986), p. 62.

of 1985 became a media event that the failure of Western aid efforts in the Third World became generally known, by the 1970s alert observers were calling for new development strategies based on technologies appropriate to the immiserated areas. The need for a change in course was striking. In 1960, Eugene Black, head of the World Bank, had christened the postwar era the "Age of Economic Development."[89] But the large-scale, capital-intensive development projects promoted by the World Bank did little for the Third World. By the end of the 1980s, Africa, which had fed itself in 1960, was importing 40 percent of its food and sending huge sums of money out of the continent to service the debts owed for a tragic series of development disasters.[90] Largely unknown in the 1960s, the concept of "appropriate technology" was commonly found two decades later in both the literature and the policies of development. In the early 1980s over one thousand groups claimed to be working on or with appropriate technology.[91] More important, both Third World governments and the "aid establishment" of the industrialized nations had accepted the principle of appropriate technology, although the proportion of investment resources devoted to appropriate technology remained small in comparison to that given to more traditional aid efforts.[92]

Schumacher stands at the center of the history of appropriate technology. His discussion of intermediate technology in *Small Is Beautiful* was for many readers their first introduction to the problem of large-scale development and its potential solution by smaller-scale technology. By 1973, however, when *Small Is Beautiful* was published, Schumacher had already devoted a number of years to the provision of appropriate technology to the developing nations. He had written his essay on Buddhist economics in 1955; in 1960, in the *Observer*, he had called for a shift to a more nonviolent technology. In 1965, Schumacher began to put his ideas into action when he founded the Intermediate Technology Development Group, a research and consultancy organization involved in Third World development. The group helped pioneer a gradualist approach to development, which, although at first much maligned by other economists, proved very successful. Supported by such well-known figures as Prince Charles, the Intermediate Technology Development Group had become in the 1980s an established and respected institution in the arena of

89 Eugene Black, "The Age of Economic Development," *Economic Journal*, June 1960, p. 268.
90 Steven Mufson, "White Elephants in Black Africa," *New Republic*, 29 Dec. 1986, pp. 18–20; Bertrand Schneider, *The Barefoot Revolution: A Report to the Club of Rome* (London: Intermediate Technology Publications, 1988), pp. 3–18. See also Jennifer Seymour Whitaker, *How Can Africa Survive?* (New York: Harper and Row, 1987).
91 Carr, *AT Reader*, pp. 3–5; see also pp. 72–9.
92 Frances Stewart, Introduction to Carr, *AT Reader*, p. xiii; Jequier, *Appropriate Technology*, pp. 24–5.

Third World aid and development.[93] One observer argued that the alternative technology movement was built "largely on Schumacher's reputation."[94] Such a statement overemphasizes Schumacher's role; yet, the fact that it was made illustrates Schumacher's effectiveness in communicating his message.

Schumacher's ability to communicate ensured the success of *Small Is Beautiful*. Published in England in June 1973, by December 1974 the book had been reprinted four times as a hardback.[95] Schumacher's argument possessed great appeal because, as Chapters 10 and 11 have shown, it emerged in a period of heightened environmental consciousness and pessimism. More than this, however, Schumacher offered a holistic analysis grounded on romantic assumptions and rooted in his own quest for religious truth. He spoke within the context of an established intellectual and cultural tradition of protest.

93 See the *Sunday Times Review*, 18 Aug. 1985, pp. 33–4. According to David Collins, ITDG's information director in 1986, the group received 60% of its budget from the British government, 30% from grants from other sources such as foreign governments and the UN, and only about 10% from public donations. Collins described ITDG as a consultancy organization that works for free (interview with David Collins, 14 Mar. 1986).

94 Krishan Kumar, *Utopia and Anti-Utopia in Modern Times* (Oxford: Blackwell, 1987), p. 406.

95 According to Satish Kumar, in 1977 *Small Is Beautiful* placed third on a list of the publications that British politicians described as having the most influence on their thought (see essay entitled "E. F. Schumacher," undated, ITDG files). I have been unable to locate Kumar's source.

Conclusion:
romanticism and the Greens

By the time of Schumacher's unexpected death in 1977, the Green movement also appeared to have come to the end of its days. Press coverage and
public awareness of environmental issues dropped dramatically after 1975,
during the era of economic recession, rising unemployment, and severe labor
unrest. Margaret Thatcher's election in 1979 seemed to sound the death
knell for the Greens. Although many Greens had demanded an end to
pragmatic politics and the restoration of principle to political life, Thatcher's
brand of conviction politics threatened to undermine the basic assumptions
of eco-activism.

Yet, despite the end to the first phase of eco-activism, the movement that it
aroused continued. Not only did publications such as the *Ecologist* and *Resurgence* remain in existence, but new ones, such as *Vole,* began.[1] Friends of the
Earth continued to agitate, accompanied after 1975 by the even more aggressive and more media-aware Greenpeace. As health issues grew increasingly
important to individuals, especially middle-class individuals with plenty of
disposable income, organic foods moved into the consumption mainstream.
Most significant, in the late 1970s the fight over nuclear energy became a
central political and social battleground. Activists from the early Green movement joined with the previously uninvolved to battle what they perceived to
be an unmitigated evil threatening their communities. Although the first
phase of the Green movement had ended by 1980, then, and had apparently
dropped out of public consciousness, its organizational structures remained
intact and were able to surface again very quickly when the second phase of
the movement began in the mid-1980s.

Three developments contributed to the resurgence of Green concern after
an extended period of apathy. First, in the summer of 1985, the Ethiopian
famine became a media event. The enormous amount of publicity given to

---

1 *Vole* began in Oct. 1977 and ceased publication in 1981. In its opening statement of
purpose, the journal declared, "The *Vole* is in favour of decentralisation and small units;
is opposed to the consumption of goods as an end in itself, and to the desire and pursuit
of unlimited economic growth. The *Vole* is interested in community action, amenity
groups, alternative technology, self-sufficiency. . . ."

the horror in Ethiopia alerted many people in the industrialized world to the failure of over three decades of development and relief programs and to the related fact of environmental devastation in the developing nations. The answers offered by E. F. Schumacher and other critics of orthodox economic development seemed more relevant than ever.

The summer of 1985 also witnessed the second key event in arousing Green concerns. On the evening of 10 July 1985, an explosion destroyed the *Rainbow Warrior,* the ship of the radical environmentalist organization Greenpeace. The bomb, which killed one Greenpeace member, was set by the French Secret Service in order to keep the *Rainbow Warrior* from interfering with French nuclear tests in the South Pacific.[2] By 1985 Greenpeace had become probably the world's best-known environmentalist organization. With its propensity for dramatic and media-oriented campaigns such as setting up human shields between baby seals and their hunters and challenging whale fleets in small rubber boats, Greenpeace proved its mastery of the "photo op" and the unforgettable image. Although its willingness to violate the law alienated the organization from many potential supporters, the linking of the French government to the *Rainbow Warrior* explosion gained Greenpeace extremely favorable publicity. It also lent validity to Green doubts about the security of democracy in a world of large-scale organizational structures.

The most important event in the resurgence of Green concern in the second half of the 1980s was the Chernobyl nuclear power plant disaster of 1986. On 25 April, the management of the nuclear power plant located in the Ukraine decided to carry out a series of tests that were afterward revealed to have been both unauthorized and poorly planned. The tests required shutting off the reactor's emergency core cooling system. At 1:24 A.M. on 26 April, two explosions occurred about three to four seconds apart. Radioactivity spewed into the atmosphere, and a fire began inside the reactor.[3] Thirty-one people died in the immediate aftermath of the accident. At least 135,000 were evacuated from a thirty-kilometer zone around the plant; the number of deaths from radiation-induced cancer is not yet known.[4] As the fallout from the explosion made its way across the world, the disaster spread beyond the Soviet Union. Produce, milk, and livestock all had to be destroyed because of radiation contamination. In the north of Britain, two to four million sheep

2 See Richard Shears and Isobelle Gidley, *The Rainbow Warrior Affair* (London: Unwin Paperbacks, 1986).

3 David Marples, *The Social Impact of the Chernobyl Disaster* (New York: St. Martin's Press, 1988), pp. 13–21; Richard Mould, *Chernobyl: The Real Story* (New York: Pergamon Press, 1988), pp. 7–11. See also Zhores Medvedev, *The Legacy of Chernobyl* (New York: Norton, 1990).

4 Marples, *Social Impact of the Chernobyl Disaster,* pp. 26–37; Mould, *Chernobyl,* p. 63.

were contaminated.[5] Chernobyl boosted the already-strong anti-nuclear movement; more important, it heightened concern about the intricate ecological web connecting the peoples of Europe and their natural environment.

The later Green movement is not the subject of this study; its emergence, however, indicates that the problems that the eco-activists recognized in the 1960s and 1970s remain acute. The early Greens studied here were, of course, better at outlining the problems than at providing solutions. One reviewer of Schumacher's *Good Work* argued that the greatest weakness in Schumacher's analysis lay in explaining how to move from the present into a Green future: Schumacher "prefers to see the world as a morality play, in which the heroic 'little people' slowly undermine the villainous world of Massive Technology from within. . . . the multinational corporations quietly wither away . . . a perfect omelette made of good intentions, and achieved without breaking a single (free-range) egg."[6] Such criticism is more than a bit unfair. In the Intermediate Development Technology Group Schumacher established a means of gradual yet fundamental change in the Third World. It is true, however, that the West's path out of the industrial present into a more sustainable future is not clearly marked in Schumacher's work, nor in the works of his fellow early Greens.

Nevertheless, such political inadequacies do not nullify the significance of the early Green critique. Many elements of the eco-activist movement were rooted in a romantic outlook. They sought a reevaluation of the benefits of industrialization and the efficacy of orthodox economic analysis. They fought to reestablish the role of nonempirical methods of perceiving truth and devising policy. They believed that the individual could develop to his or her full potential only in a community, not in the atomized, market-driven society that Margaret Thatcher idealized. And they argued that such community could be constructed only when the bonds between humanity and nature, humanity and its past, and humanity and its spiritual aspect were recognized and restored. In their protest against postwar Britain, they articulated their message in traditionally romantic terms.

5 Marples, *Social Impact of the Chernobyl Disaster*, pp. 76–8.
6 Michael Ashley, "The Enrichment of Boredom," *Encounter* 54 (Mar. 1980): 60.

13

Conclusion

In *The Making of the English Working Class*, E. P. Thompson explored the relationship between Tory paternalism and political radicalism and concluded that the "starting-point of traditionalist and Jacobin was the same. . . . Although Jacobin and Tory are at opposed political poles, sparks of feeling and of argument are continually exchanged between them."[1] Similar sparks of feeling, exchanged between individuals and groups with contrasting political beliefs, have been the subject of this work. No doubt many of the individuals discussed in the preceding pages would have been surprised and dismayed to find themselves members of the same company. For example, although George MacLeod and C. S. Lewis were both prominent advocates of Christianity, they espoused opposing political and social views. MacLeod, it is safe to say, would have been horrified at the cavalier attitude toward the Bomb displayed by Lewis, who once wrote that "when the bomb falls there will always be just that split second in which one can say 'Pooh, you're only a bomb. I'm an immortal soul.' "[2] Nevertheless, MacLeod, Lewis, and the many very different men and women who appeared above *were* part of the same company. "Sparks of feeling" flashed between and among these diverse individuals and groups and illuminated their shared romantic protest.

The tradition of romantic protest originated in Britain in the late eighteenth century as a reaction against the new society taking shape under the impact of empiricism and industrialization. At the same time that industrialization appeared to be destroying old boundaries and snapping the bonds of conviction and community, the triumph of empirical modes of analysis seemed to reduce human reality and individual experience to the limited realm of the material. Combined, these forces of fragmentation and limitation threatened to destroy both the basis of community life and the belief that an individual's actions and attitudes mattered. Romantic protesters refused to accept such a world. Compelled by a desire to save the earth from what

---

1 E. P. Thompson, *The Making of the English Working Class* (1963; New York: Vintage Books, 1966), pp. 343–4.
2 Recalled by Neville Coghill in "The Approach to English," in Jocelyn Gibb, ed., *Light on C. S. Lewis* (New York: Harcourt, Brace and World, 1966), pp. 64–5.

they perceived to be certain destruction and degradation, they embarked on a quest for reintegration.

In post-1945 British society, the task of reintegration possessed a special urgency. In Britain, as elsewhere in the industrialized world, the years after 1945 witnessed enormous economic and social change. Although Britain did not experience the astounding economic growth rates of nations such as West Germany and Italy, both the construction of the welfare state and the emergence of a consumption economy significantly changed the material structures of most people's lives. The coming of affluence, however, was accompanied by greater standardization and an increase in the size and scale of the institutions and organizations that an individual encountered daily. For some individuals, the gains of affluence could not outweigh the losses resulting from the bureaucratization, the "massness" of modern society. They sought instead an alternative path, a way that would allow them to overcome their feelings of alienation, powerlessness, and fragmentation. In their protest against contemporary society, they utilized and expanded upon the vocabulary and concepts of the romantic tradition.

The fantasies of Lewis and Tolkien stand in this tradition. These works reveal a rejection of the principal assumptions of postwar society. Such contemporary doctrines as the inherent progressivism of scientific and technological activity, the efficiency and superiority of quantitative and empirical approaches for understanding the world, and the need for expertise found no place in Lewis's and Tolkien's belief systems. In their fantasies, they sought not only to escape the empirical, technocratic, and industrial world but also to sketch a more sustainable and sustaining alternative. They created myths, subcreations that both reflected the imagination and goodness of the divine creation and revealed the ways in which it had been marred by humanity. Lewis and Tolkien believed that by attempting to sever the ties that joined the human being to God, to nature, and to other human beings, modern society had placed itself on the edge of an abyss of meaninglessness and, finally, eternal despair. Their fantasies depicted otherworlds where human heroes interacted with spiritual and natural forces. They emphasized the beauty of nature and its right to exist, apart from its utility to human beings; they stressed the heroism embedded in the individual, and the need for the individual to be a part of a community; they focused on the magical or supernatural elements of life. Thus, Middle-earth and Narnia served as embodiments of Lewis's and Tolkien's critiques of contemporary society. These critiques were essentially romantic, an assertion of the primacy of nonmaterial reality.

Lewis's and Tolkien's political views placed them in sharp contrast to the men and women who joined together in CND and the other movements against the Bomb. Yet, like Lewis and Tolkien, the anti-Bomb protesters sought to present an alternative vision of society (one that, it can be argued, was as much a fantasy as are Narnia and Middle-earth). By rejecting nuclear weapons, the epitome of materialism, technology, and expertise, CNDers sought to remake not only the world situation but also Britain itself. They argued that by banning the Bomb, Britain could reclaim its role as moral leader of the world and, with the support of the neutral nations, mediate between the superpowers and melt the cold war blocs. At the same time, such a renunciation would thaw the frozen structures of domestic political and social life. In their struggle against the apathy, materialism, and political pragmatism they perceived as dominant in postwar Britain, CNDers worked to reclaim the decision-making process for the ordinary individual and thus to restore authentic democracy to Britain. If the nation heeded the call to "ban the bloody H-bomb now," then moral fervor would return to British politics, and nonmaterial goals would assume their rightful position of priority. The high percentage of Christians in the Campaign and the involvement of such religious men as Acland and MacLeod reinforced the antimaterialism of this vision, as did the involvement of the New Leftists, with their rejection of the materialist-minded socialism predominant in Britain. The work of Thompson, in particular, exemplified the romantic currents that swept through CND and gave it its peculiar force.

Internal contradictions sapped CND of its strength and, together with changes in world affairs, ensured its decline in the 1960s. Many of its supporters, however, marched on into the early Green movement, a third manifestation of postwar romanticism. These eco-activists declared that society would soon self-destruct if it failed to change its course. Against the bigness of industrial society, they placed their ideal of a small-scale, technologically "soft," stable society. Their politics ran the gamut from Marxist to reactionary, but essential to their critique was a rejection of the growth obsession of modern society and a belief that humanity had to relearn the lessons of nature in order to survive. According to E. F. Schumacher in *Small Is Beautiful*, Western industrial society had failed to heed nature's teachings about the necessity of beauty, simplicity, and nonviolence and as a result had catapulted itself into crisis. Resolution of this crisis, Schumacher insisted, began with individual spiritual renewal. Nonviolence, beauty, and simplicity took root at a personal level and bore fruit in human-scale economic and technological structures. Schumacher's personal experiences with alternative religious traditions, particularly Buddhism, set him against British empiricism and pragmatism and shaped his romantic critique of modern society. Thus, like Lewis, Tolkien, and many CNDers and eco-activists, he took his place in the line of romantic critics that reached back to the Romantic poets, Carlyle, Ruskin, and Morris.

Several common themes linked fantasy literature, CND, and the early

Greens. The vision of the past as a guide for the future surfaced again and again. Narnia and Middle-earth rest on idealized versions of medieval and Old English society. In the idea of the past held by New Leftists like Thompson, the traditions of the English working class and its peculiar socialism could help remake the future. Schumacher, like C. S. Lewis, condemned the presentist bias of modern society and insisted that education must be grounded in the thought and literature of past ages. For eco-activists, the past became a repository of simple technologies, farming and healing methods, and guidelines for the optimum size of political and economic structures.

In all three movements, this backward orientation also indicated a rejection of the modern, degraded world status of Britain. Within CND, especially, but evident among all the players of the romantic drama, was a view of the past as a time of British – or, more often, *English* – glory and as a source of British strengths that must be revived in order to make a better world. Hence, CNDers depicted Britain as the moral leader of the world capable of guiding the other nations into a nonnuclear future. In the fantasies of Lewis and Tolkien, both Narnia and the Shire evoked an ideal Britain and proved to be the place from which salvation came. Eco-activists turned the "decline of Britain" theme on its head and insisted that slow economic growth indicated a national refusal to join the international race to destruction. In Britain, they argued, a set of values survived that could enable the island to lead the rest of the world into a sustainable future. Patriotism, at times a "Little Englander" nationalism, wove its way through these movements and served as a second unifying theme.

The sense of national identity was often accompanied by anti-Americanism. To these romantic critics, the United States represented the future to avoid, a society devoted to growth and speed and endless change, a nation without a sense of tradition, a collection of individuals rather than a community. Although anti-Americanism can be seen in the romantic tradition before 1945, it was accentuated by Britain's decline into a client state of the United States in the decades after the Second World War. The subordination of British foreign and economic policy to American demands, as well as the growing cultural hegemony of the United States, appeared to threaten not only Britain's independence but also its uniqueness. Tolkien's efforts to find a mythology for England, CND's ambivalence toward NATO, and the Green emphasis on local control indicate a concern to preserve and protect essential British or English characteristics that were seen as threatened by Americanization and standardization.

Anti-Americanism linked the concern for Britain's identity and role in the world to the third common theme in postwar romantic protest: antimaterialism. To many romantics, Americans were caught up in an endless pursuit of material wealth, to the impoverishment of their individual lives and national culture. But antimaterialism meant more than condemning the quest for goods that appeared to dominate the Age of Affluence. It also meant asserting the existence of nonmaterial realities. Even those who would fiercely resist the label "religious," such as Thompson, insisted on the importance of realizing that life transcended the material dimension. The romantic critique joined these two meanings of materialism. If society denied any reality beyond that comprehended by the five physical senses, then meaning and purpose must dwindle to matters of material consumption. Therefore, eco-activists protested against industrial society's allegiance to economic growth not only because they believed that such growth threatened to overload the earth's capacities but also because they believed that the emphasis on material production and consumption indicated that modern society was seriously ill, was in a state of spiritual as well as economic and environmental crisis. CNDers discerned a spiritual lack at the core of the nuclear defense system. By losing touch with nonmaterial realities, with the fundamentals, modern society had allowed technology to escape its proper limits and so had created the means by which to destroy humanity. This questioning of the materialist basis of twentieth-century culture is at the heart of Lewis's and Tolkien's fantasies as well. The very act of creating otherworlds is an affirmation of the nonmaterial force of imagination. In their myths, Lewis and Tolkien accented the poverty of an exclusively materialist perception of reality.

Connected to this rejection of materialism was the view that quantification is an extremely limited tool with which to apprehend the human experience. Numbers, romantics argued, like the physical senses, could not embrace the deeper levels of meaning, emotion, or significance. Hence, the impatience with statistics evident in these movements. In Narnia, Aslan knocked the numbers out of Eustace and so enabled the boy to perceive for the first time the beauty and meaning of his experience. Even Schumacher, who made his living as a statistician, fought to reduce the power of numbers in postwar society. For Thompson, the triumph of numbers meant the dominance of quantitative history and an interpretation of the past that he condemned as a paean to industrial capitalism. Against the modern obsession with quantity, romantic protesters like Lewis, Schumacher, and Thompson asserted the importance of qualitative questions. They saw the quality of life in modern society particularly threatened by the encroachments of industrialization upon the natural environment. Nature, in the romantic critique, comprised more than the material world; it was a system of relationships that transcended analytical study, an organic whole of which humanity was a part. Alienated from nature, modern men and women stumbled into such tragic absurdities as nuclear defense systems. Respect for the integrity of nature, the heart of the eco-activist protest, permeated Lewis's and Tolkien's fantasies as well. In Narnia and Middle-earth humanity and nature were in such close connection that even the trees communicated.

If nonmaterial realities did exist, then pragmatism and politics had to give way before "higher" considerations. All these movements bore witness to an anti- or apolitical mind-set. Even individuals who granted validity to party politics, such as MacLeod and various New Leftists, remained critical of the practices of orthodox politics and fought to inject "morality" into the political debate. They abhorred the fact that despite campaign rhetoric, pragmatism rather than principle ruled British politics. In the postwar period, both major parties accepted the outlines of the welfare state and the assumptions and techniques of consensus politicking. Whether Labour or Conservative, governments were both dominated and defeated by Britain's seemingly unstoppable economic decline. With political decisions shaped by economic statistics, numbers-leery romantics backed away from the world of politics. Lewis and Tolkien withdrew almost completely. For CNDers and early Greens, such extreme withdrawal was both impossible and unappealing. They believed they could change the world but found themselves stymied by political realities. Thus they sought either to reshape those realities by means of mass-movement pressure or the formation of new political parties or to bypass the political establishment by building alternative structures. Whether tackling the political structure or making an end run around it, their aim remained to restore a moral vigor to English politics.

For many romantics, the concept of participatory democracy held the key to revitalizing British politics. An essential element of both Guild Socialism and Distributism in the early decades of the century, the demand for participatory democracy stood near the center of post-1945 romantic protest as well. Although neither Lewis nor Tolkien was interested in political theory or debate, both created fantasies in which the decisions and actions of ordinary people (or hobbits) shaped the course of events. Their created worlds were monarchist and hierarchical; nevertheless, they affirmed the power of the "little people." In the fight against nuclear weapons, the theme of participatory democracy is, of course, fundamental. Frustration with the decision-making process that led to the Bomb forced some nuclear protesters, particularly those in the DAC, the Committee of 100, and the New Left, to criticize parliamentary democracy and to look for alternative ways of achieving their ideal of a truly democratic state. This search for alternatives continued in the early Green movement, as eco-activists demanded decentralization and a return to smallness as steps on the road to a more genuine democracy, based on the participation of ordinary people.

This insistence that ordinary persons could and should shape the structures of their world – the affirmation of individual agency – served as a fourth connecting strand among the three movements. Postwar romantics protested against the exaltation of the expert in contemporary society. To them, technocrats embodied a new form of tyranny, a modern means of depriving the individual of decision-making power. CND's very existence stemmed from the belief that no sane and moral individual could allow the governments of the world to continue on the nuclear path. Small was beautiful in Schumacher's eyes because of the smallness of the ordinary individual. In Lewis's and Tolkien's fantasy worlds, small and ordinary folk, children and hobbits rather than experts, saved the day. The idea that the ordinary individual counted had special appeal in the context of postwar Britain. For many CNDers and eco-activists, and perhaps for some fantasy readers, their adherence to these movements expressed their own powerlessness. They tended to cluster in professional positions outside the economic market and on the margins of political power.

The romantic affirmation of individual agency led to protest against the 'massness' of modern society. This protest often took the form of respect for hierarchy, most evident in the monarchies of Narnia and Middle-earth, in Mishan's rejections of the ideal of equality, and in Schumacher's philosophical system based on levels of being. Such hierarchicalism was more than reactionary elitism. It stemmed, first of all, from the desire to restore to modern society some of the variegated hues that colored the romantic vision of the past. It grew also out of the belief that the ordered societies of the past had been communities. Mass society was believed not only to have eradicated the power of the ordinary individual to shape his or her life but also to have distorted relationships between individuals. The give-and-take of ordinary human intercourse became difficult or contrived, and ceremonies of mourning and celebration became empty activities, fossils from an age when such events had occurred within the framework of community. With his stress on the human need for smallness, Schumacher sought to rebuild this framework. The Inklings, the Aldermaston March, and Thompson's investigations into plebeian culture were also expressions of the importance of community in the three movements.

These protesters recognized no contradiction in their dual emphasis on the individual and community. They argued that only in community could the individual be a distinct person, and they opposed mass society as the enemy of both individualism and community spirit. They failed to see, or admit, however, that the needs of the community and the rights of the individual often do conflict. These postwar romantics tended to sidestep this quagmire by their distorted remembrance of the past. The idea of a golden age, whether the medieval era, the Renaissance, the hunter–gatherer epoch, or simply the preindustrial world, colored and weakened all three movements. The golden age illusion revealed a selective and sentimental view of the past, one often not only ahistorical but escapist and elitist as well. Elitism, although rarely as explicit as, for example, in the writings of Mishan, was embedded in the assertion, common to all three movements, that the postwar era witnessed the erosion of the individual's ability to decide the direction of his or her life. Control over the structures of one's life is a privilege possessed only by elites, whether in the technocratic twentieth century, the industrializing age, or the preindustrial past. This control may have been slipping out of the hands of members of the middle classes in postwar Britain. Medieval peasants, however, were no more, and arguably less, the agents of their own destinies than modern factory hands. Of course, the romantics held no monopoly on selective memory. Their opponents, in their depiction of technology, industry, and science as the tools by which humanity had released itself from superstition and degradation into a cornucopia of material delights, betrayed the same blinkered vision.

Affirmation of the past as guide for the future, affirmation of Britain's uniqueness, affirmation of the importance of the nonmaterial, affirmation of individual agency, and affirmation of community were the threads that wove fantasy literature, CND, and the early Green movement into a colorful quilt of romantic protest. At the root of such affirmation and central to all three movements was the quest for wholeness: the effort to overcome the fragmentation of modern society. The individuals and groups examined here sought reintegration, the restoration of right relationships between humanity and its past, humanity and nature, and humanity and technology; between the individual and his or her work, the individual and his or her soul, the individual and other individuals. This critique of modern society was essentially a faith commitment, a belief neither provable nor disprovable, that these right relationships had once existed and could be restored.

Unlike their Victorian forebears in the romantic tradition, however, these protesters did not address a limited audience with whom they shared a vocabulary and an economic and political milieu. Instead, they had to try to overcome the barriers erected among academic specializations and between themselves and the new secularized mass culture. They had to find new ways in which to articulate the romantic critique of industrial society if they were to be heard and understood. In their hands, such disparate entities as fantasy literature, mass marches, narrative history, alternative economics, and environmental awareness became vehicles of protest, the means by which they sought to open the eyes of the British and so to save the earth.

Select bibliography

The footnotes contain full references to all works cited in the text. Listed below are the archival sources consulted, as well as what are, in my judgment, the key secondary sources for further reading.

Collections

Part I

British Broadcasting Corporation Written Archives Centre, Reading.
Marion Wade Collection. Marion E. Wade Center, Wheaton College, Wheaton, Ill.
Tolkien Collection. Marquette University, Milwaukee, Wis.

Part II

CND Collection. Library of Political and Economic Science, London School of Economics.
CND Collection. Modern Records Centre, University of Warwick.
Committee of 100 Papers. Modern Records Centre, University of Warwick.
George MacLeod Papers. Community House of the Iona Community, Glasgow.
George MacLeod Papers. National Library of Scotland, Edinburgh.
Victor Gollancz Archives. Modern Records Centre, University of Warwick.
In addition, Peter Cadogan holds a collection of press reports concerning the Committee of 100.

Part III

Conservation Society Archives. Conservation Society National Office, Chertsey, Surrey. (Note: This office is now closed.)
Ecology/Green Party Papers. Modern Records Centre, University of Warwick.
E. F. Schumacher Papers. Library of the National Coal Board, London. (Note: The National Coal Board has been reorganized as British Coal, and its library dis-

banded. Although many of the library's holdings can be found in British Coal's Archive Department in Mansfield, the Schumacher Papers used in this work remain in Hobart House in London.)

E. F. Schumacher Papers. Intermediate Technology Development Group, Rugby. (Note: Most of Schumacher's papers remain in private hands.)

Soil Association, Bristol.

In addition, the British Library contains a number of publications of the Conservation Society, the Ecology/Green Party, Friends of the Earth, Greenpeace, Intermediate Technology Group, and Survival International.

For further reading

Introduction and Chapter 1

Barzun, Jacques. *Classic, Romantic, and Modern.* Chicago: University of Chicago Press, 1975.

Boos, Florence, ed. *History and Community: Essays in Victorian Medievalism.* New York: Garland, 1992.

Bright, Michael. *Cities Built to Music: Aesthetic Theories of the Victorian Gothic Revival.* Columbus: Ohio State University Press, 1984.

Canovan, Margaret. *G. K. Chesterton: Radical Populist.* New York: Harcourt Brace Jovanovich, 1977.

Carpenter, L. P. *G. D. H. Cole: An Intellectual Biography.* London: Cambridge University Press, 1973.

Chandler, Alice. *A Dream of Order: The Medieval Ideal in Nineteenth-Century English Literature.* Lincoln: University of Nebraska Press, 1970.

Conford, Philip, ed. *The Organic Tradition: An Anthology of Writings on Organic Farming, 1900–1950.* Bideford, Devon: Green Books, 1988.

Corrin, Jay. *G. K. Chesterton and Hilaire Belloc: The Battle against Modernity.* Athens: Ohio University Press, 1981.

Davey, Peter. *Arts and Crafts Architecture: The Search for Earthly Paradise.* London: Architectural Press, 1980.

Ffinch, Michael. *G. K. Chesterton.* London: Weidenfeld and Nicolson, 1986.

Frye, Northrop. *A Study of English Romanticism.* New York: Random House, 1968.

Girouard, Mark. *The Return to Camelot: Chivalry and the English Gentleman.* New Haven: Yale University Press, 1981.

Glass, S. T. *The Responsible Society: The Ideas of the English Guild Socialists.* London: Longman, 1966.

Gould, Peter. *Early Green Politics: Back to Nature, Back to the Land, and Socialism in Britain, 1880–1900.* New York: St. Martin's Press, 1988.

Hardy, Dennis. *Alternative Communities in Nineteenth Century England.* London: Longman, 1979.

Heyck, T. W. *The Transformation of Intellectual Life in Victorian England.* New York: St. Martin's Press, 1982.

Holloway, John. *The Victorian Sage: Studies in Argument.* Hamden: Archon Books, 1962.

Hough, Graham. *The Last Romantics.* London: Duckworth, 1949.

Houseman, Gerald. *G. D. H. Cole.* Boston: Twayne Publishers, 1979.

Johnson, Lesley. *The Cultural Critics.* London: Routledge, Kegan Paul, 1979.

Kaplan, Fred. *Thomas Carlyle: A Biography.* Ithaca: Cornell University Press, 1983.

Lovejoy, Arthur. "On the Discrimination of Romanticisms." In *Essays in the History of Ideas.* Baltimore, 1948.

Marsh, Jan. *Back to the Land: The Pastoral Impulse in Victorian England from 1880 to 1914.* London: Quartet Books, 1982.

Mendilow, Jonathan. *The Romantic Tradition in British Political Thought.* London: Croom Helm, 1986.

Perkin, Harold. *The Rise of Professional Society since 1880.* London: Routledge, 1989.

Stansky, Peter. *Redesigning the World: William Morris, the 1880s, and the Arts and Crafts.* Princeton, N.J.: Princeton University Press, 1985.

Thompson, E. P. *William Morris: Romantic to Revolutionary.* London: Lawrence and Wishart, 1955. Rev. ed. New York: Pantheon Books, 1977.

Thompson, Paul. *The Work of William Morris.* London: Quartet, 1977.

Wiener, Martin. *English Culture and the Decline of the Industrial Spirit.* Cambridge: Cambridge University Press, 1981.

Williams, Raymond. *The Country and the City.* London: Paladin, 1975.

Culture and Society. London: Chatto and Windus, 1960.

Keywords: A Vocabulary of Culture and Society. London: Fontana, 1983.

Wilson, A. N. *Hilaire Belloc.* London: Hamish Hamilton, 1984.

Wright, A. W. *G. D. H. Cole and Socialist Democracy.* Oxford: Clarendon Press, 1979.

Part I

Aeschliman, Michael. *The Restitution of Man: C. S. Lewis and the Case against Scientism.* Grand Rapids: Eerdmans, 1983.

Beversluis, John. *C. S. Lewis and the Search for Rational Religion.* Grand Rapids: Eerdmans, 1985.

Cantor, Norman. *Inventing the Middle Ages.* New York: William Morrow, 1991.

Carpenter, Humphrey. *The Inklings: C. S. Lewis, J. R. R. Tolkien, Charles Williams, and Their Friends.* London: Allen and Unwin, 1978.

Tolkien: A Biography. Boston: Houghton Mifflin, 1977.

Christopher, Joe R., and Joan Ostling. *C. S. Lewis: An Annotated Checklist of Writings about Him and His Works.* Kent, Ohio: Kent State University Press, 1974.

Dorset, Lyle. *And God Came In: The Extraordinary Story of Joy Davidman, Her Life, and Marriage to C. S. Lewis.* New York: Macmillan, 1983.

Firsching, Lorenz Johann. "Worlds Apart: The Two Cultures Problem in Twentieth-Century Britain." Ph.D. diss., State University of New York at Binghamton, 1982.

Green, Roger Lancelyn, and Walter Hooper. *C. S. Lewis: A Biography.* New York: Harcourt Brace Jovanovich, 1974.

Griffin, William. *Clive Staples Lewis: A Dramatic Life.* San Francisco: Harper and Row, 1986.

Hadfield, Mary Alice. *Charles Williams: An Exploration of His Life and Work.* Oxford, 1983.

Johnson, Judith Anne. *J. R. R. Tolkien: Six Decades of Criticism.* Westport, Conn.: Greenwood, 1986.

Kilby, Clyde. *The Christian World of C. S. Lewis.* Grand Rapids: Eerdmans, 1964.

Lewis, W. H. *Brothers and Friends: The Diaries of Major Warren Hamilton Lewis.* Edited by Clyde Kilby and Marjorie Lamp Mead. San Francisco: Harper and Row, 1972.

Patrick, James. *The Magdalen Metaphysicals: Idealism and Orthodoxy at Oxford, 1901–1945.* Macon, Ga.: Mercer University Press, 1985.

Sayer, George. *Jack: C. S. Lewis and His Times.* London: Macmillan, 1988.

Shippey, T. A. *The Road to Middle-earth.* London: Allen and Unwin, 1982.

Sibley, Brian. *Shadowlands: The Story of C. S. Lewis and Joy Davidman.* London: Hodder and Stoughton, 1985.

West, Richard. *Tolkien Criticism: An Annotated Checklist.* Kent, Ohio: Kent State University Press, 1981.

Wilson, A. N. *C. S. Lewis: A Biography.* New York: W. W. Norton, 1990.

Part II

Bess, Michael. *Realism, Utopia, and the Mushroom Cloud.* Chicago: University of Chicago Press, 1993.

"Rebels against the Cold War: Four Intellectuals Who Campaigned to Recast World Politics, 1945–1985." Ph.D. diss., University of California at Berkeley, 1989.

Collins, L. John. *Faith under Fire.* London: Leslie Frewin, 1966.

Driver, Christopher. *The Disarmers: A Study in Protest.* London: Hodder and Staughton, 1964.

Duff, Peggy. *Left, Left, Left: A Personal Account of Six Protest Campaigns, 1945–1965.* London: Allison and Busby, 1971.

Edwards, Ruth Dudley. *Victor Gollancz: A Biography.* London: Victor Gollancz, 1987.

Ferguson, Ron. *Chasing the Wild Goose.* London: Collins, Fount Paperbacks, 1988.

George MacLeod: Founder of the Iona Community. London: Collins, 1990.

Groom, A. J. R. *British Thinking about Nuclear Weapons.* London: Frances Pinter, 1974.

Holden, David Richard. "The First New Left in Britain, 1956–1962." Ph.D. diss., University of Wisconsin at Madison, 1976.

Inglis, Fred. *Radical Earnestness: English Social Theory, 1880–1980.* Oxford: Martin Robertson, 1982.

Jones, Mervyn. *Chances.* London: Verso, 1987.

Kaye, Harvey. *The British Marxist Historians.* Oxford: Polity Press, 1984.

The Education of Desire: Marxists and the Writing of History. New York: Routledge, 1992.

Kaye, Harvey, and Keith McClelland, eds. *E. P. Thompson: Critical Perspectives*. Philadelphia: Temple University Press, 1990.

Minnion, John, and Philip Bolsover, eds. *The CND Story: The First Twenty-five Years of CND in the Words of the People Involved*. London: Allison and Busby, 1983.

Palmer, Bryan D. *The Making of E. P. Thompson: Marxism, Humanism, and History*. Toronto: New Hogtown Press, 1981.

Parkin, Frank. *Middle Class Radicalism: The Social Bases of the British Campaign for Nuclear Disarmament*. Manchester: Manchester University Press, 1968.

Rose, Clive. *Campaigns against Western Defence*. New York: St. Martin's Press, 1985.

Taylor, Richard. *Against the Bomb: The British Peace Movement, 1958–1965*. Oxford: Clarendon Press, 1988.

"Green Politics and the Peace Movement." In *A Socialist Anatomy of Britain*, edited by David Coates et al. Cambridge: Polity Press, 1985.

Taylor, Richard, and Colin Pritchard. *The Protest Makers: The British Nuclear Disarmament Movement of 1958–1965, Twenty Years On*. Oxford: Pergamon Press, 1980.

Taylor, Richard, and Nigel Young, eds. *Campaigns for Peace: British Peace Movements in the Twentieth Century*. New York: St. Martin's Press, 1987.

Taylor, Robert. "The Campaign for Nuclear Disarmament." In *The Age of Affluence, 1951–1964*, edited by Vernon Bodganor and Robert Skidelsky. London: Macmillan, 1970.

Thayer, George. *The British Political Fringe*. London: Anthony Blond, 1965.

Widgery, David, ed. *The Left in Britain, 1956–1968*. New York: Penguin, 1976.

Young, Nigel. *An Infantile Disorder? The Crisis and Decline of the New Left*. London: Routledge and Kegan Paul, 1977.

Part III

Arndt, H. W. *Economic Development: The History of an Idea*. Chicago: University of Chicago Press, 1987.

The Rise and Fall of Economic Growth. Melbourne: Longman Cheshire, 1978.

Bramwell, Anna. *Ecology in the Twentieth Century: A History*. New Haven: Yale University Press, 1988.

Church, Chris. *Coming of Age: The First Twenty Years of Friends of the Earth in Britain*. London: Gollancz, 1992.

Cotgrove, Stephen. *Catastrophe or Cornucopia: The Environment, Politics, and the Future*. New York: Wiley, 1982.

Evans, David. *A History of Nature Conservation in Britain*. London: Routledge, 1992.

Graham, Frank, Jr. *Since "Silent Spring."* Boston: Houghton Mifflin, 1970.

Hays, Samuel. *Beauty, Health, and Permanence: Environmental Politics in the U.S., 1955–1985*. New York: Cambridge University Press, 1987.

Kimber, Richard, and J. J. Richardson. *Campaigning for the Environment*. London: Routledge and Kegan Paul, 1974.

King, Roger, and Neill Nugent. *Respectable Rebels: Middle Class Campaigns in Britain in the 1970s.* London: Hodder and Stoughton, 1979.

Lowe, Philip, and Jane Goyder. *Environmental Groups in Politics.* London: Allen and Unwin, 1983.

McCormick, John. *Reclaiming Paradise: The Global Environmental Movement.* Bloomington: Indiana University Press, 1989.

Nash, Roderick Frazier. *The Rights of Nature: A History of Environmental Ethics.* Madison: University of Wisconsin Press, 1989.

Nicholson, Max. *The New Environmental Age.* New York: Cambridge University Press, 1987.

Nicholson-Lord, David. *The Greening of the Cities.* London and New York: Routledge and Kegan Paul, 1987

O'Riordan, T. *Environmentalism.* London: Pion, 1976.

Parkin, Sara. *Green Parties: An International Guide.* London: Heretic Books, 1989.

Payne, Virginia. "The History of the Soil Association." Master's thesis, University of Manchester, 1972.

Pepper, David. *The Roots of Modern Environmentalism.* London: Routledge, 1989.

Porritt, Jonathon, and David Winner. *The Coming of the Greens.* London: Fontana, 1988.

Rivers, Patrick. *Politics by Pressure.* London: Harrap, 1974.

Rowland, Wade. *The Plot to Save the World: The Life and Times of the Stockholm Conference on the Human Environment.* Toronto: Clarke, Irwin, 1973.

Rudig, Wolfgang, and Philip Lowe. "The Withered 'Greening' of British Politics: A Study of the Ecology Party." *British Political Studies* 34 (1986): 262–84.

Sandbach, Francis. *Environment, Ideology, and Policy.* Montclair: Allanheld, Osmun, 1980.

Schnaiberg, Allan, *The Environment: From Surplus to Scarcity.* New York: Oxford University Press, 1980.

Smillie, Ian. *Mastering the Machine: Poverty, Aid, and Technology.* Boulder: Westview Press, 1992.

Weintraub, Andrew, et al. *The Economic Growth Controversy.* New York: International Arts and Sciences Press, 1973.

Weston, Joe, ed. *Red and Green: The New Politics of the Environment.* London: Pluto Press, 1986.

Winner, Langdon. *The Whale and the Reactor: A Search for Limits in an Age of High Technology.* Chicago: University of Chicago Press, 1986.

Wood, Barbara. *Alias Papa: A Life of Fritz Schumacher.* London: Jonathon Cape, 1984.

Worster, Donald. *Nature's Economy: A History of Ecological Ideas.* San Francisco: Sierra Club Books, 1977.

Index

Works by a given author are included at the end of that author's index entry.